# Britain's Retreat from Empire in East Asia, 1905–80

The decline of British power in Asia, from a high point in 1905, when Britain's ally Japan vanquished the Russian Empire, apparently reducing the perceived threat that Russia posed to British interests in India and China, to the end of the twentieth century, when its influence had dwindled to virtually nothing, is one of the most important themes in understanding the modern history of East and South-East Asia. This book considers a range of issues that illustrate the significance and influence of the British Empire in Asia and the nature of Britain's imperial decline. Subjects covered include the challenges posed by Germany and Japan during the First World War, British efforts at international co-operation in the interwar period, the British relationship with Korea and Japan in the wake of the Second World War and the complicated path of decolonization in South-East Asia and Hong Kong.

**Antony Best** is an Associate Professor in International History at the London School of Economics, UK.

# Routledge Studies in the Modern History of Asia

**Voices from the Shifting
Russo–Japanese Border**
Karafuto/Sakhalin
*Edited by Svetlana Paichadze and
Philip A. Seaton*

**International Competition in China,
1899–1991**
The rise, fall, and restoration of the
Open Door Policy
*Bruce A. Elleman*

**The Post-war Roots of Japanese
Political Malaise**
*Dagfinn Gatu*

**Britain and China, 1840–1970**
Empire, finance and war
*Edited by Robert Bickers and
Jonathan Howlett*

**Local History and War Memories
in Hokkaido**
*Edited by Philip A. Seaton*

**Thailand in the Cold War**
*Matthew Phillips*

**Early Modern Southeast Asia,
1350–1800**
*Ooi Keat Gin and Hoang Anh Tuan*

**Managing Famine, Flood and
Earthquake in China**
*Lauri Paltemaa*

**Science, Technology, and Medicine
in the Modern Japanese Empire**
*Edited by David G. Wittner and
Philip C. Brown*

**Street Performers and Society in
Urban Japan, 1600–1900**
*Gerald Groemer*

**Suicide in Twentieth
Century Japan**
*Francesca Di Marco*

**Treaty Ports in Modern China**
Law, land and power
*Edited by Robert Bickers and
Isabella Jackson*

**Kyoto Visual Culture in the Early
Edo and Meiji Periods**
The arts of reinvention
*Edited by Morgan Pitelka and
Alice Y. Tseng*

**Health Policy and Disease in
Colonial and Post-Colonial
Hong Kong, 1841–2003**
*Ka-che Yip, Philip
Yuen-sang Leung, and
Timothy Man-Kong Wong*

**Britain's Imperial Retreat from
China, 1900–1931**
*Phoebe Chow*

**Constitution Making in Asia**
Decolonisation and state-building
in the aftermath of the
British empire
*H. Kumarasingham*

**Britains's Retreat from Empire in
East Asia, 1905–80**
*Edited by Antony Best*

# Britain's Retreat from Empire in East Asia, 1905–80

Edited by
Antony Best

LONDON AND NEW YORK

First published 2017
by Routledge
2 Park Square, Milton Park, Abingdon, Oxon OX14 4RN

and by Routledge
711 Third Avenue, New York, NY 10017

*Routledge is an imprint of the Taylor & Francis Group, an informa business*

© 2017 Antony Best

The right of Antony Best to be identified as the author of the editorial
material, and of the authors for their individual chapters, has been asserted
in accordance with sections 77 and 78 of the Copyright, Designs and
Patents Act 1988.

All rights reserved. No part of this book may be reprinted or reproduced or
utilised in any form or by any electronic, mechanical, or other means, now
known or hereafter invented, including photocopying and recording, or in
any information storage or retrieval system, without permission in writing
from the publishers.

*Trademark notice*: Product or corporate names may be trademarks or
registered trademarks, and are used only for identification and explanation
without intent to infringe.

*British Library Cataloguing in Publication Data*
A catalogue record for this book is available from the British Library

*Library of Congress Cataloging in Publication Data*
Names: Best, Antony, 1964- editor of compilation.
Title: Britain's retreat from empire in East Asia, 1905-1980 / edited by
    Antony Best.
Description: Milton Park, Abingdon, Oxon ; New York, NY : Routledge,
    2017. |
Series: Routledge studies in the modern history of Asia ; 122 | Includes
    bibliographical references and index.
Identifiers: LCCN 2016017513| ISBN 9780415705608 (hardback) | ISBN
    9781315889603 (ebook)
Subjects: LCSH: Great Britain–Foreign relations–East Asia. | East  Asia–
    Foreign relations–Great Britain. | Decolonization–East Asia–History–
    20th century. | Great Britain–Colonies–Asia–History–20th century. |
    Imperialism–History–20th century. | World politics–1900-1945. | World
    politics–1945-1989.
Classification: LCC DS518.4 .B75 2017 | DDC 325/.3410950904–dc23
LC record available at https://lccn.loc.gov/2016017513

ISBN: 978-0-415-70560-8 (hbk)
ISBN: 978-1-315-88960-3 (ebk)

Typeset in Times New Roman
by Taylor & Francis Books

This book is dedicated to the memory of our friend, colleague and mentor Peter Lowe

# Contents

| | |
|---|---|
| *List of tables* | ix |
| *List of contributors* | x |
| *Acknowledgement* | xii |
| *Note* | xiv |
| *Abbreviations* | xv |

Introduction: Peter Lowe and the history of the British presence in East Asia and South-East Asia  1
ANTONY BEST

1 Early retirement: Britain's retreat from Asia, 1905–23  8
IAN NISH

2 Imperial Germany's strategy in East and South-East Asia: The campaign against British India  21
T.G. FRASER

3 Japan's Twenty-One Demands and Anglo-Japanese relations  35
SOCHI NARAOKA

4 Britain, intelligence and the Japanese intervention in Siberia, 1918–22  57
ANTONY BEST

5 Britain, the League of Nations and Russian women refugees in China in the interwar period  71
HARUMI GOTO-SHIBATA

6 Defending the 'Singapore strategy': Hankey's Dominions tour, 1934  87
ANN TROTTER

viii  *Contents*

7  Conquering press: coverage by the *New York Times* and the
   *Manchester Guardian* on the Allied occupation of Japan, 1945–52    100
   ROGER BUCKLEY

8  In search of regional authority in South-East Asia: The
   improbable partnership of Lord Killearn and Malcolm
   MacDonald, 1946–8                                                   117
   A.J. STOCKWELL

9  Anglo-American relations and the making and breaking of the
   Korean phase of the 1954 Geneva Conference                         135
   ROBERT BARNES

10  A withdrawal from Empire: Hong Kong–UK relations
    during the European Economic Community enlargement
    negotiations, 1960–3                                               152
    DAVID CLAYTON

11  From Vietnam to Hong Kong: Britain, China and the everyday
    Cold War, 1965–7                                                   171
    CHI-KWAN MARK

12  Towards 'a new Okinawa' in the Indian Ocean: Diego Garcia and
    Anglo-American relations in the 1960s                              190
    YOICHI KIBATA

    *Index*                                                            204

# List of tables

| | | |
|---|---|---|
| 10.1 | Destination of exports from Hong Kong, 1936–8 to 1960 (%) | 156 |
| 10.2 | Hong Kong's exports and re-exports as a relative share of UK and German import classes, 1965–7 | 157 |
| 10.3 | Average per unit import price of 'drills, jeans and gaberdines' into the UK, and market share of imports by country of origin, 1959–62. | 158 |
| 10.4 | Average per unit import price and import market share in the UK of Hong Kong and Japanese underwear, 1959–62 | 158 |

# Contributors

**Robert Barnes** studied for his undergraduate and Master's degrees at the University of Manchester where he was taught and supervised by Peter Lowe. He went on to receive his PhD in International History at the LSE in 2011 before being appointed a Lecturer in History at York St John University. His first monograph titled, *The US, the UN and the Korean War: Communism in the Far East and the American Struggle for Hegemony in the Cold War*, was published by IB Tauris in 2014. He has also published a number of journal articles and chapters in collections relating to the Korean War.

**Antony Best** is Associate Professor of International History at the London School of Economics. His most recent single-authored book is *British Intelligence and the Japanese Challenge in Asia, 1914–1941* (2002), and he is one of the co-authors of *International History of the Twentieth Century and Beyond*, 3rd edition (Routledge, 2015).

**Roger Buckley** is an academic visitor at St Antony's Oxford, and was previously professor of international history at International Christian University, Tokyo.

**David Clayton** is a Senior Lecturer in History at the University of York and has written extensively on the history of the British Empire, with a particular focus on Hong Kong. He has written on changes to patterns of colonial production and consumption, and on laws regulating economic life. His new project is an economic-cum-environmental history of water in Hong Kong, 1945–80.

**T.G. Fraser** is Emeritus Professor of History at Ulster University and former Provost of its Magee campus. He edited, with Peter Lowe, *Conflict and Amity in East Asia: Essays in Honour of Ian Nish* (Palgrave, 1992), and is a Fellow of the Royal Asiatic Society.

**Harumi Goto-Shibata** is Professor in International History in the Department of Advanced Social and International Studies, Graduate School of Arts and Sciences, at the University of Tokyo. She is the author of *Japan and*

*List of contributors*  xi

*Britain in Shanghai, 1925–31* (1995) and 'The International Opium Conference of 1924–25 and Japan', *Modern Asian Studies*, vol. 36, part 4 (2002).

**Yoichi Kibata** is Professor of International Relations at the Faculty of Law, Seijo University. His publications in English include: (ed. with Ian Nish) *The History of Anglo–Japanese Relations, 1600–2000, Vol. 2, The Political Dimensions, 1930–2000* (Macmillan, 2000) and (ed. with Philip Towle and Nobuko Kosuge) *Japanese Prisoners of War* (Bloomsbury, 2000).

**Chi-kwan Mark** is Senior Lecturer in International History at Royal Holloway, University of London. He is the author of *Hong Kong and the Cold War: Anglo–American Relations, 1949–1957* (Clarendon Press, 2004) and *China and the World since 1945: An International History* (Routledge, 2012).

**Sochi Naraoka** is Professor of History within the law faculty of Kyoto University. He is the author of *Katō Takaaki to seito seiji: Nidai seito-sei he no michi* (2006) and *Taika Nijuikkajyo Yokyu towa Nandattanoka: Daiichiji Sekaitaisen to Nicchutairitsu no Genten* (2015), which won the Suntory Prize. His works in English include 'Katō Takaaki and the Russo-Japanese War', in J.W.M. Chapman and C. Inaba (eds), *Rethinking the Russo-Japanese War, 1904–05*, Vol. II (2007), 'A New Look at Japan's Twenty-One Demands: Reconsidering Katō Takaaki's Motives in 1915', in T. Minohara, T.-K. Hon and E. Dawley (eds), *The Decade of the Great War: Japan and the Wider World in the 1910s* (2014), and 'Japan's First World War-Era Diplomacy, 1914–1915', in Oliviero Frattolillo and Antony Best (eds), *Japan and the Great War*, Basingstoke: Palgrave Macmillan, 2015, pp. 36–51.

**Ian Nish** is Emeritus Professor of International History and Hon. Senior Research Fellow, STICERD, London School of Economics.

**A.J. Stockwell** is Emeritus Professor of Modern History, Royal Holloway, University of London.

**Ann Trotter**, ONZM, is Emeritus Professor, University of Otago, Dunedin, New Zealand. She is a graduate of the University of New Zealand and the University of London where she completed an MA at the School of Oriental and African Studies and her PhD at the London School of Economics. She is interested in the history of international relations in northeast Asia and in the development of international organizations in the wider Pacific region. Her publications and contributions to collections and various academic journals reflect these interests.

# Acknowledgement

It is a pleasure on behalf of all of the contributors to this volume to show our appreciation to those who have assisted us in the writing of this book. First, I would like to thank the staff at the following institutions for their kind assistance: the British Library, London; the Dwight David Eisenhower Library, Abilene; the *Gaimushō gaikō shiryōkan* (The Diplomatic Record Office of the Ministry of Foreign Affairs) Tokyo; the League of Nations Archive, Geneva; the National Archives, Kew; the National Archives and Records Administration, Washington DC; the National Archives of Australia and the National Library of Australia, Canberra; Princeton University Library; and the archives of the School of Oriental and African Studies, London. Records from the Public Record Office appear by permission of the Controller of Her Majesty's Stationary Office.

Second, I would like to thank the staff at Routledge for their usual efficient support for this volume, and especially the work of the commissioning editor, Peter Sowden, who does so much to contribute to the study of East Asian history and politics.

The major figure, though, who all of the contributors would like to acknowledge is Peter Lowe. For those who have written a chapter for this volume, Peter represented many things. He was a colleague, a supervisor, a teacher and an examiner, but for all of us he was someone whose keen intelligence we could admire and whose helpfulness, friendliness and enthusiasm we will never forget. For myself, I first met Peter in late 1986 when I had just moved on from an undergraduate degree at Leeds to start a doctorate at the LSE under Professor Ian Nish. In my first conversation with Peter he told me, much to his amusement, that he had been the external examiner for my Leeds degree and that he had enjoyed reading my dissertation on British relations with Japan in 1941 (a subject that Peter knew rather a lot about!) From that point on, I got to know Peter well both as a mentor and a friend. In 1992 he acted as my external examiner once again, this time for my thesis. I well remember the broad smile he had on his face when I walked into the 'lion's den', because it struck me as an immediate assurance that I had, thank goodness, passed. Peter typically gave me a good grilling that day and pushed me to make more of the recent intelligence releases that were by then reaching

*Acknowledgement* xiii

the Public Record Office at Kew. This was most useful advice and my subsequent publications owe much to his guidance and example. Since Peter passed away in January 2012 I have missed bouncing ideas off him, telling him of recent archival discoveries and most of all regret that I can no longer share his companionship. I know that I am not alone in this, because I was much struck by the speed with which those who were his colleagues, students and admirers offered chapters for this volume. Peter's family in Wales, and especially his niece, Alison McDuffy, were very keen to see a volume come out in his memory, and I hope that they see this book as a suitable testament to the esteem in which he was held and the warmth with which he is remembered.

# Note

This book follows the Japanese style of putting the family name first (except in the acknowledgements and when referring to the Japanese authors of work in English); Chinese names are given in Pinyin, except in cases where other contemporary usages continue to be familiar, such as Kwantung and Manchukuo. The following abbreviations appear in the text and endnotes:

# Abbreviations

| | |
|---|---|
| AMSH | Association for Moral and Social Hygiene |
| BCOF | British Commonwealth Occupation Force |
| BDEE | British Documents on the End of Empire |
| BDOFA | British Documents on Foreign Affairs |
| BIOT | British Indian Ocean Territories |
| BL | British Library |
| CER | Chinese Eastern Railway |
| CET | common external tariff |
| CID | Committee of Imperial Defence |
| CUL | Cambridge University Library |
| DBFP | Documents on British Foreign Policy |
| DDEL | Dwight David Eisenhower Library |
| DPRK | Democratic People's Republic of Korea |
| DRC | Defence Requirements Sub-Committee |
| EEC | European Economic Community |
| FED | Federation of Hong Kong Industries |
| FRUS | Foreign Relations of the United States |
| GATT | General Agreement on Trade and Tariffs |
| GCCS | Government Code and Cypher School |
| GFM | German Foreign Microfilms |
| GHQ | General Headquarters |
| HC | House of Commons |
| HKA | Hong Kong Association |
| HKGCC | Hong Kong General Chamber of Commerce |
| IJA | Imperial Japanese Army |
| IOLR | India Office Library and Records |
| LNA | League of Nations Archive |
| LNd | League of Nations documents |
| MG | *Manchester Guardian* |
| NAA | National Archive of Australia |
| NARA | National Archives and Records Administration |
| NCNA | New China News Agency |
| NLA | National Library of Australia |

xvi  *Abbreviations*

| | |
|---|---|
| NMR | North Manchurian Railway |
| NNRC | Neutral Nations Repatriation Commission |
| NYT | *New York Times* |
| OSA | Office of Systems Analysis |
| PID | Political Intelligence Department |
| POW | Prisoner of war |
| PRC | People's Republic of China |
| PUL | Princeton University Library |
| R&R | rest and recreation |
| ROK | Republic of Korea |
| SCAP | Supreme Commander Allied Powers |
| SACSEA | Supreme Allied Commander South-East Asia |
| SEAC | South-East Asia Command |
| SIS | Secret Intelligence Service |
| SOAS | School of African and Oriental Studies |
| SORO | United Russian Public Organization |
| TNA | The National Archives, Kew |
| TSR | Trans-Siberian Railway |
| TWC | League of Nations Advisory Committee on Traffic in Women and Children |
| UN | United Nations |
| UNGA | United Nations General Assembly |
| VER | voluntary export restraint |

# Introduction
## Peter Lowe and the history of the British presence in East Asia and South-East Asia

*Antony Best*

When the British Empire reached its zenith in the early-twentieth century, the most distant of its significant possessions, aside from the settler states in the antipodes, were those in East and South-East Asia. Within the former of these two regions, Britain's formal territorial presence was extremely limited, consisting only of the Crown Colony of Hong Kong, a number of leased concessions in some of the major Chinese cities and a lease over the small naval base at Weihaiwei. It was, however, the first among equals within the quasi-imperial treaty-port regime that the West as a whole had established and it dominated both the Chinese Maritime Customs Service and the most flourishing of China's ports, the idiosyncratically-governed International Settlement in Shanghai. This rather minimalist formal presence provided a number of safe havens from which Britons could indulge, in the primary reason to come so far from home – trade.

The facts that commerce was the only real interest and that the region was so distant from Europe always raised questions about Britain's willingness to defend its stake. One should recall, for example, that it only occupied the Korean port of Geomondo for two years (1885–7), that it agreed in 1894 to end the treaty-port regime in Japan in the face of concern about Japanese unilateral action, and between 1898–1900 failed to prevent Russian encroachment into southern Manchuria. This then was the British Empire's furthest and most fragile shore. It is therefore no surprise that the twentieth century was marked by a series of retreats, in terms of both territory and outlook, from this imperial high tide. At first these shifts were almost intangible and not necessarily irrevocable, but as the challenges to British power grew more varied and serious, with the rise of Chinese nationalism, Bolshevik infiltration and Japanese expansionism, the retreat steadily gathered pace until, after the Second World War, only Hong Kong remained.

In South-East Asia British interests were more substantial. Its territorial possessions consisted of formal colonies such as Burma and the Straits Settlements, the protectorates of North Borneo, Brunei, the Federated and Unfederated Malay States, and another nebulous entity, the kingdom of Sarawak, which was personally ruled by the Brooke family. In addition, it benefitted from the free trade regime that it had established in Thailand [Siam]

## 2   *Antony Best*

and had considerable influence over that country's finances. Its greater physical presence in this region compared with East Asia was mirrored by the diversity of its interests. South-East Asia was not just valuable as a market for British exports, it also produced vital commodities such as rubber, tin, iron ore and oil. Moreover, it possessed, in Singapore, the most important natural harbour in the region which added a strategic imperative to the British presence. Here, in contrast to East Asia, the pre-Second World War period saw no evidence of retreat, but in the aftermath of that conflict the same pattern would emerge and a withdrawal began.

This collection of essays is an attempt to provide new insights into the challenges to British power that influenced the process of retreat over a period of seventy years. In doing so, it is also a volume that pays tribute to one of the important chroniclers of Britain's relationship with East and South-East Asia in the modern era, the late Peter Lowe, who spent his working life as a historian at the University of Manchester. Over a period of forty years, Peter produced four monographs that outlined the history of the British presence in these regions, beginning in his first book with a study of the period just before the First World War, before moving on to the origins of the Pacific War, and then the early Cold War in East Asia, and lastly looking at South-East Asia in the 1950s.[1] In addition, he produced surveys of Britain's regional role in the modern period, and of the origins and the course of the Korean War, and edited a volume of essays on the Vietnam War.[2] Peter's work was always based on a comprehensive knowledge of the archival record and a thorough understanding of how British diplomacy worked. He used this solid foundation to construct detailed and judicious analyses of the forces that shaped British policy. In addition, he always kept in mind the wider context, namely that the problems in East Asia were only one of the many challenges facing Whitehall and never the most important.

Peter's scholarship had a significant place in the evolution of the international history scholarship on East Asia. One vital contribution was that his work reminded the wider audience of the dangers of the American-centric view of regional history, which not only privileges the United States over all the other non-Asian powers, but at its worst almost fails to acknowledge that any other players existed. In the 1960s and 1970s Peter, along with Ian Nish, William Roger Louis, Christopher Thorne, Ann Trotter and Stephen Endicott, led the way in stressing that Britain was no less a power in East Asia than America and that the former's role could not be ignored if one was to come to any kind of understanding of regional politics.[3] At the same time, though, Peter's studies clearly demonstrated the difficulties that Britain faced in keeping hold of its stake in East Asia as its resources became over-stretched and the challenges to its imperial and home security deepened in their severity.

In his first book, which dealt with the period between 1911 and 1915, Peter outlined the tensions that were emerging in the Anglo–Japanese alliance primarily over the two signatories' very different attitudes towards the 'open door' in China and the difficulty that Britain faced in defending its economic

*British presence in East & South-East Asia* 3

stake in the Yangzi valley. He ended the book with the first archive-based analysis of Britain's role in the 'twenty-one demands' and detailed its frustrations with its maverick ally while it was forced to concentrate on the war in Europe. Britain was not yet in retreat, but the limitations to its power were already clear. His next study dealt with the even more serious crisis of the late 1930s. By this stage Britain had been able to adapt itself to the rise of Chinese nationalism as represented by the establishment of the Guomindang government in Nanjing in 1927 by compromising on some of its treaty rights, but Japan posed a far more existential threat. Endangered by simultaneous challenges from Germany and Italy, Britain had no choice but to keep as low a profile as possible.

In the latter part of his second book and all of his subsequent work, Peter added another theme to his work, Anglo–American relations in East Asia and the frustrations that built up as the one came to dominate over the other. In regard to the origins of the Pacific War, Britain's irritation largely arose from Washington's prickliness about taking advice and its refusal at first to take a firm stand. In his third book, the first of these problems still existed but the second had been replaced by something more disturbing, a new-found inflexibility and ideological fervour that frightened British policy-makers who prided themselves on their pragmatism. This was especially evident in regard to the Korean War, where the United States appeared at times to be determined to engage in dangerous brinksmanship with the People's Republic of China (PRC). Convinced that its reading of the situation was more nuanced, Britain ached to exercise more power in its own right, and in his last book on Southeast Asia, Peter detailed how Anthony Eden was able briefly to achieve this goal at the Geneva Conference deliberations on Indochina in 1954, where the continuing American refusal to engage with the PRC allowed the Foreign Secretary room to cooperate with his Soviet counterpart to negotiate a settlement.

This was, however, to be Britain's last hurrah, for by the 1950s the imperative to retreat had extended itself to South-East Asia as well. This, of course, had its roots not so much in the deep decline in British influence in East Asia but in the end of the Raj in 1947. With India having gained independence, it was inevitable that Burma would rapidly follow, which it did in 1948. Peter's last book was then an investigation into how Britain attempted to maintain some kind of influence in a region that was being transformed by nationalism and communism and how ultimately it was forced to compromise with the former in order to resist the latter.

While Peter's work took in most of the key twists and turns in British policy towards these two regions, this volume consists of a series of snapshots of a number of important but often neglected moments or innovations that comment on the process of retreat. In the first chapter, Ian Nish discusses a number of the small retreats, or as he describes them, 'retirements', that Britain made in regard to its relations with Japan during the period following the signing of the second alliance treaty in 1905 and the termination of the alliance in 1923. He notes, for example, that Britain was forced to drop all

4  *Antony Best*

reference to Korea in the alliance of 1905, to agree to higher Japanese tariffs in 1911, and that at the Washington conference of 1921–22 it gave up its lease over the Chinese port of Weihaiwei. These were all planned rationalizations of its commitments and did not constitute a radical change, but they took place against a disturbing background that was raising awkward questions about British power and prestige.

The next three chapters look at case studies of the difficulties that Britain faced in the region. In his contribution, T.G. Fraser looks at a serious but often neglected challenge to British power in the region, namely Germany's attempt, following the fall of Qingdao in 1914, to use what resources remained to it in Asia to disrupt Britain's most important imperial possession, India. He outlines how the Germany tried, using its consuls in Shanghai and Bangkok and the German community in the Dutch East Indies, to support a dispersed, but determined, network of Indian revolutionaries. Assisted by German officials in the United States, four unsuccessful attempts were made to send arms to India: two from America, one from the Philippines and one from China. Plans were also prepared to raid the Andaman Islands and to enter Burma from Thailand. In the end, British resources proved too strong and the plans were betrayed from within, but this episode underlines the point that Britain did not have a monopoly on power in East Asia and implicitly demonstrates the dangers that might have emerged if Germany had engaged in a concerted campaign to weaken the ties of the alliance.

Naraoka Sōchi in his chapter draws on his recent prize-winning book in Japanese to look anew at the much more familiar crisis that marked the First World War for Britain in East Asia – the twenty-one demands. He outlines how the Chinese government leaked news of Japan's démarche to the foreign press and how this, in turn, led to the latter and the government in Britain to press Japan to modify its terms and how this episode led to increasing distrust regarding Japanese motives.

Antony Best deals with another source of tension in Anglo–Japanese relations, but again one that is less familiar, namely the distrust that arose out of the Allies' involvement in the Siberian intervention of 1918–20, which marked the furthest ever extension of British power in the region. His chapter notes that the issue of Siberia was a particularly difficult one for the British government. At one level, it sought Japanese intervention to thwart German and Bolshevik activities, but at another it was concerned that Japan was seeking to create a new sphere of influence over the Maritime Provinces, north Manchuria and Outer Mongolia rather than assisting with the Allied goal of helping the Whites to defeat the Bolsheviks in the Russian Civil War. The evidence of Japanese machinations that British intelligence gathered, when added to concerns about China and pan-Asianism, led within Whitehall to a further loss of confidence in Japan as an ally and provoked a number of officials into believing that the alliance had run its course.

In her contribution, Harumi Goto-Shibata looks at one facet of a very different but important trend in British policy in the interwar period, namely

*British presence in East & South-East Asia*  5

its involvement in sponsoring new internationalist approaches to political problems as a way of ameliorating them. In other words, her focus is on the shift away from imperialism as a frame of mind rather than dealing with a territorial retreat. She examines the plight of 'White' Russian women refugees in China in the interwar period and how international society, including Britain, endeavoured to assist them. While not dealing with retreat in its high political sense, this chapter is significant for the light that it sheds on concerns about upholding European prestige in the interwar period and the counter-veiling desire not to offend Chinese opinion.

Ann Trotter's chapter returns to strategic matters but at the same time deals with a key symbolic episode. She analyzes the visit that one of the most powerful men in Whitehall, Sir Maurice Hankey, who was both Cabinet Secretary and secretary to the Committee of Imperial Defence, made to the Dominions in 1934. This was a significant event, for his job was to brief South Africa, Australia, New Zealand and Canada on the recent debate in London about imperial defence policy and to reassure them that the British commitment to their security remained in place. This was especially important in regard to the Royal Navy's 'main fleet to Singapore' strategy. However, it is clear that this exercise in public relations did not work, for Hankey's words could not disguise the unreality of the Singapore strategy and the vulnerability of Australia and New Zealand to a seaborne attack. In other words, a major British retreat was only a matter of time.

The chapter by Roger Buckley takes us into the post-war period. He looks at an episode that again marks more of a symbolic than a material retreat by providing a comparative analysis of the Allied occupation of Japan through looking at the voluminous reportage carried by the *New York Times* and setting it against the less impressive quantity and quality of articles printed in the *Manchester Guardian*. In this essay he underlines the critical importance of the Allied press in presenting conflicting first-hand pictures of events on almost a daily basis to an international readership, and concludes by assessing the influence that American and British journalism had in regard to reinforcing existing national stereotypes and presenting fresh images of the new Japan. What is particularly noticeable about his contribution is the degree to which after 1945 the British perspective on Japan narrowed in scope with its focus almost exclusively on trade competition.

A. J. Stockwell in his contribution takes up one of the themes running through Peter Lowe's last book, namely the emergence of South-East Asia as a distinct region and how Britain responded to that phenomenon by constructing after 1945 a series of regional authorities to project British power and to co-ordinate civil administration and military planning. His essay therefore examines the British attempt to revive its presence in the region, through the appointment of a Special Commissioner (Lord Killearn) and a Governor-General of Malaya (Malcolm MacDonald), and the surprisingly successful cooperation that emerged from what might seem a cumbersome administrative structure. He argues that the success of these officials and their

6    *Antony Best*

organizations lay ultimately as much in assisting Britain's orderly withdrawal from South-East Asia as in asserting its continuing regional authority.

Robert Barnes builds on Peter Lowe's extensive coverage of the Korean War by looking at one of the few episodes he overlooked, namely the development of British and American policies during the period between the signing of the armistice in July 1953 and the collapse of the Korean phase of the 1954 Geneva Conference. His chapter demonstrates that the tensions that had existed in the 'special relationship' throughout the conflict did not end with the fighting but continued over the following twelve months. It reveals that the opening days of the Geneva Conference were focussed on trying to reach a settlement over Korea rather than Indochina and that, behind-the-scenes, much disagreement existed between the British and American delegations as the foreign secretary, Anthony Eden, supported by his Commonwealth colleagues, wanted to put forward proposals that stood a chance of settling the Korean question. It was only when it became clear that neither side was prepared to compromise and global attention shifted to Indochina because of the crisis over Dien Bien Phu, that the British delegation reluctantly accepted the de facto division of Korea. If Geneva thus marked a revival of British power in regard to Indochina, the more familiar pattern of compromise and retreat applied to events in East Asia.

In his chapter David Clayton looks at one of the conundrums posed by Britain's loss of influence in East Asia, namely what should Britain do about its commitment to Hong Kong. Typically this is treated as a political problem but in this essay he looks at the economic ramifications and specifically the Crown Colony's place in the British talks to accede to the European Economic Community (EEC). This was a difficult issue because the EEC's member states wanted to prevent Britain, which had lower levels of protection against Hong Kong imports than other parts of Europe, from becoming a conduit for low-cost Asian manufactures. This, however, posed a major threat to the viability of Hong Kong's export-orientated economy, and created major new challenges for the colonial state. Hong Kong's colonial authorities, liaising closely with the organised business community, therefore sought to influence commercial policy-making in London.

Chi-Kwan Mark examines the 'everyday Cold War' between Britain and the PRC at the height of the Vietnam War and the Cultural Revolution. Informed by the concept of 'everyday life', he focusses on Britain's diplomacy and the daily measures taken to deal with the Chinese Communists at the international and local levels. Rather than a failed policy of appeasement, he argues that British politicians and diplomats regarded persistent and patient engagement with China as the best way of fighting the 'everyday Cold War'. This, he notes, proved particularly important during the provocations associated with the Cultural Revolution when relations could have spun out of control. Britain's patient diplomacy at this point, which maintained an eye on the long term, meant that tensions were kept within bounds.

Lastly, in his chapter Yoichi Kibata deals with the final irony of British policy towards Asia in the twentieth century, which is that while the mid-1960s marked the apogee of the period of decolonization, symbolized above all by the decision announced in 1968 to withdraw from East of Suez, at the same time a new British colony was created in the Indian Ocean. On the eve of independence, the Chagos archipelago, which had until then been a part of Mauritius, was separated from the latter and turned into the British Indian Ocean Territories (BIOT). This measure, which ran completely counter to the spirit of the age, was undertaken jointly by the British and American governments as the result of their negotiations about securing a new site for US military facilities in the Indian Ocean. The BIOT were then leased to America and in the 1970s large-scale military facilities began to be constructed on one of the islands, Diego Garcia. During this process, all the inhabitants of the Chagos archipelago, about 1,500 people, were forcibly ousted from their homes and condemned to harsh lives in Mauritius and the Seychelles.

The essays in this volume thus highlight the variety of British interests in East Asia, the challenges to them and the complexity of the process of withdrawal. They do this by looking both at the diplomacy of imperial retreat and the changing attitudes of Britain towards the region. Moreover, behind these individual episodes, it is possible to discern some consistent themes that are familiar from Peter Lowe's work: the steady expansion of American power into the region and Britain's ambivalence towards it; the British desire to balance its interests with those in other areas of the Empire; and the need to protect Britain's commercial stake by not acting precipitously or alienating potential partners in a region in which it was so difficult to project power due to its sheer distance from home. It is hoped therefore that this volume will be seen as a suitable testament to Peter's memory.

## Notes

1 Peter Lowe, *Great Britain and Japan, 1911–1915: A Study of British Far Eastern Policy*, London: Macmillan, 1969; idem., *Great Britain and the Origins of the Pacific War: A Study of British Policy in East Asia, 1937–41*, Oxford: Clarendon, 1977; idem., *Containing the Cold War in East Asia: British Policies towards Japan, China and Korea, 1948–53*, Manchester: Manchester University Press, 1997; and idem., *Contending with Nationalism and Communism: British Policy towards Southeast Asia, 1945–65*, Basingstoke: Palgrave-Macmillan, 2009.

2 Peter Lowe, *Britain in the Far East: A Survey from 1819 to the Present*, London: Longman, 1981; idem., *The Origins of the Korean War*, London: Longman, 1986 and 2nd edition 1997; idem., *The Korean War*, Basingstoke: Macmillan, 2000; and idem. (ed.), *The Vietnam War*, Basingstoke: Macmillan, 1998.

3 Ian Nish, *The Anglo–Japanese Alliance: The Diplomacy of Two Island Empires, 1894–1907*, London: Athlone, 1966; and idem., *Alliance in Decline: A Study in Anglo–Japanese Relations, 1908–23*, London: Athlone, 1972; Wm Roger Louis, *British Strategy in the Far East, 1919–1939*, Oxford: Clarendon, 1971; Stephen Endicott, *Diplomacy and Enterprise: British China Policy, 1933–1937*, Manchester: Manchester University Press, 1975; and Ann Trotter, *Britain and East Asia, 1933–1937*, Cambridge: Cambridge University Press, 1975.

# 1 Early retirement
## Britain's retreat from Asia, 1905–23

*Ian Nish*

### Introduction

Peter Lowe was a leading chronicler of Britain's retreat from Asia in the middle of the twentieth century. Often mistakenly thought of as a Japanese specialist, he was in fact an expert on the international history of East Asia, covering China, Korea and Japan. His books generally bear the sub-title 'British far eastern policy' and tell how Britain's fortunes changed, some would say declined, over half-a-century. The span of Lowe's original research concentrated on the period from the third Anglo–Japanese alliance treaty in 1911 to the Twenty-One Demands 1915, though in fact his book runs up to 1922. In this early period, British retreats did take place but they were comparatively modest and its projections for the future remained generally optimistic. It was a question of partial retreat, in some cases planned retreat.[1]

This essay will follow the same trajectory but will examine the longer chronological period from 1905 to 1923. Its emphasis, like Lowe's, will be on Britain's relations with Japan and we shall reflect on the nature of the Anglo–Japanese Alliance. There are three broad periods which have to be examined: the pre-1914 period of the alliance with its doubts and dismays; the First World War when Britain wanted to preserve the status quo in East Asia till the conflict was over; and the post-war period when new factors emerged, notably the rise of nationalist China and the increasing activity of the United States.

### Before 1914

Britain's alliance with Japan, which was inaugurated in 1902, was a relationship between an established power and a rapidly growing Asian country which had won a high reputation because of its successes in the war with China and its spectacular industrial development over a few decades. It was inevitable that there should be tensions in this relationship and that these should grow the longer the alliance lasted. In the case of Japan it was always vigorously independent and had fought off Western challenges in the past. When Japan showed itself to be increasingly ambitious for spheres of interest on the Asian continent, the clash of interests inevitably increased. Britain may have wanted to curb some of the ambitions of its ally but it did not have the power any longer to influence the situation. The alliance was too fragile an instrument to effect such a purpose.

Britain's approach to foreign relations tended to be mercantile. Trade with Japan was important but necessarily secondary to that of Britain's global trade. Bilateral trade with Japan was asymmetrical with the balance being in favour of Britain. Britain was ready to increase the volume of its trade with Japan, while the latter, feeling the effects of the post-war depression, was desperate to increase her exports to the former. On the other hand, British industrialists at the turn of the twentieth century were worried about future trading prospects: the export of cotton yarn from UK to Japan, which had been £1,042,000 in 1889, fell to £580,000 in 1899 and to £71,000 in 1909. The decline was due to the development of cotton spinning in Japan, based on imports of cotton from British India. The cotton traders were concerned that this would lead to the closure of British mills in the future. The coming of war in 1914 offered Japan the long-awaited opportunity to increase its exports around the world and it did so successfully as to convert itself from a debtor to a creditor nation.[2]

Britain had benefited from the favourable tariff rates which had applied in Japan for half a century; but they were due to lapse in 1911 when the Anglo–Japanese commercial treaty of 1894 was due for reconsideration. In view of the acute financial difficulties caused by its war with Russia in 1904–5, Japan prepared a scheme for full tariff autonomy without delay. It asked for an extension of the existing trade subject to Japan's standing on a footing of absolute equality with the Powers. When the proposed new tariff rates were published, mercantile opinion in UK was unanimously opposed to the substantial increases in import duty. The merchants in the treaty ports of Japan, who were noted for their strong anti-Japanese feelings, were even more strongly opposed. Since Japan's proposals were likely to have a heavier impact upon British trade, which operated under free-trade arrangements, than on countries which were protectionist, the British government asked specially for mitigation of the high duties which were allegedly due to be imposed on British goods. The Foreign Secretary, Sir Edward Grey, pleaded with the Japanese ambassador for special consideration. Addressing a delegation from the North of England chambers of commerce, he reported that he had told the Anglophile ambassador, Katō Takaaki, that:

> ... our relations with Japan are so cordial it has produced a feeling of surprise and disappointment in this country that there should have been such an increase of the new Japanese tariff on goods subject to export from this country.[3]

But Grey also informed his audience that, while the Japanese:

10  *Ian Nish*

> ... ought to be ready to meet us in a most friendly way in regard to commercial negotiations, it also implies that we must recognize their point of view is one of complete equality. The foundation of our cordial relations with Japan is that we were the first to recognise [in 1894] that they take a place of complete equality in the comity of nations.

In other words, the British government tried to persuade the merchant community that it had to give up some of the nineteenth-century privileges and concessions which the traders had enjoyed in Japan. In the end, Tokyo did accept the thrust of these arguments and introduced a tariff in 1911 which was much less hurtful to British interests than had originally been thought. Nonetheless Britain's exports to Japan and East Asia generally declined with the coming of the war.

Britain's security in East Asia depended on the Royal Navy. But the British government had to overcome problems connected with the drain on its resources from maintaining an elaborate China squadron so far from home. The navy was essential for the maintenance of Britain's trade with the region and the key defence against signs of Russian expansion into Asia and the Pacific. To that end it had concluded the Anglo–Japanese alliance in January 1902. In a secret diplomatic note added to the treaty Britain promised to maintain its naval strength in East Asian waters, providing its vessels could be readily available for concentration there without necessarily being physically present: '[Each ally] has no intention of relaxing its efforts to maintain as far as possible available for concentration in the waters of the Extreme East a naval force superior to that of any third Power.' The ambiguity of the wording here suggests that the withdrawal of naval resources from this region was built into Britain's understanding of the alliance from the start, although the Japanese took a diametrically opposed view.

The other pillar of Britain's policy was the Anglo–French entente of April 1904. Though these French treaties made no mention of East Asia (if one excepts Siam), they were in part a device to prevent Britain, the ally of Japan, and France, the ally of Russia, being drawn into the Russo-Japanese war, which had started two months previously. Though there were no specific clauses dealing with the east, it was in the mind on both sides that they wanted to stay well clear of involvement in the war.

These two connections were bound to lead to misunderstanding and dispute. Britain and France each sought to abet its ally without violating benevolent neutrality. The war took a maritime dimension when the Russian government decided to send its Baltic fleet around the world to far eastern waters, calling on French naval installations for coal and food. The main squadron reached Camranh Bay in Indochina in May 1905. It moved out every two days in order to comply with international law and pacify the French colonial administration. But it had to wait for the auxiliary fleet, a smaller, slower fleet under Admiral Nebogatov. This delay did in fact raise prickly issues, as France was inevitably blamed for assisting its ally, Russia, despite its proclamations of neutrality.

*Britain's retreat from Asia, 1905–23*  11

This led to a bizarre event which illustrates the complexity of Britain's policy of economy and withdrawal. Japan, which was observing the movements of the Russian ships, complained to Britain about the presence of the Russian fleet in Indochinese waters and asked the Foreign Office to protest to France. Britain duly appealed to France to be very careful over how it interpreted its obligations as a neutral, as it might have implications for the outcome of the impending naval struggle. France did tell the Russians to evacuate the anchorage – but compliance was slow to take effect.

At the same time the Admiralty, fearing 'an incident' over France, sent two ships to the South China Sea for observation. Admiral Sir John Fisher, the First Sea Lord, wrote:

> ... to be on the safe side we are sending out two more battleships as if to relieve two others due to be relieved in China, and six good destroyers as if to relieve others defective. This is all in the usual course of movements of ships, so won't attract attention.[4]

He called this 'a palpable pledge of good faith [to Japan] by our reinforcement of the China fleet'.[5] However, John Chapman has drawn attention to the anomaly that the Admiralty chose this moment to withdraw the four British battleships of the China squadron from Hong Kong some three weeks prior to the decisive naval battle at Tsushima. This bizarre episode seems to indicate that Whitehall was in a state of uncertainty and pessimism about Japan's prospects at this late stage of the war.[5]

It was of course understandable that the Admiralty should give the orders for the return home of the four battleships of the China squadron in June 1905 immediately after the decisive battle of Tsushima, even though this was done without consulting Japan and was in flagrant violation of the naval clauses of the alliance. The inappropriateness of maintaining a fleet with so many battleships in her China squadron had been a long-standing issue for Admiralty pundits. A withdrawal of part of the fleet from East Asia was therefore not unexpected, in spite of protests from the admiral on that station, and served the more immediate purpose of reinforcing naval strength in European waters in the name of 'naval consolidation'. However, this stealthy withdrawal from the west Pacific was, of course, displeasing to the antipodean members of the British Empire; and complaints were raised by Australia and New Zealand at the regular Colonial conferences. There is no evidence of any Japanese complaint. Indeed, the recall of the five battleships could be regarded as a token of trust in, and dependence on, Japanese naval help in the future. In spite of these apparent inconsistencies, Admiralty policy was clearly aimed at the substantial withdrawal of its naval strength from the east in the long term. It signified the end of British naval ascendancy in eastern waters.[6]

Another feature of this period was the end of Japan's dependence on Britain's shipyards for the building of its navy. This was a Japanese withdrawal from an accustomed market, which demonstrated that Japanese shipyards had come of age and were able to build all but the most sophisticated warships. The building of the battle cruiser *Kongo* in the yards of Vickers Maxim at Barrow (launched 1913) was an important turning-point in Anglo–Japanese relations; it was the last major capital ship to be so built. Britain recognized that its role as builder for Japan was about to stop. As Tadashi Kuramatsu has put it, 'it signalled that the period of the Imperial Japanese Navy's tutelage under the Royal Navy was almost over.' While Japan still continued to purchase naval equipment from British suppliers, shipbuilding orders were reduced. This was an example of Britain's ally coming of age.[7]

## The alliance and China

The renewal of the alliance took place in the summer of 1905, what the Japanese called 'the re-negotiation of the alliance' – so radical were the changes envisaged. By this time the Japanese army was in occupation of Korea; and Japan wanted to ensure its continued supremacy there. So instead of 'the territorial integrity of Korea' which had been stipulated in the preamble to the 1902 treaty, the preamble of the new agreement promised to ensure 'the maintenance of the territorial integrity of the Possessions of the Contracting Parties' in the area. After some heart-searching, Britain sacrificed Korea's independence. During the negotiations, the Japanese asked for a guarantee that Britain would maintain its navy at the same strength in eastern waters as had been the case in 1902–5. But the Foreign Secretary himself said that this would lead to 'a superfluously large number of ships in the Far East'. Britain refused and no such commitment was included in the revised treaty when it was renewed for ten years on 12 August.[8]

In 1911 the two governments decided to renew the Anglo–Japanese alliance which was not due to expire until 1915. This involved a revaluation of Britain's security position. The Committee of Imperial Defence, in advocating a renewal of the alliance without any delay, gave a projection for the future:

> At present we maintain only a small naval force in the Far East relying on our alliance with Japan. [If we were to give up the alliance,] the reinforcement of our China Fleet to anything commensurate with the strength of the Japanese Navy would imply an important increase in our building programme.[9]

The prospect of increasing the shipbuilding budget even more did not appeal to British politicians. The security position was referred to a Colonial conference where it was agreed that the alliance should be renewed early. Again heart-searching took place over the position of Korea, which had been annexed by Japan during the previous year; and mention of it was dropped from the text. In the new treaty, Britain made clear that it was not prepared to accept any commitment to get involved in any war which happened to take

*Britain's retreat from Asia, 1905–23*   13

place between Japan and the US. The link-up was renewed for ten years and duly signed on 13 July.

Within three months a revolution took place in China. This is too great a subject to be tackled here. The political situation under the new republic and the Yuan Shihkai presidency was chaotic; and in Britain's view some elements in Japanese society, especially the military and the *zaibatsu*, appeared to wish to take advantage of it to achieve their purposes in central China. On the political/diplomatic front, Britain was aware of the Japanese urge for continental expansion and feared the inevitability of Anglo–Japanese competition for the markets of China. It was a recurring theme in Japanese dialogue that it wanted the Anglo–Japanese Alliance to become 'an alliance of commerce'. This was one of the themes of the vast Japan-British exhibition in London in 1910.[10] But there are countless other examples in speeches of Japanese politicians of the time, recommending cooperation, even joint ventures in China, in which Britain would supply the capital and the Japanese would supply the enterprise. Could the allies unite in economic and industrial cooperation in China proper? Though the Japanese aim was to secure a share in the markets of south and central China, Britain was determined to hold on to the exclusive privileges that it had acquired during the nineteenth century in the Yangtse valley where the revolutionaries were taking control. Britain was preoccupied in preventing industrial enterprises and railway building being taken over by any other Power, even its own ally. The instability in China brought about a change in Britain's confidence in Japan.

Britain was less interested in Japan's aspirations in Manchuria, the northeastern provinces of China where the war of 1904–5 had been fought and Japan had expended much in terms of blood and specie. On 3 and 10 January 1913 Sir Edward Grey held a critical personal conversation on this subject with Katō Takaaki, shortly before the latter returned to Japan in order to become foreign minister. Katō explained that three years after France, Germany and Russia had forced Japan to give back Port Arthur in 1895, Russia had taken a lease on the same territory for twenty-five years. Under the Russo-Japanese treaty of September 1905 Japan had obtained the residue of this lease, which meant that at the time of this conversation, there were only ten years yet to run before the lease would revert to China. Katō stressed that, when the lease expired, no Japanese government would be strong enough to give the leased territory back to China. Grey recognized the force of this argument, but, since the matter would not arise imminently, he promised merely to put on record what the ambassador had said. Katō's version of the conversation suggests that Grey's response was warmer than the Foreign Office version; at the very least Katō could take comfort that Grey did not explode at the idea of Japan's continental ambitions. Indeed, it was recognized on Britain's part that Japan was a populous power and, if it did not expand in Manchuria, it might expand into the southern Pacific. Moreover there was a view that, if Japan could be encouraged to go into Manchuria, it was less likely to intrude into the Yangtse valley. Various formulae were

14 *Ian Nish*

brought forward around this time whereby both countries could enjoy rights in Manchuria or the Yangtse valley or, alternatively, that one country would not encroach in the 'sphere of influence' of the other. But Japan would not allow Britain to have rights in Manchuria so the formula lapsed; the Manchurian problem would then re-surface at regular intervals over the next two decades.[11]

## Wartime developments

Britain's worries about the future of its stake in China surfaced in the major crisis over the Twenty-One Demands which Japan placed before the weakened regime of Yuan Shihkai early in 1915. These were only partially about Manchuria, but there was a clause which called for the lease to be extended indefinitely. These demands were the responsibility of former Ambassador Katō who had again been invited to become foreign minister in April 1914. The British ambassador, Sir Conyngham Greene, who had moved to the Tokyo embassy in 1912, gave London his impressions:

> The real 'power behind the curtain' is Baron Kato who has been chiefly instrumental in the formation of the Ministry, and who is looked upon with confidence by the people as a public servant of high intelligence and good repute. Strong, almost rough at times, and very direct in his manner of address, I know that he has not always been *persona grata* to some of my colleagues.... If, however, we may rely upon his friendship for England, and on his public utterances in support of the Anglo–Japanese Alliance, we may I hope look forward to a fair, and indeed sympathetic, handling of the many difficult problems which face our two Empires in the Far East.[12]

After a great deal of irritation with Japan and Katō, Britain tried to restore the situation to normality as soon as possible. Grey laid down that:

> ... our right policy is to efface ourselves over the demands, as far as is consistent with any actual British rights which they may affect, and bide our time in China till the war is over and trust to being then able to repair the damage.[13]

Grey was determined that 'we should not intervene in any way in regard to the 21 demands.'[14] Whatever might Britain have done or said a decade earlier, she was now powerless to carry much weight with the Japanese. Britain's position had declined from a position of strength in East Asia, even if illusory strength, to one of comparative impotence. The theme tune was: till the war is over!

Britain was divided in its loyalties. Diplomats admitted that a grave injustice had been done to China without Britain being able to offer any practical help. At the same time, they appreciated the dilemma of having to deal with the rising power of Japan which was not ready to be restrained by outsiders in its segment of the world. There were also repeated expressions of sympathy for Japan: 'Japan is barred from every other part of the world except the Far East and the Anglo–Japanese alliance cannot be maintained if she is to be barred from expansion there also.'[15] Japan's wartime expansion was about to threaten the alliance and this might in turn imply sacrifices on the part of Britain.

By 1917 Britain's plight in the war brought it to realize how much it had to rely on Japanese support. It made a positive appeal to Japan for assistance with naval convoys and patrol vessels for the Mediterranean station. There was a feeling that Japan was not pulling its weight as an ally in the global struggle and that some Japanese wanted to do more. (This was probably an example of Britain's limited vision about how the Japanese were looking at the war.) In response to Britain's appeal, Japan in January 1917 agreed to give naval assistance. In return Britain agreed to rather severe terms which the Japanese imposed in secret undertakings. These mainly related to the support which Britain promised at a final peace conference for the Japanese to take over the former German part of the Chinese province of Shandong. This went against the grain in London but the exigencies of wartime food supply across the Atlantic were such that the home front in Britain was desperate.

As the minister responsible for the 1917 secret agreements, the Foreign Secretary, Arthur Balfour, later commented that Grey's perception about Japan's legitimate ambitions was right but he probably expressed it too strongly. So it was by no means Grey's particular idiosyncrasy. Balfour as a conservative/unionist minister was also involved in re-thinking Britain's position in the east and taking a more relaxed view of Japan's ambitions.[16]

## Post-war settlement

On the surface, the focus in the years 1919 to 1923 was on the two great conferences, the Paris Peace Conference and the Washington Naval Conference of 1921. But, underlying these, two factors were at work: the greater involvement of the United States in East Asian affairs and the influence of China.

The peace conference of world leaders which assembled in Paris in early 1919 introduced a new force on the international scene, the United States. The newcomer which was in a position of extraordinary authority because of its wartime prosperity had great interest in Pacific affairs. Under the influence of a new spirit of nationalism, China was looking forward to the conference, hoping for signs of leadership from world statesmen which would enable it to rectify its relations with Japan. In particular the Chinese wanted the international assembly to cancel the treaty with Japan of 1915 which, they alleged, had been signed under duress, and the Sino–Japanese treaty of 1918 (voluntarily signed by China's leaders but weighted heavily towards Japan). President

16 *Ian Nish*

Wilson, who had just proclaimed his Fourteen Points, was China's main supporter. But the schedule during the hectic months of the deliberations at Paris did not leave enough time to consider East Asian problems thoroughly and Wilson was to find British leaders far from visionary. Balfour took the line that he could not defend the Sino–Japanese treaty of 1915 but that the 1918 treaty was valid: the powers at Paris could not overrule treaties which had been signed with due process.[17]

At the eleventh hour of the deliberations, the delegates turned to the problem of the future of the German lease in the Chinese province of Shandong. Balfour was given the brief on behalf of the Council of Three (Italy having opted out of the Council of Four). His recommendation was in favour of Japan being granted the lease of the former German concession, now in the occupation of the Japanese army. This recommendation was adopted by the leaders and incorporated in the Versailles treaty. Britain, which generally supported Japan's contribution to the war effort, observed the important undertakings it had made in the secret agreements of 1917. But after the war ended, it was not persuaded that the Paris solution to the China problem was the best outcome. After the treaty had been signed, Britain was no longer bound by its commitment to support Japan; and Curzon, Balfour's successor at the Foreign Office, was openly critical to the Japanese about their post-war policies towards China over Shandong.[18]

On the surface it appeared that Britain's star still shone brightly in the firmament. Because of President Wilson's retirement and illness, Britain, finding itself in a prominent position at Paris and the later European settlements, appeared to be restored to its former authority. Of course, it did not get all it wanted from the ultimate Versailles peace treaty but it, and the British Empire more generally, did benefit greatly. There was no obvious sign of Britain being in retreat. Is this true if we look at Asia?

By the time of the Washington Conference which opened in November 1921, Britain's position was less secure. The British mission was led by Arthur Balfour, now Lord President of the Council. The British Cabinet gave the delegates little advice except that the Anglo–Japanese alliance should be preserved if at all possible and that global naval disarmament was essential to Britain for financial reasons. Travelling by the *Empress of France*, the delegation studied the documents about the alliance throughout the voyage and tried to find a formula which would reconcile the two allies with their opponents. Balfour knew that the Chinese and the Americans as a whole were hostile to the alliance and wanted to see it ended, but he hoped to find a solution whereby the United States could be brought into some sort of triangular relationship, while preserving the core of the old alliance. Arriving at Quebec, he was met by Maurice Peterson of the Washington embassy and briefed about the latest developments over the conference.[19]

The new Republican administration which had taken office under President Warren Harding in March held the view that the United States had been beaten by Britain and 'Old Europe' at Paris and mounted a new radical

American initiative for world peace. Over East Asian problems this was an initiative influenced by the newly emerging Chinese nationalism. Accordingly, Balfour found that it was impracticable to convince fellow-delegates to support the continuation of a pre-1914 treaty. Thus the alliance was ultimately submerged in a Four-Power Pact which joined together the United States, Britain, Japan and France (which was admitted as a latecomer). It was an example of the idealism of the post-war period which surmised that disputes could be resolved by consultation and negotiation. It was explicitly stated that the Anglo–Japanese Treaty of 1911 'shall terminate' after ratification of the Washington treaties. The alliance, which had been advantageous to both Britain and Japan, was ended with barely a whimper of concern in London. However, the Tokyo government, while declaring its own satisfaction, was confronted with hostile public opinion expressing disappointment.

This is not the place to discuss those many-sided aspects of the Washington conference devoted to naval power and to China. The United States introduced an audacious scheme for reduction of the tonnage of the world's navies and steered it through the conference. Although Britain was surprised, politicians were not displeased by the prospect of reducing the expenditure on naval building. Balfour specially praised the 'bold statement' with which the US launched the naval initiative:

> This was conceived in a spirit of high statesmanship which raised the whole level of our debates... By no other approach could we have reached the self-denying policy with regard to Naval bases in the Pacific which provides one of the great securities for Naval peace in that vast area.[20]

By other self-denying ordinances, the conference took steps to improve the lot of 'the new China', in response to the signs of a new sense of nationalism there. China received back its rights in Shandong, not of course from Britain but from Japan. In view of this, Balfour thought it expedient, using the personal discretion given to him, to announce Britain's intention to give up the territory of Weihaiwei. The lease under the treaty of 1898 was due to lapse in 1923 and Balfour thought it appropriate to 'abandon' or 'surrender' it (using his own words).[21] The Nine-Power Pact 'relating to principles and policies to be followed in matters concerning China' took the first steps to clear up many outstanding problems including treaty revision and raised the present tariff rates to an effective 5 per cent. While Britain hoped to re-establish its position in pre-war trade, there was a serious fall in British exports, especially in cotton piece goods, only partly compensated for by increasing its machinery exports. An expert on British trade in Asia, E.M. Gull, concluded that 'Great Britain ceased to be cock of the walk in China, falling commercially to third place behind the United States and Japan.'[22]

Britain did not admit publicly that there had been a decline in its fortunes. It saw itself as trying to win back the position it had possessed in East Asia

18    *Ian Nish*

before 1914. But the world had changed and it was not so easy to recover its pre-war standing. It was important that the calculated concessions made should not be seen as a sign of weakness, least of all as a defeat. A positive gloss had to be put on concessions in the name of peace and stability in the region.

During the Washington deliberations the US had shown a new interest in Asian affairs and assumed a leadership role. Many of its initiatives were acceptable to Britain, while others were timely in the sense that the nineteenth-century privileges enjoyed by British nationals were no longer appropriate. It suited Britain – and the British Empire – to cooperate with the Americans on this occasion and support its leadership. But it remained to be seen whether that leadership role would be sustained.

## Conclusion

We have already seen that, as Japan's ambitions and population grew, the alliance treaties had to be flexible and to reflect these changes. The revised treaties of 1905 and 1911 had to give up any reference to Korea as an independent state. Second, the increase of Japanese tariffs under the 1911 treaty was a substantial concession to Japan. Needless to say this was not popular among the mercantile community and only accepted grudgingly by the powerful chambers of commerce involved. Britain admitted that Japan, as a leading world power, had aspirations which were justified and could not be circumscribed by restraints. Nonetheless, it fought its corner to preserve its sphere of interest in central China. But bit by bit Britain had to conciliate Japan. Grey held back many unpleasant issues 'till the war is over'; and Britain had to accept awkward undertakings in 1917 which it had no choice but to honour at the Paris peace conference. Finally at Washington Britain found itself required to make uncomfortable self-denying gestures. These did not amount to a retreat from East Asia but they represented a decline in the preponderant position which Britain had occupied in the area during the nineteenth century.

The signs of British retreat in East Asia described in this essay are small by comparison with those which Peter Lowe chronicled in his later studies. The former were generally what he called 'planned retreats'. Later Britain was forced to make desperate retreats on a larger scale in times of emergency. Thus in his study on the Pacific War, he acknowledged such elements of retreat as the Burma Road crisis of 1940 and the surrender of Singapore in 1942.[23] Again, because of the circumstances of the Pacific war, Britain – and even the British Commonwealth – had a negligible role in the military and civilian occupation of Japan after 1945. Nonetheless Britain tried desperately to have a voice in the peace settlement with Japan which led up to the San Francisco treaty and, according to Lowe, in some measure succeeded.[24] In his last two monographs his conclusion is that Britain appeared 'centre stage for the last time in 1965'.[25]

'Retreat' is an extreme word with military overtones and does not seem appropriate for the period down to 1923. 'Retirement' suggests a more gentle process, a calculated recognition that the wave of nineteenth-century expansion in which Britain had indulged in East Asia could not continue indefinitely and that it was appropriate that it should stage a slow, planned withdrawal and try to keep alive its special relationship with Japan as long as it could.

## Notes

1 Peter Lowe, *Great Britain and Japan, 1911–1915: A Study of British Far Eastern Policy*, London: Macmillan, 1969.
2 Ayako Hotta-Lister, *The Japan-British Exhibition of 1910*, Richmond: Japan Library, 1999, pp. 87–90; and Janet Hunter and S. Sugiyama (eds), *Anglo–Japanese Economic and Business Relations*, Basingstoke: Palgrave, 2002, pp. 36–42.
3 Manchester Chamber of Commerce, *Monthly Record*, 30 Nov. 1910, p. 311.
4 Fisher to Lansdowne 28 Apr. 1905, in A.J. Marder (ed.), *Fear God and Dread Nought*, vol. II, London: Jonathan Cape, 1956, doc. 20, fn. 1.
5 John Chapman, 'The Secret Dimensions of the Anglo–Japanese Alliance, 1900–1905', in Phillips Payson O'Brien (ed.), *The Anglo–Japanese Alliance, 1902–22*, London: Routledge, 2004, p. 90.
6 *British Documents on Foreign Affairs (BDOFA)*, part I, series E, vol. 12, contains information on the movements of the Russian squadrons.
7 Tadashi Kuramatsu, 'A Great Ordinary Man: Saitō Makoto (1858–1936) and Anglo–Japanese Relations', in J.E. Hoare (ed.), *Britain and Japan: Biographical Portraits*, vol. 3, Richmond: Japan Library, 1999, p. 190.
8 Ian Nish, *The Anglo–Japanese Alliance*, London: Athlone, 1966, pp. 330–3.
9 The National Archives (TNA), Kew, CAB38/19/46.
10 Ayako Hotta-Lister and Ian Nish (eds), *Commerce and Culture at the Japan-British Exhibition*, Leiden: Brill, 2012, p. 58.
11 *BDOFA*, Part I, series E, vol. 9, doc. 15, Annual report on Japan for 1913, p. 355.
12 *BDOFA*, IE, vol. 10, doc. 128, Greene (Tokyo) to Grey p. 406.
13 TNA, Jordan papers, FO350/14, Alston (FE Dept) to Jordan (Peking) 19 Mar. 1915.
14 TNA FO800/158, Campbell to Tyrrell 4 Nov. 1915.
15 British diplomats' reactions are given in Lowe, *Great Britain and Japan*, pp. 255–8.
16 Ian Nish, *Alliance in Decline: A Study in Anglo–Japanese Relations, 1908–23*, London: Athlone Press, 1972, pp. 202–3.
17 R.H. Fifield, *Woodrow Wilson and the Far East*, Hamden, CN: Archon, 1965, p. 279.
18 Margaret MacMillan, *Peacemakers*, London: John Murray, 2001, p. 339.
19 *Documents on British Foreign Policy 1919–39 (DBFP)*, first series, vol. 14, doc. 415. Maurice Peterson, the private secretary to Balfour, left an account in his autobiography, *Both Sides of the Curtain*, London: Constable, 1950, pp. 20–30.
20 Ibid., doc. 585 Balfour (Washington) to Lloyd George 6 Feb. 1922.
21 Ibid., doc. 415 Balfour to Lloyd George 11 Nov. 1921.
22 E.M. Gull, *British Economic Interests in the Far East*, Oxford: Oxford University Press, 1943, p. 104.
23 Peter Lowe, *Great Britain and the Origins of the Pacific War: A Study of British Policy in East Asia, 1937–41*, Oxford: Clarendon, 1977, and Peter Lowe and Ian Nish, 'From Singapore to Tokyo Bay, 1941–45', in Ian Nish and Yoichi Kibata (eds), *The Political-Diplomatic Dimension*, vol. II, *1931–2000*, Basingstoke: Palgrave, 2000, pp. 135–48.

20　*Ian Nish*

24　Peter Lowe, 'Britain's Labour Government and the Japanese Peace', in Ian Nish (ed.), *The British Commonwealth and the Allied Occupation of Japan, 1945–52*, Leiden: Brill, 2013, p. 246.
25　Peter Lowe, *Containing the Cold War in East Asia: British Policies towards Japan, China and Korea, 1948–53*, Manchester: Manchester University Press, 1997, and idem., *Contending with Nationalism and Communism: British Policy towards Southeast Asia*, Basingstoke: Palgrave-Macmillan, 2009.

# 2 Imperial Germany's strategy in East and South-East Asia

## The campaign against British India

*T. G. Fraser*

When war broke out in 1914 Germany possessed two major assets in East Asia. The first was Qingdao on the coast of China's Shandong peninsula which had been acquired in 1898 and developed as a base for naval operations in the Pacific. The other was the East Asiatic Squadron of the two powerful armoured cruisers *Scharnhorst* and *Gneisenau* and four light cruisers commanded by Admiral Maximilian Graf von Spee. Both were hostages to fortune. While von Spee's command could have given a good account of itself against the ships of Admiral Thomas Jerram's China Station, once Japan had entered the war on Britain's side on 23 August he stood scant chance against its powerful fleet, which had demonstrated its prowess at Tsushima nine years before. Deciding not to have his ships bottled up in Qingdao, Spee set off across the Pacific to his eventual destruction at the Battle of the Falklands on 8 December. By then, after a spirited defence by the small German garrison, assisted by men of the Habsburg cruiser *Kaiserin Elisabeth*, Qingdao had fallen to an overwhelmingly superior Japanese force, aided by some British and Indian troops, its governor Clemens Friedrich Meyer-Waldeck surrendering on 7 November. Two days later, the cruiser *Emden*, which had detached itself from von Spee's squadron, was destroyed by the Australian cruiser *Sydney* at the Cocos Islands. Under its enterprising commander Karl von Mueller, the *Emden* had ranged across the Indian Ocean, and on 22 September had bombarded the port installations of Madras. As the year 1914 ended, Germany's presence in the region seemed to have collapsed, but there were hopes maturing in Berlin that such assets as remained could be used to advantage, the focus of these activities being to help foment unrest in India, which Benjamin Disraeli had rightly described as the 'brightest jewel' in Britain's imperial crown.[1]

Compared with the preponderant power of Britain and Japan in the region these German assets were meagre, but they did hold some potential. Germany's plans rested on its ability to operate from the territory of neutral countries, where revolutionary activity could be organized and coordinated by diplomatic officials assisted by patriotic exiles. Siam [Thailand] offered possibilities, since it had a land frontier with Burma, then part of the Indian empire, and had a large Indian minority. So, too, did the Netherlands East

22    *T.G. Fraser*

Indies where there was a sizeable German expatriate community of some 600 males, whose patriotism could be enlisted. Their leaders included the consul-general at Batavia, Erich Windels, and the brothers Emil and Theodor Helfferich. The last two were especially important, since their brother Karl was a senior political figure at home.[2]

Nor did the fall of Qingdao entirely eradicate the German presence in China since the latter country remained neutral until 1917. Able to operate out of the International Settlement, the consul-general in Shanghai, Hubert Knipping, was designated to control attempts to assist the Indian revolutionaries.[3] The other neutral country which held the key to the German plans was the United States, partly because of its control of the Philippines, but more importantly through its embassy in Washington and its network of consular agents. Franz von Papen, the military attaché, and the consul in San Francisco, Franz Bopp, were to become central figures. Key communications to Berlin went through the ambassador, Johann Graf Bernstorff.[4] Moreover, a potentially invaluable Indian revolutionary party based in San Francisco had been founded in 1913. It will be obvious that since vast distances had to be overcome, the coordination and implementation of any plans from Berlin would be immensely difficult, especially since the lines of communication were dominated by the British and Japanese. Once the British were alerted to such activities, success would inevitably become problematic. Moreover, any clandestine operation is potentially vulnerable to betrayal from within. Nevertheless, it was out of this network of diplomats and expatriates in East and South-East Asia and in the United States that officials in Berlin hoped to disrupt Britain's position in India.

It would be difficult to overstate how important control of India was for Britain's war effort, not least as a source of manpower. Although the Indian Army had never been intended, trained or equipped for European warfare, on the outbreak of war it was Britain's sole reserve of organized troops. On 24 August 1914 the 3rd Lahore Division embarked for France, followed a month later by the 7th Meerut Division. On 26 October leading elements of the Lahore Division, 57th Wilde's Rifles (Frontier Force), 129th Duke of Connaught's Own Baluchis, and 1st Battalion Connaught Rangers, deployed in the trenches for what became known as the First Battle of Ypres. The presence of the Connaughts emphasizes the fact that the use of the Indian Army also involved regular British, or in their case Irish, battalions. All of them were invaluable and timely reinforcements.[5] Once the Ottoman Empire was at war with Britain on 5 November, the Indian Army could be looked upon to take up much of the strain of the war in the Middle East, freeing British troops for the main front in Europe. By 1918 some 1,218,000 Indians and Nepalese Gurkhas had enlisted.[6] There was, therefore, every incentive for Germany to seek to undermine India's key role in Britain's war effort. The question was not whether, but how?

The answer seemed to lie with Indian groups which were prepared to mount an armed challenge to British rule. The two main political organizations, the

*Germany's campaign against British India*   23

Indian National Congress and the Muslim League, were committed to constitutional politics, and leading Indian politicians were prepared to wait for the British to grant substantial political progress in return for the country's support in the war. But the pace of political life had quickened appreciably since Lord Curzon had announced the partition of Bengal in 1905, which had enraged political opinion, encouraging others to emerge who were impatient with such a gradualist approach. It was not surprising that the focus of such activity was to be found in Bengal where a series of violent incidents began the following year. Recruits for such a campaign came forward from amongst young men of the educated Hindu *bhadralok* community. Between 1906 and the outbreak of war a string of violent attacks, often against Indian police officers who were investigating revolutionary activities, took place in Calcutta and other parts of Bengal. Three Bengali revolutionaries who were to feature in subsequent German activities stood out as leaders of especial talent and enterprise. The most dynamic figure in Calcutta was Jatin Mukherji, a former shorthand typist with the Bengal government. Associated with him was Narendra Nath Bhattacharya, who was to achieve later fame as the leading communist M.N. Roy. A third Bengali, Rash Behari Bose, the head clerk of the Forest Research Institute at Dehra Dun, was the organizing hand behind the bomb attack on the Viceroy, Lord Hardinge, as he made his ceremonial entry into the newly proclaimed imperial capital of Delhi on 23 December 1912, after which he evaded the attempts of the Indian Police to find him.[7]

If by 1914 Bengal was known to be the centre of armed revolutionary activity, areas of the Punjab were also in the process of becoming affected. That such a thing might happen was especially disturbing to the British since the province was the principal recruiting ground for the Indian Army. The figures speak for themselves. By the end of the war some 480,000 Punjabis had been recruited, supplying some 40 per cent of the combatant troops from a province which contained only a thirteenth of the Indian population. Of these, the Jat Sikhs of the central Punjab were particularly prominent. Numbering just 12 per cent of the Punjab's population, by January 1915 the community was supplying 39.6 per cent of its combatants. In all, 97,016 Sikhs served in the course of the war.[8] Even so, by 1914 a section of the Sikh population originating in these critical recruiting areas of the central Punjab had become seriously disaffected. The reason is to be found in the racial discrimination encountered by Sikh migrants on the Pacific Coast of the United States, and, more pertinently, in the Canadian province of British Columbia. Taking advantage of the north Pacific shipping routes, between 1905 and 1907 some 5,000 Jat Sikh males had migrated to British Columbia, their arrival coinciding with that of 7,000 Japanese. Their presence triggered a demand amongst the white population for immigration controls on Asian immigration, to which the government in Ottawa responded by passing an Order in Council preventing entry into Canada of anyone who had not come by a continuous journey from their country of origin. Since there was no steamship service from India to Canada the measure brought Indian

## 24   *T.G. Fraser*

immigration to an abrupt end. By 1913, when all attempts in Ottawa and London to reverse this measure had failed, the Sikhs of British Columbia, as well as their compatriots on the American west coast, were turning to thoughts of revolution.[9]

They were aided in this by a number of Indian revolutionaries who were living in the United States. Chief amongst them was Har Dayal. Born in Delhi in 1884, he had pursued a brilliant academic career at the Government College in Lahore before deciding to resign his Government of India scholarship at St John's College Oxford in 1907, turning instead to nationalist politics, latterly in the United States.[10] In the spring of 1913 he joined a number of Sikh leaders, prominent amongst whom were Sohan Singh Bhakna of Bridal Veil, Oregon, and Jawala Singh of Stockton, California, to form the Hindi Association of the Pacific Coast, dedicated to the overthrow of British rule in India. Sohan Singh was made president, with Har Dayal as secretary.[11] From its headquarters in San Francisco, on 1 November 1913 the association published the first issue of its newspaper, *Ghadr* ('Mutiny'), the name by which the movement became known. Har Dayal's association with the party was short-lived, since in 1914 the American authorities took steps to deport him and he fled to Switzerland. By the outbreak of war there therefore existed in the neutral territory of the United States a revolutionary organization whose predominantly Jat Sikh membership came from precisely the key recruiting grounds in the Punjab which were so vital to the British war effort.[12]

It was not until the war was a month old that a campaign to assist the Indian revolutionaries was sanctioned. On 4 September the Chancellor, Theobald von Bethmann Hollweg, wrote to the *Auswaertiges Amt* that since Britain had apparently decided to wage war *à outrance*, one of their main tasks was gradually to wear Britain down through agitation in India and Egypt.[13] In fact, Bethmann Hollweg's wishes had already been anticipated.[14] The initial impetus appears to have come from Baron Max von Oppenheim. Born into a wealthy banking family in 1860, Oppenheim had been fascinated by the Islamic world, conducting archaeological excavations and travelling widely in the Ottoman Empire. In October 1914 he prepared a memorandum, '*Denkschrift betreffend die Revolutionierung der islamischen Gebiete unsere Feinde*', in which he advocated harnessing the Islamic sentiments of the Muslim peoples of the British, French and Russian empires behind the German war effort. Such a policy could come into its own once Turkey entered the war alongside the Central Powers on 5 November and the Sultan proclaimed Holy War. As the memorandum's title indicates, Oppenheim's experience and interest were in the Muslim world, and after making for Istanbul in 1915 he featured little in the Indian plans which were maturing.[15] The real driving force behind the attempts to arm the Indian revolutionaries was a young official of the *Auswaertiges Amt*, Otto Guenther Wesendonck. A member of a highly cultivated family, he was the grandson of the poet Mathilde Wesendonck, whose verses had gained immortality by being set to music by Richard Wagner as the *Wesendonck Lieder*.[16]

*Germany's campaign against British India*  25

The first task facing Oppenheim and Wesendonck was to recruit Indians who could help further their plans. There were two possibilities. The first was to engage the sympathies of the small Indian community of around 100 then living in Germany, most of them studying in Berlin, Hamburg, Dresden and other university cities.[17] It was out of this group that a committee was formed in Berlin in late August and early September.[18] However keen they might be, these young men were political novices, and for political leadership the Germans turned to members of the Indian revolutionary diaspora. An early recruit was Chempakaraman Pillai, adopted son of the Yorkshire baronet Sir Walter Strickland, who was living in Switzerland writing anti-British articles. On 8 August he left Zurich for Berlin and quickly became involved with the fledgling organization, which by January 1915 was known as the Indian Independence Committee.[19]

Living in the Friedenau district of Berlin was Virendra Nath Chattopadhyaya, born in 1880 into a remarkable family of Bengali origin. After a brilliant scientific career in Edinburgh, his father became founder and Principal of the New Hyderabad College, later called the Nizam's College, and was active in the formation of the Indian National Congress. His sister, Sarojini Naidu, earned fame as a poet, and after the war worked closely with Mahatma Gandhi in his non-violent campaigns. Chattopadhyaya's career took a different turn. Coming to London to study for the Middle Temple, by 1909 he was involved in revolutionary politics, which in various forms engaged him for the rest of his life.[20]

Even so, the Germans failed to recruit or enlist the sympathies of any major Indian political figure. The closest they came was Har Dayal, who had made his way to Geneva. At the suggestion of Hans Freiherr von Wangenheim, the ambassador to Turkey, he initially went to Istanbul to investigate the possibility of setting up an Indian organization there, but soon returned to Geneva. Wangenheim apparently was not impressed by him.[21] It seems that Har Dayal was in two minds about involving himself with the Germans. On 25 October he was issued with a passport and money to travel to Berlin, but returned them to the consul an hour later, explaining that he feared being isolated in Germany and that he could contribute nothing to the committee's work.[22] It took a personal visit from Chattopadhyaya in mid-January 1915 to persuade him to travel to Berlin by which time the committee's plans were well advanced.[23] In fact, relations between the two men were poor, and by early 1916 Har Dayal had become estranged from the committee. Forbidden by the Germans from returning to Switzerland, he lingered in the country until permitted to travel to Stockholm in October 1918. In 1920 he published in London *Forty-Four Months in Germany and Turkey*, in which he dismissed his erstwhile Indian colleagues and mounted a bitter denunciation of the Germans for their arrogance, leaving no doubt that his experience in the country had been a chastening one.[24]

If Har Dayal proved to be a disappointing recruit, a much greater setback for the Germans and their Indian colleagues was their failure to attract the

## 26   T.G. Fraser

leading Punjabi politician Lala Lajpat Rai, since he carried immense prestige and influence. Lajpat Rai's political credentials were impeccable, having been exiled to Burma in 1907 during agrarian disturbances in the Punjab. In 1914 he came to Britain as part of an unsuccessful Indian National Congress delegation, sailing for the United States in mid-November. Several attempts were then made to persuade him to join the revolutionaries, but from the start of his time in the country he repeatedly made clear his view that, while he was an Indian patriot, he preferred India to be a self-governing part of the British Empire rather than be ruled by the Germans.[25] In their rather different ways Har Dayal and Lajpat Rai had spotted the fundamental contradiction in Germany's support for Indian revolution; namely, that its record showed that it was every bit as imperialist as Britain.

While the Indian Independence Committee might have carried out useful work in the area of propaganda, Oppenheim and Wesendonck could not lose sight of the fact that the only way they could further Germany's objectives was to furnish arms to the Indian revolutionaries. In late September Bernstorff reported that Ghadr representatives and the San Francisco consulate had been in contact with a view to Germany's providing arms.[26] Two weeks later Indian revolutionaries in New York reported that an American company was prepared to ship a large consignment of arms to India on a neutral ship, but that they needed $30,000 security.[27] This proposal was dismissed at a meeting between Wesendonck and two naval officers, but the key decision was made that a major supply of arms to the Indian revolutionaries was to go ahead. Bernstorff was instructed to work with his military and naval attachés to purchase between ten and twenty thousand rifles with ammunition at a budget of between one and three million marks and to ensure that the weapons reached India.[28] By then Papen had already been at work with the Krupp representative in the United States, Hans Tauscher, and his manager, Henry Muck. By the first week in December the two men had used their contacts in the country to assemble 8,080 single-loading Springfield rifles, 2,400 Springfield carbines, 410 Hotchkiss repeating rifles, all of matching calibre with 4,000,000 cartridges and 5,000 cartridge belts, as well as 500 Colt revolvers with 100,000 cartridges.[29] Although the Springfields were by then obsolete, this armoury was clearly capable of mounting a serious challenge to the British, but two key questions remained. How were they to get to India and to whom?

The answer to the latter was not quite as obvious as it might have appeared since by the time Papen and his men were able to organize the shipment of the arms and ammunition to India in March 1915 the main effort by the Ghadr party to set off a revolution in the Punjab had already foundered. The revolutionary enthusiasm of the Ghadr members in Canada and the United States had been spurred by the unhappy *Komagata Maru* affair in the summer of 1914. On 23 May the *Komagata Maru*, a Japanese vessel chartered by a wealthy Sikh businessman called Gurdit Singh, arrived in Vancouver harbour with 376 Punjabis, mostly Sikhs, on board in an attempt to challenge

*Germany's campaign against British India*   27

Canadian immigration legislation. The ship was effectively quarantined offshore, Gurdit Singh's legal challenge failed and, just as the crisis in Europe was heightening, on 23 July the *Komagata Maru* was escorted out of Canadian waters. On its arrival at Budge Budge harbour outside Calcutta on 29 October, rioting broke out in which 20 of the passengers were killed.[30] During the two months that the ship was moored off Vancouver its fate was the subject of Ghadr meetings there and in California and Oregon. On 9 and 11 August the movement of revolutionaries to India was agreed at meetings in Fresno and Sacramento, the first large group of 60 to 70 sailing from San Francisco on 29 August, while hundreds of others followed. Some Ghadrites were intercepted by the Indian police on arrival, but others succeeded in reaching the Punjab where contact was made with Rash Behari Bose. Under Bose's leadership a rising based in Lahore in conjunction with men in some army units was planned for 19 February 1915, but the police had penetrated the movement and the attempt failed. Although isolated acts continued for a time, the main Ghadr organization in Punjab had effectively been broken. In short, Germany's most obvious ally in the United States and India had made its most serious move before assistance could be arranged. Amongst those who left for India were the party's early leaders, Sohan Singh Bhakna and Jawala Singh. The party was thus left in the hands of what proved to be the divisive and ultimately tragic leadership of Ram Chandra. It was to him, however, that Papen's agents had to turn for advice on the situation in India.[31]

The initial phase of the arms plan had gone well, but the accumulation of such a large armoury by German agents was inevitably going to catch the attention of the American Bureau of Investigation and of Captain Guy Gaunt's British intelligence network, making it imperative that its true purpose and destination be disguised. Shipment was entrusted to Frederick Jebsen, son of a former member of the *Reichstag*, a keen German patriot and owner of a shipping line in Seattle which had trading links with Mexico.[32] Through intermediaries Jebsen engaged the services of Marcos Martinez, a custom house broker, to arrange shipment of the arms to Topolobampo in Mexico. Martinez knew nothing of the shipment's true nature and purpose. Having been assured by the customs authorities that the shipment would be legal, Martinez set about arranging for the arms to be shipped from San Diego to Mexico on 19 January 1915 chartering the little schooner *Annie Larsen* and its crew. Also on board was to be a German merchant naval officer, Hermann Othmer, who was to assume command of the operation. At this point, the plan suffered its first, and ultimately fatal, setback, since the schooner Martinez had innocently chartered was quite incapable of reaching the cargo's real destination.[33] On 8 March 1915 Othmer embarked at San Diego on the *Annie Larsen*, informing its captain that he was not to sail for Topolobampo but head instead for the uninhabited Mexican island of Socorro in the Revilla Cigado group.[34] The schooner reached Socorro ten days later to await the arrival of another vessel which would take the arms to their real destination.[35]

28   *T.G. Fraser*

As an alternative to the *Annie Larsen*, Jebsen found the *Maverick*, an elderly oil tanker up for sale by the Standard Oil Company of California, but he was not able to complete the purchase until 16 March and the vessel then needed a lengthy refit.[36] The *Maverick* only sailed on 23 April. On board was a young American, John B. Starr-Hunt, who had been briefed on the plan, together with five Ghadr members. Starr-Hunt was instructed to rendezvous with Othmer at Socorro where the arms would be transferred to the *Maverick*. Othmer would then sail to Anjer in the Netherlands East Indies where he would be given instructions by agents of the Helfferich brothers. Starr-Hunt was to take the *Annie Larsen* to Topolobampo where he would have to explain why she had no arms on board.[37]

Actually, the *Maverick*'s destination was somewhat hazy, dangerously so. If no one met him at Anjer, Othmer was to proceed to Bangkok, and if he was not contacted there, he was to sail to Karachi, where it was believed the arms would be taken off in fishing boats. Papen told Berlin that the destination was Bangkok, but in his memoirs recalled it being Karachi.[38] The Helfferichs were thinking of a different destination. Karachi was not a particular centre of revolutionary activity and its choice may have been inspired by Ram Chandra who admitted to Lajpat Rai that he had told the Germans that there would be hundreds and thousands of revolutionaries there to receive the arms but that he was afraid that there might be nobody. His confession did nothing to enhance the revolutionaries in the veteran politician's eyes.[39] Fortunately for Ram Chandra he was spared embarrassment, since the Germans' plan proceeded to go further adrift. What finally foxed them was that the *Annie Larsen* had limited water capacity, and that Socorro proved to be waterless.[40] On 17 April her captain insisted that the schooner sail for Acapulco to take on water.[41] Twelve days later the *Maverick* berthed off Socorro to be informed by two stranded American seamen of the *Annie Larsen*'s departure.[42] On 27 April Othmer left Acapulco for Socorro, but here, too, the fates were against him, since the *Annie Larsen* could make no progress in the face of three weeks of head winds and calm seas. By then, her captain had had enough, informing Othmer on 19 May that his supplies meant that he had to return to the United States. On 29 June the vessel, with her cargo intact, berthed at the little timber port of Hoquiam, near Seattle.[43] Papen's scheme had fallen apart. Not only that, but the British were evidently now aware that something was being planned, two of their warships calling at Socorro to search the *Maverick*.[44] With no sign of the *Annie Larsen*, the *Maverick* sailed for Anjer and Batavia, reaching there on 19 July where its arrival without its expected cargo was a major blow to the ambitious plans which the Helfferichs had been maturing in conjunction with Jatin Mukherji.[45]

Just as this scheme was foundering, Papen was at work on another. At the end of January 1915 a representative of the Berlin committee, Heramba Lal Gupta, arrived and at a meeting in New York discussed the question of arms supplies. In March he requested that an additional 8,000 rifles, 2,000 revolvers and machine guns be sent to the Bengali revolutionaries.[46] His

*Germany's campaign against British India* 29

proposal was agreed on at the end of March, and once again Tauscher set to work, assembling a formidable armoury of 7,300 Springfield rifles, ten Gatling machine guns, 2,410,000 rounds of matching ammunition, and 920 Colt revolvers with 368,640 rounds of ammunition.[47] This time the plan was to be simpler. On 31 May Papen, who was still convinced that the other shipment was safely on its way to Java, informed Berlin that the second consignment would leave New York for the Netherlands East Indies on 15 June on the Holland-America vessel *Djember*.[48] By then, the intelligence network run by the British consul-general in New York, Sir Courtenay Bennett, was fully alert, tracing the arms to Tauscher and informing the shipping company. When the trucks carrying the arms arrived to be loaded, Tauscher's agent was informed that the contract was cancelled. A second major arms consignment had got no further than the American coast.[49]

It was in the expectation that arms would be forthcoming that the Hellferichs and Jatin Mukherji were making their plans. The offer of German help was conveyed to Mukherji by Jatindra Nath Lahiri who made the dangerous journey from Berlin to Bengal in early 1915, informing him that he should send an agent to Batavia to make arrangements for arms and money.[50] In April Narendra Nath Bhattacharya travelled to Batavia and arranged with the Hellferichs that the *Maverick*'s cargo should be landed on the Rai Mangal river in the Sunderbans.[51] Unfortunately for the revolutionaries, on his return to India Bhattacharya sent a telegram to a fellow revolutionary which was intercepted by the police.[52] Just as the police in Calcutta were being alerted, the scheme was being betrayed in Batavia by a close associate of the Helfferichs. In June the British consul-general in Batavia, W.R.D. Beckett, was contacted by someone who claimed to have knowledge of a steamer loaded with munitions, and that for the sum of fs 500,000 he could provide information which could frustrate a general rising.[53] At a subsequent meeting, the informant would only identify himself as 'Oren', born in Russia of mixed German-Swedish parentage. In addition to confirming that the *Maverick* had arrived empty, 'Oren' provided vital details of the links between the Helfferichs and Mukherji, down to the precise coordinates on the Rai Mangal river where Othmer was to have landed the arms. He also revealed details of the addresses in Calcutta where the Hellferichs had been sending money to Mukherji's organization.[54] As a result of this information, the police raided a house, finding a map of the Sunderbans and a paper referring to the *Maverick*.[55] In an operation on 9 September led by the Irish-born member of the Intelligence Branch, Charles Tegart, Mukherji and a colleague were killed and three others captured.[56]

By this time, the British had been made aware of a second German enterprise being incubated in the Netherlands East Indies. The idea was that a volunteer corps should be recruited from the local German community. These men would embark on a German steamer from Sabang off the north coast of Sumatra and attack the Andaman Islands on Christmas Day, freeing hundreds of political prisoners from the penal settlement at Port Blair, which held some of the most prominent and determined revolutionaries who had been

30    *T.G. Fraser*

sentenced to transportation, including the brothers Vinayak Damodar and Ganesh Damodar Savarkar. Some 2,000 armed men would then be landed on the Indian coast.[57]

Since this scheme never took place, it might readily be dismissed but for the extraordinary career of its author, Vincent Kraft. Kraft first contacted Wesendonck from a military hospital at Lille on 12 April 1915, announcing himself as a war volunteer from Batavia of German descent.[58] His ideas clearly impressed the Indian Committee and Wesendonck, who sanctioned his proposed Andamans scheme.[59] Immediately on his arrival at Medan in mid-July, Kraft offered his service as an informer to the British vice-consul, who passed the information to Beckett. Beckett then granted him a visa for Singapore, where he was arrested, as he had clearly intended.[60] When the officer commanding, General Dudley Ridout, offered him the choice of either being tried as a spy or working for the British, Kraft simply demanded money, and it was apparently agreed that he would work for the British for £2 a day.[61] Now in British pay, Kraft went to Shanghai to liaise with Knipping, who informed him that he had acquired a large stock of arms for shipment to India. Knipping agreed to land the arms at an island in the Little Nicobars for use in the projected Andamans project.[62] Even this endeavour came to grief, since Knipping's plans for the arms were betrayed to the British by a dissident Austro-Hungarian.[63] Although Kraft returned to the Netherlands East Indies to work on his Andamans scheme, both Knipping and the Indian Committee had decided that in view of these setbacks it should not proceed.[64] No further attempts to aid the revolutionaries came from this direction.

One further endeavour was attempted. This plan was based in Siam and its target was Burma, which contained a large ethnic Indian minority. This scheme seems to have originated with the arrival in Berlin from the United States of the Ghadr leader Barakatullah in early January 1915 and a meeting with Oppenheim.[65] In February 1915 the consul in Bangkok, Dr Remy, was informed that Knipping was responsible for Indian revolutionary affairs and that he was to follow his instructions.[66] Three men were recruited in the United States to aid the Ghadrites. Albert Wehde was an art dealer from Chicago who was to set himself up in Calcutta as a purchaser of Indian art but whose purpose was to finance the revolutionaries. He was to travel with two others who were to train revolutionaries on the Siam-Burma border, George Boehm, a German army veteran, assisted, it seems, by another German-American called Sterneck.[67] They got no further than the Philippines, where they transferred cases of arms from two ships, the *Sachsen* and *Suevia* which were in Manila harbour, to a motor schooner, the *Henry S,* with a view to smuggling them into Siam. But when they applied to American authorities for customs clearance on 10 July, this was refused and the arms were unloaded. Four days later they left Manila and took no further part in the enterprise.[68]

Siam now became the main focus of Ghadr activity, with several hundred revolutionaries gathering in the jungle at Pakho for the projected invasion of

*Germany's campaign against British India* 31

Burma. To train them, Knipping informed Remy that he was sending three former members of the Beijing embassy guard, Haeusing, Ecks and Jaenigen. On arrival, however, the last two were kept under surveillance by Siamese officials and only Haeusing made it to Pakho. Remy found an efficient conduit for arms to the revolutionaries, his agent persuading a Norwegian ship's officer trading between Swatow and Bangkok to smuggle in revolvers and ammunition on every trip. A substantial armoury was supplied to the revolutionaries.[69] However, the movement of Sikhs into the country could hardly go unnoticed, especially since three British officers on secondment from Burma were in senior police positions.[70] As information accumulated of Indians entering the country, an Indian secret agent was sent from Singapore, who soon became aware of the details of the plan. Acting on this intelligence, on 21 July the British *charge d'affaires*, Herbert Dering, secured the agreement of the Siamese government for the extradition of the suspected leaders. The police proceeded to arrest six leading Ghadrites.[71] Their arrest was enough to scuttle the plan, Remy concluding that it had collapsed.[72] Six other Ghadrites did enter Burma, but when they attempted to contact an Indian mountain battery they, too, were arrested.[73]

Although the Indian Independence Committee remained in existence until the end of the war, the Germans gave up on their plans of assisting the Indian revolutionaries from East and South-East Asia after their succession of setbacks in 1915. With limited experience of such work, German officials and their agents had tried hard with what assets they had, but it had been a costly exercise, the purchase and kitting out of the ill-starred *Maverick* alone costing $86,000.[74] Despite their endeavours they had never been able to overcome the logistical problems facing the supply of weapons to the revolutionaries, informers had undermined their plans, and the British were alert to any threat to their rule. Moreover, German activities in the United States had exposed them to unwelcome attention from the authorities, ultimately revealed in the so-called 'Ghadr Trial' in San Francisco of party leaders and their German associates. On its last day, 24 April 1918, Ram Chandra was shot dead in court by one of his fellow accused.[75] What German expectations were remains unclear. In his memorandum of 4 September 1914 Bethmann Hollweg had merely spoken of harassing Britain in India, and in his memoirs von Papen admitted that Indian independence could not be achieved with German help but that by fomenting local disorders the number of Indian troops being sent overseas might be limited.[76] Despite all the efforts made, even this modest goal eluded them, as did the hopes they had aroused in their Indian allies.

## Notes

1 For a discussion, see Hew Strachan, *The First World War, Volume I: To Arms*, Oxford: Oxford University Press, 2001, Chapter 6. The events in this chapter are discussed in the author's University of London doctoral thesis, 'The intrigues of the German government and the Ghadr party against British rule in India, 1914–1918',

32   *T.G. Fraser*

completed at the London School of Economics in 1974. I am grateful to my successive supervisors David Dilks and Ian H. Nish, and to W.N. Medlicott and James Joll. An earlier version of this chapter is the author's 'Germany and Indian Revolution, 1914–1918', *Journal of Contemporary History*, 12/2, 1977, pp. 255–72. See also Richard J. Popplewell, *Intelligence and Imperial Defence: British Intelligence and the Defence of the Indian Empire 1904–1924*, London: Frank Cass, 1995. I am grateful to Grace Fraser and Professor Alan Sharp for their helpful comments on my drafts.

2  The National Archives, Kew (TNA), FO371/3065(60854) 'List of Germans, Austrians, Turks and Pro-Enemy Residents in the Netherlands East Indies', Singapore, 1917.

3  TNA, German Foreign Microfilms (hereafter GFM) 21/397/00461–8 *'Eine kurze Zusammenfassung der Plaene des indischen Committees'* (Dec. 1914).

4  TNA GFM/21/397/00390–00391 Wesendonck memo 18 Oct. 1914.

5  J.W.B. Merewether and Sir Frederick Smith, *The Indian Corps in France*, London: John Murray, 1918, pp. 9–13, 21–2.

6  M.S. Leigh, *The Punjab and the War*, Lahore: Superintendent Government Printing, Punjab, 1922, (Reprints from the University of Michigan Library), p. 41.

7  The activities of the Bengali revolutionaries are chronicled from the official British perspective in the *Sedition Committee 1918 Report*, Calcutta: Superintendent Government Printing, 1918, (reprinted Nabu Public Domain Reprints), pp. 15–62.

8  Leigh, *The Punjab*, pp. 41–4.

9  T.G. Fraser, 'The Sikh Problem in Canada and its Political Consequences', *The Journal of Imperial and Commonwealth History*, vol. VII/1, 1978, pp. 35–55.

10  Dharmavira, *Lala Har Dayal and Revolutionary Movements of His Times*, New Delhi: Indian Book Company, 1970, pp. 40–50, and E. Jaiwant Paul and Shubh Paul, *Har Dayal: The Great Revolutionary*, New Delhi: Lotus Collection, Roli Books, 2003, pp. 7–106.

11  Sohan Singh Josh, *Baba Sohan Singh Bhakna: Life of the Founder of the Ghadar Party*, New Delhi: People's Publishing House, 1970, pp. 25–8.

12  See T.G. Fraser, 'The Intrigues of the German Government', Chapter 1. A recent analysis of the Ghadr movement is Maia Ramnath, *Haj to Utopia: How the Ghadar Movement Charted Global Radicalism and Attempted to Overthrow the British Empire*, Berkeley: University of California Press, 2011.

13  TNA GFM/21/397/00326 Bethmann Hollweg to *Auswaertiges Amt* 4 Sept. 1914.

14  TNA GFM/21/397/00461–00468 *'Eine kurze Zusammenfassung der Plaene des indischen Committees in Berlin'*, (Dec. 1914).

15  See Lionel Gossman, *The Passion of Max von Oppenheim: Archaeology and Intrigue in the Middle East from Wilhelm II to Hitler*, Cambridge: Open Book Publishers, 2013, *passim*.

16  Personal information.

17  TNA GFM/21/397/00352 Polizeirat Henning to Oppenheim 15 Sept. 1914, *'Inder und Perser in Deutschland'*.

18  TNA GFM/21/397/00318 Oppenheim to Prittwitz 31 Aug. 1914, and GFM/21/397/00461–00468, *'Eine kurze Zusammenfassung der Plaene des indischen Committees in Berlin'*, (Dec. 1914).

19  TNA FO371/2784(25020) Bertie (Paris) to Grey 5 Feb. 1916, enclosing French intelligence note on 'Piliai Chempakaraman' 29 Jan. 1916, and FO371/2786(8834) 'History of Sir Walter Strickland', Quinn (SB) 3 May 1916.

20  Tara Ali Baig, *Sarojini Naidu*, New Delhi: Publications Division, Ministry of Information and Broadcasting, Government of India, 1974, pp. 6–11, and James Campbell Ker, *Political Trouble in India 1907–1917*, New Delhi: Superintendent, Government Printing, 1917, pp. 69 and 265.

## Germany's campaign against British India   33

21  TNA GFM/21/397/00365 *Auswaertiges Amt* to Wangenheim 24 Sept. 1914, GFM397/00358 Wangenheim to *Auswaertiges Amt* 21 Sept. 1914, and GFM/21/397/00379 Wangenheim to *Auswaertiges Amt* 15 Oct. 1914.
22  TNA GFM/21/397/00405 Romberg to *Auswaertiges Amt* 25 Oct. 1914.
23  TNA GFM/21/397/00565 Romberg to *Auswaertiges Amt* 13 Jan. 1915.
24  TNA GFM/21/398/00530–00531 Singh (Berlin) to Indian Independence Committee 25 Jan. 1916, and Har Dayal, *Forty-Four Months in Germany and Turkey*, London: King and Son, 1920, (reprinted Forgotten Books, 2012).
25  'Indian Revolutionaries in the United States and Japan', 6 June 1919, in B.R. Nanda (ed.), *The Collected Works of Lala Lajpat Rai*, vol. 8, New Delhi: Manohar Publishers, 2006, pp. 173–92.
26  TNA GFM/21/397/00371 Bernstorff to *Auswaertiges Amt* 30 Sept. 1914.
27  TNA GFM/21//21/397/00383 Bernstorff to *Auswaeriges Amt* 16 Oct. 1914.
28  TNA GFM397/00390–00391 Wesendonck memo 18 Oct. 1914.
29  TNA GFM/21/397/00473 Bernstorff to *Auswaertiges Amt* 7 Dec. 1914, and British Library (BL), India Office Records (IOR), MSS.EUR.C.138, Ghadr Trial, vol. 2, p. 929, Muck testimony (Tauscher statement, 8 Feb. 1916).
30  See Fraser, 'The Sikh Problem in Canada'.
31  See Fraser, 'The Intrigues of the German Government', especially Chapters 3 and 4.
32  TNA FO371/2787(109254) Note on Frederick Jebsen,(c. June 1916).
33  BL IOR MssEur138, Ghadr Trial, vol. 4, Martinez testimony, pp. 1953–4, 1958–9, and vol. 8, Schluter testimony, pp. 3799–801; and TNA GFM/21/397/00622 Bernstorff to *Auswaertiges Amt*, 25 Jan. 1915.
34  BL IOR MssEur138, Ghadr Trial, vol. 8, Schluter testimony, pp. 3801–2.
35  BL IOR MssEur138, Ghadr Trial, vol. 2, Kotzenberg testimony (Othmer diary), p. 983.
36  BL IOR MssEur138, Ghadr Trial, vol.1, Opening statement for the United States, pp. 30–2.
37  BL IOR MssEur138, Ghadr Trial, vol. 6, Starr-Hunt testimony, pp. 3084–6.
38  TNA GFM397/00772 Papen to *Auswaertiges Amt*, 11 Feb. 1915; Franz von Papen, Translated by Brian Connell, *Memoirs*, London: Andre Deutsch, 1952, p. 40; and BL IOR, MssEur138, Ghadr Trial, vol. 6, Starr-Hunt testimony, p. 3085.
39  'Indian Revolutionaries in the United States and Japan', 6 June 1919, in Nanda (ed.), *The Collected Works of Lala Lajpat Rai*, vol. 8, p. 179.
40  BL IOR MssEur138, Ghadr Trial, vol. 2, Kotzenberg testimony (Othmer diary), p. 983.
41  BL IOR MssEur138, Ghadr Trial, vol. 2, Kotzenberg testimony (Schluter to Othmer), p. 984.
42  BL IOR MssEur138, Ghadr Trial, vol. 6, Starr-Hunt testimony, pp. 3100–1.
43  BL IOR MssEur138, Ghadr Trial, vol. 2, Kotzenberg (Othmer diary and Schluter to Othmer, 19 May 1915), pp. 983, 983–4, and vol. 8, Schluter testimony, p. 3810.
44  TNA ADM53/45610 Log of HMS *Kent* 13–14 May 1915.
45  TNA FO371/2494(105318) Beckett (Batavia) to Grey 2 Aug. 1915.
46  TNA GFM397/00798 Bernstorff to *Auswaertiges Amt* 1 Mar. 1915, and GFM/21/398/00011 Bernstorff to *Auswaertiges Amt* 25 Mar. 1915.
47  BL IOR MssEur138, Ghadr Trial, vol. 2, Muck testimony, (Tauscher statement, 8 Feb. 1916) p. 930.
48  TNA GFM/21/398/00176 Papen to *Auswartiges Amt* 31 May 1915.
49  TNA FO115/1895 CG (NYC) memo 1 July 1915, and BL IOR, MssEur138, Ghadr Trial, vol. 2 Muck testimony, p. 920.
50  TNA GFM/21/398/00608–12 Indian Independence Committee to Wesendonck 7 Apr. 1916, enclosing report from Harish Chandra, and J. Campbell Ker, *Political Trouble in India*, Calcutta: Superintendent, Government Printing, India, 1917, p. 277.
51  TNA FO371/2788(152538) P.K. Chakravarti statement 17 Dec. 1915.

## 34 T.G. Fraser

52 Ker, *Political Trouble in India*, p. 278.
53 TNA FO371/2494(106706) Beckett to Grey 2 July 1915 (copy of anonymous letter).
54 TNA FO371/2494(103192) Beckett to Grey, Hardinge and Jerram 29 July 1915, and FO371/2495(126500) Beckett to Grey 4 Aug. 1915.
55 Ker, *Political Trouble in India*, pp. 278–9.
56 Ker, *Political Trouble in India*, pp. 279–80, and Sir Percival Griffiths, *To Guard My People: The History of the Indian Police*, London: Ernest Benn, 1971, pp. 409–11.
57 TNA GFM/21/398/00079–83 Indian Committee memo 29 Apr. 1915, GFM/21/398/00090 'Andamanen' memo 4 May 1915, and FO371/2497(188834) Beckett to Grey 5 Nov. 1915, enc. Statement by 'Oren'. For the background to the Savarkar brothers see *Sedition Committee 1918 Report*, pp. 5–14.
58 TNA GFM/21/398/00057 Kraft letter, *Festungslazarett*, Lille 12 Apr. 1915.
59 TNA GFM/21/398/00055 Wesendonck memo 28 Apr. 1915, GFM/21/398/00079–83 Indian Committee memo 29 Apr. 1915, and GFM/21/398/00090 'Andamanen' memo 4 May 1915.
60 TNA FO371/2495(124971) Beckett to Grey 30 July 1915.
61 TNA FO371/2492(109593) Ridout (GOC Singapore) to WO 3 Aug. 1915, FO371/3422(6821) Ridout to DNI 5 Jan. 1918, and FO 371/3423(51442) French (MI1s) to Sperling (A. Dept) 16 Feb. 1918.
62 TNA FO371/3069(223) Biographical sketch of Kraft 13 Nov. 1917, and FO371/2495(136663) Ridout to WO 23 Sept. 1915.
63 TNA FO371/2496(153442) Alston (Peking) to Balfour 16 Mar. 1917, and FO228/2642 De Saumarez to Grey 15 Jan. 1916.
64 TNA GFM/21/398/00368 Indian Independence Committee to Wesendonck 14 Nov. 1915, and GFM/21/398/00576–8 Windels to *Auswartiges Amt* 5 Jan. 1916; Kraft's subsequent career is studied in Antony Best, 'The Double Agent's Tale: Vincent Kraft and Anglo–Japanese Relations, 1915–18' in John Fisher and Antony Best (eds), *On the Fringes of Diplomacy: Influences on British Foreign Policy, 1800–1945*, Aldershot: Ashgate, 2011, pp. 111–26.
65 TNA GFM/21/397/00563–4 Oppenheim memo 9 Jan. 1915.
66 TNA GFM/21/400/00142–54 '*Betrifft: Foerderung der indischen Aufstandsbewegung von Siam aus*' Remy (Berlin) 11 Nov. 1917.
67 TNA GFM/21/398/00088 Bernstorff to *Auswartiges Amt* 9 Apr. 1915, FO115/2067 Sperling to Spring-Rice (Washington) 14 Jan. 1916, enc. Note on Siam-Burma expedition, FO371/2784(8266) Singh statement 15 Nov. 1915, and FO371/2784 (8266) Boehm statement 16–17 Nov. 1915.
68 TNA FO371/2495(130787) Harrington (Manila) to Jerram (C-in-C China) 22 July 1915, and FO371/2784(8266) George Boehm statement 16–17 Nov. 1915.
69 TNA GFM/21/400/00142–54 '*Betrifft*' 11 Nov. 1917, and FO371/2884(8266) Sukumar Chatterji statement.
70 TNA FO628/32 Crosby memo 28 Dec. 1914, and FO371/3068(176681) Dering (Bangkok) to Balfour 27 July 1917.
71 TNA FO371/2493(99108) Dering to Grey 21 July 1915, FO371/2495(128631) Dering to Grey 6 Aug. 1915, FO371/2496(149891) Dering to Grey 8 Sept. 1915, and FO 628/32 Dering to Govts of India and Singapore 6 Aug. 1915.
72 TNA GFM/21/400/00142–54 '*Betrifft*' 11 Nov. 1917.
73 F.C. Isemonger and J. Slattery, *An Account of the Ghadr Conspiracy, 1913–1915*, Lahore: Superintendent, Government Printing, 1919, p. 135.
74 BL IOR MssEur138, Ghadr Trial, vol. 6, Rudbach testimony, p. 2791.
75 Isemonger and Slattery, *Account of the Ghadr Conspiracy*, p. 137.
76 Von Papen, *Memoirs*, p. 40.

# 3  Japan's Twenty-One Demands and Anglo–Japanese relations

*Sochi Naraoka*

## Preface

This chapter examines the impact that Japan's Twenty-One Demands towards China in 1915 had on Anglo–Japanese relations, mainly focussing on the conflict that emerged in diplomatic negotiations and newspaper reports. The Twenty-One Demands were presented by the Ōkuma Shigenobu government to the Yuan Shikai administration in order to enlarge Japanese interests in China. They consisted of five groups, and the main contents were as follows.

Group I confirmation of Japan's seizure of German ports in Shandong Province

Group II expansion of Japan's interests in southern Manchuria and eastern Mongolia

Group III Japanese control of the Hanyeping mining and metallurgical complex in central China

Group IV the prohibiting of China from giving any further coastal or island concessions to foreign powers except for Japan

Group V the compelling of China to hire Japanese advisors on finance and policing, empowering Japan to build three major railways, establishing a joint police organization of China and Japan and so forth

Groups I–IV were proposed with the intention of expanding Japan's existing interests. It was natural that China was opposed to them. However, they were not unacceptable to the Allied Powers, considering that Japan had declared war against Germany on the basis of the Anglo–Japanese alliance in August 1914. On the other hand, most of the articles of Group V were not based on existing interests and were likely to conflict with the equality of commercial opportunity among all nations in China and the preservation of its territorial integrity. Therefore, not only China but also Britain, Japan's main ally, and the United States, which had in 1899 required all foreign powers to agree to the above-mentioned principles, were strongly opposed to the demands. Japan succeeded in having China accept Groups I–IV in return for deleting Group V from the demands, but the relations between Japan and other countries became unprecedentedly worse. Therefore the issue of the Twenty-One Demands was a major turning point in Japanese diplomatic history.[1]

36  *Sochi Naraoka*

There have been a lot of previous studies on this topic, many of which have focussed on US-Japan relations. The Wilson administration was much concerned about this crisis, and the then Secretary of State, William J. Bryan, issued a statement that refused to recognize the treaties concluded on the basis of Japan's demands. This so-called '(First) Bryan Statement' is regarded as the beginning of the American 'non-recognition' policy, which was revived in the 1930s. In America, some books on the 'Demands' were published straight after the First World War[2], and scholars such as Arthur Link and Noel H. Pugach produced further studies after the Second World War.[3] Since then, Horikawa Takeo, Hosoya Chihiro, Kitaoka Shin-ichi, Shimada Yoichi, Takahara Shusuke and Kawashima Shin in Japan and Frederick Dickinson and Noriko Kawamura in the US have expanded the historiography.[4]

In contrast, there have been relatively few studies focussed on Anglo–Japanese relations. One of the exceptions is Peter Lowe's *Great Britain and Japan*, which was published in 1969.[5] He produced as comprehensive a survey of public and private documents in Britain as possible, and analyzed the issue of the Twenty-One Demands in the context of the history of Anglo–Japanese relations. His study, based on clear evidence, succeeded in presenting a persuasive interpretation, and faults cannot be found with his conclusions. However, there is room for expansion of his study through the examination of Japanese primary resources which Lowe did not survey and to build on other recent studies. This paper attempts to re-examine how the diplomatic negotiations concerning the Twenty-One Demands proceeded and what impact they had on Anglo–Japanese relations.

In this paper, I will focus on the British newspapers and journalists which have been neglected in previous studies. British newspapers were in a serious dilemma in the face of Japan's demands. Japanese expansion in China clearly had the potential to damage existing British interests, but Japan was a British ally and Japanese support was necessary for maintaining the war against Germany. The *Manchester Guardian*, whose position was near to that of the radicals and which reflected the interests of the commercial community of Lancashire, was critical of Japan's demands and insisted that British interests in China should be protected. On the other hand, *The Times*, which was conservative and friendly with the Foreign Office, basically reported in favour of Japan.

The director of the Foreign Department of *The Times* in those days was Henry Wickham Steed. He took the lead in reporting on East Asia, gathering information from correspondents in the field and consulting other principal members of the company, including Sir Valentine Chirol, a former head of the Foreign Department. The correspondent responsible for East Asia was David Fraser.[6] Although based in Beijing, he was practically a Tokyo correspondent as well, as he often moved between China and Japan collecting news material.[7] Another correspondent, William Donald, worked in Beijing under Fraser's guidance.[8] This Australian journalist was clearly pro-Chinese and communicated closely with other pro-Chinese sympathizers such as George Morrison,[9] another Australian journalist who was a former Beijing correspondent of *The*

*Times* and was now employed as a political advisor to President Yuan Shikai since 1912, and Paul Reinsch,[10] the American minister in China.[11] This paper examines their influence on the way in which *The Times* reported on the Twenty-One Demands, using documents from the News International Archives and the George Morrison Papers in the State Library of New South Wales.

## The submission of the Twenty-One Demands

The Japanese government declared war on Germany on 23 August 1914 and took control of German possessions in Asia and the Pacific within three months. The German colonies in the Western Pacific north of the equator were occupied in October, and Qingdao – the German concession in China – fell in November. The biggest objective that the Japanese government wished to achieve on this occasion was to extend the privileges that it had acquired in Manchuria after the Russo-Japanese War. In the peace treaty it had gained the right to lease Port Arthur and Dalian and to manage the South Manchurian Railways, but these rights were granted on a fixed-term basis and some of them were scheduled to expire in 1923. Faced with this troubling situation, Katō Takaaki, the Japanese foreign minister, thought that the Chinese might agree to extend the terms of the Japanese rights in Manchuria if Japan would return Shandong to China's sovereignty.

However, the domestic political situation made it difficult for the Japanese government to act upon Katō's blueprint. After the initial military success in Asia and the Pacific, many individuals within Japan started to advocate that their government should take this occasion to expand its interests in China. These individuals argued against the idea of handing Qingdao back. The Imperial Japanese Army (IJA) also advocated that the government should take assertive measures to expand Japanese interests in China. Although Katō was critical of these opinions, he and the Japanese Foreign Office (Gaimushō) could not ignore them. It was due to strong pressure from the IJA that he ended up inserting the seven articles which belonged to the fifth group of demands – which were by far the harshest requests that the Japanese made towards the Chinese government. The Twenty-One Demands were drawn up by 3 December and the document was submitted to Yuan on 18 January 1915.

Katō was fully aware that the demands in Group V might induce a sharp reaction not only from the Chinese but also from the Western powers. Therefore he emphasized to the Chinese that the real demands lay in the first four groups (Group I–IV), and that the fifth group (Group V) were only 'requests'. In addition, when Katō disclosed the contents of the Japanese conditions to the British, Russian, French and American governments, he showed them only the first four groups of demands, and deliberately concealed the articles which belonged to Group V. He was hoping that he could conclude the negotiations with the Chinese government as secretly and swiftly as possible, before the Western governments could learn about the contents of the Japanese demands.

## 38  *Sochi Naraoka*

Such negotiation tactics might have worked during the time of the Qing dynasty. However, the Japanese demands were extremely difficult for the new Chinese government to accept. China was, after all, going through a rapid growth of nationalism after the Xinhai Revolution of 1911–12. Yuan immediately leaked the contents of the demands, including the fifth group which had not been revealed to the Western governments, to journalists in China. By late January 1915 the fact that the Japanese had submitted twenty-one demands had become fully revealed, and resulted in unleashing widespread criticism towards Japan in the Chinese press. The phrase 'Japan's Twenty-One Demands' started to gain a negative connotation during this period. In addition, the Japanese demands began to catch the attention of American newspapers around the same time. Before the Japanese government could make counterarguments against such reports, numerous newspaper stories – including inaccurate ones – circulated around the press, and they contributed to creating a 'rumour' that Japan was intending to take drastic measures to expand its interests in China.

### The Chinese leak of Group V and the rise of anti-Japanese opinion

Yuan attempted to arouse the suspicion of the Western governments against Japan by leaking the contents of Japanese demands, in the hope that these countries would intervene on his behalf. Therefore Yuan's government continued to leak the information even after late January. The accurate details of the demands were communicated to Morrison by Yuan and his confidant, Cai Tinggan, sometime between 4 and 5 February. The information was then passed on to Sir John Jordan, the British minister to China. Around the same time, Donald gained the same information from Zhou Ziqi, the finance minister of the Chinese government, and Paul Reinsch, the American minister to China. On 7 February Donald telegraphed this information to Fraser, who at this time was in Tokyo, and the latter showed this document to Katō in an interview that they had the following day. The Japanese foreign minister had no alternative but to admit to the existence of Group V of the demands. In his memorandum, Fraser wrote as follows:

> I ventured my surprise that his office had formulated such proposals, for he, with his knowledge of international politics, must have known quite well that all the foreign offices of the Powers concerned would be horrified to realize what Japan was aiming at. He interrupted me at once. 'The demands were not formulated in my office; They were passed over to me by the military with instructions to have them presented to Yuan Shi-Kai without delay.'[12]

Fraser also informed Sir Conyngham Greene, the British ambassador to Japan, about Group V. Greene then visited the Gaimushō on 9 February to strongly protest.

Donald forwarded a detailed report about Group V to London, which reached *The Times* headquarters by 10 February. As the Foreign Office and the Japanese embassy in Britain both denied the existence of the group, Steed decided to censor this section of Donald's report before publication.[13] In addition, *The Times* argued on 13 February through its editorial that the Japanese demands did not violate the territorial integrity of China and the principle of open door.[14]

Eki Hioki, the Japanese minister to China, used these articles to inform the Chinese government that the British supported the Japanese demands.[15] There also were many Japanese newspapers, such as *Tōkyō Nichi Nichi Shimbun*, which referred to *The Times*' criticism of China's attitude over this issue.[16] In contrast, the newspaper articles of *The Times* sparked a strong reaction in China. The *Peking Gazette*, an English newspaper that was sympathetic to the Yuan administration, published an editorial on 16 February which argued that *The Times*, steered by Japan, was leading the world in the wrong direction. Morrison, Donald and Jordan all supported this contention.[17] Even in Britain, there were newspapers such as the *Manchester Guardian* which were critical towards Japan. This newspaper was read principally by individuals in the commercial and industrial sector of Lancashire, who paid great interest to trade in China. On 17 February it posted an editorial titled 'Japan and China' and, after reporting that there were currently many unofficial rumours circulating about the Japanese demands, raised its concern about the fact that 'Japan's action is in some ways scarcely compatible with the declared object of the Anglo–Japanese Alliance'.[18]

Despite the fact that *The Times* forwarded articles which were somewhat supportive of the Japanese stance over this issue, most of the other newspapers were becoming increasingly critical towards Japan. In this environment, Yuan handed the full translation of the twenty-one demands to Morrison on 15 February.[19] Morrison immediately forwarded this to Jordan, who passed it on to the Foreign Secretary, Sir Edward Grey, the next day.[20]

## The failure of Katō's attempt for swift conclusion of the negotiations

As Katō wanted to ensure confidentiality over this issue, he did not relay information about the existence of Group V even to his ambassadors, including Inoue Katsunosuke, the ambassador to London. However, information about this issue was becoming an open secret by mid-February, and on 17 February the Japanese foreign minister decided to inform Inoue about Group V through a telegraph. In the subsequent communication, he added that he had chosen not to disclose the existence of the fifth group because it was fundamentally different in its substance from the first four groups.[21] Inoue belatedly understood the situation, and forwarded three important telegrams to Tokyo two days later.[22]

The first telegraph informed Katō that there had been a rapid growth of anti-Japanese sentiment in Britain. Inoue pointed out that while *The Times* and the *Daily Telegraph* had not yet objected to the recent Japanese diplomatic manoeuvres in China, the *Manchester Guardian* was becoming increasingly critical towards Japan, and the ambassador duly forwarded a copy of the editorial on 17 February. Inoue added that the Japanese actions in China 'could induce a strong reaction from the British public. ... If the [Japanese] imperial government fails to deal with this issue in a satisfactory manner, then it could be put into a very difficult situation in terms of diplomacy.'

The second telegraph pointed out that, if the fifth group of the demands were presented simultaneously with the other demands and became a focal part of the negotiations, then it would be difficult to convince the Western governments that there was a fine distinction between the fifth and the other groups of demands. Inoue also suggested that it was highly likely that the Chinese government had already leaked the full contents of the Japanese demands, and feared that the British government might accuse Japan of duplicity.

The third and the last telegraph reported on the interview that Inoue had with Steed, who visited him on the day this telegraph was sent to Japan. Steed had a close relationship with many Japanese diplomats in London, and held a relatively favourable opinion of Japan.[23] This sentiment had led him to conceal some of the contents of Donald's report about the Japanese demands, and post an editorial that showed sympathy towards the Japanese position. Yet, even Steed felt compelled to inform Inoue that he was deeply concerned about the recent actions that the Japanese government had taken in China, as Steed had already been informed by Jordan that Donald's report was accurate. He also told Inoue that British residents in Beijing were infuriated by the fact that the Japanese were utilising the opinion of *The Times* to support their case. After this interview, Inoue realized that the British government knew about the details of the Japanese demands, and requested Katō for instructions.

The Japanese foreign minister duly permitted his ambassador in Britain to provide information about Group V,[24] and Inoue did so in a meeting with Beilby Alston of the Foreign Office on 20 February and with Steed on the following day.[25] Upon learning this, Grey decided on 22 February that he should revise British policy towards East Asia which had been based upon the belief that Group V did not exist, and communicated to the Japanese government through Greene that his government wished that British interests and the spirit of the Anglo–Japanese Alliance be respected.[26]

Katō complied with this request, but he also argued that 'there was no particular intent to hide' Group V as he hitherto had done, and also requested the British government not to intervene in the Sino–Japanese negotiations.[27] He also reiterated to the Russian, American and French ambassadors that the fifth group 'was not a demand', and also that it 'was not intended to violate the territorial integrity of China'.[28] Yet, the Sino–Japanese negotiations had seen virtually no progress even after a month after the Japanese government had submitted its demands. Meanwhile, the Chinese criticism and the suspicion of the West towards Japan had become stronger. Katō's initial tactics to

*Japan's Twenty-One Demands* 41

conclude the Sino–Japanese negotiations as quickly as possible and present them as *fait accompli* to the Western governments had failed.

## Continuing difficulties

Hioki, who was facing strong resistance from the Chinese, considered it impossible to settle this issue unless the Japanese government softened its attitude. On 12 February he advised Katō that the latter should prioritise the negotiations over the first four groups of demands, and leave the fifth group until the talks concluded.[29] However, Katō rejected Hioki's suggestion the next day and replied that there were 'precedents' for the Chinese government accepting demands similar to those in Group V when the Japanese government had requested them in the past. He therefore instructed his minister in Beijing not to back down over these demands until the Chinese considered them in a positive spirit.[30]

While Hioki did not raise any objections to these instructions, there is evidence that suggests he was disappointed. When he met Fraser after the latter's return to China in March, he said that he thought 'the [Japanese] government had made a serious mistake'.[31] However, the domestic political situation was making it increasingly difficult for the government in Tokyo to make compromises in the negotiations. As the contents of the demands had now been thoroughly leaked, Japanese newspapers sharply criticized the Chinese attitude, and demanded that the government be firm. Being the leader of the ruling party, Katō could not make compromises that might induce a public outcry, especially as a general election was scheduled to take place on 25 March. On 16 February the Ōkuma administration had approved a new draft of demands with only minor amendments, and authorized Hioki to promise that the Japanese government would give back Jiaozhou Bay around Qingdao, the German concession in China that was currently under the Japanese occupation, if the Chinese government would accept the Japanese demands.[32] The administration recognized that this was 'practically the only bargaining card that it had', and instructed its minister in Beijing that he should utilize it at his discretion.

There were no particular changes to the stance of the Japanese government towards Group V. Katō's uncompromising attitude over this issue might also have been affected by the fact that the reaction of the Western governments towards these demands seemed much weaker than he had expected. When he communicated the contents of the fifth group to Greene, he believed that Britain would react adversely against the fifth article within Group V, which demanded concessions on railroads in south of China, and the sixth article which demanded that the Chinese government not concede Fujian province to any other power. However, Greene did not raise any particular objections towards these two articles, and he even said that he thought there was 'no reason to think that the British government would consider anything particularly problematic' about the Japanese demands over Fujian.[33] The Russian and French ambassadors in Japan showed interest in the fourth article within Group V, which mentioned Japanese arms sales to China, and the American ambassador showed concern about the third article which demanded joint Sino–Japanese police institutions in China, but they too did not raise strong objections. Perhaps this reaction made Katō somewhat optimistic that he could push through at least some of the demands in Group V. In face of the public outcry that the Twenty-One Demands had caused, it would not be surprising if Katō was looking for measures to appease public opinion and recoup the political influence of his party and administration by pushing the articles which initially were intended to be only 'desired conditions'. As a result, Katō's stance over the issue of the demands became inconsistent and inflexible; he would persist in pushing for some of the articles in Group V until May, when he submitted an ultimatum to China.

Yet, it was impossible for the negotiations to proceed as long as the Japanese government remained firm over the demands in Group V and the Chinese continued to be adamant that they would not discuss them. Under these circumstances, the next initiative that Katō took up was to resort to military intimidation. On 10 March he suggested in a Cabinet meeting that the Japanese government should postpone its planned withdrawal of troops from Manchuria and the Shandong peninsula, and send in another division. Yamagata Aritomo, one of the genrō who cast strong influence over the army, criticized this decision.[34] However, Katō feared that under the current situation, even the negotiations over the interests in Manchuria might fail if he did not take any additional measures. The foreign minister's suggestion was approved by the Cabinet, and thus the Japanese military presence in China was reinforced by mid-March.

This only resulted in hardening Chinese attitudes even further, and also made Western governments more suspicious about Japanese intentions. When Jordan met with Yuan on 13 March, the latter told him that the negotiations were proceeding smoothly, but he could not be responsible for what might come of any resort to force.[35] On the other hand, the criticism within Japanese political circles and media against the Chinese attitude towards the Japanese demands also became stronger after the military reinforcement. The ruling party, the Dōshikai, managed to win a landslide victory in the general election which was held under conditions of strong excitement, as if the country were in the midst of a war. However, the negotiations still showed no sign of progress even in April, and hit deadlock.

## Rising British mistrust of the Japanese

The negotiations reached an impasse, but ultimately a compromise was reached. Viewed from the outside, it seems that Britain might have helped bring about that compromise, but from the perspective of those involved directly the compromise was a result of pressure from Japan's elder statesmen. First let us consider the way in which Britain handled the situation.

*Japan's Twenty-One Demands*  43

As the details of the demands Japan had issued to China came to light in Britain, members of the Foreign Office and the press quickly became more critical of Japan. Unfavourable articles about the Japanese demands began to appear in newspapers in mid-February, leading to a barrage of questions about the Twenty-One Demands in Parliament.[36] The members asking questions were all 'backbenchers', and they elicited no more than curt replies from Foreign Secretary Grey and Neil Primrose, the under-secretary of state for foreign affairs. Thus Ambassador Inoue initially reported that the issue would have negligible political impact.[37] Of course, as Grey explained to Inoue, it would put him in a very difficult position if a breakdown in Sino–Japanese relations led to a situation developing that was opposed to the objectives of the Anglo–Japanese alliance; a rise in anti-Japanese sentiment inside Britain was certainly not something he could afford to ignore.[38]

In fact, from March to April the Foreign Office was inundated with letters from companies and groups with deep connections to China insisting on a halt to the Japanese advance into China and the protection of British profits. Chief among the groups that applied such pressure were: the British-American Tobacco Company (2 March); the China Association (24 March, 1 April); the Manchester Chamber of Commerce (27 March); the London Chamber of Commerce (12 April); and the Liverpool Chamber of Commerce (15 April).[39] On 6 April the Chinese representatives on the Legislative Council adopted an emergency measure asking the British government to support China on the grounds that Japan's demands violated the principles of equal trading opportunity and Chinese territorial integrity.[40]

On 8 March Grey met with Counsellor Honda Kumatarō to inform the latter of his own views of the Twenty-One Demands.[41] As he had done in the past, Grey expressed his understanding – up to a point – of Japan's expansion of its position in Manchuria. He went on to state that the only Japanese demands with a direct impact on British interests were related to railways, suggesting that, with the exception of Article V of Group V, none of the other demands were particularly problematic. He was most concerned about the possibility that a collapse in the negotiations would cause instability in China that could harm British interests. Grey expressed those reservations clearly, putting Japan on warning:

> The concessions related to the British railways are, as it were, minor points. What causes me anxiety is the possibility of political developments arising out of the Japanese negotiations with China. ... I think that China should make concessions. At the same time, I do hope that Japan will attempt to persuade China patiently in order not to cause a breakdown in the negotiations.[42]

Although Grey adopted a reserved tone during this meeting, claiming that the fifth article of Group V was a 'minor point', he actually took the matter quite seriously. On 10 March he had Greene deliver a memorandum to Katō insisting that Japan should respect Britain's railroad interests in southern China, revealing Britain's absolute opposition to Group V, Article V.[43] Katō did not respond to the document, but he must have felt the need to take British views into consideration.

On 15 March Secretary of State Bryan delivered the first 'Bryan Statement', a memorandum dated 13 March, to the Japanese ambassador Chinda Sutemi. Based on Bryan's goal of peacefully resolving the conflict, the memorandum, produced with revisions from within the State Department, expressed objections to four of the articles in Group V.[44] Compared to the British response, it raised objections to more of the items, but it did not object to the demands Japan was making in regards to Manchuria or Shandong; in contrast to previous American efforts to keep Japan's interests in Manchuria in check, the note had a placatory tone that implied the Americans had retreated.[45] Accordingly, Katō did not find the document especially threatening. When Greene met with Katō on 17 March, he observed that Katō did not seem to be taking the note very seriously.[46]

After the existence of Group V came to light, however, British journalists grew increasingly mistrustful of the Japanese. When Steed met Counsellor Honda on 24 February, he promised not to publish editorials on the Sino–Japanese talks in his paper for the time being, in the interest of promoting mutual Anglo–Japanese understanding.[47] Yet in a letter to Fraser he revealed that his confidence in Japan was already crumbling, although he felt that the whole question of their relations with Japan would depend on the war and there was very little use in quarrelling with the Japanese now.[48]

Perhaps that explains why *The Times* published an article entitled 'Japanese Pressure on China: Fear of a Crisis' on 12 March, with additional reporting on the story appearing on 16 and 19 March.[49] Between 1 and 16 April the paper frequently featured stories on the Sino–Japanese negotiations: 'Japanese Demands On China: Six Points Settled' (1); 'The Japanese Claims On China: Extra-Territorial Rights' (2); 'Supply Of Arms To China: Japanese Demands Resisted' (3); 'Japanese Interests In China: Important Statement by Count Ōkuma' (5); 'Japanese Trade Policy: Conflicts with British Interests, The Demands on China' (6); 'The Japanese Claims On China: Embargo on the coast' (13); and 'Japanese Demands Of China: The Railway Concessions' (16).[50] Unlike other newspapers, the editorial section of *The Times* was not critical of Japan, but it was clear that the paper's overall tone had changed; Katō began to perceive that *The Times* was featuring more 'sensational' stories that were inconvenient for Japan.

Katō responded by sending a telegram to Inoue on 17 April, instructing the latter to explain to Steed the issue surrounding the railways in southern China (the fifth article of Group V) that were of concern to the British and to request that he stop publishing articles that were unfavourable towards Japan.[51] Based on those directives, a meeting between Honda and Walter Scott, the deputy chief of the foreign news desk, was scheduled for 30 April. From that meeting until the final stage of the negotiations, *The Times* would continue to refrain from publishing strong criticisms of Japan.

## Japan's Twenty-One Demands    45

Fraser, the correspondent then in Tokyo, did not agree with Steed on this point. Meeting with Katō for a second time on 22 February, Fraser questioned him further on the details of Group V. According to Japanese accounts, Fraser agreed with Katō's explanation, replying that all of the Japanese demands seemed reasonable and the problems of the British railways would be easily solved between Britain and Japan in the future.[52] Unlike his predecessor Morrison, Fraser was not necessarily biased towards China, which led Katō to hope that he would write articles that showed an understanding of the Japanese point of view. He told Hioki to win Fraser over and 'manipulate' him when he returned to Beijing in April.[53]

As he watched the negotiations unfold, however, and as criticisms mounted against the Japanese, Fraser adopted a more critical stance towards Japan. He was particularly concerned about the issue of the railways in southern China. When he met with Hioki on 19 April, Fraser criticized Japan, insisting that the Japanese demands regarding the railways in southern China were a challenge to British interests, and that the ways of the Japanese government could hardly be justified.[54] After returning to Peking, Fraser wrote articles based on his reporting in Japan, but Hioki observed that he had been forced to change his outlook because those articles were attacked and mocked by British living in China. It appeared to Hioki that Fraser regretted meeting with Katō as he felt deceived by him. In fact, Fraser wrote in a letter to Steed dated 17 March that he thought the British Foreign Office had not realized that Katō was a 'pretty slippery gentleman' and Hioki a 'certain little liar'.[55]

In contrast to *The Times*, the *Manchester Guardian* was strongly critical in its stories on Japan. It continued actively reporting on the Sino–Japanese negotiations well into March,[56] and published an editorial on 13 March entitled 'The Japanese Demands', which argued that, 'What we have to do is to interpret the Japanese Demands in the light of Anglo–Japanese Treaty.'[57] In that context, the paper sent the Japanese government into a panic when, on 18 March, it suddenly published a scoop entitled 'A Complete List of Japan's Demands on China: Formidable Programme in Five Sections, Comparison with the Version First Given by Japan', which compared the full text of the demands Japan had submitted to China with the unofficial list of demands (which excluded Group V) that Japan had released to the Great Powers, including Britain. Inoue sent a telegram to Katō on 20 March, reporting that, 'Ever since the exposure in the *Manchester Guardian*, radical papers, including that publication, have gradually become increasingly aggressive.'[58] Since the Chinese government was exerting pressure on the British government, Inoue was concerned that 'this may lead to a troublesome situation for Japan'.[59]

On 30 March Inoue met with Walter Langley, the assistant under-secretary at the Foreign Office who supervised the Far Eastern Department, and asked him to try to find out who had leaked the information to the *Manchester Guardian*. Langley assured him the leak did not come from within the British government. The true source of the leak was never revealed, but, as the article

46  *Sochi Naraoka*

carried the byline 'from our correspondent', it seems likely that its special correspondent in China, Bertram Lenox Simpson, had obtained the information from someone in Yuan Shikai's administration.

Throughout the months of March and April, the paper continued its daily coverage of the Sino–Japanese negotiations. The main articles were: 'Japan and China: The United States Note' (19 March); 'United States & Japan: The Chinese Agreement of 1908' (23 March); 'China and Japan: An Army of Defence Round Pekin' (24 March); 'China and Japan: Military Measures Round Pekin' (30 March); 'Japan and China: Tokio's Reply to American Note' (31 March); 'Japan and China: A Favourable Turn' (3 April); 'Japan's Demands upon China: The Premier's Statement' (5 April); 'Japan and China: A Suave Comment in Pekin' (7 April); 'Japan and China: British Railway Interests' (14 April).[60] In a meeting with Ambassador Greene, Katō lamented, 'This sort of information leak is terrible. Now it will be difficult to reach a compromise.'[61]

### The settlement caused by the final notification

In late April the Sino–Japanese talks appeared to have stalled, and within the Japanese government those arguing in favour of taking a hardline stance against China were gaining momentum. In an editorial on 22 April, the *Tōkyō Asahi shimbun* called for a 'firm resolution', insisting that it was time to prepare for the opening of hostilities.[62] Other national papers like the *Tōkyō Nichi Nichi Shimbun* and the *Jiji shimpō* also adopted a tough stance, although they did not go so far as to insist on a declaration of war.[63] The party publication of the ruling Dōshikai party, the *Hōchi shimbun*, blamed the Chinese for the breakdown in the negotiations, while the opposition Seiyūkai party paper, the *Chūō shimbun*, criticized the government for its 'failure of diplomacy' and spoke out strongly against compromising with the Chinese.[64] After meeting on 21 and 24 April, respectively, members of the Dōshikai and the Seiyūkai resolved that the Ōkuma Cabinet should carry out its demands.[65] Stirred on by the ultranationalists Tōyama Mitsuru and Uchida Ryōhei, the Kokumin Gaikō Dōmeikai (People's Diplomacy League; a political group formed the previous year that supported an uncompromising foreign policy) sponsored a social gathering on 27 April devoted to discussion of the 'China problem', and it was attended by over two hundred activists.[66]

Yamagata Aritomo, Matsukata Masayoshi, Inoue Kaoru, and Ōyama Iwao, the four senior statesmen with the most political power, all lamented the situation that had developed, but there was nothing they could do about it. When Matsukata met with Hara Takashi, president of the Seiyūkai, on 19 April, he claimed that he and Yamagata had read about the demands that Japan had issued to China in the newspaper; neither of them had seen any of the diplomatic documents. Several days earlier, Prime Minister Ōkuma had visited Matsukata to report that the issue in China would soon be resolved, but now there was no sign of a resolution. Matsukata told Hara, 'I am overcome with dread when I think about the future of our diplomacy.'[67] Somehow, information on the state of affairs in the Ōkuma Cabinet made its way to the senior statesmen either via Home Minister Ōura Kanetake, Yamagata's trusted friend, or Mochizuki Kotarō, a Dōshikai-affiliated member of the Diet who acted as Inoue Kaoru's private secretary.[68] Nevertheless, there was hardly any mutual understanding between the government and the senior statesmen. Thus, the senior statesmen remained in the dark as the negotiations moved into their final stage.

At a Cabinet meeting on 20 April, Katō proposed offering the 'return of Jiaozhou Bay' to the Chinese, and his proposal was accepted. Of course it would not be an unconditional return; four conditions would be attached, including the right to develop a harbour in the former German leasehold in Jiaozhou Bay and to build an exclusive Japanese concession, as well as concessions to be shared with the other Great Powers. Katō hoped that this compromise would finally bring the negotiations to an end. The following day, Katō and War Minister Ichinosuke Oka visited Yamagata's residence together to read him the text of the revised proposal that had been adopted by the Cabinet (they did not give him a copy of the document).[69] Yamagata believed that the Japanese demands were still too unreasonable, even in the revised proposal, and he responded with the following candid remarks:

> As I have already explained, I fundamentally disagree with you. As I peruse the list of demands, I see many items that could be easily achieved if Sino–Japanese relations improved, without any particular need to stipulate them in a treaty. The great powers, in particular, are not likely to greet any of these demands favorably. Looking back over the last forty-odd years of imperial diplomacy, in the days when Itō (Hirobumi) and Inoue (Kaoru) were in charge, the utmost care was given to all matters involving Europe and the United States. The cabinet was consulted even on issues that individual bureau chiefs decide today based on their own discretion, and those issues were discussed in cabinet meetings that lasted into the night. Now, after the Sino–Japanese and Russo-Japanese wars have established Japan as one of the world's great powers, it may not be necessary to show as much consideration to the Western powers as we did in the past, but it would be too vain of us to consider Japan's current status to be equal to that of Great Britain.
>
> As far as these demands on the Chinese are concerned, it would have been appropriate to design them so that one or two of the items would bring mutual benefits for the Western powers too, but the current list of demands is too heavily skewed toward Japan's own interests. When dealing with the Westerners, it is not advisable to give them the impression that Japan is bullying the weak. It may be necessary to make a final resolution if our demands regarding Manchuria and Mongolia are rejected, but as I already told you, we should not go to war simply because the items in Group V were not accepted.

Katō responded optimistically, arguing that 'China will happily agree to most of our demands' because Japan was going to return Jiaozhou Bay. In the event that China rejected the revised proposal, Yamagata asked, 'Do you intend to declare war immediately?' Although Yamagata was slightly relieved when Katō replied, 'No, we will continue our discussions', he went on to caution the latter on a number of additional points. Katō sought the senior statesmen's approval so tenaciously that, on the following day, he was ultimately able to obtain their consent to the Cabinet resolution after Yamagata contacted Matsukata and Inoue.

Subsequently, Katō kept in contact with Hioki as he re-evaluated the revised proposal, which was approved by the Cabinet on 26 April. In that revision of the document, the third article of Group V (merger of Chinese and Japanese police forces) was retracted. As for the rest of the items in Group V, however, although they were supposed to be excluded from the treaty and concessions were supposed to be made along the lines of the Chinese government's demands and official exchange notes, the same demands, strongly reflecting the spirit of the original Japanese text, were still being made.[70]

When he submitted the revised proposal to the Chinese, Katō simultaneously delivered an unofficial announcement to the British via Ambassador Inoue. His goal in doing so was to gain British understanding of the conclusion of the Sino–Japanese treaty in regards to the issue of the railways in southern China (the fifth article of Group V), which had caused so much agitation among the British. Inoue announced to Grey that the revised proposal represented the greatest compromise Japan was willing to make, arguing, 'However the situation develops from this point, it is entirely up to the Chinese.' Grey responded by saying, 'In the unfortunate eventuality that these events should lead to a rupture, I implore you to ensure that they do not, as a result, clash with the objectives of the Anglo–Japanese Alliance.'[71] On the grounds that the demands were so numerous and so complex, he refrained from stating his personal opinion until the Foreign Office had a chance to inspect them carefully.[72] According to Langley, Grey had originally 'expected more of Katō', but now he had lost faith in him: 'He could not hide his opinion that the alliance was faltering.'[73] Grey was becoming increasingly mistrustful of Japan, and he had no intention of taking the Japanese explanation at face value. He intended to scrutinize the Japanese to ascertain their true intentions.

On 1 May China's foreign minister, Lu Zhengxiang, gave Hioki the Chinese response to the revised Japanese proposal. The document was adamant in its rejection of almost all of Group V, arguing that 'all of those items violate the sovereignty of the Republic of China, the treaty rights of the Western powers, and the principles of equal opportunity.' There was still a wide gap between the Chinese position and the terms contained in Japan's revised proposal. When Katō read the Chinese response on the morning of 2 May, he began thinking about resolving the situation with a final notification.[74]

At a Cabinet meeting held on 3 May Katō proposed a plan to issue a final notification insisting that China concede to the revised document of 26 April, and the Cabinet members agreed to this suggestion. When the Cabinet met with the senior statesmen at the Prime Minister's residence on 4 May, however, all three of them – Yamagata, Matsukata, and Ōyama – objected to the plan.

Yamagata began the disagreement during the meeting. As soon as he took his seat in a room full of Cabinet ministers sitting in a row, he began grumbling at Ōkuma and Katō in a tone that was both provocative and derisive: 'What a mess! Now that we're in this situation, it might be tough for you, Mr. Foreign Minister, but how about if you go to Beijing and sort things out personally?' The silence continued, and when Navy Minister Yashiro Rokurō said that the foreign minister could not leave the country during a national emergency, Yamagata shouted, 'Stop quibbling!' Finance Minister Wakatsuki Reijirō, who was in attendance at the time, said, 'It felt like a fire was going to break out.'[75] Since the outbreak of First World War, Katō had rushed into entering the war against Germany and issuing the Twenty-One Demands without sufficiently discussing those decisions with the senior statesmen, and Yamagata was disgusted with him. Yamagata's reprimand at the meeting was an eruption of the dissatisfaction he had been feeling towards Katō since the previous year.

Katō had no intention of visiting Beijing as an ambassador, but he asked Yamagata what he thought the government's next step should be. Yamagata responded, 'If we can make concessions that do not cause problems, we should compromise. Surely we cannot compromise on the Manchuria question, but there must be items in Group V that we could compromise over without making trouble.' Matsukata agreed with Yamagata's view. Next, Yamagata said, 'I merely stated my opinion for your reference', and, after asking for 'the Cabinet to resolve the matter for itself', he left the room. Without reaching a consensus, that morning's meeting was adjourned.

In a subsequent account by the industrialist Takahashi Yoshio, Yamagata was recorded as being resigned to the idea of committing troops to 'matters of life and death for the nation', such as Manchuria, but he viewed all of the items in Group V as nothing more than 'trivialities'. Convinced that mobilizing troops over such insignificant issues would cause Japan to lose face on the world stage, Yamagata put all of his energy into stopping 'such shameful negotiating tactics'.[76] Yamagata had distanced himself from the Ōkuma Cabinet, but now that Japan had finally come to the brink of war with China, he began doing everything in his power to influence the government. Inoue had been keeping the Cabinet under his tutelage, but since illness prevented him from attending the meeting he contacted the Ōkuma Cabinet by telephone from his villa in Okitsu. He criticized the government for submitting 'unnecessary conditions' and asked the Cabinet to return Qingdao and seek accord with the Western powers.[77]

After the 4 May meeting between the senior statesmen and the Cabinet ministers ended, the ministers remained in the room and continued their

50 *Sochi Naraoka*

deliberations; in the middle of the night, an important telegram arrived from Grey. It was more sternly written than any of the previous British messages, effectively demanding that Japan remove Group V.[78] What follows is a quotation from the main section of the telegram:

> I earnestly hope there will not be rupture between Japan and China, if, as I believe, the only outstanding question now is Part v of the Japanese demands. ... I hope, therefore, that Japan will either not press these points or make it clear that her demands do not bear the construction that is being placed upon them in some quarters.

At that point, the Cabinet ministers' agenda focussed on whether or not to remove Group V from the final notification. Their discussion continued until the dawn, but ultimately, after a proposal from Home Minister Ōura, they decided to remove Group V. After the draft of the final notification was formally approved by the Cabinet on 5 May, Ōura visited the three senior statesmen – Yamagata, Matsukata, and Ōyama – to gain their informal consent.[79] On 6 May another meeting between the Cabinet ministers and the senior statesmen was held at the prime minister's residence, and the text of the final notification was formally approved. Based on that decision, a meeting was held with the Taisho emperor in attendance, during which it was determined that the final notification would be submitted to the Chinese. Hioki handed the final notification to the Chinese foreign minister on 7 May.

During that time, Grey reached out to the Japanese once again, asking them on 6 May to bear in mind the spirit of the Anglo–Japanese alliance and resolve their negotiations with the Chinese amicably. On the other hand, Jordan, joined by the ministers from Russia and France, visited Lu Zheng-xiang on 5 May, and together they pressed him to accept the demands. The Chinese government maintained its bold stance in the face of Japan's final notification, but once it had been delivered and it was clear that the American intervention the Chinese were counting on was not forthcoming, they despairingly agreed to the demands. Foreign Minister Lu notified Hioki of the decision to consent to the final notification on 9 May. The Chinese and Japanese governments worked together to consolidate and revise the phrasing of the document, and on 25 May the treaty and attached official notices were signed. Thus, the Sino–Japanese negotiations that had continued for roughly four months ended in a compromise.

## Evaluation of the Twenty-One Demands

On 10 May the *Manchester Guardian* argued that China had yielded to the Japanese ultimatum and had saved itself from the violent action which was being threatened by Japan. Both were 'congratulated' in an editorial titled as 'China's decision'. The newspaper highly rated the deletion of Group V as follows:

*Japan's Twenty-One Demands* 51

We gladly acknowledge that Japan, in presenting her ultimatum, has substantially modified her demands. She has, in particular, postponed 'until a suitable opportunity in the future' those demands in clause 5 which were an undoubted attack on China's independence ...[80]

Nevertheless, it also expressed its anxiety as it thought that the demands which Japan had not withdrawn and China had accepted were serious enough. It was obvious that the newspaper was still wary of Japan, although it expressed a welcome for the compromise reached by the two countries.

Taking a contrary approach, *The Times* highly praised the way in which the Japanese government had conducted itself in the final stage of the negotiations. In an editorial titled 'The Far Eastern Compromise' on 10 May, the newspaper argued that 'China and Japan have adjusted their differences, and the war cloud in the Far East has been dispersed', and 'all the questions in Group V, of these proposals, except the Fukien [Fukian] question, on which a compromise had been already reached, disappeared.' The following sentences in the editorial indicate that *The Times* still had confidence in Japan, Britain's ally, to some extent:

While the courage and the good sense of the Japanese statesmen in making these extensive modifications in their first proposals are deserving of the highest praise, the reflection is inevitable that more caution in formulating their original demands and greater tact in the conduct of the negotiations might have ensured them the advantages they have acquired without resort to so drastic a step as the issue of the ultimatum. ... The masses in Japan may be disappointed at the compromise to which the EMPEROR and his advisers have come, but friendly observers abroad will see in it a fresh proof that her statesmen fix their gaze upon the far-off future, and have the sagacity and the courage, even in moments of popular excitements, not to prejudice it by grasping in the present for more than the present can safely yield.

However, contrary to the editorial, some journalists on *The Times* already felt a deep-rooted distrust towards Japan. After the negotiations were concluded, Fraser summarized the whole process as follows.[81] Being the only Western journalist who had interviewed both Katō and Hioki, his views are worthy of attention:

The conclusion at which I have arrived, after watching things in Tokyo for six months, is that Japanese Government have no policy in regard to China. Nor does there seem to me to be any individual statesman in Japan possessed of convictions as to the line Japan ought to follow in China – That is to say, any revealed statesman, with convictions founded on knowledge & understanding of the situation. Every politician in Japan thinks Japan ought to do certain things in China, but the opinions of most of them are based on blissful ignorance of outside considerations, such as the feelings of the Chinese and the interests of other Powers.

## Conclusion

This paper has examined the various impacts of Japan's Twenty-One Demands on Anglo–Japanese relations, mainly focussing on diplomatic negotiations and newspaper reports. The Japanese government required the Yuan Shikai administration not to leak the contents of the demands to the outside world and failed to inform the Great Powers, including its ally, Britain, of Group V which might conflict with Chinese sovereignty. Group V included demands to expand Japanese influence over the Chinese government, thus outmanoeuvring Britain. It breached the trust between the two countries. Foreign Minister Katō Takaaki was conscious of this, but was compelled to attempt such an unreasonable tactic because of the pressure from the hard-liners in Japan.

Yuan Shikai leaked information on the negotiations in order to arouse an anti-Japanese movement in China and create distrust towards Japan among the Great Powers. Yuan did this to break the ties between Japan and the Great Powers. The leak was remarkably effective, and China succeeded in inviting international criticism of Japan at the beginning of the talks.

From the present point of view, China's leaking of this information was reasonable, and so Katō, who did not predict this move, appears to have been inept. However, it can be said that he was only following precedent. In the Sino–Japanese negotiations immediately after the Russo-Japanese War, the Chinese government had agreed not to leak information to the outside and no other countries had intervened. The Chinese broke the practice of the last ten years and resisted fiercely as the Twenty-One Demands were much greater than the ones required before then. The media, which was increasingly developing after the Revolution in 1911, supported the government and stimulated Chinese nationalism. One of the reasons why the negotiations over the demands came to a deadlock was that the Japanese government did not recognize both the excessiveness of its policy and the changes in Chinese politics and society.

This paper has also analyzed in detail the final stage of the negotiations after the leak of the Chinese government. The British government trusted the Japanese and did not believe in the rumours about the demands when the negotiations started, but its attitude became more severe after it became clear that it had been kept in the dark. After this, it attempted to restrain the Japanese government by repeatedly insisting that the objectives of the Anglo–Japanese alliance should be kept in mind. Among the British newspapers, the *Manchester Guardian* stood at the forefront of attacks on Japan. On the other hand, *The Times* refrained from criticism, but the journalists who had treated Japan with favour to some degree, such as Henry Wickham Steed and David Fraser, lost their confidence.

The negotiations between China and Japan came to a deadlock at the end of April, and some of the Japanese newspapers began to insist on war in case of their complete breakdown. But the elder statesmen, particularly Yamagata

*Japan's Twenty-One Demands* 53

Aritomo, urged Katō to moderate the demands and the British government reiterated its interpretation of the terms of the alliance. Katō therefore made the decision to delete Group V and attempted to make a compromise with Yuan by sending an ultimatum requiring China to accept the fixed demands. Some Chinese politicians insisted on continued resistance, but Yuan, with no prospect of American intervention and with the Entente Powers, including Britain, recommending the avoidance of war, eventually yielded. As a result the Chinese government accepted the principal demands of Groups I–IV.

The Japanese government thus succeeded in securing the interests which it had thought the most important by concluding an agreement with the Chinese government. Therefore it can be seen that the negotiations ended in a Japanese victory. That is why Yuan Shikai has been unfortunately regarded as a traitor to his country.[82] Nevertheless, Japan lost Chinese confidence during this crisis and many Chinese began to regard Japan as an 'enemy' standing in the way of the construction of a new country. It is doubtful therefore whether the methods the Japanese government used to secure its interests were reasonable. In addition, British politicians and diplomats began to distrust Japan through their experience of this episode.[83] While the value of the Anglo–Japanese alliance was not fundamentally questioned as the Great War continued, the Twenty-One Demands severely damaged British confidence in Japan and contributed to the termination of the alliance in 1922.

## Notes

1 For the details of the Twenty-One Demands, see Naraoka Sochi, *Taika Nijuikka-jyo Yokyu towa Nandattanoka: Daiichiji Sekaitaisen to Nicchutairitsu no Genten,* Nagoya: Nagoya daigaku shuppankai, 2015, and idem., 'A New Look at Japan's Twenty-One Demands: Reconsidering Katō Takaaki's Motives in 1915', in Tosh Minohara, Tze-ki Hon and Evan Dawley (eds), *The Decade of the Great War: Japan and the Wider World in the 1910s,* Leiden and Boston, MA: Brill, 2014, pp. 189–210; and idem., 'Japan's First World War-Era Diplomacy, 1914–1915' in Oliviero Frattolillo and Antony Best (eds), *Japan and the Great War,* Basingstoke: Palgrave Macmillan, 2015, pp. 36–51.
2 Thomas F. Millard, *Democracy and the Eastern Question: The Problem of the Far East as Demonstrated by the Great War, and Its Relation to the United States of America,* New York: Century, 1919; Stanley K. Hornbeck, *Contemporary Politics in the Far East,* New York: Appelton, 1919; and Paul H. Clyde, *International Rivalries in Manchuria, 1689–1922,* Columbus: Ohio State University Press, 1926.
3 Arthur Link, *Wilson: The Struggle for Neutrality, 1914–1915,* Princeton, NJ: Princeton University Press, 1960; Russell H. Fifield, *Woodrow Wilson and the Far East: The Diplomacy of the Shantung Question,* Hamden, CN: Archon, 1952; Roy Watson Curry, *Woodrow Wilson and Far Eastern Policy, 1913–1921,* New York: Bookman, 1957; Noel H. Pugach, *Paul S. Reinsch: Open Door Diplomat in Action,* New York: KTO Press, 1979.
4 Horikawa Takeo, *Kyokuto Kokusaiseijisi Josetsu,* Tokyo: Yuhikaku, 1958; Hosoya Chihiro, 'Nijuikkajyo Yokyu to Amerika no Taio', *Hitotsubashi Ronso,* vol. 43–1, 1960 (see also idem., *Ryotaisenkanki no Nihon Gaiko,* Tokyo: Iwanami shoten, 1988); Kitaoka Shin-ichi, 'Nijuikkajo Yokyu: Nichibei Gaiko no Sogosayo', *Nenpo Kindainihon Kenkyu,* vol. 7, 1985 (see also idem., *Monkokaihoseisaku to Nihon,*

54   *Sochi Naraoka*

Tokyo: Tokyo daigaku shuppankai, 2015); Shimada Yoichi, 'Taika Nijuikkajo Yokyu', *Seijikeizai Shigaku*, vol. 259–60, 1987; Takahara Shusuke, *Wilson Gaiko to Nihon: Riso to Genjitsu no Aida 1913–1921*, Tokyo: Sobunsha, 2006; Kawashima Shin, 'Nijuikkajo Yokyu to Nicchukankei Saiko' in Kawashima Shin (ed.), *Kindai Chugoku omeguru Kokusaiseiji*, Tokyo: Chuokoron shinsha, 2014; Frederick R. Dickinson, *War and National Reinvention*, Cambridge, MA: Harvard University Asia Center, 1999; Noriko Kawamura, *Turbulence in the Pacific: Japan-U.S. Relations during World War I*, Westport CT: Greenwood Press, 2000.

5   Peter Lowe, *Great Britain and Japan, 1911–1915*, London: Macmillan, 1969. Ian Nish also examined Katō Takaaki's diplomatic leadership on presenting the Twenty-One Demands in his *Japanese Foreign Policy, 1869–1942: Kasumigaseki to Miyakezaka*, London: Routledge & Kegan Paul, 1977.

6   David Fraser (1869–1953) was originally from Scotland and adopted as correspondent by *The Times* in 1904. He became a Beijing correspondent, succeeding George Morrison, in 1912. He was the author of *A Modern Campaign, or War and Wireless Telegraphy in the Far East*, London: Methuen & Co., 1905.

7   Another Tokyo correspondent was J.H. Penlington, but he was not trusted by London and left to only less important news.

8   William Donald (1875–1946) was a Beijing correspondent of *The Times* from November 1914 to March 1915. Afterwards he worked as a Beijing correspondent of the *New York Herald* and the editor of the *Far Eastern Review*. He later became a political adviser to Zhang Xueliang and Chiang Kai-shek. His biography is E.A. Selle, *Donald of China*, New York: Harper & Brothers, 1948.

9   George Ernest Morrison (1862–1920) was a Beijing correspondent from 1897 to 1912. He was one of the most influential journalists in China. His biography is Cyril Pearl, *Morrison of Peking*, Sydney: Angus & Robertson, 1967. For recent studies of Morrison, see Eiko Woodhouse, *The Chinese Hsin Han Revolution: G. E. Morrison and Anglo–Japanese Relations, 1897–1920*, London: RoutledgeCurzon, 2004, and Antony Best, 'G. E. Morrison (1862–1920) and Japan, (1862–1920)', in Hugh Cortazzi (ed.), *Britain & Japan: Biographical Portraits*, Vol. VIII, Kent: Global Oriental, 2013.

10   For his activity in China, see Pugach, *Paul S. Reinsch* op. cit. and Paul Reinsch, *An American Diplomat in China*, Garden City, NY: Doubleday, Page & Company, 1922.

11   J.O.P. Bland (1863–1945), the former Shanghai correspondent, was also a regular contributor to *The Times*, but seems not to have reported on the Twenty-One Demands.

12   Times Newspapers Limited Archive, News UK and Ireland Limited (TNL), London, Fraser Papers, autobiography (draft), file 5.

13   Inoue (London) to Katō, 13 Feb. 1915, *Nihon Gaiko Monjo, 1915 Vol.3–1* (hereafter *NGM*), Tokyo: Gaimusho, 1968, pp. 563–6.

14   *Times*, 13 Feb. 1915.

15   Morrison to Steed, 17 Feb. 1915, in Lo Hui-min (ed.), *The Correspondence of G. E. Morrison, vol. II*, Cambridge: Cambridge University Press, 1978.

16   *Tōkyō Asahi Shimbun*, 14–15 Feb. 1915.

17   *NGM* Katō to Hioki (Beijing), 15 Feb. 1915; Hioki to Katō, 16 Feb. 1915, pp. 161–4; The National Archives, London (TNA), FO371/2322 Jordan (Beijing) to Grey, 16 Feb. 1915, tel. 31; and Mitchell Library, Sydney (ML), G.E. Morrison Papers, Morrison to Tsai Ting-Kan, 16 Feb. 1915.

18   *Manchester Guardian*, 17 Feb. 1915.

19   ML, Morrison papers, diary entry 15 Feb. 1915, and Morrison to Tsai Ting-Kan, 15 Feb. 1915.

20   TNA FO371/2322 Jordan to Grey, 16 Feb. 1915, tel. 32, and Jordan to Grey, 18 Feb. 1915, tel. 33.

Japan's Twenty-One Demands   55

21  *NGM* Katō to Inoue, 17 Feb. 1915, pp. 570–1.
22  *NGM* Inoue to Katō, 19 Feb. 1915, pp. 573–5.
23  Shidehara Kijuro, *Gaiko Gojunen*, Tokyo: Chukobunko, 1987, pp. 258–9.
24  *NGM* Katō to Inoue, 19 Feb. 1915, pp. 575–7.
25  *NGM* Inoue to Katō, 21 Feb. 1915, pp. 585–7.
26  *NGM* Minute on Katō's interview with Greene, 22 Feb. 1915, pp. 587–90.
27  *NGM* Inoue to Katō, 23 Feb. 1915, pp. 592–4.
28  *NGM* Minute on Katō's interviews with the Russian ambassador, 15 and 25 Feb.
    1915, with the American ambassador, 20 Feb. 1915, and with the French ambassador,
    27 Feb. 1915, pp. 569–70, 577–81, 597–9, 601–3.
29  *NGM* Hioki to Katō, 12 Feb. 1915, pp. 152–3.
30  *NGM* Katō to Hioki, 13 Feb. 1915, pp. 158–9.
31  TNL, Fraser Papers, DSF/3 autobiography (draft), file 5.
32  *NGM* Katō to Hioki, 16 Feb. 1915, pp. 164–8.
33  *NGM* Minute on Katō's interview with Greene, 22 Feb. 1915, pp. 587–90.
34  Shoyu Kurabu (ed.), *Taishoshoki Yamagata Aritomo Danwahikki Zoku*, Tokyo:
    Fuyoshobo shuppan, 2011, p. 24.
35  TNA FO371/2323 Jordan to Grey, 13 Mar. 1915, tel. 55.
36  Lowe, *Great Britain and Japan*, p. 244.
37  *NGM* Inoue to Katō, 20 Mar. 1915, pp. 650–1.
38  *NGM* Inoue to Katō, 8 Mar. 1915, pp. 606–7.
39  TNA FO371/2322, British-American Tobacco Company to Grey, 2 Mar. 1915,
    No. 24893; FO371/2323, Jordan to Alston (FO), 25 Mar. 1915, No. 34695; Man-
    chester Chamber of Commerce to Grey, 27 Mar. 1915, No. 36360; China Association
    to Nicholson (PUS FO), 1 Apr. 1915, No. 39098; London Chamber of Com-
    merce to Grey, 12 Apr. 1915, No. 43268; Liverpool Chamber of Commerce to
    Grey, 15 Apr. 1915, No. 45143.
40  TNA FO371/2323 Colonial Office to Nicolson, 7 Apr. 1915, No. 41009.
41  *NGM* Inoue to Katō, 8 Mar. 1915, pp. 606–7.
42  Ibid.
43  *NGM* Minute on Katō's interview with Greene, 10 Mar. 1915, pp. 607–11.
44  Takahara, *Wilson Gaiko*, Ch. 1.
45  Hosoya, 'Nijuikkajyo Yokyu to Amerika no Taio', Kitaoka, 'Nijuikkajo Yokyu',
    and Takahara, *Wilson Gaiko*.
46  *NGM* Minute on Katō's interview with Greene, 17 Mar. 1915, pp. 638–40, TNA
    FO371/2323 Greene (Tokyo) to Grey, 18 Mar. 1915, tel. 112.
47  *NGM* Inoue to Katō, 24 Feb. 1915, pp. 595–6.
48  TNL, Steed papers, TT/ED/HWS/1/David Fraser, Steed to Fraser, 12 Mar. 1915.
49  *Times*, 12, 16 and 19 Mar. 1915.
50  *Times*, 1, 2, 3, 4, 5, 13 and 16 Apr. 1915.
51  *NGM* Inoue to Katō, 17 Apr. 1915, p. 686.
52  *NGM* Katō to Inoue, 23 Feb. 1915, pp. 592–4.
53  *NGM* Inoue to Katō, 17 Apr. 1915, p. 686.
54  *NGM* Hioki to Katō, 19 Apr. 1915, pp. 334–5.
55  TNL, Steed papers, TT/ED/HWS/1/David Fraser, Fraser to Steed, 17 Mar. 1915.
56  *Manchester Guardian*, 1, 3, 4, 5, 9, 10, 12 and 17 Mar. 1915.
57  *Manchester Guardian*, 13 Mar. 1915.
58  *Manchester Guardian*, 18 Mar. 1915.
59  *NGM* Inoue to Katō, 20 Mar. 1915, p. 651.
60  *Manchester Guardian*, 19, 23, 24, 30, 31 Mar. 1915 and 3, 5, 7 and 14 Apr. 1915.
61  *NGM* Minute on Katō's interview with Greene, 15 Apr. 1915, pp. 681–3.
62  *Tōkyō Asahi shimbun*, 22 Apr. 1915.
63  *Tōkyō Nichi Nichi Shimbun*, 24 Apr. 1915, *Jiji shimpō*, 25 Apr. 1915.
64  *Hōchi shinbun*, 24 Apr. 1915 and *Chūō shinbun*, 23 Apr. 1915.

56  *Sochi Naraoka*

65  Horikawa, *Kyokuto Kokusaiseijisi Josetsu*, pp. 240–1.
66  *Tōkyō Asahi shimbun*, 28 Apr. 1915.
67  The description of this meeting on 19 Apr. 1915 is based on Hara Keiichirō (ed.), *Hara Takashi nikki*, Vol. 4, Tokyo: Fukumura Shuppan, 1965.
68  Mochizuki to Inoue, 26 Feb. and 22 Apr. 1915, in Yamamoto Shirō, (ed.), *Dainiji Ōkuma naikaku kankei shiryō*, Kyoto: Kyoto Joshi Daigaku, 1979, pp. 261–4.
69  For this meeting, see Shoyu Kurabu (ed.), *Taishoshoki Yamagata Aritomo*, pp. 24–7.
70  Horikawa, *Kyokuto Kokusaiseijisi Josetsu*, pp. 241–50.
71  *NGM* Inoue to Katō, 28 Apr. 1915, pp. 705–6.
72  TNA, FO371/2323 Grey to Greene, 29 Apr. 1915, tel. 112.
73  TNA Jordan papers, FO350/14 Langley to Jordan, 30 Apr. 1915.
74  For the final stage of the negotiations, see Naraoka, *Taika Nijuikkajyo Yokyu*, pp. 240–7.
75  Wakatsuki Reijirō, *Meiji Taishō Shōwa seikai hishi: Kofŭan kaikoroku*, Tokyo: Kōdansha, 1983, p. 206.
76  The description of 14 May 1915 is in Takahashi Yoshio, *Banshōroku: Takahashi Sōan nikki*, Vol. 3, Kyoto: Shibunkaku Shuppan, 1986.
77  Matsumoto Tadao, *Kinsei Nihon gaikōshi kenkyū*, Tokyo: Hakuhōdō Shuppanbu, 1942, pp. 269–70.
78  TNA FO371/2324 Grey to Greene 3 May 1915, tel. 119.
79  Shōyū Kurabu (ed.), *Taishoshoki Yamagata Aritomo*, pp. 30–1.
80  *Manchester Guardian*, 10 May 1915.
81  TNL, Steed papers, TT/ED/HWS/1/David Fraser, Fraser to Steed, 1 Aug. 1915.
82  However, this evaluation of Yuan Shikai is recently changing even in China and Taiwan. For the detail, see Kawashima, *Kindai Chugoku*, and Yo Kaitei, *Nicchu Seijigaikokankeisi no Kenkyu: Daiichijisekaitaisenki o Chusinni*, Tokyo: Fuyoshobo shuppan, 2015.
83  For the views of Grey and British diplomats, see Lowe, *Great Britain and Japan*, pp. 255–8.

# 4 Britain, intelligence and the Japanese intervention in Siberia, 1918–22

*Antony Best*

If the history of British policy towards East Asia in the twentieth century can be categorized as one of gradual retreat then it is important to see that this process was inextricably interwoven with the changing nature of Anglo–Japanese relations. As long as the alliance that had been first signed in 1902 was in a healthy state, the close relations between Britain and Japan camouflaged the fact that British power in the region was operating at the very limit of its capabilities. Once, however, the alliance went into a state of decline, the profound differences over regional policy that existed between London and Tokyo revealed the limited degree to which Britain could extend its power into East Asia. To a degree this was evident even before the outbreak of the First World War in August 1914, but that conflict helped to speed up that process and placed considerable strain on the alliance.

The majority of studies that deal with the gradual decline of the Anglo–Japanese alliance, including Peter Lowe's first book, *Great Britain and Japan, 1911–1915: A Study of British Far Eastern Policy*, quite rightly concentrate on China as the major source of disunity between Britain and Japan.[1] China was, though, not the only area which led to the development of tensions between the two allies. As T.G. Fraser (in this collection and elsewhere) and Richard Popplewell have demonstrated, the growing British suspicion of Japan that arose during the First World War was also linked to the belief that the latter was in some way connected to the radical Indian nationalist movement that caused concern in London and New Delhi.[2] Another aspect to the decline of British faith in its ally, and one that has attracted relatively little attention, relates to an issue that reinforced the fear that Japan had unlimited ambitions for the domination of East Asia, namely its role in the Allied intervention in Siberia.[3] Between 1918 and 1922, when Japanese troops were present in mainland Russia, Britain perceived Japanese policy in Siberia as having very little to do with developing an effective White Russian coalition against the Bolsheviks. Instead, it believed that Japan was far more concerned with establishing a puppet regime that would allow it to exercise political and economic control of the area between Vladivostok and Chita and to take over the former Tsarist Russian sphere of influence in north Manchuria centred on the Chinese Eastern Railway (CER).

Crucial to the development of this negative image of Japan was the intelligence that entered British hands through the activities of the British consular service in the region, the local Secret Intelligence Service (SIS) network and the early activities of the Government Code and Cypher School (GCCS). As with all intelligence, the information derived from these sources was not without its problems. In the case of the Siberian intervention, the rudimentary nature of the intelligence-gathering operations in the region and the doubtful reliability of some of their sources left policy-makers uncertain about the degree to which an accurate picture of Japanese actions and intentions was being relayed and whether some information was, in fact, invented by outside forces specifically to play on British fears. In other words, intelligence both clarified and confused thinking in Whitehall.

\*\*\*

The irony in regard to the Siberian intervention, considering the suspicion that it was to sow, is that the initial Allied idea that Japan should play a major role in that region was intended to give the Japanese a chance to demonstrate that they were pulling their weight in the anti-German coalition. In 1917, with the outcome of the war still uncertain, Britain felt that Japan needed to make a greater contribution to the war effort. At first the focus of attention was on the Imperial Japanese Army (IJA) committing troops to the campaign against the Ottoman Empire in either Mesopotamia or Palestine. This plan had, however, foundered on the long-standing prejudice against deploying Japanese troops to defend British interests in Asia and the attendant harm that this might do to the empire's prestige.[4] Against this background, the opening of a power vacuum in eastern Siberia in the autumn of 1917 offered a more fertile field for Japanese activity. Intervention in Siberia was necessary because of the danger that Germany might be able to extend its influence into a region where the port of Vladivostok was over-flowing with unused military hardware. Thus suddenly a military front had appeared in which Japan could make an important contribution to the fight against the Central Powers without impinging on the interests of its allies. Siberia's close proximity to Japan also meant that Tokyo was more likely to comply with any request for action, and that its intervention would not require it to draw on the over-stretched resources of Allied shipping. Lastly, of course, there were the simple facts that not only did Britain have many other more important priorities for its own forces, but that Siberia was about as distant a front as one could imagine from the corridors of Whitehall and that there were few British commercial interests there that needed protecting from the avarice of others.

Accordingly in December 1917 discussions began in Whitehall about the possibility of a Japanese intervention in Siberia. This was not an uncontroversial issue, for the use of the Japanese military clearly had some difficult and complicated strategic implications. Naturally one reason for concern was

*Japanese intervention in Siberia, 1918–22*  59

how the Russian people would react to the appearance of Asian troops on their soil, and in particular the Japanese army which had been responsible for the traumatic defeat of 1905. It was feared that this might outrage Russian opinion and only perhaps make the delicate situation in that country even worse.[5] In addition, concern was expressed on the basis of Japan's wartime record to date and especially the disquiet that its wartime machinations in China had already created. For example, in January 1918 a report put together by MI2, the branch of the War Office's Military Intelligence Directorate that dealt with Asia, expressed the view that once the 'coveted' Maritime Provinces of Siberia, which included the area between Vladivostok and Khabarovsk, came under Japanese occupation, it could 'prove difficult to persuade her to evacuate'.[6] Similarly, one Foreign Office official noted:

> ... the Japanese are a people 'vindictif et réaliste' – practical and selfish to the last degree. They care nothing for the general purposes of the alliance &, if they took action, would take it in their own interest & not in that of Russia or of the Allies.[7]

From this perspective, therefore, grave dangers might arise if Japan was pressed to intervene.

Not everyone, though, was disposed to see Japan in a bad light. Most notably, Lord Milner, who was minister without portfolio and a member of the War Cabinet, observed to the Foreign Secretary, Arthur Balfour, that he did not share the general suspicion of the Japanese and argued that 'the defence of the interests of the Alliance in that region of the globe is Japan's natural job'.[8] Moreover, in a meeting of the War Cabinet in February Milner warned that Britain had up to now been treating Japan 'as a convenience' and that 'it was most essential that we should take such action as would remove this sense of grievance'.[9] This was also a view shared by the Parliamentary Under-Secretary at the Foreign Office, Lord Robert Cecil, who wondered 'if we are not over-suspicious of Japan'.[10] Others took a simple realpolitik view of the situation. For example, within the War Office, Lord Stanhope, who was a Major in the Allied and Neutral Branch, argued that as there was nothing that the Allied powers could do to prevent Japan's seizing control of Vladivostok, it was best to accept the fact and turn it into a virtue.[11]

The argument of those who were prepared to trust Japan was strengthened by events in the region, or at least what was thought to be happening there. The situation at the time of the Bolshevik revolution in November 1917 was that Britain had few reliable sources of information on Siberia at its disposal. It had a consul in Vladivostok, Robert Hodgson, but in the chaos ensuing from the collapse of the Provisional Government's authority he had no means of communicating with London, and nor had the vice-consul in Irkutsk. Thus, in early January Cecil was forced to admit to Balfour that 'Vladivostok ... is a mystery' and that it was unclear if it was in Bolshevik or moderate hands.[12] One of the few witnesses to the scene was a former military control officer at Vladivostok, a Canadian named Major Mackintosh Bell. In December 1917 Bell passed through Tokyo en route to London and recommended to the British ambassador to Japan, Sir William Conyngham Greene, that Britain should land a force at Vladivostok.[13] Unfortunately Bell was hardly a reliable source; he had just been dismissed from his previous post 'because he was quite incompetent'.[14] Indeed, the news that he had relayed his thoughts to Greene led the head of MI1c (the forerunner of SIS), Admiral Mansfield Cumming, to inform the Foreign Office that:

> I do not think you should place too high a value on this officer's opinion ... He is the most determined conversationalist I have ever met but the opinion which he disburses upon every subject on the smallest provocation are much more remarkable for quantity than quality.[15]

In the circumstances, the quickest solution to the information vacuum was to draw on the China consular staff stationed in Manchuria and the military personnel attached to the legation in Beijing and to order those that could be spared to cross the border into Siberia.[16]

While the Foreign Office waited for these men to report on the situation, the air was filled with alarming rumours from a variety of sources. Not surprisingly, the best placed people to provide information were the Japanese themselves, but the question naturally arose of whether their intelligence was accurate or was being manipulated to present a self-serving picture of conditions. Certainly the news that they relayed to Greene bolstered the case for Japanese intervention, for it suggested that the tens of thousands of German and Austro-Hungarian prisoners-of-war (POWs) stationed in Siberia were being freed from custody and receiving arms.[17] News from MI1c sources added to the sense of panic. On 21 February 1918 an agent at Dairen was reported as stating that the Bolsheviks intended to transport the voluminous stores at Vladivostok, which were thought to include munitions, into the interior of Russia, leading one official in Whitehall to note tersely, 'This should clinch matters.'[18] French intelligence also pointed to the same general conclusion, as did the British consular reports emanating from Siberian cities such as Irkutsk and Krasnoyarsk.[19] Some observers, however, took a much less alarming line. For example, a Captain Hicks, who toured Siberia in the early months of the year, claimed to find no evidence that POWs were being armed.[20] As one Foreign Office official noted, this tide of conflicting information had not arisen simply because the truth was difficult to ascertain, but also because 'nearly everyone who reports has an axe to grind'.[21]

The influence of one other source is impossible to assess. It is known that from 1916 Britain began to intercept and try to read Japanese diplomatic traffic. Indeed, a document from 1919 includes the statement that in 1917 George Sansom of the Japan consular service was given the job of finding a 'solution of all existing Japanese codes and cyphers'.[22] However, the degree to which this source was able to provide useful insights into Japanese thinking is

*Japanese intervention in Siberia, 1918–22* 61

unclear because there are very few references to intercepts in the general correspondence of the Foreign Office and the GCCS's monthly collated records of all telegrams translated and circulated around Whitehall only begin in November 1919.[23] The only indication that intercepts had a role to play comes from a passing remark by the Permanent Under-Secretary at the Foreign Office, Lord Hardinge, who observed on one telegram from Washington which referred to Japan's limited ambitions in Siberia, that 'we know from secret information that the Japanese have an entirely different scheme of intervention in their heads'.[24]

Against this troubled and unclear background, the general view in the War Cabinet, and indeed of an inter-allied diplomatic conference held in France in March, was that, despite the doubts about whether it could be trusted, Japan should intervene.[25] As is well known, the obstacle to this scheme was the attitude of the United States, which was opposed to any unilateral Japanese occupation of Siberia. It was not until August 1918 that President Wilson finally relented and even then he only agreed to the idea that the United States and Japan should send 7,000 men apiece with the object of covering the retreat of the Czech Legion along the Trans-Siberian Railway (TSR).[26] IJA troops thus only officially landed in Vladivostok in mid-August, where they were soon joined by the Americans and small detachments of British and French troops. The British contingent was under the command of Brigadier-General Alfred Knox, who had formerly been the military attaché at the Petrograd embassy. The nature of the intelligence staff under him is not exactly clear, but one person who did not serve on it was Mackintosh Bell. The latter had returned to Vladivostok in June under Foreign Office auspices as a passport control officer to gather political intelligence, but once again 'his zeal outran his discretion' with the result that the military pushed successfully for his dismissal.[27]

With Allied troops now on the ground in Siberia, the British had got what they had initially wanted. However, even as these forces landed, the nature of the intervention began to change in an example of the phenomenon of 'mission creep'. By the autumn of 1918 the 'White Russian' resistance to the Bolsheviks was becoming more coherent. Accordingly, the Western Allies were prepared to use their troops in Siberia to intervene directly into the Russian civil war in support of Admiral Kolchak who was as the standard-bearer for the Whites in that region. The only problem with this policy was whether the Japanese would sign up to this consensus. The difficulty here was that ever since the first months of the year, it had become clear that the IJA was developing close links with Grigory Semenov, another regional military leader. Semenov had no aspirations towards Russian national leadership, but was interested in creating a new greater Mongolia and, as such, desired Japanese sponsorship of his ambitions in return for giving Japan economic concessions. Thus if Japan wanted to create a new sphere of influence for itself, it made sense for it to back Semenov.[28]

With the intervention underway and Germany on the brink of defeat, the British were hopeful that the Japanese would prove move amenable and assist

## 62 Antony Best

in Allied efforts against the Bolsheviks. As far as Whitehall was concerned, the most positive move that Japan could make in this regard was to send its forces, which had quickly expanded to 70,000 men thus dwarfing the size of the other Allied contingents, into west Siberia in order to cover the rear of the Czech Legion. This would then free the latter to fight west of the Urals.[29] However, the Japanese would not play ball, for while they were happy to garrison east Siberia, they were not prepared to send their forces west of Lake Baikal to assist Kolchak.[30] Moreover, contrary to Allied policy, they insisted on continuing to provide subsidies to Semenov. This undermined Allied policy for Kolchak as Semenov's lieutenants had seized control of the TSR around Chita and were preventing the railway from working effectively.[31]

This uncooperative attitude, together with the general high-handedness of the IJA, led to an urgent analysis of Japan's aims in Siberia. In September 1918 at the instigation of Cecil, the Political Intelligence Department (PID) at the Foreign Office produced a memorandum on Japanese pan-Asianism and Siberia, which concluded that Japan hankered after turning Vladivostok into an open port and probably also wanted control of the northern half of Sakhalin due to its rich coal reserves. It also raised the possibility that Japan might use any future agreement to withdraw from Siberia as a bargaining chip for recognition of the extension of its commercial rights in China.[32] Events in Siberia soon suggested that even this might be too conservative an evaluation. Japan's obvious interest in fishing rights, raw material extraction and control of the railways led one of the British diplomats in Vladivostok to observe in November that the methods it was following were reminiscent of its policy in China and that, 'From the moment the Japanese disembarked on Siberian soil, they have proceeded methodically with their usual tactics of establishing themselves as if they had come to stay.'[33]

This sense of foreboding soon came to be shared at the highest levels. In late 1918 General Henry Wilson, the Chief of the Imperial General Staff, produced a memorandum for the War Cabinet which noted the need to persuade Japan to cease providing subsidies to Semenov and to pass aid only to the Kolchak regime at Omsk.[34] There was, however, no evidence that Japan was prepared to change its stance. Thus, on receiving a MI1c report which stated that the Japanese opposed Kolchak because he was the only Russian willing to stand up to them, Wilson was reduced to lamenting in early 1919 that, 'The Japanese have lost no opportunity to exploit Eastern Siberia, with a view to their economic advantage, and have been guilty of innumerable acts of extremely high-handed action.'[35] The PID concurred with his judgement. In February 1919 it produced a new memorandum that drew on the latest MI1c reports coming into London which detailed the way in which Japan was using Semenov to shore up its own interests. Based on this information, the PID report warned, 'Her [Japan's] purpose ... is hegemony in the Far East and recognition of herself as the guardian of the Yellow Races together with acknowledgement of preferential rights in China.'[36] Coming at the same time as Japan was seen as being uncooperative at the Paris peace conference, its

*Japanese intervention in Siberia, 1918–22*  63

general attitude suggested both to the Foreign Office and the War Office that its policies required 'careful study'.[37]

Worse was to come, for intelligence sources at the end of February reported that Kolchak, feeling that the allies were wavering in their support for his cause, was in desperation ready to turn to Japan for help and prepared to hand over mining rights and northern Sakhalin in return for its assistance.[38] Over the next few months evidence accumulated that Japan was ready to respond to Kolchak's overtures and to tame Semenov in return for its own pound of flesh.[39] This led to a new fear developing in the mind of one British diplomat, namely that the Japanese would push Kolchak to adopt an even more reactionary direction than hitherto with the eventual aim of creating an autocratic alliance between Japan, Germany and Russia.[40]

For the rest of 1919, as Kolchak's regime started to crumble under the weight of Bolshevik assaults, rumours continued to circulate about Japan's nefarious activities. In November Henry Sly, the consul at Harbin, reported that a Japanese syndicate had been established to acquire from Semenov all of the forests and mines between the river Argun and Lake Baikal.[41] Meanwhile, a visit to Urga carried out by one of the young consuls in China, Harry Steptoe (who would soon transfer to the SIS), revealed that the Japanese were selling weapons to the Mongols and encouraging Semenov to expand his sphere of influence into Outer Mongolia.[42] In addition, the position of the CER emerged as a matter of concern when it became paralyzed by a Bolshevik-inspired strike in August 1919, for this raised the issue of whether Japanese troops might intervene to re-establish law and order, which would, in turn, lead the railway to come under Japanese control.[43]

One might expect that further evidence of the Japanese inclination to fish in troubled waters would have raised hackles in London. The reality, though, was somewhat different, for while many of the British diplomats in the region expressed concern about Japan's actions, the reaction in Whitehall was more muted. This was the result of a number of different factors. In part, it was a response to the changing circumstances in Siberia. At the start of the year there had been a genuine hope that Kolchak might be able to lead a successful campaign against the Bolsheviks, and Japan's attitude had been criticized because its obstructionism threatened to compromise this Allied goal. By the summer, though, it was apparent that Kolchak's moment had passed and that the priority now was merely to keep his regime in being. If the Japanese were willing to help with this, then the inevitable price would be worth paying. Indeed, some observers openly argued that Japan should be bribed with commercial concessions in order to shore up Kolchak's regime. For example, in August the War Office raised the idea that, in return for the IJA sending its troops to the front, Japan might be allowed to engage in a temporary occupation of the CER.[44] The Foreign Office rejected this proposal, but its grounds for doing so notably rested on the danger that a Japanese seizure of the CER would pose to Chinese interests in Manchuria and Mongolia rather than any fear of Japan's ambitions in Siberia.[45]

64　*Antony Best*

In addition, the British response was cautious because larger issues were now being played out in the region. In regard to China, the focus of British and American diplomacy was now on trying to revive the international banking consortium that oversaw loans to the Chinese government and to inveigle Japan into cooperating with this goal. This was by no means easy, but there was a sense that, following the decision at Paris in May 1919 to transfer the German concession in Shandong to Japan, the latter was now willing to follow a more moderate line towards China.[46] Moreover, it was inferred from recent Japanese actions that its attention was shifting away from Shandong towards its more long-standing sphere of influence in Manchuria, which Britain was more prepared to tolerate.[47]

Another important concern was the future of the Anglo–Japanese alliance. It was recognized, in the light of the rise of American power and the creation of the League of Nations, that the nature of the alliance would need to change, but there was a lingering fear that if Japan were dissatisfied that it might in the long run opt for a new alignment with Germany and Russia. This meant that its ambitions needed to be treated with kid gloves lest it look for new unscrupulous friends.[48] It is interesting to note in this context that the new Foreign Secretary, Lord Curzon, in December 1919 circulated a memorandum to his Cabinet colleagues by an anonymous expert on Russian affairs. In this report, the writer was damning in his indictment of the Japanese, referring to them as 'aggressively patriotic ... individually truculent, fundamentally deceitful, [and] imbued with the idea that he is under an obligation to impose his own particular form of kultur on his neighbours'.[49] At the same time, however, the expert argued that Japanese expansion in Siberia should not overly concern Britain, for if Japan had to expand anywhere then it was clearly better for it to go north rather than south.

The trend of events in the last six months of 1919 thus helped to place Japan's manoeuvring in Siberia in context. Clearly Japanese adventurism was not particularly welcome, but in the wider scheme of things Britain could live with an increase in the former's influence in the Maritime Provinces and northern Manchuria if this made Japan more amenable in regard to China. More broadly still one can discern a clear sense of the limits to British power and the need for compromise if the goal was to return stability to the region in the near future.

The collapse of Kolchak's government and his subsequent execution by the Bolsheviks in early 1920 brought an end to any final Allied hopes that Siberia could be a launching pad for a White victory in the Russian civil war. Consequently, Britain, France and the United States withdrew their respective forces with only the Japanese staying on. The fact that Japan's troops stayed on the ground naturally led to renewed debate about its motivations. At least in public the Japanese government proclaimed that it intended to withdraw in the medium term.[50] However, the intelligence reports that Whitehall received from the region at this time suggested that more was going on underneath the surface and that Japan was determined to establish some kind of buffer state in eastern Siberia centred on Vladivostok. This puppet regime would have the dual aim of perpetuating Japanese economic predominance and denying the Bolsheviks the chance of controlling an area that bordered on the Japanese colony in Korea. This, it was speculated, might well involve a permanent Japanese occupation of the southern end of the Maritime Provinces.[51]

The prospect of such an occupation becoming a reality was reinforced by the events of the spring of 1920. In early March a clash took place between Bolshevik and Japanese forces in the town of Nikolaevsk at the mouth of the Amur River. In the subsequent fighting some 700 Japanese soldiers and civilians lost their lives, thus demonstrating to Tokyo the need for a demonstration of force to secure Japan's interests. The result in early April was that Japanese forces seized control of Vladivostok and other cities such as Khabarovsk and Nikolsk and overthrew the provisional Zemstvo government which was seen as too sympathetic towards the Bolsheviks.[52]

British intelligence did not provide any substantive forewarning of this event, but in its wake an apparently new source of information emerged on the scene when Sly in Harbin began to forward to the Beijing legation intelligence that he was receiving from a man of either Baltic or Czech background called John Liubek.[53] This material was in Russian and purported to be translations of Japanese diplomatic telegrams and despatches. On the face of it, this evidence suggested that the Japanese had launched the coup at Vladivostok to aid Semenov and that at the same time they were working for a change of leadership in Beijing. Sly was impressed by this information, but its veracity was brought into doubt by Hodgson in Vladivostok, who noted 'John is known to us for some time past and is an unmitigated humbug with an astoundingly fertile imagination' and that he had been responsible for 'innumerable ludicrous rumours'.[54] This tendency to discount the sensational was also evident in the Foreign Office itself, where the more scandalous SIS reports were now treated with a large measure of caution.[55]

The Foreign Office could afford to do this, in part, because it was now able to turn to a much more reliable source of information, namely the GCCS's decryptions of Japan's diplomatic telegrams. These documents revealed that, contrary to the more sensational gleanings from human intelligence, the Japanese Cabinet had, indeed, decided on a partial withdrawal of forces from Siberia and that its continued occupation of cities such as Khabarovsk was closely tied to a satisfactory settlement of the Nikolaevsk incident, and that it had been agreed to stop any future joint operations with Semenov.[56] Furthermore, some rather more down-to-earth reports that were being received from the SIS representative in Vladivostok indicated that this moderating of Japan's stance was predicated on the changing political circumstances. Realizing that the Japanese and their puppets would never deal with them directly, the Bolsheviks had in April 1920 created a Far Eastern Republic (FER) as a nominally independent state. Japan's new policy therefore was to engage with this new regime and persuade it to accept the permanent existence of a non-communist buffer state that would control the south-eastern Siberian littoral.[57]

For the rest of 1920 and into early 1921 Siberia therefore became much less of a concern than hitherto even though the future of the region was not entirely clear. However, in February 1921 one of Kolchak's former colleagues told Sir Beilby Alston, the new British minister in Beijing, that the anti-Bolshevik elements in Siberia planned to unite and launch a military offensive against the FER and that they expected to receive military aid from Japan.[58] This news was relayed to Alston in the hope that Britain too might wish to get involved. This, however, was not the case. Instead the Foreign Office informed Alston that, 'We are completely opposed to any further adventures in Siberia, and you should make it clear that we regard the whole move with the utmost disfavour.'[59]

From his post in Tokyo, the British ambassador, Sir Charles Eliot, refuted the inference that the Japanese would support this latest escalation of tensions.[60] However, once again in the months that followed the SIS intelligence coming into London suggested that the Japanese were cooperating with Semenov and the right-wing Kappelist forces in planning a reactionary coup against the moderate government in Vladivostok.[61] The question, though, was whether this was actually Japanese government policy or simply an initiative being undertaken by its forces in Vladivostok without orders from Tokyo; SIS suspected that it was the latter.[62]

The long-awaited coup finally took place on 26 May. Shortly afterwards the local SIS representative observed that 'The Japanese are affording the new Government moral support, and are maintaining order', while a later report stated that the Kappelist forces could not have achieved victory, 'had not the Japanese literally made it impossible for the other side to interfere'.[63] At one level, it therefore appeared that the Japanese were complicit. However, once again the diplomatic intercepts provided a different picture of events. On 26 May the GCCS circulated a Gaimushō telegram that indicated that a top-level conference in Tokyo had reached agreement on the need to open trade talks with the FER preparatory to a withdrawal of Japanese forces, which suggested that the government was adhering to its moderate policy.[64] Then on 7 and 10 June further Gaimushō communications revealed that the recent coup had been planned by Semenov from Dairen and that the Kwantung Army had tried to get him to desist. Moreover, they showed that the Japanese government had protested to their protégé about the embarrassment his behaviour had caused them and warned him that he would receive no assistance.[65] Thus, while it might have been the case that there had been some sympathy for the coup within the Japanese high command in Vladivostok, it seems that such sentiments did not exist in Tokyo. Moreover, it appears that the government in Japan soon decided to exert its authority over the local military forces, for when Semenov arrived in early June in Vladivostok harbour on a ship from Dairen he was not allowed to disembark.[66]

The contradictory picture produced by the disagreements between the authorities in Vladivostok and the government in Tokyo left the Foreign Office in some confusion. In a memorandum written at an unspecified date in

*Japanese intervention in Siberia, 1918–22* 67

June 1921 the official in day-to-day charge of overseeing events at Vladivostok and future Conservative MP, Paul Emrys-Evans, observed that there was no direct evidence of Japanese complicity in the coup, but noted that he felt that they were clearly sympathetic. However, in this note for his seniors he made no attempt to draw any distinction between the local Japanese in Vladivostok and the government in Tokyo, and being undated it is not clear if this was written before he saw the intercepts noted above.[67]

What is clear, though, was that this was just a blip in the trend of events in Siberia, for in mid-August the Japanese government announced that it had decided to hold formal talks at Dairen with the FER in an attempt to pave the way for withdrawal. Then at the Washington Conference which took place towards the end of the year they committed themselves publicly to a policy of evacuation.[68] The Dairen talks opened in late August 1921, but made only fitful progress during the autumn and collapsed completely in the spring of 1922. In the late summer they reconvened at Changchun, but again progress proved impossible, for the FER representatives demanded a Japanese withdrawal from north Sakhalin while rejecting the idea of any compensation for the Nikolaevsk incident. Events on the ground, however, dictated that Japan had no choice but to honour its promise, as during 1922 the forces of the FER were able to push back the White Russians until the only stronghold that remained was Vladivostok. With Japan's buffer state in terminal decline, it was forced to accept the inevitable and in October the Japanese army evacuated its last remaining forces from Siberia bar the units that remained in occupation of north Sakhalin. Thus in late October 1922 Vladivostok fell to the Red forces, and in the following month the Bolsheviks, no longer needing their puppets, abolished the Far Eastern Republic and exerted their own authority over the whole of Siberia. It was, however, to be another three years until the Soviet Union and Japan finally settled their differences over Nikolaevsk and north Sakhalin and agreed to open diplomatic relations.

\*\*\*

Taking place during a crucial period in Anglo–Japanese relations, the Siberian intervention can be seen as another nail in the coffin of British trust in Japan. While clearly not as significant as the tensions that developed over Japanese policy towards China, the events in Siberia in 1918–19 revealed Japan to be a self-serving power that was not prepared to exert itself for what Britain saw as the common good. Instead, Japan's whole policy appeared to be motivated by its desire to gain economic and political advantages. It was, however, the failure to cooperate, rather than the nature of Japanese ambitions, that most disturbed the British government. In the autumn of 1918 the British government was convinced that the Allied powers should come together and support the Kolchak regime. The failure of the Japanese to do so, added to their unwillingness to send their forces beyond Chita, created a negative impression in British minds and raised serious questions about Japan's utility as an ally. Nor, it should be

68 *Antony Best*

added, was this the first time that Japan had acted directly against the primary goal of British policy; in the autumn of 1915 Japan, to Britain's fury, had vetoed the Chinese breaking off of diplomatic relations with Germany.[69]

At the same time, however, the history of the Siberian intervention has more to tell us about the nature of British power in East Asia than just that this event contributed to the decline of the alliance. It is also important as an episode that revealed some of the limitations of British influence in the region. This is apparent at a number of levels. First, one can note that from the start of the intervention until its end British policy was hamstrung by its under-developed intelligence presence in North-East Asia and the difficulty that its consular staff had in sorting the wheat from the chaff. It was only once a regular stream of intercepts came on line that it was possible to have reliable insights into Japanese policy. Second, it is notable that, while Britain felt that Japan's policy was cynical and unwise, there was at the same time a sense developing that if the Japanese were to expand anywhere it was better that it should take place in Siberia than in China or, heaven forbid, that it should engage in a southward advance. The Japanese presence in Siberia was thus seen in a similar way to the hold that it exercised over Manchuria both before and after the First World War. In the best of all possible worlds, Britain would have preferred it if Japan upheld the 'open door' and did not seek spheres of influence. However, if that were not possible, then Britain could live with the Japanese exercising influence over North-East Asia in the hope that this would satisfy its expansionist appetite and stop it looking further afield. Implicit in this reluctant compromise was the recognition that if Japan did decide to seek treasure elsewhere that this might well pose a substantial threat to British interests that the Empire would be ill-equipped to resist. Japan's expansion was therefore beginning to pose some uncomfortable questions.

## Notes

1 Peter Lowe, *Great Britain and Japan, 1911–1915: A Study of British Far Eastern Policy*, London: Macmillan, 1969; Ian Nish, *Alliance in Decline: A Study in Anglo–Japanese Relations, 1908–23*, London: Athlone, 1972; Ian Nish & Kibata Yoichi (eds), *The History of Anglo–Japanese Relations: The Political and Diplomatic Dimension*, 2 vols, Basingstoke: Macmillan, 2000; and Phillips Payson O'Brien (ed.), *The Anglo–Japanese Alliance, 1902–1922*, London: Routledge, 2004.

2 T.G. Fraser, 'India in Anglo–Japanese Relations during the First World War', *History*, 209 (1978), pp. 366–82; Richard J. Popplewell, *Intelligence and Imperial Defence: British Intelligence and the Defence of the Indian Empire, 1904–1924*, London: Frank Cass, 1995; and Antony Best, 'India, Pan-Asianism and the Anglo–Japanese Alliance', in O'Brien (ed.), *Anglo–Japanese Alliance*, pp. 236–48.

3 The Siberian intervention's effect on the alliance is mentioned in Nish, *Anglo–Japanese Decline*, pp. 237–42 and 249–54.

4 The National Archives, Kew (TNA), CAB23/4 WC250 War Cabinet meeting 16 Oct. 1917. See also John Fisher, '"Backing the Wrong Horse": Japan in British Middle East Policy 1914–18', *Journal of Strategic Studies*, 21 (1998), 60–74.

5 TNA CAB23/4 WC294 War Cabinet meeting 7 Dec. 1917, and FO371/3020 237673/231734/W38 Hardinge minute undated [Dec. 1917].

# Japanese intervention in Siberia, 1918–22   69

6  TNA WO106/5724 'Note on the Japanese Attitude towards the Situation at Vladivostok', MI2 report 8 Jan. 1918.
7  TNA FO371/3289 30285/383/38 Lyons (N Dept) minute 19 Feb. 1918.
8  TNA, Balfour papers, FO800/203 Milner to Balfour 19 Jan. 1918.
9  TNA CAB23/5 WC353 War Cabinet meeting 25 Feb. 1918.
10  TNA FO371/3289 30285/383/38 Cecil minute undated [Feb. 1918].
11  TNA CAB25/48 'Notes on the Intervention of Japan in Siberia' Stanhope memorandum 2 Feb. 1918.
12  British Library (BL), Balfour papers, Add.Mss49738 Cecil to Balfour 8 Jan. 1918 f.201.
13  TNA FO371/3020 245416/231734/W38 Greene (Tokyo) to Balfour 28 Dec. 1917 tel. 772.
14  TNA FO371/3020 245437/231734/W38 Graham (FO) minute undated [Dec. 1917].
15  TNA FO371/3298 7713/1869/W38 Cummings (CSS) note 1 Jan. 1918.
16  This process can be followed in the files TNA FO228/2755 and 2756.
17  TNA FO371/3289 30372/383/38 Greene to Balfour 16 Feb. 1918 tel. 140, and 42745/383/38 Greene to Balfour 7 Mar. 1918 tel. 199, and FO371/3291 73853/383/38 Greene to Balfour 26 Apr. 1918 tel. 422.
18  TNA FO371/3289 35126/383/38 MI1c note 21 Feb. 1918.
19  For the French report, see TNA FO371/3290 50044/383/38 Jordan (Peking) to Balfour 18 Mar. 1918 tel. 255. The British consuls' reports are in TNA FO371/3289 28964/383/38 Lindley (Petrograd) to Balfour 13 Feb. 1918 tel. 437, and FO371/3290 50422/383/38 Jordan to Balfour 18 Mar. 1918 tel. 259.
20  TNA FO371/3291 69998/383/38 Lockhart (Moscow) to Balfour 18 Apr. 1918 tel. 106.
21  TNA FO371/3291 69998/383/38 Gregory (N. Dept) 3 May 1918.
22  TNA HW3/35 'Nominal Role of MI1b' unattributed memo 2 Aug. 1919.
23  The November 1919 intercepts are in HW12/1.
24  TNA FO371/3285 78179/6/W38 Hardinge minute undated [May 1918].
25  TNA CAB23/5 WC353 War Cabinet meeting 25 Feb. 1918, and FO371/3443 104148/104148/W50 Allied Diplomatic Conference records 15 Mar. 1918.
26  For the US-Japanese negotiations about intervention in Siberia in 1918, see Frederick Dickinson, *War and National Reinvention: Japan in the Great War, 1914–1919*, Cambridge, MA: Harvard University Press, 1999, pp. 180–200, and Noriko Kawamura, *Turbulence in the Pacific: Japanese-US Relations during World War 1*, Westport, CT: Praeger, 2000, pp. 107–29.
27  TNA FO228/2758 Greene to Jordan 16 Apr. 1918 tel.-, and FO371/3338 136121/136121/38 Campbell (FO) minute undated [Aug. 1918]. For Mackintosh Bell's reports before his dismissal, see FO228/2761 'Intelligence Report No.1' Bell report 12 July 1918 and 'Intelligence Report No.3' Bell report 15 Aug. 1918.
28  TNA FO371/3286 115256/6/W38 Jordan to Balfour 27 June 1918 tel. 541. For the Kolchak regime, see Jonathan D. Smele, *Civil War in Siberia: The Anti-Bolshevik Government of Admiral Kolchak, 1918–1920*, Cambridge: Cambridge University Press, 1997.
29  TNA CAB24/63 GT5648 'Note on the Situation in Russia and Siberia' Wilson (CIGS) note 9 Sept. 1918.
30  TNA FO228/2765 Alston (Vladivostok) to Balfour 31 Oct. 1918 tel. 50, and WO106/1288 Knox (GOC Vladivostok) to WO 24 Nov. 1918 tel. 268.
31  TNA CAB24/71 GT6460 'The Military Situation in Siberia' Wilson note 11 Dec. 1918.
32  TNA FO371/4367 PID384/384 Japan/001 'Japanese Pan-Asiaticism and Siberia' PID memo 16 Sept. 1918.
33  TNA FO228/2765 Alston to Balfour 5 Nov. 1918 no. 4.
34  TNA CAB24/71 GT6460 Wilson (CIGS) note 11 Dec. 1918.
35  TNA FO608/188 598/2/1/1320 Wilson minute 3 Feb. 1919.
36  TNA FO608/204 611/2/1/2651 Japan/003 'Japanese Activity in Siberia and Recognition of the Omsk Government' PID memo 18 Feb. 1919.

70  *Antony Best*

37  TNA FO371/3996 18032/13127/38 FO to DMI 18 Feb. 1919, and DMI to FO 21 Feb. 1919.
38  TNA FO371/4094 34330/11/57 CX.066300/P/C/642 SIS Vladivostok to London 25 Feb. 1919.
39  TNA FO371/4095 Alston (Tokyo) to Curzon 19 May 1919 tel. 196.
40  TNA FO371/4095 72390/11/57 Emrys-Evans (N. Dept) minute 13 May 1919, and 76602/11/57 Emrys-Evans minute 21 May 1919.
41  TNA FO371/4097 149323/11/57 Jordan to Curzon 3 Nov.1919 tel. 565, and FO228/2769 Sly (Harbin) to Jordan 9 Dec. 1919.
42  *Documents on British Foreign Policy 1919–1939* (hereafter *DBFP*), first series vol. VI, no. 467, Jordan to Curzon 14 Aug. 1919, pp. 670–1.
43  TNA FO228/2767 Sly to Jordan 3 Aug. 1919 tel. 31.
44  TNA WO106/1310 WO to Knox (Omsk) 12 Aug. 1919 tel. 80416, and FO371/4102 118111/956/W57 DMI to FO 19 Aug. 1919.
45  TNA FO371/4102 118111/956/W57 Tilley minute 29 Aug. 1919.
46  *DBFP*, first series, vol. VI, no. 422, FO memo 11 July 1919, pp. 602–5.
47  Ibid, no. 670, Ashton-Gwatkin memo 13 Jan, 1920, pp. 931–3.
48  Ibid, no. 522, Alston to Tilley 7 Oct. 1919, pp. 761–5, and no. 646, Alston to Tilley 30 Dec. 1919 pp. 912–14.
49  TNA CAB24/95 CP337 'Siberia' Curzon memo 20 Dec. 1919.
50  *DBFP*, first series, vol.VI, no. 779, Alston to Curzon 16 Mar. 1920, pp. 1043–4, and no. 805, Alston to Curzon 1 Apr. 1920, p. 1074.
51  TNA FO371/4099 188472/11/57 Hodgson (Vladivostok) to Curzon 23 Mar. 1920 tel. 82.
52  TNA FO228/2770 Hodgson to Curzon 16 Apr. 1920 tel. 79.
53  TNA FO228/2771 Sly to Alston (Peking) 28 May 1920.
54  TNA FO228/2771 Hodgson to Alston 30 June 1920 tel. 105.
55  TNA FO371/4099 195786/11/57 Emrys-Evans minute 5 May 1920, and FO371/4100 208652/11/57 Emrys-Evans minute 19 July 1920.
56  TNA HW12/10 BJ.002876 London to Paris 14 June 1920, circulated 16 June 1920, and HW12/12 BJ.003446 Military Attaché Paris to Komatsubara (Reval) 9 July 1920, circulated 21 July 1920.
57  TNA WO106/6144 CX/2770/V 'Siberia – The Vladivostok Government' SIS report 14 and 15 June 1920.
58  *DBFP*, first series, vol. XIV, no. 229, Alston to Curzon 3 Feb. 1921, pp. 247–8.
59  Ibid., no. 232, Curzon to Alston 14 Feb. 1921, pp. 250.
60  TNA FO371/6935 N2029/134/57 Eliot (Tokyo) to Curzon 10 Feb. 1921 tel. 64.
61  TNA WO106/6145 'Siberia' SIS report 9 May 1921, and FO371/6936 'Preparations for a Coup d'État in the Maritime Region' SIS report no. 215 19 May 1921.
62  TNA FO371/6936 N5894/134/57 'Preparations for a Coup d'État in the Maritime Region' SIS report 19 May 1921 no. 215.
63  TNA WO106/6145 'Coup D'État at Vladivostok' SIS report 1 June 1921 no. 234, and Marsden (MA Tokyo) to DMI 1 July 1920 no. 40.
64  TNA HW12/22 BJ.006651 Paris to London 23 May, circulated 26 May 1921.
65  TNA HW12/23 BJ.006831 London to Brussels 4 June, circulated 10 June 1921.
66  TNA FO371/6936 N6778/134/57 Eliot to Curzon 11 June 1921 tel. 229.
67  TNA FO371/6936 N6901/134/57 'Siberia' Emrys-Evans note undated [June 1921].
68  TNA FO371/6937 N9704/134/57 Eliot to Curzon 22 Aug. 1921 tel. 314, and FO228/2775 Balfour (Washington) to Curzon 26 Jan. 1922 tel. 302.
69  Antony Best, 'Britain, Japan, and the Crisis over China, 1915–16', in Oliviero Frattolillo and Antony Best (eds), *Japan and the Great War*, Basingstoke: Palgrave-Macmillan, 2015, pp. 52–71.

# 5 Britain, the League of Nations and Russian women refugees in China in the interwar period

*Harumi Goto-Shibata*

## Introduction

Following the Russian Revolution in 1917, it is estimated that one to two million Russians fled their native country. They took refuge in many countries, including Germany, France, Poland, the Baltic States, the Balkans and China. The refugees did not go unnoticed. The plight of Russian women refugees in China came to the attention of the League of Nations in the mid-1930s. It was found that some of these women had fallen victim to human trafficking. This chapter examines the situation of these women of Russian origin in China and how international society endeavoured to assist them. It analyzes British as well as the League of Nations' documents, mainly because Britain was the chief pillar of support for the League. Another reason is that British voluntary organizations were very much interested in the issue; furthermore, Britain had an extensive consular network in China and was extremely good at collecting and organizing information.

Let us first look at the situation of the Russian refugees as a whole. The overwhelming majority were single men of military age, as the soldiers of the defeated White Russian army constituted the core of the refugees. Most of the soldiers and the civilians came from the peasant class, which made up 80 per cent of the Russian population at the time of the revolution. The refugees included ethnic groups such as Ukrainians, Cossacks, Georgians and Jews from the former Russian Empire.[1] These Russian refugees began to arrive in East Asia from 1918 onwards, but the process sped up after the powers withdrew from the Siberian intervention in the early 1920s. Many fled to Manchuria, namely the north-eastern part of China, and the treaty ports on the Chinese coast and rivers. In later years Russian peasants also left in order to escape from forced collectivization. On 20 July 1932 the Nansen International Office representative in China reported that there were 73,882 Russian refugees in Manchuria. According to a study by C. M. Skran, Russian refugees continued to migrate to East Asia until 1935.[2]

The refugee question was relatively new. In the nineteenth century the number of refugees in Europe was limited. The typical refugees in those days were revolutionary intellectuals who knew the languages of the countries in

## 72  *Harumi Goto-Shibata*

which they took sanctuary. Neither immigration controls nor welfare systems had been developed. Governments did not have to worry about their financial obligations if they allowed refugees to settle within their borders.[3]

After the Russian Revolution, however, the refugee question became serious. The newly established League of Nations appointed Fridtjof Nansen as its High Commissioner for Russian Refugees in 1921. He had become famous as an Arctic explorer and had already had experience of organizing emergency relief to famine victims in Bolshevik Russia after the November Revolution. By 1923, as his responsibilities widened, the adjective 'Russian' was dropped from his title. He contributed greatly to improving the plight of refugees; however, the League's financial support for the refugee question was extremely limited from the beginning to the end. Nansen received no salary and had to acquire the necessary funds from outside sources. After his death in 1930, the League established the Nansen International Office for Refugees to deal with the question. The budget of the Nansen Office was also limited and covered only administrative costs. In addition, the League Assembly decided that the office should close at the end of 1938 because it was hoped that the Russian refugees in Europe would gradually be assimilated into their host countries.[4]

Contrary to this hope, the number of refugees increased drastically in the 1930s, chiefly due to the policies of Nazi Germany from 1933 onwards. At the same time, countries including France, which had accepted many European refugees, changed their policies on foreign workers because of the world-wide economic depression. With its limited budget, the League of Nations could not cope with this deteriorating situation and when the Second World War broke out, even this minimal support was terminated.[5]

In regard to the problems faced by the Russian women refugees in China, their predicament was uncovered not by the Office for Refugees but by the Commission of Enquiry into Traffic in Women and Children in the East. In its Covenant the League was made responsible for preventing trafficking in women and children and in October 1930 a Commission of Enquiry was dispatched to Asia to look into the situation there. Spending one and a half years in the region, it visited many countries, including Japan, India and the British mandate in Palestine.[6] As a result, the misery of the Russian refugees who were stranded in faraway places in East Asia was brought to light for the first time.

The sections of this paper are structured as follows: section one looks at the efforts to stop trafficking in women and children and then examines the plight of the Russian refugees in greater detail; section two explores the condition of the Russian refugees based on the information from British consuls in China and a report written by a Russian organization in Shanghai; and section three considers the opinions of British voluntary organizations. In analyzing these different perspectives, it is difficult not to notice the question of racial group-making and boundary maintenance in the period. Although what constituted the 'white' race was unsettled and the counterparts of the Russian women in the treaty ports were actually the Western men working there, many people imagined the issue to be a tragedy involving white women living among non-white men.[7] The opinions expressed were not free from the social norms of the period.[8] It should also be noted that light was shed on the problem at the time of the Manchurian Affair. Section 4 examines the effect of the sale of the Chinese Eastern Railway, which had been constructed by the Russian and Chinese Empires, to Manchukuo. As we shall see in Section 5, the League of Nations could not take up the task of rescuing Russian women refugees. The question was a difficult one, which required abundant resources and was related to the racial issue. As a result, the League came to rely on voluntary organizations.

## Background: the suppression of traffic in women and children

In Europe in the late-nineteenth century the bringing of young girls from the countryside to the cities for the purpose of engaging them in prostitution came to be noticed as a serious phenomenon. This was called 'white-slave trafficking'. Many voluntary organizations were established to tackle the problem. For example, in Britain, the Association for Moral and Social Hygiene (AMSH) developed from an organization formed by Josephine Butler in 1875, and the International Bureau for the Suppression of Traffic in Women and Children was established in 1899. The latter actively lobbied for international treaties. These efforts resulted in the first international convention signed in 1910. After the First World War, Article 23 (c) of the League of Nations' Covenant made the suppression of trafficking in women and children one of the League's tasks. Furthermore, in 1921 the League adopted the Convention for the Suppression of the Traffic in Women and Children. The crime's name was changed from the 'white-slave trade' to 'traffic in women and children' to emphasize that race was not an issue in its mission.[9]

In the following year the League's Advisory Committee on Traffic in Women and Children (TWC) was created. Based on its recommendations, an enquiry concerning international trafficking in women in Europe, the Mediterranean Basin and the Americas was carried out between 1924 and 1926 by a special body of experts whose report was published in 1927. Then in 1930 the League Council decided to extend the enquiry to Asia by establishing the Commission of Enquiry into Traffic in Women and Children in the East. Dame Rachel Crowdy, the head of the League's Social Questions Section, was authorized to be a member of the Commission. She had become the director of the continental branch of the British Voluntary Aid Detachment in 1915 and had been made a DBE for her work in 1919. In the same year, she became the head of the League's Social Questions Section. She had also been a key figure in fostering unofficial correspondence between the League and the voluntary sector.[10]

The League Council limited the responsibility of the Commission of Enquiry to the international aspect of the question, as the European colonial

74  *Harumi Goto-Shibata*

powers were reluctant to open their colonies to international view, while China and Japan stated that they would participate only if the enquiry was limited to international aspects.[11] There was an awareness that this was likely to be a difficult exercise due to the wide differences in Asian social customs from those that existed in Europe and it was feared that pointing out all the problems would result only in antagonism.

The United States was not a member of the League, but its government was approached to find out whether it would consent to the extension of the enquiry to the Philippines. A favourable reply was received. In addition, the United States assisted in another way, for a most remarkable point is that the necessary funds for the enquiry were made available to the League Council by the Bureau of Social Hygiene in New York, an institution which had already furnished funds for the previous enquiry. The assistance from this voluntary organization was indispensable, because the League was run by contributions paid by its members and its budget was strictly limited.

The League Council also appointed a travelling commission, whose chairman was Bascom Johnson, the director of the legal section of the American Social Hygiene Association. Two other members were Alma Sundquist, a Swedish physician, and Karol Pindor, a Polish diplomat, the latter having been stationed in Harbin in Manchuria from 1922 to 1928. The travelling commission left Marseilles on 9 October 1930. After spending eighteen months in various parts of Asia, Pindor wrote a report, which was signed on 10 December 1932 and submitted to the League Council.[12]

## Russian women refugees in China

The travelling commission discovered that the largest number of victims of trafficking were Chinese followed by women from the Japanese Empire. The Japanese women who were engaged in brothels in China were considered to be the victims of trafficking. The report concluded that the abolition of licensed brothels in the countries concerned was urgently required to solve the problem.[13] However, even before reporting on these more numerous victims, the report dealt with the plight of Russian women refugees in China. It divided these refugees into two categories: first, those stranded in remote parts of Manchuria, and, second, those in the railway zone of north Manchuria. It was those in the latter category who, it was believed, might have been caught up in the trafficking of human beings.[14]

The railway mentioned above was the Chinese Eastern Railway (CER), which throughout its life was a centre of political, financial and legal complications. In 1896 the Russo-Chinese Bank had been founded under a charter from the Russian Government, and an agreement for the construction of the CER concluded between the bank and the Chinese Qing Government. The railway thus began as a spearhead of Russian imperialism in East Asia. Its southern branch was ceded to Japan after the Russo-Japanese War in 1905 and became the South Manchurian Railway. In May 1924 an agreement on the status of the CER was signed in Beijing between the new Soviet and Chinese Governments. Both parties agreed that the railway was henceforth to be regarded purely as a commercial concern, and the Soviet Government agreed to transfer to China all bonds and shares in the line. Four months later the Soviet Government signed a similar agreement at Mukden with Zhang Zuolin's autonomous government in Manchuria. The Mukden agreement was then accepted by the Beijing Government and made an annex to the Beijing agreement. In July 1929 Zhang's son, Zhang Xueliang, tried to monopolize the railway using military power, but was defeated by Soviet forces. The two sides then signed an agreement at Kharbarovsk, returning to the status quo ante bellum in January 1930.[15]

Harbin was at the centre of the CER and there was a relatively large Russian community in the city. Various people lived in Harbin, including White Russians and Jews who had fled the pogroms. Many were poor, but when the League's travelling commission investigated the situation there in 1931, it found that only part of the Russian community was destitute. Some were employed by the CER and some were in business, catering for those employees, while Russian intellectuals in the city were engaged in publication. Russian institutes of higher education also existed.[16]

In the meantime, many Russian girls in Harbin longed for a fashionable life in coastal cities such as Shanghai. Many single, young Western men worked in these treaty ports and there was a huge demand for dancing partners and restaurant waitresses. Traffickers exploited this situation. The victims of the trafficking often failed to closely examine any offer which seemed to provide them with an easy means to journey to the coastal cities. By the time they reached their destination, they would be in debt for the cost of the journey and for the clothing they required for their new roles. Typically they would have given the agent their identity papers and permits to travel.[17] Charles F. Garstin, the British Consul-General in Harbin, reported that little notice was taken of the traffic in China; a man could easily take with him from Harbin a number of girls without being asked any questions by the authorities, and the examination of passports was not strictly carried out.[18]

Obviously not all Russian women in the treaty ports were victims of the traffickers. Some gave music lessons, while some others were engaged in dress- or hat-making. Some women danced with men, but did not provide them with other 'services'. Some might have lived with men outside of marriage, but there were many couples who married later. It was estimated, however, that at least 22.5 per cent of Russian women in Shanghai between the ages of sixteen and forty-five were engaged in some form of prostitution.[19]

Not only the TWC but also the Nansen International Office regarded the Russian refugee women's situation as serious. For example, the second appendix of the latter's report for the year ending 30 June 1934 was entitled 'Situation of Russian Refugee Women in the Far East' and reported that distress in Harbin had continued to increase since the commission's visit. As for Shanghai, it noted that the number of Russians, estimated at over 18,000, was

76  *Harumi Goto-Shibata*

much too large for a city where the European population was only about 20,000 and pointed out that the local supply of labour was so abundant and cheap that many occupations were not open to the Russian refugees.[20]

In September 1934 this appendix together with the report of the Commission of Enquiry in the East came under examination at the fifth committee of the League Assembly, which was in charge of social and humanitarian questions. The assembly subsequently decided to instruct the Secretary-General, Joseph Avenol, to arrange for the collection of further information from official and unofficial sources and to report the result of his enquiries to the TWC.[21]

The plight of the Russian women refugees in China thus came to the notice of the League of Nations. That the Russian refugees were not under the protection of any country might have been why such unedited information came to light, as the League Council had ordered that the enquiry should be strictly confined to the international aspect of the question. The investigators were required to obtain the consent of the authorities of the countries concerned if they wished to study national aspects of the traffic. These countries, including Japan, were shown the draft of the report before it was made public and could ask for corrections and modifications if necessary.[22]

## Information collected by British Consulates

Reading the report of the fifth committee, Sir John Pratt, an advisor to the Far Eastern Department of the Foreign Office, expected that the question of communicating Britain's consular reports to the League would arise. He had been the acting Consul-General at Shanghai between September 1924 and May 1925 and accordingly did not think there was much exaggeration in the reports that reached Geneva. As a result on 18 October 1934, the Foreign Office sent a dispatch to its posts in China calling on them to observe the trafficking of Russian women and report on the approximate number of women affected.[23]

The replies from the British consulates in China expressed their own serious concern about human trafficking. Garstin reported on the situation in Harbin. Just like Pindor, the author of the League's report, he observed that the basic problem was the existence of a large number of young Russian girls who were unable to find respectable employment locally. Traffickers, including two Russians noted down as 'B' and 'N', took advantage of this situation. Most of the traffickers were men who owned brothels in other ports in China, and among their agents were smartly-dressed girls.[24]

The Foreign Office ordered the consulates in three other cities, namely Tianjin, Shanghai and Hankou, to send reports. Among the three cities, it seems that the situation in Tianjin was the worst. It was reported that there were several brothels owned by Russian Jews outside the foreign concessions and that about forty Russian women worked there. A Russian who had the same surname 'N', as mentioned in the report from Harbin, was among the brothel owners. The chief of the British Municipal Police, who wrote the report, suspected that these 'houses' had bribed the local police. There were also some women who were dancing partners. These women moved to Yifu and Qingdao during the summer for the naval ships there. Furthermore, there were about 140 women who were the mistresses of American and French sailors. It was also reported that the number of Russians was increasing due to a recent exodus from Harbin caused by the political situation in Manchuria.[25]

In addition, Sir John F. Brenan, the Consul-General in Shanghai, forwarded a copy of a letter from Major F. W. Gerrard, the commissioner of police in the International Settlement, and a memorandum prepared by C. E. Metzler, chairman of the Russian Emigrants' Committee. Gerrard considered that the problem was not just one of the Russian women, but of the Russian community as a whole. Many Russians did not know any language other than their own and therefore it was not easy for them to find jobs; indeed, many Russian men in Shanghai earned so little that they could not afford to marry. Gerrard was of the opinion that as a result there was a surplus of girls who would otherwise have become wives.[26]

Metzler, who had been born in 1886, was a Russian diplomat before the revolution. He arrived in China in March 1912 as an attaché at the Russian Legation in Beijing, and left the service in June 1924. He had been the vice-chairman of the Russian Emigrants' Committee in Shanghai since its establishment in 1926, and risen to become chairman in October 1931. He reported that during the past year many young Russian women had arrived from Harbin. He was of the opinion that more funds for the rescue of the Russian women were necessary.[27]

Brenan, however, seems to have been worried about the effect of over-emphasizing the plight of the Russian women. He enclosed with his report an extract from *The People's Tribune* of 1 October 1934, which was entitled 'The "Shocking" Report on Russian Women in Shanghai'. The extract pointed out that racism was mixed in with the sense of sympathy towards the Russian women. The article described the League's report as shocking, but did so not because of the sympathy shown towards the Russian women in Shanghai, but rather the fact that similar concern was not evident in regard to local Chinese women or even towards Russian women in Russia itself. It also wrote that the League Committee appeared to be shocked at the possibility of 'white' women being assimilated into a people whose equality with 'whites' had been officially denied by the League of Nations from the very outset of that organization. Here the author of 'The "Shocking" Report' was obviously referring to the failure of the racial equality proposal presented by Japan at the Paris Peace Conference in 1919. The author expressed deep dissatisfaction with the League, asking whether it was simply a League of White Nations, and interested only in white women.[28]

At the end of November 1934 the request from Avenol to make an enquiry into the situation of Russian women in the concessions and settlements in

China reached Britain, together with a fairly detailed questionnaire. However, the Far Eastern Department was worried that if Britain offered too much detailed information, the Chinese, in whose country the problems were occurring, might be offended. Therefore, arguing that Avenol was presumably in direct communication with the Shanghai Municipal Council, the Foreign Office decided to supply information only on the British concessions in Tianjin and Shamian. In addition, the Foreign Office edited the information before it was communicated to the League. Britain's answer to the League was therefore short.[29]

## Report by a group of Russians in Shanghai

The League of Nations intended to collect information not only from official sources but also from unofficial ones. One example of the latter is a report prepared by the Council of the United Russian Public Organization at Shanghai, which was submitted to the League on 10 March 1935 (in the report the organization's name was abbreviated to SORO, based on its Russian name.) Brenan wrote in 1936 about the Russian community in Shanghai and SORO. According to him, a somewhat acrimonious division existed between two rival Russian factions, one under the presidency of the former diplomat Metzler and the other under General Th. L. Gleboff, a former Cossack leader who had fought under Ataman G. M. Semenov (Semenov had collaborated with Japan for about two years after November 1918). Brenan was of the opinion that Metzler was very reliable; his interests were not political; and his major concern was the welfare of the Russian community. On the other hand, Brenan did not trust Gleboff and his faction. SORO was Gleboff's association, and Brenan considered that its report was produced with self-interest on the part of some members of the committee. Some Russians also considered the report to be a gross exaggeration and a false representation of the facts in order to obtain funds from the League and were worried that the ensuing publicity would damage the image of the Russian women.[30] Thus the report of SORO was considered somewhat problematic; indeed Gleboff's covering letter to E. E. Ekstrand, then chief of the Social Section of the League of Nations, seems to reflect his racial bias and that of other members of SORO. Having the reservations in mind, let us examine the report.

Gleboff wrote that the traffic in Russian women in Shanghai was not only affecting the Russian emigrants' community, but also the foreign population in Shanghai at large. On behalf of SORO, he tried to draw readers' attention to the following claims: first, that Russian women were being driven to offer themselves to the local people; second, that the prostitution of Russian women could not but have a demoralizing effect on women of other Western nationalities in China; and third, that this would very deeply affect the prestige of Western nations in the Orient.[31] By presenting the issue as one which affected the prestige of Western nations, Gleboff was trying to incite a sense

*Russian women refugees in China* 79

of crisis among the Western people at the League of Nations. Gleboff and other members of SORO also argued that the unemployment among Russians in Manchuria had resulted in their influx into Shanghai. However, with Manchukuo already established, the Japanese Foreign Ministry could not accept SORO's observation; a cross and a question mark were put on the margin of the document in the Japanese Foreign Ministry Archives.[32]

Another problem of SORO's report was that it compared the situation of Russian refugees in Shanghai with that of foreign residents in the settlements, not with that of the local Chinese. Foreign residents in China in the interwar period usually enjoyed affluent lives which they could not have dreamed of pursuing in their home countries. Hoping to enhance the possibility of Russian refugees being employed by these foreign residents, the report emphasized that Russian refugees should learn English and French, but the Chinese language was not mentioned. It should be noted, however, that the recent growth of Chinese nationalism had made the foreign settlements themselves unwelcome among the local population and that Britain had already started contemplating a change in their status. It was therefore utterly impossible to provide Russian refugees with funds to let them live like the other Westerners in the treaty ports.

## The opinions of the British voluntary organizations

A meeting of the TWC was held between 2 and 9 May 1935. It debated whether a conference on trafficking in women and children in the Far East should be convened and discussed the British colony of the Straits Settlements as one possible venue.[33] The Committee then went on to consider the plight of the women of Russian origin in the Far East. The results of the enquiry which Avenol made the year before were submitted to the committee. Sidney W. Harris of the British Home Office said that, while the situation of Russian women was deplorable, members of the TWC must not overlook the fact that it was no more miserable than that of women in many other countries who were not able to find respectable employment. He also observed that it appeared impossible, in the absence of funds, to make any definite proposals for the assistance of the Russian women. The committee agreed therefore that it would expect voluntary organizations to increase their efforts.[34]

In July 1935 the British Social Hygiene Council, one of the voluntary organizations established at the beginning of the twentieth century, sent a memorandum to the Foreign Office. The memorandum was entitled 'The Position of the White Russian in Manchukuo' and was sent under the name of Dame Rachel Crowdy. Crowdy had, after recently retiring from the League, attended the fifteenth international conference of the Red Cross in Tokyo from 20 to 29 October 1934 and had made the most of this opportunity to visit several cities in Manchuria including Harbin.[35] Based on her experiences, the memorandum reported that at one time the shops and cafes run by the White Russians had been used by the Red Russians working for the CER.

## 80  *Harumi Goto-Shibata*

Now, however, with the CER having been sold to Manchukuo, the Red Russians had started to return home and the small shops were gradually being taken over by the Japanese or Koreans; more White Russians, therefore, were being thrown out of employment.[36] Under the circumstances, Crowdy wrote, there was no other choice for Russian women but to become 'dancing partner prostitutes' or 'concubines to the Chinese farmers'. In her memorandum, there is also a description of a house lived in by a woman where there was no sign of any bread-winner. Crowdy wrote that after leaving the house, she was told that 'the Russian woman was ashamed of the man who supported her and of the fact that she was a concubine to a Chinese farmer.'[37] There is no doubt that both Crowdy and the British Social Hygiene Council acted with good intentions to rescue Russians in Manchuria. Crowdy's memorandum, however, showed that even a person like herself was not free from the attitudes of the period and that she understood the problem from the perspective of white people's prestige.

The British Foreign Office found Crowdy's memorandum too alarmist. It was of the opinion that, although Russian women were in fact arriving in large numbers in Shanghai and the other treaty ports, they were forced there more by economic pressure than by any white-slave organization in Harbin. It also observed that the majority of the Russian women obtained occupations such as chef's assistants or typists.[38]

In addition to the limits of the arguments made so far by the voluntary sector, there was also one case in which a non-government organization made an utterly unrealistic proposal. In 1935 the AMSH suggested that the League should make a strong appeal for funding from the Chinese municipalities and elsewhere to solve the problems surrounding the Russian women. However, the economic situation of China in the 1930s was not good and if the AMSH had been clearly aware of the plight of numerous poor Chinese women, some of whom were also victims of human trafficking, it would not have easily made such a proposal. The Foreign Office only acknowledged the letter.[39]

## The impact of the sale of the CER to Manchukuo

The plight of the Russian refugees was not unrelated to the Japanese Empire, because Harbin was then under the rule of Manchukuo. The most relevant development was the sale of the CER to Manchukuo. Manchukuo argued that its coming into existence changed the legal status of the railway, while both the Soviet and Chinese Governments insisted that its position remained unchanged, because they had not recognized Manchukuo. The Foreign Office observed that once recognition was granted, the Soviet Government would be entitled to assume that the Manchukuo Government was the rightful successor to the Chinese Government and could then freely proceed to modify the old agreements in mutual accord with its new partner.[40]

The Soviet Union was placed in a difficult position by the conflict that developed in 1931 between the Chinese and the Japanese in Manchuria. Some

Chinese sought refuge in Soviet territory and attacked the railway from there. The Japanese Kwantung Army, in turn, regarded them as 'bandits' and used the CER in order to suppress them.[41] There were also a number of new unsettled issues, such as a dispute regarding the ownership of the warehouses and railway-sidings in Harbin, and the question of the return by the Soviet Government of railway rolling stock and locomotives removed from the CER into Soviet territory after the Manchurian Incident. An attempt to reach an agreement on these latter questions was made on 28 March 1933 at a meeting at Harbin between the Manchukuo Government and the directors of the CER, but no settlement was reached. Indeed, it was reported in the local Russian and Chinese press that the Soviet vice-director had affirmed that not only the locomotives in dispute but the whole of the CER was the property of the Soviet Government. The Chinese director of the railway disagreed, of course, with this claim that the Soviet Union was the sole owner of the railway.[42]

However, the Soviets wanted to avoid a military clash with the Japanese in this period.[43] Therefore on 2 May 1933 Maxim Litvinov, the People's Commissar for Foreign Affairs, mentioned the possible sale of the CER to the Japanese ambassador in Moscow. In addition, the Soviets agreed to change the railway's name to the North Manchurian Railway (NMR) from 1 June 1933.[44] Subsequently a conference of Soviet and Manchukuo delegates convened to negotiate the sale of the Russian rights in the CER to Manchukuo in Tokyo on 26 June. The negotiations continued for about a year and a half. The greatest obstacle was the huge disparity between the price named by the Soviet Government and that which Manchukuo was prepared to offer. Manchukuo only admitted Russia's claim to half-ownership in the railway; the remaining half, according to its interpretation, was rightfully its own property as heirs to the rights of China in Manchuria.[45] The sale of the CER was brought to a successful end in March 1935. E. G. Jamieson, the acting British Consul-General in Harbin, observed that Soviet Russia had made the best of a bad bargain and sold its interest in the railway, the value of which was steadily depreciating.[46]

The sale brought about a change in the situation in North Manchuria. Jamieson observed that the White Russian population, numbering some 35,000, was now confronted with the prospect of unemployment and even starvation as a result of growing Japanese penetration. The Soviet employees of the NMR and their families left for Soviet Russia at the expense of Manchukuo by the beginning of August. The number of the people departing amounted to a little over 20,000. Manchukuo paid the Soviet employees' retirement allowances, which amounted to about ¥30,000,000. Spending resulted in an astonishing but short-lived boom. Then the slump began because the new purchasers were Japanese. For example, the ready-made clothes that had been made for the physically large Russians were oversized and entirely unsuitable for the Japanese market.[47] Sir John Hope Simpson of Chatham House wrote as follows:

## 82   *Harumi Goto-Shibata*

[Harbin's] importance as the centre of the refugee community in the Far East has disappeared, and it has been replaced in this respect by Shanghai. Harbin is now a Japanese town, and the Russians have been ousted from many occupations which were their monopoly. Those with sufficient means left Harbin after the Japanese occupation.[48]

### Relying on the voluntary organizations

As many Russians were leaving Harbin in the summer of 1935, the League Secretariat prepared a new memorandum on the position of Russian women in the Far East. This document was based on the information collected at the request of the Secretary-General and was to be submitted to the Assembly in September that year.[49] The contents of the memorandum are mostly the same as the information which has already been introduced in this chapter. In addition, however, the memorandum mentions the existence of many voluntary organizations which were endeavouring to improve the situation of women of Russian origin. The shortcomings of those organizations were considered to be that they tended to concentrate on one geographical area and that there were very limited links between them. Therefore, it was considered essential that an agent be appointed who could co-ordinate the activities of the various organizations and areas.[50]

Just around this time the number of refugees worldwide began to dramatically increase. After September 1935 more than 100,000 Jews fled Germany, and the League's budget was utterly insufficient to cope with the new situation. The League was run by subscriptions from its member countries, but some countries, including China, failed to pay the allocated amount. It fell to the British and the French to make up any budget deficit.

In September 1935 the fifth committee of the League Assembly agreed to authorize the Secretary-General to secure the services of a competent person to act as the agent of the League of Nations. The British and Chinese delegates expressed reservations even at this proposal to find someone on the spot who would undertake the work without entailing extra expenditure by the League. The former pointed out that the appointment of a League agent without funds to supervise the problem in so large an area as China did not appear likely to enhance the reputation of the League.[51]

On 2 February 1937 a conference on traffic in women and children in East Asia was opened in Bandung in the Dutch East Indies. Before the conference, there were again some British charities which considered the problem of Russian women refugees from the viewpoint of white people's prestige and lobbied the Foreign Office accordingly. However, the latter did not think likewise. It was of the opinion that the prostitution of white women in the Far East, deplorable though it was, was a less important factor in the loss of prestige than the general degradation of large sections of the Russian community, particularly in Manchuria.[52]

Presented with the drastic increase in refugees and the innate lack of a sufficient League budget, no spectacular solution was proposed at the Bandung conference. The question of assisting the Russian women was again considered essentially to be one for voluntary organizations; the League's role was merely to appoint an agent who would co-ordinate the activities of the various voluntary organizations. Even the money needed to employ such a person was hoped to be found from private sources. Although the appointment was approved at the Assembly in 1937, it was suspended by the Council in January 1938 due to the deterioration in the situation of East Asia.[53]

## Some concluding thoughts

This chapter has examined the problems faced by Russian women refugees in China and how international society tried to tackle these issues. The League of Nations was established largely in order to maintain world peace, but its economic, social and other humanitarian sections also gradually came to play significant roles in the interwar period. Several commissions of enquiry, including that into trafficking in women and children, were despatched to various parts of the world.

Originally, East Asia was by no means a major concern of the League of Nations. It was a place where several empires including the British Empire still held special interests, and neither Japan nor Britain welcomed this new actor on to the scene. Once established, however, the League started to have its own will and momentum that went beyond the control even of Britain which was the chief pillar of support for the League. International civil servants from smaller countries, which did not have any existing relations with East Asia, were attracted by the new opportunities offered by the League of Nations. They hoped to utilize their own expertise fully in East Asia, especially in China, and to fulfil their ambitions at the same time.[54]

The problem of Russian refugees in China came to be noticed thanks to this expanding role played by the League of Nations. The Russian refugees were impoverished if they did not have some special talent or knowledge of foreign languages. Therefore some women became engaged in prostitution, and some probably supported their families by so doing. It seems while there were some unfortunate women who had fallen victims of human traffickers, there were also some who worked as recruiting agents of the traffickers.

It was surely necessary to help these impoverished people, but its innate lack of resources made it impossible for the League to take initiatives. The League was run by contributions paid by its member countries, but some failed to pay the allocated amount. The budget of the League of Nations as a whole was limited. As a result, there was some imbalance between what some international civil servants aspired to do and what the League could actually achieve. Regarding the issue of the Russian women refugees, the League had to rely on the efforts of the voluntary organizations. These organizations had played a significant role to solve the problem of human trafficking from the

## 84 *Harumi Goto-Shibata*

very beginning, and had lobbied to make the suppression of human trafficking one of the tasks of the League of Nations. These organizations were therefore indispensable when the League needed detailed information on the situation of Russian refugees in China and some offered funds to support the League's mission. Indeed, some people, such as Crowdy, were active in both official and private organizations.

In the end, the League of Nations did not succeed in solving the problem of Russian women refugees. However, it at least provided a venue for gathering and analyzing information and a forum to discuss ways to rescue them. This was a significant first step and, building on this foundation, efforts to help refugees were carried on and strengthened after the Second World War and are continuing even today.

## Notes

\* This chapter is based on the author's 'Chūgoku no Roshia jin josei nanmin mondai to Kokusai Renmei' in Yōichi Kibata & Harumi Goto-Shibata (eds), *Teikoku no Nagai Kage*, Kyoto: Minerva shobo, 2010, pp. 203–27. The earliest English version was presented at the Oxford-Kobe workshop on 'Civil Society – Violence and Order' held on 28–30 March 2009 in Kobe, Japan. The author would like to thank its participants from various places of the world for their valuable comments to improve the paper.

1 Barbara H.M. Metzger, 'The League of Nations and Refugees: the Humanitarian Legacy of Fridtjof Nansen', in United Nations, *The League of Nations 1920–1946*, New York: United Nations, 1996, p. 74; Claudena M. Skran, *Refugees in Interwar Europe*, Oxford: Clarendon Press, 1995, pp. 33, 109. See also Michael R. Marrus, *The Unwanted*, Philadelphia, PA: Temple University Press, 2002.

2 Sir John Hope Simpson, *The Refugee Problem*, Oxford: Oxford University Press, 1939, p. 497, and Skran, *Refugees*, pp. 35–6.

3 Metzger, 'The League of Nations', p. 75; see also John Torpey, *The Invention of the Passport*, Cambridge: Cambridge University Press, 1999.

4 Skran, *Refugees*, p. 74, and Zara Steiner, *The Lights that Failed*, Oxford: Oxford University Press, 2005, pp. 365–7.

5 Skran, *Refugees*, pp. 26, 123, 131, 133; Metzger, 'The League of Nations', pp. 78–80.

6 On the investigation in Japan, see Onozawa Akane, *Kindai Nihon shakai to kōshō seido*, Tokyo: Yoshikawa kōbunkan, 2010.

7 Brian Donovan, *White Slave Crusades*, Chicago, IL: University of Illinois Press, 2006, pp. 6–9, 15.

8 Concerning the limits of the period, see also Susan Pedersen, 'The Maternalist Moment in British Colonial Policy', *Past and Present*, 171, 2001, p. 182; Margherita Zanasi, 'Exporting Development', *Comparative Studies in Society and History*, 49/1, 2007, pp. 143–69.

9 F. S. L. Lyons, *Internationalism in Europe 1815–1914*, Leiden: A.W. Sythoff, 1963, pp. 274–84, and Daniel Gorman, *The Emergence of International Society in the 1920s*, Cambridge: Cambridge University Press, 2012, pp. 53–7.

10 League of Nations documents (LNd), C.849.M.393.1932. IV, League of Nations, Commission of Enquiry into Traffic in Women and Children in the East, Report to the Council, p. 11 and List of members. See also B. Metzger, 'Towards an International Human Rights Regime during the Inter-War Years' in K. Grant et al. (eds), *Beyond Sovereignty*, New York: Palgrave-Macmillan, 2007.

11 Gorman, *Emergence*, p. 87. The significance of the issue of international vs national or imperial has been raised in Stephen Legg, 'Of scales, networks and assemblages: the League of Nations apparatus and the scalar sovereignty of the Government of India,' *Transactions of the Institute of the British Geographers*, 34, 2009, pp. 234–253.

12 LNd C.849.M.393.1932. IV, Commission of Enquiry, Report, pp. 3, 12; and The National Archives, Kew (TNA), FO371/17387 W858/263/98 from LN, C.50.1933. IV, 23 Jan. 1933.

13 LN, *Commission of Enquiry into Traffic in Women and Children in the East: Summary of the Report to the Council*, Geneva, 1934, pp. 10, 12, 39–40.

14 LNd C.849.M.393.1932. IV, Commission of Enquiry, Report, pp. 7–8, 29–37, 97–8.

15 Gaimushō Gaikō Shiryōkan (ed.), *Nihon Gaikō-shi Jiten*, Tokyo: Yamakawa shuppansha, 1992.

16 *Harbin and Manchuria*, special issue of *The South Atlantic Quarterly*, Durham, NC: Duke University Press, 2001.

17 LNd C.849.M.393.1932. IV, Commission of Enquiry, Report, pp. 22, 34–7.

18 TNA FO371/18534 W11137/43/98 Garstin (Harbin) to Simon 4 Dec. 1934.

19 Marcia R. Ristaino, *Port of Last Resort*, Stanford, CA: Stanford University Press, 2001, p. 94.

20 LNd A.12.1934, Nansen International Office for Refugees, Report of the Governing Body for the Year Ending June 30th, 1934, Appendix II.

21 LNd A.12.1935. IV, LN, Position of Women of Russian Origin in the Far East, pp. 1–2.

22 LNd Report, pp. 11, 14; Onozawa, *Kindai Nihon shakai to kōshō seido*, pp. 225–8, 306–7.

23 TNA FO371/18534 W8702/43/98 Pratt minute 8 Oct. 1934, and Simon to China posts 18 Oct. 1934.

24 TNA FO371/18534 W11137/43/98 Garstin to Simon 4 Dec. 1934.

25 TNA FO371/19668 W1472/26/98 Beare (Tianjin) to Simon 27 Dec. 1934.

26 TNA FO371/19668 W1467/26/98 Brenan (Shanghai) to Simon 29 Dec. 1934.

27 TNA FO371/19668 W1467/26/98 Brenan to Simon 29 Dec. 1934.

28 TNA FO371/19668 W1467/26/98 Brenan to Simon 29 Dec. 1934. See also Naoko Shimazu, *Japan, Race and Equality*, London: Routledge, 1998.

29 TNA FO371/18534 W10263/43/98 LN 11B/14387/13457 21 Nov. 1934; and League of Nations Archives, Geneva (hereafter, LNA), 11B/14387/13457, Harris (HO) to Ekstrand 15 Jan. 1935; LNd A.12.1935.IV, p. 3.

30 TNA FO371/20480 W4395/172/98 Brenan to Peking, no. 134, 1 Apr. 1936; and Ristaino, *Port of Last Resort*, p. 94.

31 JACAR (Ajia rekishi shiryō centre, Japan), Ref. 04122142300, p. 86. Pages 67 to 89 of this record are SORO's report sent by Ishii (Shanghai) to Hirota, 22 Apr. 1935.

32 Ibid.

33 As the Straits government objected to the suggestion that the conference should be held at the same time as the meeting of the Advisory Council of the Eastern Bureau of the Health Organization, Bandung in the Dutch East Indies was finally chosen. LNA, 11B/15411/13661, 13 May 1935, Ekstrand to Rajchman.

34 TNA FO371/19668 W4217/26/98 Harris to Makins (FO) 16 May 1935; W4677/26/98, minutes of the 86th session of the LN Council, 23 May 1935; JACAR, Ref. 04122142300, pp. 230–1, Sei-shōnen hogo shimon iinkai keika hōkokusho.

35 Bristol University, special collections, DM1584/12/B, unpublished autobiography of Dame Rachel Crowdy, part V, Chapter 3, p. 35 and Chapter 4, pp. 43–66.This material is used with the permission of the University of Bristol Library Special Collections.

86   *Harumi Goto-Shibata*

36  TNA FO371/19677 W5908/356/98 British Social Hygiene Council to Hoare 4 July 1935.
37  TNA FO371/19677 W5908/356/98 British Social Hygiene Council to Hoare 4 July 1935.
38  TNA FO371/19677 W5908/356/98 minutes 18 July 1935.
39  TNA FO371/19677 W6993/356/98 from AMSH 29 July 1935, and Makins minute 9 Aug. 1935.
40  TNA FO371/17082 F3302/43/10 FO memo 19 May 1933.
41  TNA FO371/17066 F914/27/10 Garstin to Simon enclosure 29 Feb. 1933, and FO371/17067 F2919/27/10 Garstin to Simon 31 Mar. 1933.
42  *Nihon Gaikō Bunsho*, Shōwa-ki II, vol. 2, part 2, documents nos. 326–8; Satō Motoei, 'Hokuman Tetsudō jōto mondai wo meguru Nisso kankei', Komazawa daigaku bungakubu kiyō, no. 54, 1996, p. 130; and TNA FO371/17067 F2919/27/10 Garstin to Simon 31 Mar. 1933, FO371/17069 F5199/27/10 Garstin to Simon 30 June 1933, and FO371/17134 F3488/2463/10 Garstin to Simon 9 May 1933.
43  On the negotiation concerning the sale of the CER, see Satō, 'Hokuman Tetsudō', and Nihon Kokusai Seiji Gakkai (ed.), *Taiheiyō Sensō he no Michi, 4, Nicchū Sensō, Ge*, Tokyo: Asahi shimbunsha, 1987 (originally published in 1963); Steiner, *The Lights that Failed*, pp. 744, 749–50.
44  TNA FO371/17133 F3182/2463/10 Strang (Moscow) to Simon 12 May 1933, and FO371/17082 F4423/43/10 Garstin to Simon 22 June 1933.
45  *Nihon Gaikō Bunsho*, Shōwa-ki II, vol. 2, part 2, document no. 352; and TNA FO371/17134 F5273/2463/10 Snow (Tokyo) to Simon 7 July 1933, and F5945/2463/10, Snow to Simon 13 Aug. 1933.
46  TNA FO371/19302 F2688/298/10 Jamieson (Harbin) to Simon 8 Apr. 1935.
47  TNA FO371/19302 F2688/298/10 Jamieson to Simon 8 Apr. 1935, FO371/19290 F5515/119/10 Jamieson to Hoare 7 Aug. 1935, FO371/19302 F2688/298/10 Jamieson to Simon 8 Apr. 1935, and FO371/19303 F4695/298/10 Jamieson to Hoare 6 July 1935.
48  Simpson, *The Refugee Problem*, p. 495.
49  LNd, A.12.1935. IV, LN, Position of Women of Russian Origin in the Far East, p. 1.
50  Ibid., p. 16.
51  *British Documents on Foreign Affairs*, part 2, series J, vol. 10, doc. 132, 1 Oct. 1935; TNA FO371/19694 W10383 5 Dec. 1935; FO411/19 part XXII no. 2, 9 Aug. 1935; and Skran, *Refugees*, p. 144.
52  TNA FO371/21244 W272/272/98 Knatchbull-Hugessen (Peking) to Eden, 4 Jan. 1937; and W14819/272/98, FO Minutes, 24 July 1937.
53  TNA FO371/22521 W1426/62/98 20 Dec. 1937, From LN, no. C. 516.M357.1937. IV, Report on work of the Bandeong Conference, p. 66.
54  See also Harumi Goto-Shibata, 'Kokusai Renmei no tai Chū gijyutsu kyōryoku to Igirisu, 1928–1935: Rajchman eisei buchō no katsudō to shikin mondai wo chūshin ni', in Hattori Ryūji et al. (eds), *Senkanki no higashi Ajia kokusai seiji*, Tokyo: Chūō daigaku shuppan bu, 2007, pp. 131–95; and idem., 'Kokusai Renmei to Nihon: Manshū jihen ki no tai Chū gijyutsu kyōryoku wo megutte', in Hosoya Yūichi (ed.), *Global Governance to Nihon*, Tokyo: Chūō kōron shin sha, 2013, pp. 15–56. Harumi Goto-Shibata, *Kokusai Shugi to no Kakutō: Nihon, Kokusai Renmei, Igirisu Teikoku*, Tokyo: Chūō kōron shin sha, 2016.

# 6 Defending the 'Singapore strategy'
## Hankey's Dominions tour, 1934

*Ann Trotter*

The effect of the expansion of the Japanese empire into Manchuria in 1931, the Japanese attack on Shanghai in 1932 and move into Jehol [Rehe], north China, in 1933 was to expose the relative decline of the British Empire and to raise difficult questions for the future of Britain's role in the Far East. Peter Lowe has described these events as 'a watershed'. Japanese expansionism had replaced Chinese nationalism as the greatest threat to British authority in East Asia.[1]

In fact, British power in the east had been declining since the beginning of the twentieth century, but the extent of that decline had been disguised by the existence of the Anglo–Japanese alliance, which Lowe has described as 'a cornerstone of international order in East Asia'.[2] From 1901 to 1921 this alliance enabled Britain to maintain its standing within the region by leaning on Japanese naval power, enjoying, as Ian Nish suggests, 'some glory without power in the area'.[3] While the implications of the disappearance of the alliance for international order were not immediately apparent, the consequences for Britain's naval position in the east soon were. The years of war from 1914–18 had accelerated the decline of Britain's power and wealth and any hope of restoring the naval situation was quashed when Lord Jellicoe's proposal, in 1919, for a Pacific Fleet to be based in Singapore, was rejected as too costly.

One part of Jellicoe's proposal was, however, taken up. It was decided to build a naval base at Singapore from which a British fleet might be deployed in some future emergency. Work began in 1923. It proceeded with stops and starts but was not near completion by 1932. The Singapore strategy appeared to be a demonstration of imperial solidarity. In retrospect, however, it can be seen as evidence of the chronic weakness of British power. Nevertheless, it became the basis of the defence policy of the empire east of Suez.

The mantra, 'main fleet to Singapore', guided the defence policies of the southern Dominions, Australia and New Zealand through the 1920s. They had been assured at imperial conferences that Britain would protect them and that a fleet would be sent in the event of a crisis in the east. British political leaders were, as Lowe has noted, 'extremely reticent when it came to spelling out the facts of life to the Dominions'.[4] Promises were reiterated. The Dominions were not made aware of the reality of British weakness.

## 88  Ann Trotter

The Shanghai crisis in 1932 altered perceptions in Britain. The Chiefs of Staff reported that Shanghai, where British gunboats were based, and Hong Kong, were vulnerable. They wrote, 'Recent events in the Far East are ominous. We cannot ignore the Writing on the Wall.'[5] At the same time, in Australia and New Zealand, the first doubts about the policy of reliance on imperial defence began to be expressed.

In New Zealand the Chief of Staff ordered a report on requirements for the defence of the country. In August 1933 a committee of five senior officers recommended a modest programme of rearmament and pointed out that, 'if the Main Fleet for any reason is unable to reach Singapore, New Zealand is driven entirely by her own resources ... and could not in any case defend itself against a protracted attack'.[6] New coastal and anti-aircraft artillery was ordered, along with torpedo bombers and reconnaissance planes for the air force as part of a six-year defence programme. The establishment in New Zealand of this 'miniscule' air force (which was part of the military forces) encouraged a muted debate among those who questioned reliance on imperial strategy and believed importance should be given to protecting New Zealand's shores from invasion.[7]

In Australia this debate was carried on much more forcefully and presented problems for the Commonwealth Minister for Defence, Sir George Pearce. Pearce's position had been made clear. He declared in 1933 that the government was confident that any attacker would have to reckon with the whole naval and military power of the British Empire.[8] This confidence was not shared by Pearce's military advisers. They maintained that, instead of cooperating in the maintenance of the Empire's sea power, Australia would do better to build up its army and air force to resist invasion.[9] Since the discussion appeared to be deadlocked, it was suggested that some informed advice from Britain might assist the minister in resolving the important question of future defence policy.

It happened that the Australian state of Victoria was to celebrate its centennial in 1934. The Commonwealth government saw this as an opportunity to invite some distinguished persons from Britain to the country. The most celebrated guest was to be the Duke of Gloucester but the government suggested that senior officers from each of Britain's defence services might also become official guests who, at the same time, could advise on matters of local defence.[10] The British reply to the feelers put out by the Australian High Commissioner in London on this possibility was that none of these gentlemen could be made available to visit Australia.[11]

An alternative solution was then found. The Commonwealth Treasurer, R. G. Casey, proposed that Sir Maurice Hankey, the Cabinet Secretary, secretary to the Committee of Imperial Defence (CID) and chairman of the Defence Requirements Committee (hereafter DRC), be invited. Hankey was well known to both Casey and Pearce, who had attended imperial conferences in the past, and Hankey had maintained correspondence with both men. Claiming that he had been 'slogging away for years thinking about and trying to promote unity within the empire', Hankey was pleased to accept the invitation.[12] This Australian initiative soon led to an invitation from the New Zealand government.[13] The Australian government paid all expenses and allowed Hankey to choose his route. For personal reasons Hankey chose to go first to South Africa, then to Australia, New Zealand and Canada – a formidable journey then, around the world by sea and steam. He arranged to depart after the parliamentary recess in July 1934.[14]

Discussions on problems in the east, on how best to respond to Japan's activities in China, on the preservation of Britain's interests there, and on Britain's significant naval weakness in relation to these, had occupied the Foreign Office and the Treasury from 1933. The Chiefs of Staff annual review that year had emphasized the urgent need to find solutions to the defence problems in the east and stressed Britain's significant naval weakness. The appointment of Hitler as Chancellor of Germany in January 1933 and evidence of German intentions to rearm added uncertainty about the future in Europe and raised the question, in government circles, of local, as distinct from imperial, defence.

Inevitably, the discussions in Whitehall on defence requirements centred on priorities and costs. In these discussions a gulf appeared between what might be called the 'European menace' school, which stressed the need for increased airpower and a smaller navy based at home (of which the Chancellor of the Exchequer, Neville Chamberlain, was the chief exponent), and the 'Empire, big navy' school that insisted that naval expenditure to defend Britain's worldwide interests was the priority. In this school, Sir Maurice Hankey was the inspiration and the *eminence gris* in support of the Admiralty.

The DRC, which was established in November 1933 to consider the Chiefs of Staff's review, reported in February 1934.[15] It accepted the view of the Chiefs of Staff, identifying Japan as the source of immediate concern, and recommended that, while efforts should be made to improve relations with the Japanese, Britain should 'show a tooth' in East Asia, that is, demonstrate an ability to use force if required. This was envisaged as a preliminary to a policy of accommodation and friendship with Japan. Germany was, however, recognized as the ultimate potential enemy.[16]

For Chamberlain, who had introduced the lowest defence estimates in the inter-war years in 1932, the DRC report was a threat to his plans for a balanced budget and gradual economic recovery. He could see no point in 'showing a tooth' in the Far East if the real enemy was closer to home. The idea that Britain could simultaneously prepare against war with Germany and war with Japan was, he argued, 'an impossibility', nor was the prospect of building and sending out a fleet capable of containing the Japanese realistic. He could not accept the 'staggering prospect' of the expenditure of £85 million on the five-year defence programme that the DRC report recommended. Given its financial weakness, he maintained, only by concentrating on defence in Europe could Britain achieve security through its own strength. Japan's friendship and goodwill, he thought, might best be secured through diplomatic effort.[17]

90  *Ann Trotter*

Chamberlain's views and his readiness to minimize Britain's imperial role placed him at odds with the Admiralty, which was concerned to preserve as much as possible of the naval aspects of the DRC report, and with Hankey, the chief architect of that report. Like many in Britain, Hankey thought of the Empire as a family whose members must be held together. With this idea went the responsibility to protect the family members. Chamberlain's proposals for such a radical change in defence policy and in particular in the role of the navy caused 'a flutter in many dovecotes', Hankey reported, including, of course, his own.[18] Between March and July 1934 the arguments raged in the Cabinet and its Disarmament Committee to which the former had given the task of considering and making recommendations on the DRC Report.

In this debate the Dominions were a bargaining chip rather than a key factor. In fact for both Australia and New Zealand the policies of 'showing a tooth' in the Pacific and of accommodation and friendship with Japan were in their interests. They were both vulnerable, both desirous of enjoying the security that would be reflected by a strong British presence in the east, and both anxious to foster favourable trading relationships with Japan.

At the end of May 1934 Ramsay MacDonald, the Prime Minister, met the Dominion High Commissioners and told them 'very privately' that, 'as a result of a number of things happening in Germany and elsewhere,' the government had decided that a comprehensive survey of the whole defence position should be made before any big decisions were taken. He assured them that before any such decisions were made the Dominions would be called into consultation.[19]

Hankey lobbied all key ministers to argue against the priority that Chamberlain gave to home defence and to the air force over the requirements of the navy and imperial defence; affirming his view that a rapprochement with Japan would be more likely to be effected if Britain's interests were seen to be defended; maintaining that Singapore would be without value without a strong and mobile navy. He dwelt on the effect on Australia and New Zealand and Britain's 'valuable far eastern colonies' if the Japanese navy was allowed to expand and war was forced on Britain and the Empire. He quoted General Smuts' description of the British navy as 'the greatest instrument in the world, the shield spread over the entire Commonwealth and over South Africa'.[20]

The result of this lobbying and Hankey's coaching of the First Sea Lord, Admiral Sir Ernle Chatfield, was that Chamberlain's proposal to set aside the threats from Japan was not found acceptable. Chamberlain, however, succeeded in reducing the overall DRC programme to £50.3 million. The general priorities in the DRC report were accepted. The cuts demanded by Chamberlain to expenditure on the army were accepted and the allocation to the air force was slightly increased. The position regarding the navy was obscured by digressions regarding a new naval limitation treaty to be negotiated in 1935, and this enabled the hard decision to be postponed. The naval construction and naval deficiencies programme was left to be discussed between the Chancellor and first lord 'in the early autumn' of 1934.[21] This was the situation in July 1934 when Hankey was due to start out on his journey to Australia.

# Hankey's Dominions tour 1934    91

It had been agreed at the Imperial Conference in 1926 that the Dominions should be kept informed of imperial defence policy and MacDonald had assured the Dominion High Commissioners three months earlier that they would be kept informed of the outcome of the discussion on defence policy then going on. As the conclusions on the DRC were 'tentative and incomplete' and the 'naval issue' had not been settled when Parliament was due to go into recess in July 1934, the Cabinet decided that the DRC report was not to be sent to the Dominions. Instead, Hankey was, as he commented, 'landed with the rather delicate task of telling the [Dominion] Prime Ministers ... how the matter stands'.[22] He was to take with him on his forthcoming visit to the Dominions copies of both the DRC report and the ministerial decisions on it. He was to make a statement to the prime ministers about the general results of the enquiry up to date, so that there might be no misunderstanding of the failure of the report to deal with the navy, in which the Dominions were principally interested.[23]

The role of confidential envoy for the government on a difficult issue was one for which Hankey was well qualified. On the matter of the unresolved question of the role of the navy in defence, however, he was not disinterested. The stalled naval deficiency and construction programme was a problem on which his views were well known. He wanted to see a progressive advance in construction and the repair of deficiencies. He believed there could be 'no greater blow to the unity of the Empire' than a failure to assert Britain's sea power in the Pacific in an emergency and he felt 'it would help' if he could 'get Dominions' opinion right' before the Dominion prime ministers came to London in the spring of 1935.[24]

Given the delicate matter of the unresolved 'naval question' and his known views on this, Hankey recognized the importance of having the insurance of a statement clarifying the government's objectives on naval matters. Before he left for South Africa, therefore, Hankey had a 'long and full discussion' with the Chancellor of the Exchequer. He told Chamberlain that he could not recommend the Australian government support Pearce's proposal, which involved spending £6 million additional to the budget, to carry out a scheme for naval expenditure, on the fundamental basis of which the Chancellor appeared to have doubts. He asked for the Chancellor's support for a formula outlining the British position.[25] This formula represented the naval position as the DRC, which Hankey had chaired, wished to see it, and was in line with the desiderata for Far Eastern defence recommended by the ministerial committee, which had considered the report. It stated:

With the object of enabling the fleet to proceed to Singapore in any major emergency in the Far East, it is the intention of His Majesty's Government in the United Kingdom

1    to complete the first stage of the deficiencies of the Singapore base by 1938

2   to proceed with plans for the defence of fuelling stations east of Suez
3   to make good the deficiencies of the navy as financial conditions permit.

The naval construction programme, however, cannot be determined until after the naval conference, 1935.[26]

Hankey argued that he needed this document in order to assure the Australians that Britain would be able to fulfil its part of the bargain in the event of an emergency in the Pacific, but no cabinet decision had been reached on these matters. Chamberlain was, therefore, not prepared to sign. He finally agreed, however, that if Stanley Baldwin, as chairman of the ministerial committee that had considered the DRC report, authorized Hankey to use the formula, he would withdraw his opposition. Hankey therefore drew up an *aide memoire* that he asked Baldwin to initial. He explained to Baldwin:

The principle on which all reports have been based has been that there will be a naval base at Singapore sufficiently strongly defended to hold out *until the arrival of the main fleet of capital ships, which thereafter provides the shield to cover the whole of our interests in the south Pacific and Indian Ocean.*[27]

Hankey declared he could not conceive of any alternative system of imperial defence that was not based on 'the centuries old assumption of sea power'. Failure on Britain's part, he was convinced, would break up the empire and, he wrote to Baldwin, 'nothing would induce me to be a party to that.' Baldwin signed the *aide memoire* without comment. Chamberlain signed reluctantly. Hankey felt the authority this gave him had 'immense effect'.[28]

Before he left, Hankey wrote to MacDonald to tell him of the *aide memoire*. He claimed the document gave him 'moral backing' to discharge the task of advising the Dominions on defence.[29] He also wrote to Baldwin both officially and privately while he was away urging that the bearing of naval defence on the preservation of the unity of the Empire should not be overlooked and warning him against the influence of Warren Fisher, the permanent head of the Treasury, who, he claimed, had, 'never been sound about the navy or about defence questions in the Pacific'. Any weakening of the intention to assert British sea power in the Pacific would have 'an absolutely shattering' effect on the Empire, he suggested.[30] He wrote:

I am glad to have obtained from you, and the chancellor of the exchequer, that little bit of paper about the Far East (Singapore etc.) Without it I should feel I was walking on a bog and with it I shall have to tread warily.[31]

Hankey also carried with him an assurance from Chatfield that Singapore's gun defences would be completed by the spring of 1937, although the barracks and store houses would still have to be built. No promises could be made about the fleet. Hankey's 'little bit of paper' represented the most optimistic view possible of the future for the navy in the Pacific.

Hankey's tour was officially announced in August 1934. In those days a visit to the distant Dominions by a prominent British civil servant involving a series of long sea voyages was rare indeed. In a discreet interview with the *Evening Standard*, Hankey explained that he was going to Australia as a guest of the government for informal talks, would be visiting South Africa en route and New Zealand and Canada on the return journey. The 'quality papers' accepted this version, but the *Daily Express* headline read 'Empire Tour Mystery' while the *Daily Herald* produced a triple headline: 'Secret Defence Tour by Cabinet Chief. Sounding Dominions on New Policy. Talks on Vital Matters of Strategy'. The communist *Daily Worker* and the weekly, *New Leader*, both suggested that the tour signalled that 'war was in the air'. More surprisingly, *Izvestiya* reported the tour and described Hankey, unsurprisingly, as 'one of the chief partisans of British Imperialism'.[32] Rumours of his 'secret' purpose followed Hankey at every stage of his journey.

In South Africa Hankey first reviewed coastal defences in Cape Colony. He then proceeded to Pretoria to meet General Hertzog, the Prime Minister. Hankey had been warned that Herzog was 'rather inclined to underrate the German menace' and inclined to Germany rather than France. He prepared carefully for an interview that proved to be bizarre rather than challenging. General Hertzog was a silent recipient of Hankey's presentation of the British government's defence policy including the DRC report and ministerial committees' decisions on it. He reported on the Cabinet's decisions on defence requirements and the position as regards naval deficiencies, emphasizing that there was no change in British policy and that efforts were being made to minimize the risk of war in the east or in Europe. He spoke uninterruptedly for an hour. After this, Hertzog said he understood Britain's policy and had no comments on, or criticisms of, the policy to offer.[33]

Hankey's friend, General Smuts, the Deputy Prime Minister and Minister of Justice, proved a much more responsive and enthusiastic listener. He expressed approval of the British decision to rearm, showed a 'lively awareness' of the perils looming in East Asia and 'hoped the strength of the navy would be maintained' as it was 'the shield of the whole empire'. This was, of course, exactly Hankey's view.[34] But Smuts' enthusiasm represented a minority view in South Africa. The future of the navy and Singapore and British defence policy in general was, for historical, geographical and ethnic reasons, of less central interest to the South African government than it was to the southern Dominions, Australia and New Zealand.

After a long, tedious and predictably stormy journey across the southern Indian Ocean, the Hankeys arrived in Perth in mid-September 1934. His unofficial discussions on defence began with Pearce, until recently the

Minister of Defence, whom Hankey knew well from meetings of wartime imperial cabinets as well as imperial conferences. The Hankeys then went on by train, another tedious journey, via Adelaide to Melbourne. There, a large gathering of state dignitaries was assembled to meet him. The press gave prominence to the arrival of 'The Mystery Man of Britain', and the left-wing press, suspicious of his visit, suggested it was a definite sign of preparations for war.[35] In all Hankey had six meetings with the Defence Committee, and also saw the Federal Prime Minister, J. A. Lyons. He also met the recently appointed Minister of Defence, R. A. Parkhill, who, he thought, 'knew very little about his portfolio'. In Canberra Hankey produced a draft of a long paper, 'Higher Organisation for Defence in Australia'. He had found Australians 'ignorant of the principles of defence, liable to imagine all kinds of dangers' and, he thought, they 'had the wind up' about Japan.[36] There was considerable anxiety in Australia as to whether the British fleet in eastern waters really did provide security, or whether an army and air force were needed in Australia for defence against invasion in the event of simultaneous trouble in Europe. Hankey re-emphasized the importance of naval defence and cooperation with the Royal Navy both directly by the Royal Australian Navy and indirectly by Australian military and air forces. He assured the Australians that the plans of the Admiralty were framed on the defence of British interests in the Pacific Ocean, that it had been decided to spend 'a lot of money' on Singapore and that Britain was unlikely to let its vast interests go by default.[37]

Hankey described the Australian people as 'incredibly pro-British' and reported that the government and officials had treated him 'marvellously': 'Every secret is confided to me as though I was a member of the cabinet,' he wrote. He believed the home government's policy was 'understood by them all' and that the reasons for postponing the decision on a long-range naval programme were fully appreciated. Hankey felt he had won the battle for Australia's cooperation in an imperial naval programme.[38]

Hankey could feel his accomplishments in Australia had been positive, but the courtesy of those people who treated him so 'marvellously' and apparently accepted the policies of Whitehall as expounded by their distinguished visitor, frequently disguised their scepticism. Hankey might have been surprised by the private comments of his host in Melbourne, Sir John Latham, the Deputy Prime Minister and a former Minister of External Affairs. Writing to Pearce, whom Hankey described as 'our best friend in Australia', Latham noted:

> It would be a good thing if Great Britain had a more definite policy about Oriental Affairs and if the Dominions actually knew what that policy was ... Great Britain is quite prepared to say in flowing language what the *objectives* of her policy are – such as cooperation, coordination and friendship etc. etc. with the great nations of the East. Such statements remind me of the noble candidate who states that he will not be deterred from pursuing at all costs the welfare of the people.[39]

Pearce replied that he agreed 'absolutely' with these remarks about British policy.[40]

Hankey's task in New Zealand was simpler than in Australia. New Zealand's geographical isolation and small population made it effectively defenceless. The country had of necessity to stand or fall with the empire as a whole. New Zealand's security depended ultimately on the success in the Pacific of the general scheme of imperial defence. New Zealand's Chief of General Staff, Major General Sinclair Burgess, a soldier for whom Hankey had a high regard, had, in October 1933, however, initiated the formation of a CID modelled on the British CID. The arrangements were still largely on paper at the time of Hankey's visit.[41] Informal talks with ministers and service chiefs were held. Hankey's statement of British policy and plans followed closely that which he had made in Australia. At a ministerial meeting, Hankey took the opportunity to remind his hosts of the apparently prophetic statement that the Prime Minister, George Forbes, a man of limited imagination, had made at the 1930 Imperial Conference when he had deprecated the decision to slow down the work at Singapore. Neither the Prime Minister nor Hankey felt the need to inform his audience that the latter had actually written this speech at Forbes' request.[42] There was 'great satisfaction' with, and no criticism from, the New Zealand team of the British defence requirements policy. Hankey also found there was 'warm support' for a policy of better relations with Japan. He reported that both Australia and New Zealand were basing their system of defence on the assumption that Singapore could be maintained until the British fleet could proceed there to 'shield the whole of the empire east of Suez' in the event of an emergency.[43] The New Zealand experience, with his hosts' unqualified support of the policies he espoused, left Hankey ecstatic. He found the country, he reported, 'really the land of my dreams. Everything was perfect for us, the people, the accommodation and the weather.'[44] The machinations of the Treasury, his report implied, should not be allowed to let these 'incredibly patriotic people' down.

Hankey had always realized that Canada was likely to be the most delicate part of his mission. As was the case in South Africa, historical, geographical and ethnic factors helped explain a lack of enthusiasm in Canadian circles for Hankey's mission, but after the 'fervid imperialism of Australia and New Zealand', the 'calculating aloofness' of Ottowa struck a chilly note. Hankey entered Canada in rather 'anxious circumstances' as the country was on the eve of a general election. Neither the government nor the people were much interested in questions of collective security. In addition, some weeks before Hankey arrived in Canada the press had suggested he would come as the official emissary of the British government to promote a common plan of defence within the Empire. This suggested that Hankey was part of some imperialist plot. Hankey was warned that there was a growing body of opinion in Canada in favour of keeping the country out of the next war at all costs and he was therefore aware he must tread warily when it came to discussing British rearmament with Canadians.[45]

96    *Ann Trotter*

The Canadian Prime Minister, R. B. Bennett, with whom Hankey had a two-hour talk, appeared to understand the necessity for the defensive provisions Britain was making, but the Canadian view of Japan and the shifting balance in northeast Asia and the Pacific was inevitably different from that of Britain or Australia or New Zealand. The evident growth of Japanese power and ambitions appeared to leave the Canadians unmoved. The United States could be expected to protect the Canadian Pacific coast, and 'collective security' would look after Canada's eastern trade. Maritime defence as a worldwide issue simply was not understood by most Canadians, Hankey thought, and on 'imperial relations' opinion as a whole was unformed. Major General MacNaughton, Canada's 'tremendously able' chief of general staff, to whom Hankey outlined British defence plans and proposals, thought Canada would 'come along' if the cause were just and every effort to maintain peace had been exhausted. He stressed to Hankey the importance of Canada's relationship with the United States and warned that any sign of friendliness on Britain's part to Japan was taken in America as unfriendly to the United States. This conversation led Hankey to emphasize in his report on the Canadian tour that, from the point of view of imperial policy, 'if we estrange the United States we shall estrange many people in Canada.' He urged that, in cultivating good relations with Japan, the United States should not be alienated. It was his impression that 'all the Dominions' attached importance to the closest possible relations with the United States.[46] When Sir Robert Vansittart, permanent head of Foreign Office, read this, he commented tartly on the Canadian attitude and Hankey's conclusion from it: 'Our policy must necessarily be to cultivate good relations with both USA and Japan. There is no present prospect of doing more with them. This is friendly realism.'[47]

Hankey returned to London in January 1935. It was plain that the tour had not been a purely 'social junket', and alarmist accounts of his activities in the Dominions appeared in the press suggesting the tour was about preparations for another war. By the time Hankey returned, the Treasury-inspired movement for an Anglo–Japanese rapprochement had collapsed as a result of Japan's lack of enthusiasm for such an agreement.[48] The Japanese had announced their abrogation of the Washington naval treaties, and Admiral Kato Kanji had announced that the Japanese navy was 'reborn'. This prospect put the British in a position of greater vulnerability. The American naval negotiators, with whom preliminary naval talks had been held in June, were not sympathetic to the British assessment of their naval requirements. The talks were adjourned.[49] The prospect of creating the kind of imperial defence 'shield' for which Hankey had led the Dominions to hope was remote. The problem of imperial defence had to be reassessed in the light of a possible arms race. As one Foreign Office official wrote to Latham:

> The problem seems to be whether we should trust the feeble uncertain American or the predatory Jap (sic). General Smuts wants us to go wholeheartedly with America. It is very difficult to know which horse to

*Hankey's Dominions tour 1934* 97

back. For the sake of Australia and New Zealand, the Jap (sic) would be the better partner.[50]

The Dominion factor in calculations about imperial defence simply underlined the dilemma of a power with a greater stake in the external world than it was capable of defending.

Hankey had fulfilled his mission to keep the Dominions informed of British policy as efficiently as could be expected without dwelling on the reality of British naval weakness. His experience showed that there was no such thing as a 'Dominion opinion' on imperial defence matters. Except for New Zealand, which had no alternative to the 'main fleet to Singapore' scenario and whose contribution to imperial defence would inevitably be small, there was neither enthusiasm nor capability in the Dominions to assist in sustaining the myth of British power in the Pacific in 1934. Rather, a reluctance to spend on defence and preoccupation with local issues were the shared characteristics. General Smuts may have been an advocate for Anglo–American cooperation but his views were his own, rather than those of the South African government. The Canadians had made it clear they had no wish to be involved in the problems of imperial defence. Australia's vast territory and relative proximity to the Dutch East Indies and to Singapore made it, geographically, the Dominion the most immediately vulnerable to hostilities from Japan. In spite of his 'marvellous' reception there, it is clear that many in Australia's defence circles were sceptical of Britain's intentions and its capacity to deliver naval protection. Soon after Hankey's departure the bogey of a Japanese invasion that had been fostered by the Australian chiefs of staff was revived and with it the contention that local rather than imperial defence was of paramount importance. Advice from London, it was suggested, should be treated with reserve since the problem of the protection of Australia had never been considered there; all thought in Whitehall was really centred on the United Kingdom.[51] This cynicism was less than fair to Hankey and others who were determined to preserve Britain's imperial role, unrealistic as their aspirations may, in hindsight, appear.

Far from being a 'mystery tour' or a preparation for war, Hankey's tour was essentially an exercise in public relations. In this role Hankey was an able and well-informed salesman who made the best of the case for Britain's capacity to defend the Dominions through the power of its ageing and yet to be refitted and expanded fleet. Hankey was always 'skating on thin ice' on this tour, but he undoubtedly believed that the navy was the key to the maintenance of Britain's imperial position to which he gave priority in spite of the changes in power balances in Europe and East Asia. Hankey was warmed by his contact with so many loyal and friendly citizens, but it is evident that many of those citizens were not as impressed as he supposed by the imperial and naval policy he propounded. 'Dominion opinion' was a weapon that could be used by British ministers to strengthen their arguments in Cabinet, but on naval, as on other issues, each Dominion had a particular

## 98  Ann Trotter

point of view. In 1934 goodwill was the most that any Dominion could offer the British in their problems in sustaining an imperial defence programme.

Stephen Roskill, Hankey's biographer, suggests that the 'whole-hearted and generous contribution' of Australia and New Zealand to the war effort after 1939–41, when the dangers that Hankey foresaw so clearly actually came to pass, may have been the 'fruits' of his efforts.[52] It seems more likely that the loyalty, sentiment, old-fashioned patriotism and the self-interest which Hankey had witnessed in those countries in 1934, were the prevailing forces in decision-making in Australia and New Zealand in that time of crisis.

## Notes

1  Peter Lowe, *Great Britain and the Origins of the Pacific War*, Oxford: Oxford University Press, 1977, p. 6.
2  Lowe, *Great Britain*, p. 4.
3  Ian H. Nish, *Alliance in Decline: A Study in Anglo–Japanese Relations 1908–23*, London: Athlone, 1972, p. 394.
4  Lowe, *Great Britain*, p. 9.
5  W. David McIntyre, *New Zealand Prepares for War*, Christchurch: University of Canterbury Press, 1988, p. 124.
6  See W. David McIntyre, *New Zealand*, p. 130.
7  W. David McIntyre, 'New Zealand, Japan and the Twenty Year Last Contest of Empires 1931–1951', in Roger Peren (ed.), *Japan and New Zealand: 150 Years*, Palmerston North: Massey University, 1999, p. 94.
8  The National Archives, Kew (TNA), Hankey papers, CAB 63/71 CID/392-C 'The Defence of Australia' Pearce memo 15 Nov. 1933.
9  TNA, Hankey papers, CAB 63/71 'Remarks of Australian Chiefs of Staff' 16 Jan. 1933.
10  TNA, Hankey papers, CAB 63/70 Bruce to Hankey 14 Dec. 1933.
11  National Archive of Australia, Canberra (NAA), A981 DEF/173 Bruce to Lyons 23 Jan. 1934.
12  TNA, Hankey Papers CAB 63/70 Hankey to Bruce 17 Feb. 1934.
13  TNA, Hankey Papers, CAB 63/77 Parr to Hankey 18 July 1934.
14  Lady Hankey was a member of the South African family, de Smidt. The Hankeys had planned to stay with her relatives. Before the cabinet decision Hankey had simply proposed to pay a courtesy call on the prime minister.
15  The committee was made up of Hankey, Sir Robert Vansittart, the permanent under-secretary of the Foreign Office, Sir Warren Fisher, the permanent secretary to the Treasury, and the Chiefs of Staff.
16  TNA CAB 24/247 CP 64(34) DRC report 28 February 1934.
17  TNA CAB27/511 DCM (32) 120 Note by the Chancellor of the Exchequer on the report of the DRC 20 June 1934; and Stephen Roskill, *Hankey: Man of Secrets*, vol. 3, London: Collins, 1974, p. 111.
18  TNA, Hankey papers, CAB 63/21 Hankey to MacDonald 3 Aug. 1934.
19  Roskill, *Hankey*, p. 109.
20  Roskill, *Hankey*, p. 126; and TNA FO372/3005 T6326 UKHC Pretoria to Thomas 14 May 1934.
21  Roskill, *Hankey*, pp. 109–12
22  Roskill, *Hankey*, p. 116.
23  Roskill, *Hankey*, p. 112; and TNA CAB23/79 31(34) Cabinet conclusions 31 July 1934.

## Hankey's Dominions tour 1934  99

24 National Maritime Museum, Greenwich, Chatfield papers, Hankey to Chatfield 9 Aug. 1934.
25 TNA, Hankey papers, CAB 63/66 Hankey to Baldwin 30 July 1934, and CAB 21/398 Hankey to MacDonald 3 Aug. 1934.
26 TNA, Hankey papers, CAB 63/66 Hankey *Aide Memoire* 30 July 1934; and Roskill, *Hankey*, pp. 114–15.
27 TNA, Hankey papers, CAB 63/66 Hankey to Baldwin 30 July 1934. The prime minister, MacDonald, was in poor health and on holiday at this time.
28 Roskill, *Hankey*, p. 113.
29 TNA CAB 21/398 Hankey to MacDonald 3 Aug. 1934.
30 Cambridge University Library (CUL), Baldwin papers, vol. 1, Hankey to Baldwin 23 Aug. 1934.
31 CUL, Baldwin papers, vol. 1, Hankey to Baldwin 23 Aug. 1934.
32 See Roskill, *Hankey*, p. 119.
33 Roskill, *Hankey*, pp. 125–6.
34 Roskill, *Hankey*, p. 126.
35 Roskill, *Hankey*, p. 128.
36 TNA, Hankey papers, CAB 63/70 Hankey to Howarth 13 Oct. 1934.
37 TNA, Hankey papers, CAB 63/70 'Notes of meetings of defence committee held for discussions with Sir Maurice Hankey', 19 Oct.–13 Nov. 1934.
38 Roskill, *Hankey*, pp. 127–32.
39 National Library of Australia, Canberra (NLA), Latham papers, MS1009, series A, general correspondence, Latham to Pearce 19 Dec. 1934.
40 NLA, Latham papers, MS1009, series A, general correspondence, Pearce to Latham 21 Dec. 1934.
41 McIntyre, *New Zealand*, pp. 131–3.
42 TNA, Hankey papers, CAB 63/78 Hankey to Harding (DO) 29 Nov. 1934.
43 Roskill, *Hankey*, pp. 132–5.
44 See McIntyre, *New Zealand*, p. 133.
45 Roskill, *Hankey*, pp. 138–9.
46 TNA, Hankey papers. CAB 63/81 Hankey to MacDonald 2 Jan. 1934 and Roskill, *Hankey*, p. 140.
47 TNA, Hankey papers, CAB 63/81 Vansittart (FO) to Hankey 14 Jan. 1935.
48 Ann Trotter, 'Tentative steps for an Anglo–Japanese Rapprochement in 1934', *Modern Asian Studies*, 8/1, 1974, pp. 59–83.
49 Ann Trotter, *Britain and East Asia 1933–1937*, Cambridge: Cambridge University Press, 1975, pp. 92–4, and Roskill, *Hankey*, p. 143.
50 NLA, Latham papers, MS 1009, series A, general correspondence, Wigram to Latham 3 Jan. 1935.
51 TNA, Hankey papers, CAB63/70 Hyde to Hankey 27 Mar. 1935.
52 Roskill, *Hankey*, p. 136.

# 7 Conquering press: coverage by the *New York Times* and the *Manchester Guardian* on the Allied occupation of Japan, 1945–52

*Roger Buckley*

The twin aims of the Allied occupation of Japan were to alter the latter for the better and to fit a reformed nation into an American-designed arc of friendly Asia-Pacific states. Such ambitions proved to be controversial, complicated and highly protracted. Given that it had taken years of bitter fighting on land and sea to gain the much delayed surrender of Imperial Japan, it was hardly surprising that interest around the world on what might follow was intense. Publishers and editors of newspapers, magazines, newsreels, radio stations and photo-journals immediately scrambled to get their men and a few women into Tokyo to report at length on vital events. The surrender scenes on the USS *Missouri* generated headline stories across the globe that were, in turn, followed by saturation coverage of Japan by papers such as the *New York Times* (*NYT*) for the remainder of the year and beyond. Yet little, however, appears to have been published in English on this theme, and the admirable, standard account of the occupation years makes no mention of reportage by *NYT* journalists between late September 1945 and April 1952.[1]

Overnight war correspondents shed their uniforms and became civilian reporters. They might still find themselves subject to the whims of General MacArthur's staff but their opportunities were greatly expanded by the ending of the war in the Pacific. The exact rules and regulations that they were expected to follow were fluid; though all required permission from the Supreme Commander Allied Powers General Headquarters (SCAP GHQ) to land in Japan, their copy could be censored and individuals on occasion were required either to leave or were barred from returning for perceived infringements by military officials. Yet all this was a two-way street. SCAP GHQ might well take umbrage at what Allied journalists were reporting but equally the American authorities were anxious to see that their version of events was receiving due attention both at home and internationally. The process was far from easy, with journalists taking professional pride in outwitting what they held to be petty restrictions now that the conflict was over and a more relaxed era was supposedly at hand.

The first months were chaotic. Attempts to organize a rudimentary Press Club were difficult, and some strait-laced journalists thought that the behaviour of certain of their colleagues bore closer parallels with that of the 'wild

*Press and the occupation of Japan, 1945–52*  101

west' than a disciplined military occupation following a gruelling and pitiless world war.[2] Communications and accommodation were necessarily ad hoc. GHQ saw elements of the press corps as irresponsible, while reporters complained of hide-bound junior officers concealing information, stalling over facilities for all but the sycophantic and limiting access when stories were breaking. Yet, despite the foul-ups and horse-play by larrikins, the stories poured out to slake the public's thirst on what was going to happen to the Emperor, how General MacArthur was running the show and whether or not the varied responses of the Japanese nation to their new Shogun and his foot soldiers were appropriate.

Any brief overview of such a vast subject involving journalists for papers across the political spectrum representing each and every Allied country over more than half a decade is surely impossible. This survey merely looks at portions of the press coverage of key events as reported by two serious, liberal, newspapers: one American, the *New York Times*, and one British, the *Manchester Guardian*, as a tentative first step towards perhaps establishing something more comprehensive and analytical. For now, though, the activities of journalists from such key states as the Soviet Union, China and Australia, to say nothing of Indian, French, Dutch and Scandinavian reporters, are brutally excluded.[3]

Even when the topic is reduced to merely two out of the dozens of competing papers that attempted to report on occupied Japan, the amount of material is vast. This is particularly the case for the *NYT* where readers might well expect to find three lengthy articles on differing aspects of the occupation in the paper on any one morning; only when it came to the pressing subject of present and future trade policies could the *Guardian's* loyal Lancastrians be said to find coverage of comparable depth. The *NYT* was both a national and, indeed, international paper, while the *Manchester Guardian* (it changed its title and base in 1959) had yet to stray very far from its regional roots. It should be noted, however, in the interests of fairness that the initial rationing of newsprint in postwar Britain makes any direct comparison somewhat flawed, though the combined influence, resources and readership of the *NYT* were the envy of the world in an era when it could comfortably print an edition of 52 pages and was in the process of burying its only real city rival, the *New York Herald-Tribune*.[4]

Both papers regarded themselves as providers of substantial and accurate overseas news; we shall see whether such claims had substance when it came to reporting on post-surrender Japan and ask if either or both enhanced their reputation by stories filed during the occupation. Since American journalists had long-established contacts with MacArthur and his inner circle through extensive coverage of the Pacific theatre, it was only to be expected that they would swamp those from all other nations combined in any American-controlled occupation. The *NYT* responded with alacrity to the challenges of making some sort of sense of fast-developing events, knowing full well that its readership was intensely interested in what would become of the occupation.

## 102  Roger Buckley

The way in which the paper handled the details of the surrender underlines the skill with which it put together a host of stories with by-lines from Tokyo, Chungking, Manila, Guam, Washington, New York and London on successive front pages in August and September 1945. For example, almost the entire front page for 7 August 1945 was linked to its banner headline announcing the dropping of the first atomic bomb on Hiroshima.[5] Such extensive reporting was then seen again when Japan formally surrendered to the Allies on 2 September 1945.[6] The collective result stands as testimony indeed to the *NYT*'s resources and professionalism under the pressure of reporting minute-by-minute developments set against merciless deadlines, something perhaps best illustrated by William Laurence's lengthy, later much anthologized, exclusive piece entitled 'Atomic Bombing of Nagasaki Told by Flight Member'. This was by-lined 'With the Atomic Bomb Mission to Japan' and opened with the stark sentences:

> We are on our way to bomb the mainland of Japan. Our flying contingent consists of three specially designed B-29 'Superforts', and two of these carry no bombs. But our lead plane is on its way with another atomic bomb, the second in three days, concentrating in its active substance an explosive energy equivalent to 20,000 and, under favorable conditions, 40,000 tons of TNT.[7]

The paper also had another advantage. In addition to closely following the intricate negotiations and drama of imperial Japan's inglorious defeat, the *NYT* was quick to capitalize on its prewar roots by opening once again a fully-fledged bureau in Tokyo with accredited American staff members covering politics, economic developments and how Japanese society was adapting to imposed change. Nothing remotely comparable was attempted by the British press where reporting appears to have been largely a fluid mix of reliance on news agencies plus journalists on short-term contracts and the use of freelancers who might be available when a particular story broke. Those hoping to trace the British side have also to confront the disadvantage that the convention was to head items by words such as 'from our own correspondent' or alternatively 'by our special correspondent' in an era where journalists might well be switching posts frequently. To give two examples: the Australian reporter Richard Hughes, who had known Shanghai and Tokyo before the war, would find himself back in Japan after the surrender doing a host of jobs from being the first manager of the near unmanageable Foreign Press Club to filing for the Kemsley group, while Hessell Tiltman, another experienced prewar figure, would write for anyone in the US or Britain willing to take his stories before later landing a more permanent post with the *Guardian*. (Tiltman became the doyen of foreign correspondents in Tokyo; his stories would be closely followed by Peter Lowe in subsequent decades.)

From the outset the *NYT*'s coverage of occupied Japan was both remarkably extensive and generally careful to present the establishment's view of developments. It took seriously its responsibility to provide detailed stories, though giving greater attention to what MacArthur and GHQ claimed to be doing rather than wishing to look too closely under the stone. Its staff would not go on to write anything comparable in style or substance to Mark Gayn's 'Tokyo Diary',[8] preferring instead to be seen as representing the paper of record when the phrase is understood to mean the full transmission of news often favourable to the United States government and its agencies in Japan. Readers of its stories could hardly fail to gain the impression that General MacArthur was succeeding in his tasks and that his critics were in error if they noted shortcomings. Yet, even if the paper hesitated to criticize SCAP policy, the volume of information sent from Tokyo is remarkable and must surely have been without equal during this period.[9]

Once the occupation began the *NYT*'s division of labour was broadly three-fold. Lindesay Parrott, as bureau chief, necessarily concentrated on reporting the shifting and entangled political story, while his deputy, Burton Crane, dealt with the changing economic and financial situation, leaving the freelancer Ray Falk with the opportunity to write at length on how both Japanese society and Americans (military and civilian) were responding to the occupation. The result is often an amalgam of hard news and more leisurely features that combined to inform readers of both the key points of high politics in Tokyo and its impact on life in the backwaters of Ibaraki or how sailors felt inside an enlisted men's club at Yokosuka. It was through Falk's stories, for example, that the curious might gain some insight into the contradictions of rural Japan. He noted that Ibaraki was invariably defined as the nation's 'most feudalistic and stubborn' prefecture, yet it could happily host Hollywood films under the delightful advertisement: 'Come and see American motion pictures-leaders of world culture. Now showing: Abbott and Costello. Coming: Tarzan and the Oklahoma Kid.'[10]

At this distance from the occupation such feature articles often appear of greater interest than the hard political news, which tended at times to be a rehash of what SCAP GHQ's own public relations people had released to the waiting press corps moments earlier. Indeed it is hard not to note that from the first days of September 1945 onwards the volume of material was so overwhelming that it was difficult for foreign journalists to begin even to question what they were being told from American and Japanese official sources. This led, to give but one early example that appeared as a small item in most Allied papers, to a planted story by the Imperial Household Agency in which it was claimed that the Emperor was both a devout Christian and confirmed teetotaler, without finding it necessary to furnish a shred of evidence to a ruse that was patently intended to reinforce his image in the eyes of Allied readers. The crush of events clearly worked to the advantage of MacArthur's own publicity machine. Its operators were felt by sections of the Allied press to be reproducing similar tactics to those that they had deployed during the Pacific War in order to garnish their chief's record. Then reports were sent out on how beaches were forever being stormed without mishap,

104    *Roger Buckley*

and countless victories won thanks entirely to MacArthur's military genius, now it was a case of the faultless viceroy saving a demoralized nation from starvation and communism. The result, if SCAP's critics are to be believed, was a smouldering, endless guerrilla campaign between the powers-that-be and defenders of the Western journalism's right to speak out on all but matters of the highest security. General Willoughby as chief intelligence officer to MacArthur argued that 'unjustified criticism' was to be deplored, yet when challenged to answer whether he held that all criticism of the Occupation might be deemed unjustified Willoughby is said to have replied, 'Certainly.'[11] Some of the issues doubtless appear petty today, yet the fact that MacArthur was at times rebuked by his superiors in Washington for seemingly restricting information and by refusing to permit the return to Tokyo of reporters who were held to have written stories critical of SCAP GHQ suggests that print journalism was seen to be a powerful tool for all parties in the final pre-television years. General MacArthur certainly felt so and would personally pen lengthy rebuttals to any offending editor if he reckoned that his handiwork was being traduced.[12] Since few publications in the United States were prepared to ignore such rebuttals, MacArthur was invariably granted perhaps undue prominence in the shape of thousands of words of flowery prose, thanks to his reputation as the man who was successfully remaking Japan without bloodshed along American lines.

Yet it is not easy to assess with any degree of accuracy what impact all this mega-reportage on occupied Japan had at the grass roots either in the United States or Britain. From the outset it would appear that those already holding firm views on what the Allies ought to be doing to Japan may well have been reluctant to shift their opinion despite the barrage of generally positive news that appeared in the press. The *Far Eastern Survey* for 12 September 1945 was already noting that American public opinion polls of late August had strongly felt that an invasion, conquest and subsequent occupation of Japan would be necessary, even if Tokyo were to offer a negotiated peace surrender; insistence too on the execution of the Emperor rather than to deploy him as 'a puppet to run Japan for Allies' was the overwhelming choice of those polled.[13] Yet, by the autumn, official policy had shifted in quite the opposite direction. By then MacArthur and his ever-sensitive aides were correct to note that domestic opinion was strongly in favour of the earliest possible demobilization of US forces around the globe and a careful husbandry of men and materiel. This led General Sutherland, SCAP's initial chief of staff, to bluntly tell the *Saturday Evening Post*'s surprised correspondent that, '[i]n order to get a minimum commitment of people and resources here, we're going to continue to exercise authority through the emperor's government.'[14] The contradictions between 'the cut-rate peace' that relied on the cooperation of the Japanese state and the understandable wish to remember Pearl Harbor and punish Japan for its sins would only be resolved in the future. For the moment though the American public wanted its boys back home immediately and yet expected its government to wield the big stick in newly occupied

Japan. It may be that the shift in American public opinion followed some considerable way behind SCAP GHQ's remarkably determined and ambitious reform programmes. Only later, once MacArthur was reported by most of the media to be making a success of Allied policies and after he had also announced punitive measures, such as reparations, the purge and the Tokyo war crimes trials, was the occupation viewed in a particularly positive light.

The gradual swing in American opinion towards the support of a less vindictive set of occupation policies may well have rested on positive reportage gleaned from US wire services and Allied correspondents in Tokyo. While there was almost certainly a time lag between initial action and later approval for what was already taking place, the fact that the American public continued to accord General MacArthur high praise suggests that the Truman administration and the US Army had little to fear from reactionary elements at home. Widespread trust in MacArthur and his lieutenants coupled with what readers may have gathered over the degree of cooperation from Japanese officials and people towards their occupiers reinforced a sense that all was going well in Japan. Genuine understanding of the transformation being enacted throughout Japan by SCAP GHQ may have been shallow, but the steady flow of encouraging news probably left many readers satisfied that their government had got it right.

Few papers contributed more to this generally up-beat analysis than the *NYT*. An examination of its initial reportage underlines both the serious and positive characteristics of its coverage at a time when the occupation was still finding its feet amidst political uncertainties and a critical food situation that left MacArthur directing a confused and unstable nation. Readers were certainly informed of the difficulties of the opening months of the occupation, yet the underlying message was one of guarded confidence that MacArthur, the Imperial Palace and certain reformist politicians might well be able to push Japan gradually in a more liberal direction. The *NYT*, for example, heralded the rescript that announced the renunciation of the Emperor's 'divinity' as ranking 'with the most important state papers in Japanese history'. It supported the measure by suggesting that it accorded with the 'quiet though determined American attack, not on the position of the Imperial throne but on the method in which the "Tenno system" has been used by the military clique'.[15] It also added that this move was, in addition, part of the equally 'quiet attempt in certain Japanese circles close to the throne to bring the Emperor closer to the people and to strip the Imperial incumbent of some of his forbidding majesty'.[16]

Similar caution can be seen in highly conservative stories by the *NYT*'s correspondent that clearly relied on insider contacts. These spoke, for example, of the Emperor's 'anxiety' over Prime Minister Shidehara's failure to keep his Cabinet together; indeed, the idea was floated that an imperial intervention might 'reap credit abroad as having helped the Japanese smoothly to carry out the Allied [purge] directive in the face of the Government's inability to do so'.[17] Since the language used by the paper when discussing the

106   *Roger Buckley*

Emperor was thoroughly deferential, it is probable that Parrott appreciated that his columns would be carefully digested on both sides of the palace moat and that there were perhaps grounds for making haste slowly. Journalism had consequences in January 1946.

Somewhat similar caution is in evidence when the *NYT* reported on the lesser mortals attempting to obey General MacArthur at a time when 'the average Japanese, after his generally hungry, heatless, cheerless New Year's Day' had little indeed to celebrate. At issue was the purge programme. It was here that the paper ran a lengthy story on 4 January 1946 that summarized MacArthur's key orders on both the removal of individuals judged to be ultranationalists and the banning of all political parties associated with Japanese imperialism under the headline of 'M'Arthur Purges Japan of Jingoes in Public Office'.[18] Yet it also noted that 'the order constitutes one of the most sweeping political purges ever made by a democratic regime', which rather begs the question of how far Shidehara's weak and unelected cabinet with its prewar nationalist members could be said to be democratic in more than outward form. Parrott saw the instructions from SCAP as long anticipated but 'beyond even the broadest expectations of the Japanese'.[19] In this instance, as with other crises of early 1946, Prime Minister Shidehara Kijūrō got more sympathy from the paper than he received from the domestic press. Thus the food crisis facing Japan in early 1946 was described by Burton Crane as partly the consequence of a national belief that a 'sympathetic' United States would automatically take care of its new ward come what may. Shidehara's reluctance to tackle the farmers' refusal to carry out its rice delivery schemes 'since it might provoke riots' was explained in broader terms as merely being one instance of Japan's tradition of 'in loco parentis' with SCAP GHQ now widely expected to be the solver of industrial problems and rampant inflation and the feeder of the entire nation. The Japanese media, as *NYT* journalists were careful to note, took a much harsher line than this over Shidehara's bumbling. On 6 January Parrott wrote of public anger at 'Baron Shidehara's "do nothing" Cabinet' that 'continued to cling tenaciously to power', while underlining that the 'new Japanese parties and the Japanese press, which since the occupation has been consistently more liberal in tone than the government, are busily canvassing the situation with every sign of glee'.[20] The result was an almost farcical situation whereby SCAP GHQ was demanding that heads should roll in across-the-board purge campaigns that, in theory, would have decimated Shidehara's government and left the premier and Yoshida Shigeru as possibly the only remaining cabinet members still standing. Opportunities for a spot of humour on this score – never perhaps the paper's strongest point – were missed.

Although the full ramifications of the purge directives' impact on Japanese politics would only become clear later, the *NYT* appears to have had little inkling of the drastic constitutional reforms that would shortly be demanded by General MacArthur and General Whitney's Government Section. The paper's earlier analysis of the proposed gentle tinkering with the House of

Peers appears somewhat ludicrous in the light of what would soon occur, and its apparent sympathy with the dilatory remaking of the Shidehara cabinet suggests that its sources of information were more Japanese than American. When reporting SCAP's ruling that a general election should be called in the spring Parrott noted that any such election 'may give something approaching a popular mandate as a basis for whatever Cabinet succeeds that of Baron Shidehara' and added that, '[a]t last there may be revealed, on a national basis, a broad scale picture of what courses the Japanese wish to follow in the reconstruction of their defeated nation.'[21] Events, of course, quickly took a diametrically different course when overnight a small team from General Whitney's section dictated a model constitution that left the Emperor in a tightly-controlled box, simply abolished the House of Peers and the peerage, granted votes to women, and insisted that the purge be enacted regardless of its consequences for existing political parties. The entire exercise ought to have left no one in doubt as to who was running the occupation and what would be required of Japanese officialdom; prevarication, special pleading and the floating of balloons favouring the Emperor were out; purges, reparations and improved rice collection now took priority. And as if to underline the seriousness of all this, MacArthur ordered the establishment of the International Military Tribunal for the Far East on 19 January 1946 for suspected major war criminals, without prejudicing 'the jurisdiction of any other tribunal, established in Japan or in any territory of the United Nations wherewith Japan has been at war, for trial of war criminals'.[22]

The relative conservatism behind the *NYT*'s reportage to this date came somewhat unstuck later in 1946. Its support for a modest degree of reform, on the unspoken assumption that anything beyond this would never easily take root, hardly fitted in with the radicalism of the MacArthurian Constitution with its demotion of the Emperor and sweeping parliamentary changes. Yet once the tide began to turn again in 1948–9 towards economic and political consolidation, the paper clearly felt relieved and went out of its way to emphasize the switch in policy. Parrott filed a lengthy piece in February 1949 that opened by stating categorically that '[t]hree and a half years after the surrender the occupation of Japan has moved into a new phase that will shape the nation's destiny for a considerable period.'[23] He noted that:

> American opinion about Japan is an increasingly decisive factor here. The occupation from the beginning has been largely an American affair, the United States having provided the bulk of the troops that garrison the country and more than 90 per cent of the resources on which Japan has been forced to rely. The point is sometimes missed that within recent months it has become almost exclusively an American affair.[24]

He underscored this point by stressing that BCOF was now down to a 'token army' of a mere 2,000 Australians and that the Allied Council for Japan 'usually adjourns in a matter of minutes, finding nothing on its agenda'.[25]

108    *Roger Buckley*

Increasingly, in the view of the *NYT*, it was going to be up to Japan to take care of itself through aiming for greater economic self-sufficiency, and this it felt might be possible through the recent change in political fortunes. Parrott spoke of 'the new Government of Premier Shigeru Yoshida [as] probably the best instrument it has had in its hands since the surrender', adding that Yoshida:

> ... is an outstanding foe of communism. He has announced that he wants to crush the Communist movement in Japan and has proposed privately to put Japanese Communist leaders back in the prison cells from which the occupation liberated them immediately after the surrender.[26]

Assuming Parrott's sources were correct, this was a poor recommendation for a man also defined as supportive of a speedy re-industrialization of a nation whose strategic value to Washington might lead to its defence by US forces. The *NYT* stated elliptically that '[s]ome military opinion holds that at least a bridgehead in Japan must be held, possibly even at the cost of using Japanese as allies should war come.'[27] (Others disputed this and cautioned that Japan was vulnerable to air and naval attack as well as the risk of starvation through blockade.)

When placed against such often commendable reportage the *Guardian's* coverage of occupied Japan is a disappointment; judged by almost any criteria its scanty paragraphs on pages that juxtaposed test match cricket scores, municipal committee reports and foreign snippets come off decidedly second best. To claim that the paper had few resources and its readership only wanted detailed information on what might be the fate of the Japanese textile industry goes someway to explaining its Tokyo 'deficit', yet perhaps equally important was a general willingness (or pragmatic acceptance) to reckon with an international scene where Britain was obviously going to play a lesser role. If responsibility for fixing the postwar world would be up to the United States and the Soviet Union, then the paper too could opt out. It is unlikely, for example, that any other British quality paper would be prepared to note in November 1946 that the Soviet press saw the twin features of London's foreign policy as 'systematic and universal support for reactionary forces in countries both in the New and Old World, and, second, progressive slipping into the position of junior partner in the Anglo–American block [sic].'[28] Britain's own 'new deal', based on the Attlee government's launching of the welfare state, despite the difficulties of domestic reconstruction, clearly took priority over any particular interest in the Pacific once the POWs had arrived back at Liverpool and Southampton and order of sorts was restored in South-East Asia. Japan was now largely off the map.

For the *Guardian* there was more relief than regret that responsibility for the occupation rested largely with the United States and its agents. While the occupation remained a major news story for the *NYT* throughout the years from the belated surrender in 1945 to the much delayed peace settlements of

1951–2, it had only sporadic importance for the *Guardian* with the result that its readers had little hope of gaining a rounded view of events. There were, however, some exceptions to this disappointing picture. The first, naturally enough, was an avid interest in Japan's attempted resuscitation of its textile industry and the responses of the British Cabinet to an issue of major concern to Lancashire's once proud cotton belt; the second was the occasional printing of what would today be defined as op-ed pieces that attempted to summarize what was going on in Japan and to place the details in a broader context. This was seen, for example, in a cautious two-column article by Sir Paul Butler that was simply headed 'Democratic Japan General MacArthur's Policy'[29], and later contributions by Sir George Sansom in May 1948 that offered an historical survey of the Pacific War and the atomic bombing of Hiroshima.[30] The lack of systematic interest in covering the occupation meant that articles appeared only when the *Guardian* sensed a major story and even then it was usually beholden to Reuters and the Associated Press for coverage. Brief items, for example, on 'Hirohito Ends Divinity Myth'[31] and 'Japan's Future: No Significant Move Towards Democracy-Gen. MacArthur',[32] only gave the bare bones of what was happening. When it did offer occasional comments on MacArthur its editorial line could be short and tart, suggesting on 1 January 1946 that MacArthur's self-importance might make Allied cooperation difficult and musing on whether the Emperor's recent renunciation of his divinity could well lead the Japanese peasantry to 'now bow in another direction'.[33]

Weeks, unfortunately, could go by when there might be absolutely no news from Japan in the paper with the sole exception of multiple references to what was happening or might happen over Japan's textile industry. All this, when combined with Lancashire's own seemingly endless working parties, commissions, reports and wage tribunals on how best to revive its textiles industry, conspired to produce a highly skewered and one-dimensional picture of the occupation. The *Guardian*, it is true, could note the hypocrisy of the Commonwealth's military forces holding a ceremony marking the promulgation of the new Constitution with its war renunciation clauses at Hiroshima near ground zero in November 1946[34], and there were occasional references to 'Changing Japan-Laying the Foundations of Democracy' but this was small beer.[35]

In the immediate postwar years the *NYT* and *Guardian* were widely seen as two stolid, somewhat left-of-centre papers. Both needed no reminding of the importance of printing local news of interest to their core city readers but there the comparison ends. The *NYT* was careful to balance stories of strikes by sanitation workers and longshoremen or the machinations of New Jersey politicians with space for a great deal of national and international news, while the *Guardian*, though most certainly catering for its readers over issues in the north-west of England, failed to give equal prominence to overseas developments. In this it was obviously hampered by having only eight pages to play with (in reality seven as its front page was entirely devoted to classified ads)

110    *Roger Buckley*

and by the working assumption that foreign affairs were of secondary importance. Since interest in the occupation of Japan ranked towards the bottom of this pecking order, it followed that the *Guardian*'s coverage was frequently shallow. The only exception to this generalization was when the *Guardian* acted as a specialized trade paper. Then it fed its readers with endless stories on textiles developments and gave a prominence to cotton, rayon and silk that no other broadsheet in the Western world could begin to equal. The paper printed, for example, innumerable quasi-editorial 'Trade Notes' throughout the occupation era on Japanese textile production figures, rehabilitation measures and concern over low labour costs. On this issue alone Lancashire was obsessed with Japan. Little else mattered. Allied reform efforts and the fate of Asia counted for naught, at least until 1950, in the minds of industrialists ever fearful of renewed competition from Osaka's mills on the back of encouragement from SCAP GHQ's Economic and Scientific Section and a pressing regional demand for cheaper finished textiles.

Given the interests of its readership it would have been suicidal for the *Guardian* to come out too strongly in support of radical new thinking within Lancashire's cotton industry, yet its caution, in what to outsiders at least appears to amount almost to defeatism when reckoning with Japan's postwar textile prospects, was a disappointment. It did, admittedly, give space to those who called for an end to 'the old bogy of Japanese competition'[36] and reported, again at length, on the early resignation speech in his Stoke constituency of Ellis Smith, the parliamentary secretary to Sir Stafford Cripps at the Board of Trade, in which the MP called for the nationalization of the entire cotton industry, but the paper's tone – like its readership – was generally cautious.[37]

Timidity ruled even when profits were good, the five-day week was in operation, wages had been increased in a bid to tempt younger workers to the mills and global demand was robust; all this when the average dividends for shareholders across the industry were 'higher than those of any other year since 1920' suggests funk of a high order.[38] Lancashire feared Japan long before it had good reason to worry, preferring instead to look backwards and failing to put its own house in order through any rapid modernization of management, machinery or manpower. Even in 1946 when Osaka was struggling to get back on its feet, the *Guardian*'s anonymous correspondent in Japan was warning that SCAP's textile programme would, if implemented, ensure that 'the day when all Asiatics will again wear "Made in Japan" clothes is not far off'.[39]

Little wonder then that the Attlee Cabinet felt frustrated in its efforts to persuade Lancashire to recharge its batteries and reckon with future opportunities. The disunity  and defensiveness of the industry left ministers generally unsympathetic to its constant pleas for assistance, particularly as London had to balance wider Anglo–American ties, hopes for a generally liberal global trading system and the requirements of southeast Asian consumers for affordable cotton goods against Oldham's endless carping at Osaka.[40] It deserves to be noted too that MacArthur was invariably well briefed and persuasive when handling textile questions in front of British diplomats and visiting industrialists; he stuck firmly to his guns in resisting calls for any slower rehabilitation of what was seen as a vital currency-earner for an impoverished Japan facing large balance-of-payment deficits. Concern for the political consequences of empty stomachs that could well jeopardize the chances of bedding down a democratic Japan guaranteed that its mills would rapidly expand production, particularly when Washington was signalling after 1948 that it was not prepared to underwrite its East Asian ward indefinitely. Textiles rather than steel or shipbuilding had to be the 'essential' backbone of any export-led recovery.[41]

To conclude, both the *Guardian* and the *NYT* generally followed and commented on the occupation from a pro-SCAP perspective. The only major exception for the *Guardian* was in the key field of cotton textiles where it (and backbench constituency MPs) often opposed the more relaxed thinking of the Attlee government, at least until wider issues gained its attention on the road to the San Francisco peace settlements. For the *NYT* its reservations concerned the radical nature of SCAP's reforms that hardly accorded with Japanese conservatism and its immense respect for the Imperial institution. The paper paid great attention to the Emperor[42] and much to the obvious disappointment of SCAP's Government Section insisted that the 'Emperor's psychological influence is enormous; indeed, it is one great vital factor in Japanese life', defining him as 'the triple-distilled essence of Japan without whom the nation might fall apart and in whose name all commands must eventually be given'.[43] The *NYT*'s extensive reportage, aided by stout contacts within the Imperial Household Agency, suggests that those who have defined the occupation as largely a double-act performed by MacArthur and Yoshida may yet have to consider granting the Emperor at least a supporting role within their pantheon.[44] The enthusiasm with which Japanese crowds greeted their often nervous and tongue-tied monarch as he went about his required tours of the nation certainly points to a continuing reverence with political and social implications for both the individual and institution. The *NYT* also could be gently sceptical over the supposed ambassadorial qualities claimed by MacArthur of his GIs and question too the depth of the Japanese public's commitment to the new-fangled importation of democracy.

When, however, it came to the ending of the occupation both papers went out of their way to lavish praise on the Anglo–American sponsored peace treaty, the US-Japan security pact and the defence arrangements with Australia and New Zealand, and the Philippines associated with San Francisco. Such applause was no doubt conditioned in part by the unpleasant reality of heavy Allied casualties in the war on the Korean peninsula, it being widely sensed in Western capitals that one aim of the Communist offensive was to destabilize Japan and wreck the on-going peace process. The *NYT*'s coverage of San Francisco, which centred around pieces by James Reston that were undisguisedly fed from State Department sources, was extraordinarily detailed, in keeping with its entire handling of the occupation. Yet this

## 112    Roger Buckley

attention to the American side of the venture did not exclude fair notice of the Soviet Union's bitter criticisms that Washington was intent on a 'separate peace' thanks to the draftsmanship of 'seasoned warmonger' John Foster Dulles and that it was inadmissible to exclude the People's Republic of China from the venue. The paper devoted page after page to the speeches from states large and small, including everything from the blunt statement by Andrei Gromyko that the US was in the process of re-militarizing a potentially aggressive Tokyo to the shortest address of the entire conference-thirty-one words by the Iraqi delegate saying that since he had received no instructions from Baghdad he would be unable to comment further on the treaty.

For once, the *Guardian* – almost as if to make up for lost time – gave substantial coverage both to a series by Robert Guillain of *Le Monde* on what it titled 'Japan After MacArthur'[45] and to hour-by-hour events at the carefully stage-managed peace conference through some lengthy and rather verbose pieces from Alistair Cooke.[46] The twin themes of securing a non-vindictive peace and encouraging the Yoshida government to be vigilantly anti-communist were endorsed by the *Guardian* and the *NYT* at great length, leading the former to criticize India for boycotting San Francisco[47] and the latter to take pains to define newly-independent Japan in the summer of 1952 as both 'a vital link in our line of Pacific defenses'[48] and a prospective member 'in the Colombo economic plan developed for Southeast Asia by the sterling area countries'.[49]

The decidedly belated shift in the *Guardian*'s attitude towards Tokyo is perhaps best explained through a combination of respect for the United States' astute diplomacy in working towards granting Japan a peace of 'political generosity' and the fact that by 1950–1 Lancashire's endless complaints against Osaka had yet to ring true. The *Guardian* noted that such a peace 'is a rare spectacle in the world and one to be encouraged', which was particularly significant from a paper professing liberal, internationalist credentials.[50] When peace finally arrived the details largely confirmed what it had foreseen: Washington had indeed gained through the peace treaty and concomitant security pact 'the best of both worlds – a friendly Japan and the military outposts which it thinks necessary'.[51] Yet any change of heart by the *Guardian* was probably due more to the economic realities of the Korean War's global procurement boom than any detailed analysis of the treaty's chapters on security matters or reparations – Alistair Cooke, overwriting as usual, called this 'the thorn in the rose ... haunted by the grey-gloved ghost of Clemenceau'.[52] The fact is that Lancashire was both enjoying a sellers' market with no end yet in sight to substantial profits and relishing at least the rumour that Osaka's own high prices were beginning to work against Japanese textile exporters.[53] Such good news had to be taken on board, even by the most hardened Lancastrian mill owners and their equally sceptical older operatives, and could only dent the calls for subsidies at home and protection abroad. With world cotton production reaching an all-time high by 1951 and the *Guardian* reporting on the same morning both labour shortages in the industry and the prevalence of under-the-table cash bonuses to retain workers, no government in its right mind was going to cave in to lobbyists from the North-West.[54] The *Guardian*'s Washington correspondent underlined this reality when stating on the publication of ambassador Dulles' draft peace treaty in March 1951 that the State Department had been surprised that '[t]here has been far less resistance to the revival of Japan's textile industry than was expected' by Allied members of the Far Eastern Commission.[55] Aside from a bromide by the Attlee government on the retention of the right to deal unilaterally with extreme changes in future trading conditions, Lancashire got virtually nothing at San Francisco. Perhaps it had cried wolf too often.[56]

At heart both papers were essentially conformist and generally reported events in a 'top-down' manner favourable to the Allies. Where there was criticism of the occupation it tended to be mild and more attached to doubts over Japanese behaviour than hostility to MacArthur and his staff. Neither paper, with only rare exceptions, challenged the basic tenets of the occupation nor doubted that a pro-Western, rearming, capitalist Japan was in the process of working its way back to an important role in regional society. The *NYT*, for example, was already reporting in January 1950 how Japanese ministers were criticizing the Soviet Union for postponing any prospect of a comprehensive peace treaty through being 'over-particular about the procedural argument'.[57] Both the *NYT* and the *Guardian* saw Tokyo's future as largely dependent on close political and economic friendship with the United States and, to a lesser extent, with a declining Britain. Both papers clearly acted as media buttresses to the West's strategic objectives in East Asia. They endorsed, in effect, a return to the days of the Anglo–Japanese alliance, though in this instance through a one-sided Washington-Tokyo pact that would evolve gradually into a remarkably resilient and more equal US-Japan partnership. The arrangements initialled in 1902 found their echo once again when the peace settlements gained Senatorial ratification in 1952. This time, however, the relationship between Japan and the leading power of the moment in the Asia-Pacific would endure for three generations and more.

## Notes

1 John Dower, *Embracing Defeat: Japan in the Wake of World War II*, New York: New Press, 1999. Earlier in-house histories of the *NYT* and the *Guardian* appear to have been equally reticent when it came to coverage of the occupation.
2 John Morris, on short-term assignment for the BBC, was particularly put out by such shenanigans, but the fact that he had been an officer in the Gurkhas may have had something to do with his ire.
3 Primary-source material on the Allied press during the occupation is slim. There is one chapter in William J. Coughlin, *Conquered Press: The MacArthur Era in Japanese Journalism*, Palo Alto, CA: Pacific Books, 1952, and The Foreign Correspondents Club of Japan's own archival holdings on this era are slight; see Charles Pomeroy (ed.), *Foreign Correspondents in Japan: Reporting a Half Century of Upheavals: From 1945 to the Present*, Tokyo: Tuttle, 1998.

114    *Roger Buckley*

4 The *Herald-Tribune* lasted until April 1965 but had been leaking money for years, despite the quality of its writing; Homer Bigart and Marguerite Higgins were war correspondents for the paper during both the Pacific and Korean wars. See Richard Kluger, *The Paper: The Life and Death of The New York Herald Tribune*, New York: Random House, 1989.

5 'First Atomic Bomb Dropped on Japan: Missile is equal to 20,000 tons of TNT: Truman warns Foe of a "Rain of Ruin"', *NYT*, 7 Aug. 1945.

6 *NYT*, 2 Sept. 1945. The headline read 'Japan Surrenders to Allies, Signs Rigid Terms on Warship; Truman sets today as V-J Day'.

7 William Laurence, 'Atomic Bombing of Nagasaki Told by Flight Member', *NYT*, 9 Sept. 1945. Laurence noted that Group Captain Leonard Cheshire was on board the third plane as 'the official representative of Prime Minister Clement R. Attlee'; the other British observer was Professor William Denny of London University. Nearly sixty years later, critics would argue that Laurence had deliberately played down the effects of radiation when reporting on the victims of the atomic bombings.

8 Gayn reported for the *Chicago Sun* and was often in hot water with SCAP GHQ. His *Tokyo Diary* was published in 1947.

9 Full-length articles by the *NYT* are reprinted in Roger Buckley (ed.), *The Post-War Occupation of Japan, 1945–1952: Selected Contemporary Readings: From Pre-Surrender to Post-San Francisco Peace Treaty: Series 2: Pamphlets, Journals, Press and Reports*, vol. 2, *US Policies and Commentaries, 1946–50*, Leiden: Brill, 2013.

10 Ray Falk, 'Teaching "Demokratzi" To the Japanese', *NYT*, 12 June 1949.

11 Coughlin, op cit, p. 120.

12 See, for example, the critical article 'Two-Billion Dollar Failure in Japan', *Fortune*, April 1949 and MacArthur's later response.

13 *Far Eastern Survey*, 12 Sept. 1945, citing a Gallup Poll 'this summer'.

14 Richard Tregaskis, 'Have We Given Japan Back to the Japs?', *Saturday Evening Post*, 27 Oct. 1945.

15 Lindesay Parrott, 'Japanese Stunned By Hirohito's Move To Abjure Divinity', *NYT*, 2 Jan. 1946.

16 Ibid.

17 The paper's headline to Reuters' and Parrott's reports said 'Japanese Cabinet Has Resigned: Interest of Emperor Is Indicated'. See Lindesay Parrott, *NYT*, 11 Jan. 1946.

18 Lindesay Parrott, *NYT*, 4 Jan. 1946.

19 Ibid.

20 Lindesay Parrott, 'Japan's Ministers Clinging to Office', *NYT*, 7 Jan. 1946.

21 Lindesay Parrott, 'Election Problem Perplexes Japan', *NYT*, 14 Jan. 1946.

22 AP report in *NYT*, 19 Jan. 1946.

23 Lindesay Parrott, 'Our Japanese Policy Enters a New Phase', *NYT*, 20 Feb. 1949.

24 Ibid.

25 Ibid.

26 Ibid.

27 Ibid.

28 *Manchester Guardian* (*MG*), 2 Nov. 1946, report from Reuters in Moscow quoting the Soviet periodical *New Times*.

29 Sir Paul Butler, *MG*, 14 Nov. 1946.

30 Sansom, *MG*, 10–12 May 1948.

31 *MG*, 1 Jan. 1946.

32 *MG*, 3 Jan. 1946.

33 *MG*, 1 Jan. 1946.

34  *MG*, 4 Nov. 1946. The paper had given considerable play to the arrival of BCOF but does not appear to have followed its activities closely.

35  *MG*, 14 Oct. 1946.

36  See S.B.L. Jacks to the editor, 16 Nov. 1946, *MG*; see also A. Byer insisting that Lancashire 'stop complaining, and get on with the job of producing the right goods at the right price, and you will not need to fear Japanese, or any other, competition'; A. Byer to the editor, *MG*, 31 July 1951.

37  'Mr. Ellis Smith on "Why I Resigned"', *MG*, 14 Jan. 1946. Smith was reported by the *Guardian* to be advocating what he termed an 'industrial policy' in February 1947.

38  *MG*, 30 Dec. 1946.

39  *MG*, 8 Nov. 1946.

40  See Marguerite Dupree (ed.), *Lancashire and Whitehall: The Diary of Sir Raymond Streat*, vol. ii, *1939–57*, Manchester: Manchester University Press, 1987. Streat as the veteran head of the Cotton Board seemingly spent half his life taking the train from Manchester to Euston to lobby officials and their ministers.

41  See SCAP-based report in Department of State Bulletin, 'Significance of Textiles in the Japanese Economy', 25 Apr. 1948. This noted the difficulties of paying for raw cotton from abroad, tackling Japan's domestic problems of fuel and labour as well as 'world conditions of supply and demand for textile raw materials and finished products'. The report predicted that it would take between five and ten years for such issues to be solved. Neither this nor later SCAP-based material provided by the Army Department to Congress bothered to refer to British concerns over Japanese textile production.

42  See, for example, Lindesay Parrott, 'Japanese Receive New Constitution from the Emperor', *NYT*, 3 Nov. 1946. The *MG*'s account by its 'special correspondent' on the same morning stressed instead the nation's determination to 'set an example' to others over the renunciation of war.

43  Lindesay Parrott, 'Mr. Hirohito Is Still the "Sun God"', *MG*, 22 May 1949.

44  See, for example, Richard B. Finn, *Winners in Peace: MacArthur, Yoshida and Postwar Japan*, Berkeley: University of California Press, 1992.

45  See *MG*, 25, 28, 29, 30 Aug. and 4 Sept. 1951. Guillian warned in his last article that a poorly protected Hokkaido was 'one of the danger points of Asia, one of the points at which there is beginning to grow one of those abscesses which the Soviet Union is so skilled at creating and maintaining on the periphery of the Soviet world'.

46  See, for example, Alistair Cooke, 'Diplomatic Jamboree Opens in U.S.', *MG*, 2 Sept. 1951.

47  *MG* editorial, 'All Alone', 3 Sept. 1951.

48  'ANZUS Parley Points Up Vast Pacific Problems: Relations of the West to That Half of the World Are Still Unsettled,' *NYT*, 10 Aug. 1952.

49  Ibid. Marxist journals in Britain defined the venture as the 'Colombo Exploitation Plan'; see *Communist Review*, May 1951.

50  *MG* editorial, 'Treaty with Japan', 22 Sept. 1950.

51  Ibid.

52  Alistair Cooke, 'Treaty Analysed: The U.S. Defence', *MG*, 10 Sept. 1951.

53  See 'Prospects in Japan', *MG*, 22 Jan. 1951, and 'Japanese Plans for Cotton', *MG*, 10 Sept. 1951.

54  *MG*, 25 Nov. 1950.

55  *MG*, 31 Mar. 1951.

56  See 'The Draft Treaty', *MG*, 13 July 1951; '[i]t has never been possible to show how Japan's economic rivalry could be prevented, and, as with the still older bogy of German competition, the victors in the war have had to leave the vanquished with the means of economic livelihood.' Despite pressure from Washington, Britain did not grant most-favoured nation trading status to Japan.

57 Lindesay Parrott, 'Japan Says Soviet Alone Delays Pact', *NYT*, 29 Jan. 1950. By then Yoshida was stating that he welcomed a separate peace with the West, if the Communist camp kept refusing to negotiate. The fact that only a handful of Asian countries – Reston dubbed them the 'voice of free Asia' – were willing to sign the eventual peace treaty was downplayed by the *NYT*. See 'Four Asian Nations Support Draft of Japanese Treaty, Challenge Soviet Charges', *NYT*, 7 Sept. 1951. Support for the United States from Ceylon, Pakistan, Laos and Cambodia hardly began to balance the absence of China, India and Burma from the conference. Given the obvious hostility that Japan faced in Asia there was simply no prospect of organizing a multilateral NATO-style security structure for the region.

# 8 In search of regional authority in South-East Asia

## The improbable partnership of Lord Killearn and Malcolm MacDonald, 1946–8

*A.J. Stockwell*

One of the themes running through Peter Lowe's last book is the contribution of international conflict and diplomacy to the emergence of South-East Asia as a region. While the term was used occasionally before the Pacific War, it was Japanese militarism that was 'responsible for accelerating awareness of regional identity'.[1] Until 1941 the vast but ill-defined area between India and China was a backwater in international affairs. Although effectively the paramount power, the British pursued their interests piecemeal and made little effort to establish an over-arching organization for co-ordination and defence. The Japanese conquest transformed their approach. Determined to reassert authority, the British planned for reoccupation on a regional scale. However, their vision of South-East Asia was not entirely clear since regional borders ebbed and flowed between Ceylon and the Philippines and elided with 'the Far East'. Moreover, while Britain's presence was more marked at the end of the war than before, its power proved unequal to the demands of post-surrender tasks. Furthermore, differing priorities within the British government resulted in two regional authorities rather than one: Lord Killearn, Special Commissioner for foreign relations, and Malcolm MacDonald, Governor-General in colonial matters. Given their overlapping remits, contrasting temperaments and different backgrounds, the prospects for a successful partnership seemed unlikely. In the event, it proved remarkably harmonious.

## I

As relations with Japan deteriorated in the summer of 1941, the Prime Minister, Winston Churchill, considered sending a member of his Cabinet to serve as a resident minister in the Far East, with a remit and powers similar to those recently conferred on Oliver Lyttelton in the Middle East. Instead, however, he despatched another Cabinet minister, Alfred Duff Cooper, on a tour of investigation.[2] Duff Cooper was appalled to find that the 'the affairs of the British Empire were being conducted ... by machinery that had undergone no important change since the days of Queen Victoria'. There had been little effort to co-ordinate the policies of those Whitehall ministries with interests in the region. Since the outbreak of war in the West, confusion in the

Far East had been aggravated by the presence of more and more government departments, each with its own priorities. Duff Cooper saw the need for immediate change but cautioned against 'drastic reform' as being 'undesirable in time of crisis'. Having considered, but rejected, the establishment of either a new state department for the Far East with its own secretary of state or a regional organization led by a resident minister similar to the satrapy in the Middle East, he recommended a less elaborate scheme: the appointment of a high official entitled 'Commissioner-General for the Far East'. Supported by a small staff and permanent headquarters in Singapore, this official would co-ordinate British agencies, liaise with British allies, and regularly report to the War Cabinet and relevant ministers in London. Having despatched his report, Duff Cooper remained in Singapore and awaited further instructions. When Japan attacked, Churchill duly appointed him Resident Cabinet Minister for Far Eastern Affairs, though with limited powers. Thus he was instructed to appoint a war council but one which would neither interfere with the activities of service commanders nor infringe the responsibilities of colonial governors. Mistrusted as a 'snooper', Duff Cooper encountered mulish resistance, notably from the colonial governor, Sir Shenton Thomas, whom he tried but failed to replace. By mid-January 1942 Singapore was a battlefield and the appointment of General Wavell as commander-in-chief of allied forces made the resident minister redundant. Duff Cooper left for London, and Singapore fell a month later.[3]

Here today, gone tomorrow, Duff Cooper was dismissed by some as a dilettante. Confronting a looming crisis, though hoping for the best, he had placed his trust in the capacity of a commissioner-general to achieve regional consensus and in the determination of the Cabinet to resolve departmental differences and respond swiftly to regional needs. There had been no time to attempt anything other than shore up a shaky edifice; no time to consider in any detail the powers of a regional organization; no time to define the region any more precisely than territory bounded 'by the western seaboard of the American Continent ... the wastes of Siberia and the sub-continent of India'. His report was overtaken by events. Yet it was not forgotten. On the contrary, it would provide the point of departure for subsequent planning, as a Colonial Office report made clear in December 1942: 'We consider the value of a Regional Authority to be the prime lesson to be drawn from the fall of Malaya.'[4] There would be no return to pre-war parochialism and administrative disarray. Future planners would address the issues which Duff Cooper had identified but incompletely determined: the remit and territorial boundaries of the organization and the powers and status of its chief.

Within a few months of the fall of Singapore, the Colonial Office began to prepare for reoccupation. Responding to American anti-imperialism, they envisaged 'a new deal' whereby the interests of both rulers and ruled might be advanced. Security, efficiency, economic development and the promotion of self-government would require greater intervention, closer integration of disparate territories and a 'supreme regional authority'. Colonial planning gathered momentum from the summer of 1943 when the War Office requested information on long-term policy to guide the reoccupation of lost territories. The principles which would underpin both military administration and subsequent civil rule in British Malaya and Borneo were refined in inter-departmental discussions and approved by the War Cabinet in May 1944. They amounted to a radical departure, not least because they featured the consolidation of British dependencies under the supervision of a governor-general. Here was a regional organization of a sort, but it fell far short of being comprehensive. It omitted Burma whose future was planned in Simla by Sir Reginald Dorman-Smith's government in exile. Nor did it address the conduct of international relations, responsibility for which was for the time being vested in the Supreme Allied Commander South-East Asia (SACSEA).

## II

In August 1943 when only forty-three years old and still a naval captain, Lord Louis Mountbatten had leapfrogged his seniors to the position of SACSEA with the rank of acting admiral. This dispirited theatre was racked by inter-service and Anglo–American feuding but Mountbatten's diplomatic skill held the command together. Indeed, diplomacy became a major weapon for making war and peace in South-East Asia. Mountbatten's chief political adviser was Esler Dening. Seconded from the Foreign Office, Dening had already spent many years in East Asia. His father had gone to Japan as a missionary and stayed as a teacher and writer. After enlisting in the Aus-tralian forces in the First World War, Esler Dening had joined the consular service in Japan. He went on to posts in China, Korea and the Philippines, and would return to Japan in 1951 as Britain's political representative and then its first post-war ambassador (1952–7). 'A vast rock of a man' reputed to be able to 'bend a poker over his arm', he 'radiated security and confidence' and was regarded as 'the perfect man for a tight corner'.[5] However, as the political role of the South-East Asia Command (SEAC) expanded in mid-1945 following the re-conquest of Burma, Dening's position fast became untenable. Not only had he to serve two masters – the Foreign Office and the Supreme Allied Command – but he also lacked a brief to act in matters of concern to other departments, notably the Colonial and Burma Offices. Referring to the alternatives identified by Duff Cooper in 1941, Dening recommended that he be replaced either by a more senior official or, as he preferred, by a resident minister. Otherwise, there was a danger that 'we shall drift once more into the same position as we were before the outbreak of hostilities'.[6] In spite of this warning, the Foreign Office shelved the question of regional reorganization until after the British general election with the result that it was caught off guard when Japan collapsed.

On 14 August 1945 SEAC entered the 'troubled days of peace'. In addition to Burma, it acquired responsibility for British Malaya, Sumatra, Java, Siam and southern Indo-China. Mountbatten's tasks were now to disarm and

120   *A.J. Stockwell*

evacuate enemy forces, to find and repatriate allied prisoners of war and internees and, most difficult of all, to establish law and order.[7] Supremo in name, Mountbatten lacked the tools for this job, not least because, as Dening recorded in his final report, America remained aloof from this theatre.[8] He handled post-surrender tasks with a mixture of pragmatism and idealism, and did not shrink from political issues. He supported the restoration of colonial regimes but not a return to pre-war colonialism. He tried to accommodate nationalist aspirations without becoming entangled in the civil wars of others. Because he was inordinately confident in his abilities and accustomed to getting his own way, Mountbatten was liable to take initiatives whose consequences he was unable to control. His espousal of Aung San embittered 'old Burma hands'. Courting Malayan communists as heroes of the resistance exasperated the British military administration. Attempting an even-handed approach to the Dutch and the Indonesians forfeited him the trust of both sides. Relations between Mountbatten and Dening deteriorated rapidly, the former denouncing as insubordination the latter's attempts to give independent advice.

The legacy of problems left in the wake of the unexpected suddenness of Japan's collapse alarmed the Foreign Secretary, Ernest Bevin: 'our organisation is not yet adequately adjusted to them [but] dealing with them piecemeal and empirically.'[9] In October a hastily convened ministerial meeting chaired by the Prime Minister, Clement Attlee, accepted Bevin's proposal that an 'official of high standing' (not a resident minister) should be appointed to the region. However, the terms of the directive remained undecided while the handful of nominees who were proposed turned out to be unavailable or unsuitable. Sir Harold MacMichael (until recently High Commissioner of Palestine) could not be spared from a special assignment to conclude new treaties with the Malay rulers. Sir Bernard Bourdillon (who, as Governor of Nigeria, had worked closely with Lord Swinton, the Resident Minister in West Africa) had retired in 1943 owing to ill health. Lord Scarborough (Governor of Bombay, 1937–43) was unacceptable on political grounds.[10] Arrangements for the co-ordination of colonial administration, by contrast, were finalized more swiftly. As soon as the Japanese had signed the instrument of surrender on board USS *Missouri* in Tokyo Bay on 2 September, the Labour Cabinet endorsed the proposals which had been provisionally approved in May 1944. Then, during a visit to Ottawa in November, Attlee offered the position of governor-general to Malcolm MacDonald who was nearing the end of his term as High Commissioner to Canada.

The son of Britain's first Labour Prime Minister, Malcolm MacDonald had been swept along in the slip-stream of his father's career. Deflected from early aspirations to be a writer, he was elected to parliament in 1929 while still in his late twenties. He held ministerial office throughout the successive National Governments of the 1930s led by his father, Baldwin and Chamberlain. He was an emollient Dominions Secretary in the period of increased dominion autonomy following the Statute of Westminster, deftly minimizing

Commonwealth dissension during the abdication crisis and even winning the trust of Eamon De Valera. As Colonial Secretary he pursued progressive policies particularly towards tropical Africa and the West Indies. In 1940 Churchill moved MacDonald to the Ministry of Health and then to the British high commission in Ottawa, a pivotal position for sustaining Canada's contribution to the war effort. Although the Labour left distrusted Malcolm as the son of the man who had 'ratted' on the party in 1931, others, including Attlee, respected his enlightened approach to colonial and Commonwealth affairs. MacDonald later claimed that Attlee had offered him the choice of Viceroy of India (in place of Wavell), ambassador to Washington (in succession to Lord Halifax) or governor-general in South-East Asia, and that he had opted for the third because it appeared the most challenging.[11] However, he would not be free to take up the post until late May 1946, seven weeks after the restoration of colonial rule in Malaya and Singapore.

In January 1946 the appointment of a special commissioner for South-East Asia became a matter of urgency for Bevin. It was in vain that a relatively junior, albeit able, official at the Colonial Office attempted to steer his seniors away from the folly of dual control: 'I feel very strongly', declared Kenneth Robinson, 'that there will be a first class mess if H.M.G. persist in the creation both of a Governor-General, responsible to the S. of S. for the Colonies, and a Commissioner-General or Special Commissioner, responsible to the S. of S. for Foreign Affairs.'[12] By now, however, relations between Mountbatten and Dening had broken down over the Netherlands East Indies. As a temporary measure, Sir Archibald Clark Kerr (Lord Inverchapel) was brought in to resolve the stalemate between the Dutch and nationalists.[13] More worrying was the prospect of widespread famine in South-East Asia. On 1 February 1946 as the failure of the rice harvest threatened to plunge the region into chaos and upset the supply of cereals to the world beyond, Bevin turned to Lord Killearn.

## III

Lord Killearn (previously Sir Miles Lampson) was perhaps the doyen of the foreign service. Such was his stature that Eden had had him in mind for Berlin in 1936 but was over-ruled by Chamberlain who preferred Nevile Henderson; Lord Halifax considered him for Washington in 1938 although in the end settled for Lord Lothian; and Churchill saw him as a possible successor to Linlithgow in India before he decided on Wavell.[14] Lampson's reputation was founded in East Asia and cemented in the Middle East. He accompanied Prince Arthur of Connaught on the Garter mission to Japan in 1906, served in the Tokyo embassy in 1908–10 and returned in 1912 for the funeral of the Meiji emperor. In 1926, after a spell in Beijing (1916–20) and another as head of the Central Department of the Foreign Office (dealing with Europe), he went back to China as British minister. As the senior foreign emissary in Beijing at a time of upheaval and uncertainty, he distinguished

122   *A.J. Stockwell*

himself by renegotiating the unequal treaties and establishing a good working relationship with the Guomindang.[15] Success was rewarded with his appointment in 1933 as High Commissioner for Egypt and the Sudan. Nominally a sovereign state since 1922, Egypt was the centre of Britain's empire in the Middle East. Here, as in China, Lampson faced a rising tide of nationalism and anti-British agitation, and, as in China, he played a crucial part in securing British interests. The Anglo–Egyptian treaty of 1936 may have reiterated Egypt's independence but it also confirmed Britain's military base in the canal zone. Although Lampson's title changed from High Commissioner to Ambassador, his role and style continued as before. An imperial proconsul in a line of succession to Lord Cromer, he regarded Egyptians as children to be handled with 'firmness and determination'. The arrival of Lyttelton as resident minister in 1941 did not clip his wings. On 4 February 1942 when King Farouk was on the point of succumbing to Axis blandishments, Lampson surrounded the Abidin Palace with tanks and compelled His Majesty to appoint a prime minister sympathetic to the Allied cause. Raised to the peerage the following year, Killearn revelled in the pomp and oriental trappings of his office. With his dazzling second wife, Jacqueline, he entertained in a grand style, playing host to Churchill during wartime visits notably for the Cairo conference with Roosevelt and Chiang Kai Shek in November 1943.[16]

If anyone could get a grip on the crisis in South-East Asia, surely it would be Killearn with his record of foreign service, worldwide connections, energy and considerable presence – he weighed eighteen stone and was six-feet five-inches tall. Yet, given the care taken by the Foreign Office to avoid any hint of imperialism in the title and remit of their commissioner for South-East Asia, it might seem unwise to have chosen someone with Killearn's reputation. He had, however, become a liability in Cairo, and the Foreign Office was determined to move him. Bevin was committed to end the Killearn era, to put Anglo–Egyptian relations on a new footing and work towards disengagement. The first stage in what was bound to be a tortuous process was the renegotiation of the 1936 treaty with Egyptian leaders who loathed Killearn and whom he, for his part, despised. It was not altogether a coincidence that the offer of South-East Asia reached Killearn when Cairo was rocked by anti-British riots on the fourth anniversary of his infamous usurpation of Egyptian sovereignty.[17] Although Bevin's invitation came as 'a bombshell', Killearn was prepared to regard it as both a compliment and a challenge. On reflection, he suspected an intrigue by the palace in Cairo to remove him. He temporized, asking for details on the scope of the position and the provision of staff, and wrangling over emoluments and accommodation for his family. Pressed by Bevin and fearful that he might fall between two stools, he finally accepted. After all, South-East Asia guaranteed him what Egypt did not: two more years in service and two more years of pension rights – 'a big material point' for a man of sixty-six with a young family to support. Killearn felt trapped by the Foreign Office and his mood did not improve when he learned that he would have been retired had he not accepted: 'They really have been rather dirty dogs.'[18]

The food situation in South-East Asia was now 'desperate' and 'not a moment must be lost in tackling it'.[19] Killearn flew to London, put up at Claridge's Hotel and was briefed in Whitehall. Initial discussions with officials led by Sir Orme Sargent were not reassuring: 'All v[ery] vague! I feel they are pushing me into a wild panicky business! And getting rattled themselves! ... Personally I think they are mad – and that's all there is to it!' Although it was 'very definitely' demotion after Cairo, he recognized that 'beggars can't be choosers' and it was 'better than getting the sack!' Bevin, however, raised his spirits. 'Encouraging', 'friendly' and 'helpful', the Foreign Secretary told him he was taking on 'the biggest job in your life my dear boy'.[20] It was not until 13 March, when he was en route to Singapore, that the Prime Minister approved the final directive. He would serve for two years, report to the Foreign Secretary and be assisted with respect to the rice problem by a Whitehall committee representing relevant ministries and chaired by Lord Nathan, the junior minister at the War Office who was respected for his energy, probity and grasp of economic and financial issues.

While Killearn was dissatisfied with his 'nebulous' role – a complaint he never tired of making – he was encouraged by the choice of his team. The Foreign Office spared him Michael Wright (former head of chancery in Cairo) and William Empson (commercial counsellor, Cairo) as respectively his deputy and economic adviser.[21] His 'old friend and ally', Robert Scott, would be political adviser.[22] Scott had been Killearn's private secretary in Beijing and a member of the governor's war council in Singapore before the fall. Subsequently interned and tortured, he had emerged from the Japanese occupation weighing a mere seven stone. Ralph Murray joined the organization as public relations officer, and Dr William Clyde was seconded from the Colonial Service as food adviser.[23] Killearn's need for a residence that would suit both his status and his young family, was met by his 'old friend' Sultan Ibrahim of Johor, now once again ensconced in London's West End. Ibrahim lent him Bukit Serene overlooking the Singapore Strait, much to the chagrin of MacDonald who assumed this palace had been allocated to him. At the beginning of March Killearn left London to wind up his affairs in Egypt. He departed Cairo for South-East Asia on 9 March, breaking the journey in Delhi to meet Wavell, and in Rangoon, where he found the governor, Dorman-Smith, 'in a pretty bloody frame of mind'.[24] He reached Singapore on 16 March and established the Special Commission on the eighth floor of the Cathay Building.

Killearn's top priority was rice distribution. Within a fortnight of his arrival he had convened a preliminary food conference which was followed in April by a high-level gathering that included Mountbatten, governors of all British dependencies and senior representatives of other territories. This spawned plans for the distribution, rationing and production of rice. The main impediments to distribution were: lack of shipping; derelict ports; the collapse of transport in the 'rice basket' of Burma; Thailand's reluctance to release surpluses; and the allocation enforced by the International Emergency Food Council in Washington which in Killearn's view penalized South-East Asia to alleviate food shortages elsewhere.[25] After the April conference Killearn flew to Bangkok to negotiate rice shipments. He received a warm welcome from Prime Minister Nai Pridi, and was granted an audience with the young King Ananda, whom he urged to visit England and 'see how Monarchy was run and should be run on the best possible lines'. It seemed 'a useful and productive visit'[26] but Ananda was assassinated in June, Nai Pridi resigned in August and rice shipments did not pick up until the end of the year. Meanwhile, action plans agreed at the April conference were monitored at monthly meetings of territorial representatives and followed by conferences on nutrition (May 1946), fisheries, and social welfare (1947). Bit by bit, the Special Commission assumed responsibility for other aspects of regional rehabilitation which the over-stretched SEAC was ill-equipped to undertake. These included economic intelligence, shipping, coal distribution and health. The commission also assumed SEAC's role in foreign affairs and absorbed its Foreign Office staff, with the exception of Dening himself who returned to London. Once he had put in hand a strategy for dealing with the rice crisis, Killearn was glad to get back on his 'own professional ground' of international diplomacy. He visited Nanjing and represented Britain at the celebration of Filipino independence which struck him as equivalent to the status of Egypt following the treaty of 1936. He also replaced Inverchapel as intermediary in the negotiations between the Dutch and Indonesians.[27]

Killearn got on with SEAC 'like a house on fire from the start. Especially with Dickie Mountbatten himself.'[28] Characteristically Mountbatten claimed credit for the creation of the Special Commission, though he regretted that it had not been set up exactly as he had proposed. He told Killearn that he had wanted a minister of Cabinet rank but 'the authorities at home had funked that'. (In fact, Mountbatten had at first objected to a ministerial appointment.) The result, he said, was 'a curious sort of compromise involving several supermen, perhaps even too many of them.' Both Mountbatten and Killearn were wary of Colonial Office intentions. Killearn was convinced that it had 'fought tooth and nail' to prevent the establishment of the Special Commission because it was 'barging into their territory'. When colonial administration was restored on 1 April, his 'real troubles started', especially with Sir Edward Gent who was 'pugnacious', 'aggressive' and 'obstructive'. Gent had spent twenty-six years in the Colonial Office. He had been the architect of the incendiary Malayan Union and now, as its governor, seemed determined to be 'autocrat of Malaya' and 'centralise everything in Kuala Lumpur, despite the fact that nature has deemed that Singapore shall be the focal point'. Killearn regarded him as 'very much the black-hatted Whitehall type' and suspected that he kept 'in close touch with his chaps at Home' in order to obstruct regional policies.[29] Mountbatten, who had clashed with Gent during the planning of the Malayan Union, also came to regard the latter as 'a menace'. As the date for MacDonald's installation as governor-general drew near, Killearn and Mountbatten were apprehensive lest 'the Colonial Office mentality should once again come to dominate this vitally important area'.[30] MacDonald was sworn in on 22 May 1946. A week later Mountbatten departed South-East Asia, leaving the special commissioner and governor-general to work out a *modus operandi*.[31]

## IV

Killearn and MacDonald appeared to differ in almost every respect. Mac-Donald was the younger man by some twenty years, puckish and slightly built. Killearn was a shambling giant, 'two or three times my size' according to Twining, the burly governor of North Borneo.[32] Grandson of a baronet, Killearn was born into a well-established, upper middle class family; Mac-Donald's father was the illegitimate son of a ploughman and a domestic servant. After Eton, Killearn joined the Foreign Office without bothering with university; MacDonald was educated at Bedales, a progressive co-educational boarding school, followed by Queen's College, Oxford. An enthusiast for field sports, Killearn shot birds whereas the ornithologist MacDonald observed and wrote about them. In Egypt Killearn was domineering, paternalist and self-satisfied – the embodiment of imperial arrogance. He set great store by status and was a stickler over precedence. As in Cairo, so in Singapore the guests at his table were generally Westerners although he did delight in the company of the Tengku Mahkota of Johor, the eldest son of the absent Sultan. Yet compared with Cairo, post-war Singapore was a bit of come-down, with its food shortages, overcrowding and pestilential climate. After one 'singularly drab and depressing' evening with the Colonial Secretary where the dinner was 'very poor' with only water to drink, he could not help feeling 'how very differently and on what entirely better standards Diplomatic Missions ... are run. Parochial to a degree!'[33] Now at the end of his career and smarting at Foreign Office treatment, Killearn was inclined to cynicism and occasional bouts of self-pity.

MacDonald, by contrast, was in mid-career and irrepressibly optimistic about fashioning a new order in South-East Asia. He was a natural mixer, an instinctive conciliator and a persuasive correspondent. He made a point of declining the titles which went with high office and took the formalities of rank with a pinch of salt. His easy manner enabled him to get the best out of people, although some complained about his lack of gravitas. To break the ice at meetings he might take to walking on his hands. In Singapore he frequented backstreet restaurants and danced the conga with students at the University of Malaya. In Sarawak he allowed himself to be photographed arm-in-arm with two young, half-naked Iban women. While Killearn fretted about his health and that of his family, MacDonald courted enteric fever in up-river Borneo. In matters of public policy Killearn had easy relations with many Tory leaders as did MacDonald with those on the Labour side. They

126    *A.J. Stockwell*

had clashed over Palestine in 1938 when MacDonald (then Secretary of State for the Colonies) had complained about 'Lampson's tendency to be really very unhelpful' by 'out-Arabing the Arabs'.[34] They would be on opposing sides during the controversy over Suez in the 1950s: Killearn (a member of the ultra-conservative Suez Group) would oppose plans to withdraw from the base, while MacDonald (by then High Commissioner in New Delhi) would contemplate resignation over the Anglo–French invasion. In short, Killearn was an imperial grandee, a relic of a previous era, whereas MacDonald was a pioneer of the new Commonwealth. [35]

In South-East Asia each man was engrossed with a different set of specific problems: Killearn with rice distribution and the Indonesian dispute, Mac-Donald with the Malayan Union crisis and the campaign against Sarawak's cession to the Crown. They were, however, jointly responsible for the implementation of British policy in the region as a whole. This was managed by two small but crucial committees: the defence committee chaired by Mac-Donald, and the political committee which they co-chaired. Their contrasting backgrounds and temperaments did not bode well for collaboration which began with a squabble about the occupancy of Bukit Serene, a misunderstanding regarding office space in the Cathay Building and differences over the handling of the defence committee.[36] These proved to be minor disagreements, however, and were amicably settled. Thereafter, the partnership blossomed. They confided in each other and did not allow departmental differences in Whitehall to come between them. They enjoyed each other's company, hunting for Chinese ceramics and socializing *en famille*. Perhaps it was because their characters complemented each other that they saw eye-to-eye on all major issues. If MacDonald was more sympathetic and Killearn more pragmatic towards nationalist claims, they were as one in their commitment to dispel suspicions of British imperialism and to persuade America, the United Nations and neighbouring Commonwealth countries to underwrite the rehabilitation and security of South-East Asia.

At the end of November 1946 they celebrated 'a nice double': MacDonald had persuaded Malay leaders to accept a draft federal constitution in place of the Malayan Union while Killearn had completed his task in Indonesia. Convinced from the outset that 'the best and really only right line is to get out of that embarrassing commitment just as soon as we decently can', he had won the trust of the nationalists and persuaded both sides in the conflict to accept the Linggadjati Agreement which, although it would turn out to be short-lived, brought SEAC's responsibility to an end and allowed the last British forces to depart.[37] Reviewing the ups and downs of 1946, Killearn affirmed that MacDonald's arrival had been 'a real ray of sunlight' making things 'infinitely better':

> … what might have been a very difficult relationship has on the contrary proved an extraordinarily useful and helpful partnership. Of course there are small points when it is not always easy to split the difference between

his domain and mine... But so long as Malcolm is here personally I think he and I together should be able to make quite a good hand of running British policy in this part of the world.

For his part, MacDonald came 'to admire [Killearn's] energy, drive, experience and wisdom. Of course, he has his faults', he admitted:

He is too much concerned with his and his family's material well-being. But he is built on a grand scale, and if his vices sometimes appear large his virtues are colossal... Though 67 years old, he has the physical vigour and mental freshness of a man in his prime. He is still a sort of human dynamo.[38]

More so than MacDonald, Killearn came in 'for many kicks and very few halfpence' from the Malayan public on account of his responsibility for food. Despite his endeavours, the supply of rice sank to dangerous levels and the rice ration was further reduced before prospects brightened at the end of 1946. Notwithstanding attempts to explain that he was neither 'a fairy godmother' nor 'a food dictator', Killearn was variously dubbed the 'improvident fairy of Singapore' unable to deliver on his promises and 'the Great Lord Pooh Bah of Cathay Castle' laughing 'from his battlements upon the needs and distress of those below'. He became the butt of all sorts of other local grievances such as the shortage of accommodation which was blamed on the Commission's staff occupying 'other people's houses'.[39] Moreover, following the debacle of 1942, Singaporeans had little enthusiasm for a future in which their city would be the centre of British power in the region. They already felt over-run by the military and colonial administrators, and the ever-expanding Special Commission aggravated complaints about expensive, top-heavy government and 'a plethora of Excellencies'. Killearn set great store by public relations. He accepted some criticism as legitimate but not the malice of what he called the 'gutter press' in which he included the *Straits Free Press* edited by 'a most objectionable little bounder'. By and large, however, he took the rough with the smooth, and, notwithstanding the illness of his wife and his own emergency operation for appendicitis, by the end of 1946 he had grown to like Singapore particularly since 'the alternative of returning to England, with all the grim hardships of climate, lack of fuel, lack of food, etc, is not attractive'.[40]

What riled Killearn as much as anything were the signs of infirmity of purpose on the part of the Foreign Office after Sir Orme Sargent took over from Sir Alexander Cadogan as permanent undersecretary early in 1946. Like Gent, Sargent had spent his career in Whitehall rather than in the field. Though 'a delightful person', he was 'hardly sufficiently interested or of the right calibre to make much of an effort'.[41] 'The Foreign Office these days', Killearn railed on another occasion, 'really are beyond the ruddy limit!'[42] In December came news of the reduced standing of the 'Nathan Committee' on

128    *A.J. Stockwell*

rice as its chairmanship passed from a minister to Dening (now assistant undersecretary for Far Eastern affairs) in whom Killearn had little faith. Then his key advisers were recalled but not replaced, starting with Empson and followed by Murray, Wright and Scott. Meanwhile, periodic parliamentary questions about increasing expenditure on the Commission did little to allay his suspicions that its very future hung in the balance.[43] Unlike the governor-general's establishment, which was charged to the colonies, the Commission's costs were borne by the home government and between February 1946 and June 1947 they rose by over two and a half times the original estimates.[44]

## V

Whereas the appointment of the Special Commission had been precipitated by the South-East Asian food crisis, twelve months later it was the economic blizzard in Britain that prompted its reorganization. The terrible winter of 1946–7, fuel shortages, failing exports, exhaustion of the dollar loan were followed in the summer by the collapse of confidence in sterling. Rationing, taxation and cuts in public expenditure were the order of the day. Pressed by the Treasury to make significant savings, the Foreign Office instigated a review of the Special Commission.[45] By the end of April interdepartmental agreement had been reached regarding its future. In the light of Britain's imminent withdrawal from India, it was accepted that 'the duties performed by the Special Commissioner were of the highest importance and should on no account be discontinued'. Since significant economies were essential, however, the review recommended the merger of the Special Commission with the office of governor-general and the appointment of MacDonald as head of the reformed organization.[46] Thus Whitehall reverted to Duff Cooper's concept of a single commissioner-general for the co-ordination of all British interests in South-East Asia.

Neither Killearn nor MacDonald had expected to remain in post indefinitely: Killearn had been appointed for two years (until March 1948) and MacDonald for three (until May 1949). While they had been aware that changes were in the offing, they had remained reasonably confident that both regional offices would survive. For Killearn the merger plan came as a 'thunderbolt', just as Bevin's original offer of the South-East Asian job had hit him like 'a bombshell'. He firmly believed that there were 'really cogent reasons why [the special commission] should not be liquidated as an independent F.O. institution'. He had also clung to the hope that his service would be extended by another year so as to qualify for a higher pension. The decision to amalgamate took 'the whole glitter out of the show'.[47] His spirits were briefly lifted by the offer of the governorship of East Bengal which Mountbatten did his best to broker during his last weeks as viceroy. Having met Jinnah, however, Killearn shied away from the prospect of working for 'a megalomaniac'.[48] It seemed he would leave Singapore as he had left Cairo, in a huff although this time without a fresh challenge ahead.

## Lord Killearn & Malcolm MacDonald, 1946–8   129

Killearn's disgust at the absorption of the Special Commission in 'Malcolm's show' did not, however, tarnish his relationship with MacDonald. For his part, MacDonald made it clear that he had no desire to remain in South-East Asia beyond May 1949. Moreover, he staunchly lobbied Whitehall in support of Killearn's desperate appeal to stay on until the end of May 1948 so as to ensure a smooth hand-over as well as a gentle transition for his family. However, when the Foreign Office learned that Killearn had been spreading doubt on the international circuit about the wisdom of the merger, they were determined that he should 'not remain in post a day longer than is necessary' and, in the absence of Bevin, the Prime Minister himself sent what Killearn peevishly described as 'a very nasty telegram' rejecting his 'fervid appeal to his humanity and sense of fairness'.[49] Complaining to the end about shabby treatment by the Foreign Office – the final insult was the prospect of returning home on a troopship – Killearn wrote to Sargent:

> After sweating blood for you for 44 years it would have been much pleasanter to quit your Service with less feeling of having been scurvily treated … it is sad – very sad – to leave a Service one has worked for very nearly half a century, feeling as I now do about your Office.

Sargent did his best with a soothing reply:

> I am sorry you feel so badly about having to come away in March, but I can assure you that you entirely misrepresent our feelings towards you in the Department. The Service I can assure you takes a very personal pride in you and we all recognise how distinguished your long official life has been and in particular what a fine job you have done in Singapore. But it does fall to all of us to retire sooner or later, and for a variety of reasons it seemed undesirable that you should overlap with Macdonald [sic] until June.[50]

Notwithstanding the galloping costs of the Special Commission, admiration for its achievements was genuine. Although Killearn had been handicapped from the outset by lack of executive authority, on the one hand, and, on the other, widespread suspicion that his organization was a veiled form of imperialism, he had built from scratch machinery that not only contributed to the definition of a still inchoate region but more especially to the alleviation of its suffering. The Special Commission, Bevin pronounced in parliament, had saved South-East Asia from starvation.[51] Much of the criticism levelled at it in its early days proved to be ill-considered, as the *Straits Times* acknowledged in a tribute published on the day of his departure from Singapore: 'Had South East Asia been forced to wait for the same international effort which grasped the problems of Europe, 1946 would have been a year of disaster.'[52] The Special Commission had also laid the foundations for the solution of regional food problems upon which the UN was at last beginning

130   *A.J. Stockwell*

to build through the Economic Commission for Asia and the Far East.[53] Killearn himself looked back with pride on the achievements of the previous two years, and, as he braced himself for the return to austerity Britain, he also accepted that, 'Fate is probably right, and that it is time that we personally pulled out. The whole orbit of the Commission's activities has changed.'[54]

It would be wrong to conclude, as Killearn himself had at first supposed, that amalgamation meant take-over by the Colonial Office. The new organization was given a neutral name, 'Commission-General'. The commissioner-general would report to both the Foreign Secretary and the Colonial Secretary, and would be served in Singapore by 'colonial' staff and 'diplomatic' staff working side by side. Moreover, as the Colonial Office predicted, its interest in the Commission-General diminished as the dependent territories moved towards self-government, while that of the Foreign Office grew as the Cold War engulfed the region from 1948. The commissioner-general would play a central part in regional rehabilitation (through the Colombo Plan) and in regional security (as chairman of the British Defence Coordinating Committee Far East). And as his role expanded, the hope that amalgamation would result in economies of scale was dashed. Even before the Commission-General was inaugurated, an investigation by Sir David Monteath had warned that there was little scope for 'really substantial economies' arising from merger.[55] By February 1949 it had outgrown the Cathay Building and moved to Phoenix Park, the former Japanese race-course, where it would continue to expand at an alarming rate until it was wound up in the early 1960s.

As for MacDonald, the Killearns' departure incidentally solved his accommodation problem, at least for the time being. He moved into Bukit Serene where he and his family resided until evicted in 1953 by Sultan Ibrahim who loathed MacDonald as much as he had liked Killearn (probably on account of MacDonald's cordial relations with Malayan community leaders).[56] Although MacDonald had made clear his wish not to remain in South-East Asia much longer after 1949, he was reconfirmed in office six times. He even survived the shake-up of 1951–2 when General Templer was appointed Malayan 'supremo' and he himself was criticized (unfairly, it has to be said, since he lacked the power to intervene) for not having acted like a supremo. By early 1955, however, the Foreign Office concurred with the Colonial Office that MacDonald had outstayed his usefulness. In any case, Eden (Foreign Secretary and soon to be Prime Minister) had MacDonald in mind as High Commissioner to India. When he visited South-East Asia in February to attend the first meeting of the SEATO Council, Eden saw enough of the Commission-General to question its efficiency and instigate another review.[57] Although the Colonial Office felt no need for the commission, the review group as a whole favoured its continuation provided it was given 'substantial authority'. So it was that the status of the senior British authority in South-East Asia would derive thereafter from his appointment as the representative of the Prime Minister to whom he would be directly responsible. Given the difficulty that had been experienced in filling such positions from the political world, it was decided to appoint a Foreign Office 'trusty': Robert Scott, currently minister at the Washington Embassy, previously responsible for South-East Asia and the Far East in the Foreign Office, and, before that, political adviser to Lord Killearn.

## Notes

1 Peter Lowe, *Contending with Nationalism and Communism: British Policy towards Southeast Asia, 1945–65*, Basingstoke: Palgrave-Macmillan, 2009, p. 4.
2 Duff Cooper held office in the National Government (including the War Office and the Admiralty) but resigned in 1938 over Munich. Churchill brought him back, first for an unsuccessful stint as Minister of Information and then as Chancellor of the Duchy of Lancaster.
3 John Charmley, *Duff Cooper: The Authorized Biography*, London: Weidenfeld and Nicolson, 1986, pp. 154–62; Duff Cooper, *Old Men Forget: The Autobiography of Duff Cooper Viscount Norwich*, London: Hart-Davis, 1955, pp. 280–96; and The National Archives, Kew (TNA), CAB 66/20/9, WP(41)286 'British Administration in the Far East: Report by the Chancellor of the Duchy of Lancaster', 29 Oct. 1941.
4 Report by Sir W. Battershill, G.E.J. Gent and W.L. Rolleston, 4 Dec. 1942, in A.J. Stockwell, ed., *British Documents on the End of Empire: Malaya*, part I, London: HMSO, 1995 (hereafter *BDEE*), p. 31.
5 Obituary, *The Times*, 31 Jan. 1977; Roger Buckley, 'Sir Esler Dening Ambassador to Japan, 1951–57', in Hugh Cortazzi, ed., *British Envoys in Japan, 1859–1972*, Folkestone: Japan Society, 2004, pp. 173–8.
6 M.E. Dening, 'Political Co-ordination in South-East Asia', 26 June 1945, in *BDEE: Malaya*, I, p. 105.
7 See Vice-Admiral the Earl Mountbatten of Burma, *Post Surrender Tasks: Section E of the Report to the Combined Chiefs of Staff*, London: HMSO, 1969; Philip Ziegler, *Mountbatten*, London: Collins, 1986, pp. 305–38; Peter Dennis, *Troubled Days of Peace: Mountbatten and South East Asia Command, 1945–46*, Manchester: Manchester University Press, 1987; Richard McMillan, *The British Occupation of Indonesia 1945–1946: Britain, the Netherlands and the Indonesian Revolution*, London: RoutledgeCurzon, 2005; Peter Neville, *Britain in Vietnam: Prelude to Disaster, 1945–46*, London: Routledge, 2007; John Springhall, 'Mountbatten versus the Generals: British Military Rule of Singapore, 1945–46', *Journal of Contemporary History*, 36/4 (2001), pp. 635–52.
8 Dening to Bevin, 'Review of Political Events in South-East Asia, 1945 to March 1946', 25 Mar. 1946, *BDEE: Malaya*, I, p. 210 ff.
9 TNA CO825/43/36 Bevin to Hall, 14 Nov. 1945.
10 TNA PREM8/189, GEN97/1st meeting, 18 Oct. 1945; and FO800/461 Bevin to Attlee, PM/45/47, 13 Dec. 1945.
11 Clyde Sanger, *Malcolm MacDonald: Bringing an End to Empire*, Montreal: McGill-Queen's University Press, 1995, pp. 259–60; Peter Lyon, 'MacDonald, Malcolm John (1901–1981)', *Oxford Dictionary of National Biography*, online ed., May 2010.
12 Kenneth Robinson quoted in Nicholas Tarling, '"Some Rather Nebulous Capacity": Lord Killearn's Appointment in Southeast Asia', *Modern Asian Studies*, 20/3 (1986), p. 578.
13 Clark Kerr was about to transfer from the Moscow embassy to that in Washington.

132   *A.J. Stockwell*

14  Peter Neville, 'The Appointment of Sir Nevile Henderson, 1937 – Design or Blunder?' *Journal of Contemporary History*, 33/4 (1989), p. 610; David Reynolds, 'Lord Lothian and Anglo–American relations, 1939–1940', *Transactions of the American Philosophical Society*, 73, 2 (1983), p. 2; and TNA PREM 5/532, 'Viceroy of India: appointment of Field Marshal Sir Archibald Wavell in succession to Marquess of Linlithgow'.

15  R.A. Bickers, 'Death of a Young Shanghailander: The Thorburn Case and the Defence of the British Treaty Ports in China in 1931', *Modern Asian Studies*, 30/2 (1996), pp. 271–300; also Edmund S.K. Fung, 'The Sino–British Rapprochement, 1927–1931', *Modern Asian Studies*, 17/1 (1983), pp.79–105, and David Steeds, 'Lampson, Miles Wedderburn, first Baron Killearn (1880–1964)', *Oxford Dictionary of National Biography*, online ed., Jan. 2011.

16  See Malcolm Yapp, ed., *The Diaries of Sir Miles Lampson, 1935–1937*, Oxford: Oxford University Press, 1997; Trefor E. Evans, ed., *The Killearn Diaries, 1934–1946*, London: Sidgwick & Jackson, 1972.

17  For the end of the Killearn era in Egypt, see Wm. Roger Louis, *The British Empire in the Middle East, 1945–1951*, Oxford: Oxford University Press, 1985, p. 226 ff; John Kent, ed., *BDEE: Egypt and the Defence of the Middle East*, I, London: HMSO 1998, xliv–vi, and pp. 77–80 for Killearn's 'swan-song'.

18  Killearn papers, Middle East Centre, St Antony's College, Oxford, Archive GB165–0176, diary entry 11 Feb. 1946 (hereafter Diary). Killearn's diaries for South-East Asia continue seamlessly from Cairo. Unless he was travelling and until he departed Singapore (when he hand-wrote the record), he dictated entries to 'the admirable and excellent Elaine' who typed them up, including from time to time telegrams between Killearn and the Foreign Office. His use of an amanuensis does not appear to have inhibited comment on policies and personalities. Copies of correspondence relating to his appointment to South-East Asia are to be found in various file series at The National Archives, see for example FO 800/461, ff 122–49.

19  TNA FO800/461 Bevin to Killearn (Cairo), tel., 12 Feb. 1946.

20  Diary, 16, 18 and 19 Feb. 1946.

21  He had hoped to secure John Sterndale Bennett as his deputy but he could not be spared from the Foreign Office where he was head of the Far East Department. Bennett would serve as deputy commissioner-general for South-East Asia in 1950–3.

22  Diary, 14 Feb. 1946.

23  Murray had joined the Foreign Office from the BBC news service in 1939. Before his appointment to South-East Asia he had been on the staff of the Allied Commission for Austria. Clyde had been head of the English Department, University College Dundee until 1939 when he was drafted to the Ministry of Food. Here he flourished and in 1942 he was transferred to the Colonial Office as adviser on wartime food supplies. When the Special Commission was subsumed within the Commission-General in 1948, MacDonald made Clyde director of economic activities. His publications include a book on the struggle for the freedom of the press from Caxton to Cromwell.

24  Diary, 13 Mar. 1946.

25  The group (including Killearn, Mountbatten, Wright and Scott) that drafted the final communiqué had wanted to 'rub in' the point that 'the absurdly optimistic statements which had recently been issued in Washington were most misleading, and naturally were taken here in South East Asia as meaning that the general world food shortage had been to some extent ameliorated by penalizing this area.' On reflection, however, they decided not to include this 'indirect dig' at President Truman (Diary, 17 Apr. 1946).

26  Diary, 29 Apr.–1 May 1946.

27  See Killearn to Bevin, 'South-East Asia: Work of the Special Commission during 1946', 12 Apr. 1947, *BDEE: Malaya*, I, p. 307ff.

## Lord Killearn & Malcolm MacDonald, 1946–8   133

28  Diary, 1 Jan. 1947.
29  Criticism of Gent permeates Killearn's Diary from 1 April until the end of the year when, he reported, 'our relations are very much better' (Diary, 1 Jan. 1947).
30  Diary, 20 May 1946.
31  Lt-General Stopford acted as Supreme Allied Commander until SEAC ceased on 30 Nov. 1946.
32  Edward Twining quoted in Darrell Bates, *A Gust of Plumes: A Biography of Lord Twining of Godalming and Tanganyika*, London: Hodder & Stoughton, 1972, p. 195.
33  Diary, 30 July 1946.
34  Quoted in Michael J. Cohen, 'Direction of Policy in Palestine, 1936–45', *Middle Eastern Studies*, 11/3 (1975), p. 240.
35  When the Commonwealth Secretariat was set up in 1965 (to take over many of the functions of the Commonwealth Relations Office) MacDonald was suggested as its first secretary-general, but prudence dictated that the holder should be chosen from outside the UK and the Canadian diplomat Arnold Smith was appointed.
36  With the Killearn family in possession of Bukit Serene, MacDonald withdrew to the Penang Residency, staying at Mount Nassim on visits to Singapore. When his new wife and stepchildren arrived in January 1947, the family moved into Woodneuk in the grounds of the Sultan of Johor's former Tyersall Palace.
37  Diary, 2 May 1946.
38  MacDonald (Singapore) to Arthur Creech Jones, personal & secret 26 Sept. 1947, quoted in Louis, *British Empire*, p. 49.
39  For example, *Straits Times* 14 June, 26 Aug., 12 Sept. 1946, 25 Jan., 28 Aug. 1947; *Singapore Free Press*, 22 Aug. 1946.
40  Diary, 1 Jan. 1947.
41  Diary, 15 May 1946.
42  Diary, 2 Oct. 1946.
43  For example, ministers made statements about staff and costs in answer to Parliamentary Questions in July and Oct. 1946 and in Mar., May, June and Nov. 1947.
44  Tilman Remme, *Britain and Regional Cooperation in South East Asia, 1945–49*, London: Routledge, 1995, pp. 111–14
45  See TNA FO 371/63543 F1147/1147/61 Wright paper, 15 Jan. 1947; F7571/1147/61/G 'Future of the Special Commissioner in South East Asia' Allen memo, 15 Mar. 1947, following his visit to the region in Jan.–Feb. 1947; and F4341/1147/61 Killearn's views, 19 Mar. 1947.
46  TNA FO 371/63543 Note of a meeting in the Treasury chaired by Sir Edward Bridges, Permanent Undersecretary of the Treasury and Head of the Civil Service, 24 Apr. 1947.
47  Diary, 5 July and 13–14 July 1947; and TNA FO371/63545 Killearn (Singapore) to Bevin, tel., 5 Sept. 1947.
48  Diary, 5, 13, 14 and 18 July 1947.
49  TNA CO 825/72/1 Killearn to Attlee, tel., 5 Jan. 1948; MacDonald to Seel, tel., 7 Jan. 1948; Seel minute, 7 Jan. 1948; Attlee to Killearn, tel., 8 Jan. 1948; and Diary, 9 Jan. 1948.
50  TNA FO371/69687 Killearn to Sargent, 8 Feb. 1948 and Sargent to Killearn, 24 Feb. 1948.
51  *Parliamentary Debates*, Fifth Series, HC Deb, vol. 437, 16 May 1947, cc.1958–9.
52  *Straits Times*, 27 Mar. 1948.
53  'Grouping of South-East Asia: A Turbulent Setting for Creative Work – Lord Killearn's Achievement', *The Times*, 10 Mar. 1948. See also Remme, *Britain and Regional Cooperation*.
54  Diary, 10 Mar. 1948.
55  TNA FCO 141/17142 Report by Sir David Monteath on the proposed amalgamation of the offices of the governor-general, Malaya, and the special commissioner in South-East Asia; see also CO 825/72/1.

134   *A.J. Stockwell*

56 In 1953 MacDonald moved to Mallaig House owned by Loke Wan Tho, businessman, philanthropist and chairman of the Cathay Organisation. Loke was an art collector and collaborated with MacDonald in producing an illustrated book about Angkor. When MacDonald left South-East Asia in 1955, Mallaig reverted to Loke and the British government purchased Eden Hall (Nassim Road) as the commissioner-general's residence. Eden Hall is now the residence of the British high commissioner to Singapore.

57 TNA CAB128/28, CC21(55)1, 7 Mar. 1955; and CAB130/109 Office of the United Kingdom Commissioner-General in South-East Asia: Meetings, 1955.

# 9 Anglo–American relations and the making and breaking of the Korean phase of the 1954 Geneva Conference

*Robert Barnes*

Peter Lowe wrote numerous excellent books and articles on the Korean War during his long career. *The Origins of the Korean War*, in particular, ranks as one of the seminal works on this topic.[1] In the main, though, he focused on Britain's role and Anglo–American relations during the conflict and paid little attention to developments during the eleven months between the signing of the Korean Armistice Agreement on 27 July 1953 and the termination of the Korean phase of the 1954 Geneva Conference.[2] In fact, very few historians of the Korean War have scrutinized this period and the few scholarly works that do go beyond the beginning of the ceasefire have generally focused on the implementation of the armistice on the ground in Korea and not on diplomatic relations.[3] Nonetheless, tensions continued to simmer between Washington and London and the bonds that held together the so-called 'special relationship' were tested almost to breaking point, just as they had been during the numerous crises that erupted while the fighting raged in Korea. This much-overlooked episode of unrest between the Western camp's closest and most powerful allies will thus form the focus of this chapter.

On the surface the disagreements between the United States and Britain stemmed from the terms of the Korean Armistice Agreement. This document only created a military ceasefire at the thirty-eighth parallel between the belligerents. The fundamental political issue of Korean unification was not settled. Instead, the US and Communist military negotiators at Panmunjom had only agreed to recommend that a political conference should be held within ninety days of the termination of hostilities. The date, location, agenda and membership of this conference was left undecided. While all of these issues produced strains, as will be demonstrated below, it was the composition question that proved most controversial in terms of Anglo–American relations. At the heart of this matter was whether neutral nations, specifically India, should be invited to the conference.

After months of trying both at the UN and bilaterally, a solution to the composition question was found at the US, Soviet, British and French foreign ministers meeting in Berlin in February 1954. This agreement paved the way for the opening of the Korean phase of the Geneva Conference in late April. Very little scholarly attention has been lavished on these discussions and even

136   *Robert Barnes*

less has been written on Anglo–American animosity during this stage of the conference.[4] Central to this oversight is that the Korean debates produced no positive results, and that more eventful negotiations soon took place at Geneva on Indochina. Historians have thus concentrated on this later phase of the conference since the decisions taken here are usually seen as integral to the outbreak of the Vietnam War over a decade later. The rifts between the US and British delegations were also clearer to see during these debates. Still, serious problems had already been encountered between the two allies during the Korean talks since they disagreed on what course to pursue to bring these proceedings to a timely end.

Invariably, when push came to shove the British government made the major concessions over the composition question and the handling of the talks at Geneva. Britain may have still been a global player in 1953–4 but its influence was rapidly fading and it had accepted a role as junior partner to the United States in the Western alliance. Prime Minister Winston Churchill and Foreign Secretary Anthony Eden, moreover, recognized that they had to compromise if they hoped to maintain the special relationship. President Dwight Eisenhower, in contrast, was at the peak of his powers at this time since he had ended the deeply unpopular Korean War just six months after being elected. But to say that Washington got everything its own way during this period would be to ignore the efforts it made to appease its closest friend while not upsetting its newest ally, the Republic of Korea (ROK).

Two central issues lay at the root of the fissures that formed in the special relationship during these months. To start with, Washington and London both had other international loyalties that pulled them in opposite directions on the Korean issue. For its part, the US government felt it had to work closely with the ROK after having spent three years of fighting alongside it, incurring great losses in manpower and resources, in order to maintain its existence. The Eisenhower administration, therefore, believed it could not ride roughshod over the wishes of ROK President Syngman Rhee even when he adopted a hard-line approach demanding Korean unification on his terms. The Churchill government, however, greatly disliked Rhee, who was considered to be undemocratic and manipulative. The British were also much less interested in Korea which it considered a peripheral matter that only distracted attention away from more important Cold War theatres. In consequence, London was much more interested in cooperating with its Commonwealth partners, particularly India whose friendship the British desired for strategic reasons and as a means of maintaining Third World goodwill. Indian Prime Minister Jawaharlal Nehru, nevertheless, was the one international statesman determined to find a compromise solution to the Korean problem, much to Washington and Seoul's ire.

Even more significantly, since Stalin's death in March 1953, British and American Cold War strategies had been slowly diverging. For Churchill, the subsequent 'peace offensive' launched by the Soviet collective leadership had opened an opportunity to establish some form of *détente* with Moscow and he had made attaining this his final crusade in international affairs. Ultimately, the British Prime Minister desired a three-power summit composed of the United States, the Soviet Union and Britain to resolve all outstanding problems and saw the holding of a political conference on Korea as a small step towards achieving this goal.[5] In addition, London had long been convinced that it was foolish to treat the People's Republic of China (PRC) as a pariah state, especially given Hong Kong's precarious position. Rather, the British government believed that, now the Korean War was over, the PRC should be brought into the community of nations; China would then gravitate away from the Soviet bloc. But the Eisenhower administration did not share Churchill's convictions and doubted the sincerity of the new Soviet leadership's overtures. US Secretary of State John Foster Dulles, specifically, had little desire to negotiate with the USSR and even less with the PRC which Washington continued not to recognize and considered an aggressor since its intervention in Korea.[6]

## Round one: The UN and the membership question

With the signing of the Korean Armistice Agreement a special session of the UN General Assembly was scheduled to open on 17 August 1953. All parties expected that this forum would take up the Korean political conference issue. However, to complicate matters, in the brief interim period the Eisenhower administration tied itself firmly to the ROK. Dulles and the US ambassador to the UN, Henry Cabot Lodge, travelled to Seoul almost immediately after the fighting stopped to conclude the US-ROK mutual security treaty that had been promised to Rhee a month earlier in order to convince him to accept the armistice. This pact thus made South Korea Washington's newest ally and bound America's international prestige to the continued existence of the ROK.

With Dulles and Lodge away, discussions between the US and British delegations at the UN on the Korean political conference got underway only days before the special session opened. Lodge met with the British Minister of State, Selwyn Lloyd, who was present in New York because Eden was incapacitated with a serious bile-duct problem, and duly outlined a draft resolution that had been written on the flight back from Korea. This proposal recommended a two-sided conference with the 'UN' side composed of the member states which had contributed forces and the ROK. The Communist 'aggressors' should then name their own side. The proposal also stated that the conference should take place at a time and place to be arranged in discussions between the US government, acting on behalf of the UN, and the Communist side.

On hearing this proposal, Lloyd argued that the conference should be round-table in nature and include interested non-belligerents, particularly the Soviet Union and India. Lloyd also revealed that Britain had already promised a seat to India and stressed that the Commonwealth countries all felt

138   *Robert Barnes*

that such a conference would be more acceptable to the Communists and stood a much better chance of success than resurrecting the tense cross-table talks at Panmunjom.[7] Dulles, though, instructed Lodge to refuse membership to neutral countries and only to accept Soviet participation as part of the Communist side.[8] At a meeting of the sixteen contributing states, therefore, the US delegation presented its draft resolution and all of these states, except South Africa which claimed it no longer had any interest in Korea now the fighting was over, agreed to co-sponsor it. Even Britain, in spite of its misgivings, acted as a sponsor in the interests of maintaining Western unity.[9]

Yet relations between the United States and Britain soon began to deteriorate over the issue of Soviet participation. Acting Foreign Secretary Lord Salisbury, who was temporarily in charge of British foreign policy with Churchill having recently suffered a stroke, insisted on a separate draft resolution inviting the Soviet Union as an interested party. Salisbury argued convincingly that if it was left to the Communist side to invite Moscow this would imply that the USSR was an aggressor.[10] In response, Dulles argued that the American public would not tolerate Soviet participation.[11] With tensions mounting, the inexperienced Salisbury simply instructed Lloyd to accept any procedure acceptable to Washington that would bring about Soviet membership.[12] This action, however, proved premature since Dulles eventually grudgingly accepted the need to invite the Soviet Union if the conference was to stand any chance of success.[13]

Problems over Soviet membership paled into insignificance compared to those produced concerning India's membership. Salisbury had already instructed the British delegation to sponsor a draft resolution inviting India to participate at the conference.[14] Importantly, all of the other Commonwealth members had also agreed to sponsor this proposal. They argued that India had played a key role in finding a solution to the prisoners-of-war problem, helping to bring the Korean conflict to an end, and was directly interested in a peaceful settlement as chairman of the Neutral Nations Repatriation Commission (NNRC). The NNRC was the body created by the armistice agreement to take custody of prisoners who refused to return home after the fighting stopped until a solution to this problem was found at the political conference. The Eisenhower administration, however, refused to accept Indian membership since it did not want Nehru hijacking the conference and advocating concessions in order to appease the Communists. Evidently, the US government had become exasperated with what it perceived as India's meddling in Korean affairs during the years of fighting. Furthermore, Washington was sensitive to the views of the ROK government that claimed it would not attend the conference if India was present. Rhee argued that India had no right to interfere in Korean affairs and that Nehru was sympathetic to the Democratic People's Republic of Korea (DPRK). For the Americans it was essential to have the ROK on-board or else the conference would be pointless.[15]

To try to nip this problem in the bud, Lodge decided to bypass the British and approached directly V. K. Krishna Menon, Nehru's special representative at the UN. Lodge told Menon that while his government had the 'greatest respect and admiration' for India, its participation at the conference would cause 'great embarrassment' between the United States and the ROK. The US delegation hoped, instead, that India would announce it would not pursue a place at the conference. In response, Menon cryptically stated that it would only participate if requested by both sides but stressed that India had a right to be present at the conference since it had contributed a field hospital unit to the UN action in Korea.[16] To further confuse matters, Menon then told Lloyd that India definitely did wish to participate and criticized the US draft resolution for inviting only belligerents.[17]

The special session of the General Assembly thus got underway with the US and British positions poles apart. These differences were soon made public in the First Committee. While Lodge argued against the participation of non-belligerents, Lloyd maintained that the General Assembly had the authority to recommend the membership of any nation, including India.[18] Gauging the response of the other member states, the Eisenhower administration became increasingly concerned that the Commonwealth draft resolution inviting India would win widespread support. Accordingly, Dulles instructed Lodge to make it abundantly clear to the British delegation that the US government would vote against Indian participation.[19] Nevertheless, in talks in Washington Salisbury told the US Secretary of State that the British government had made a firm commitment to India.[20] Even so, privately Salisbury was becoming increasingly concerned at the damage being done to Anglo–American relations. Consequently, he instructed the British delegation not to canvass other members to support the Commonwealth draft resolution.[21]

By the end of the first week of the special session an open split between the United States and Britain on Indian participation seemed inevitable. But at the eleventh hour Menon intervened, thus preventing this from happening. He told Lloyd that while he was practically certain that the Commonwealth draft resolution would obtain a simple majority of votes, he doubted it would receive the two-thirds majority necessary to be formally adopted. He revealed that in these circumstances India would withdraw its candidacy.[22] Menon stated in the General Assembly, moreover, that India would not seek a place at the conference unless it was clear that all the major parties desired its presence. Seizing on this point, Lodge publicly announced that the US government opposed Indian membership on the grounds that its presence would prevent the ROK from attending the conference.[23] Following these developments, Salisbury decided that if the Commonwealth draft resolution did not receive overwhelming support Britain would seek the agreement of the other co-sponsors to withdraw their proposal.[24]

After ten days of deliberation, therefore, the debate in the First Committee concluded in chaotic scenes. At the last minute, the Soviet delegation introduced a number of amendments to the various draft resolutions. After each of these amendments was decisively rejected, the fifteen-power draft resolution was voted upon and was overwhelmingly approved. Next, the draft resolution recommending Soviet participation was approved with almost all members voting for it. The Commonwealth draft resolution proposing Indian membership was then approved narrowly by twenty-seven votes to twenty-one, with eleven abstentions. Significantly, Britain and all of its Commonwealth partners supported this proposal but the United States voted against it. This represented the first time such a split had occurred at the UN over Korea. Finally, a Soviet draft resolution proposing the establishment of a round table conference composed of the two Koreas plus the Soviet Union, China, the United States, Britain, France, Czechoslovakia, Poland, India and Burma, was rejected, with the United States and Britain united against it.[25]

The Commonwealth delegations met straight after this voting had taken place. Lloyd and the other Commonwealth representatives pressed Menon to withdraw India's candidacy now it was clear that their draft resolution would not gain the necessary two-thirds majority to be formally adopted. The Indian representative grudgingly accepted this course and the four co-sponsors agreed that their proposal should not be put to the vote.[26] This plan was put into action the following day with Menon announcing that India 'declined to participate' in the conference. The New Zealand delegation then called for the Commonwealth draft resolution not to proceed to the vote. On 28 August 1953 General Assembly Resolution 711 (VII) was thus adopted, inviting the 'UN' side and the USSR to participate, as well as asking the Communist belligerents to name their side.[27]

The US and British positions had been publicly aligned during the talks but privately neither government was entirely happy with the outcome of the special session. Washington had got its way on the question of Indian membership but, partly in response to British pressure, had unenthusiastically accepted the need to invite the Soviet Union to the conference. The Churchill government was even more disappointed since it had been forced to concede, against its better judgment, on the matter of Indian participation to avoid an open split with the United States. British resentment was then amplified when, as predicted, Chinese Premier Zhou Enlai rejected General Assembly Resolution 711 (VII) on the grounds that neutrals should be present at the conference. India saw this as an opportunity to revive the composition question at the General Assembly when it met again a few weeks later. But the British government, reluctant to open old wounds, accepted the American argument that the UN should stick by its decision and not be held to ransom by the aggressors.[28] Consequently, the Korean item was placed last on the General Assembly's agenda.

## Round two: Panmunjom and the membership question

With the Korean debate at the UN postponed, Dulles sought to start bilateral negotiations between the United States and the PRC to resolve the composition question. To achieve this end he utilized the provision in General

Assembly Resolution 711 (VII) permitting the US government to discuss the time and place of the conference with the Communist side. Dulles thus transmitted a communication to Beijing suggesting a meeting of emissaries at Panmunjom. Somewhat surprisingly after his negative response only weeks earlier, Zhou Enlai accepted this proposal and a meeting was set for 26 October 1953.[29] For this task Dulles appointed Arthur Dean, a trusted former colleague from the Sullivan and Cromwell international law firm.[30]

The talks between Dean and his Chinese counterpart, Huang Hua, however, were doomed from the outset. The Communist representative refused to discuss technical details such as the date and location of the conference until the presence of neutral countries at the conference was accepted.[31] Dean, in contrast, was under strict instructions not to discuss the composition question until the date and location had been agreed.[32] As a result, these meetings quickly descended into bitter slanging matches as each side accused the other of trying to sabotage the conference. But, even though a breakthrough was very unlikely, Dulles insisted that the talks be dragged out to head off debate at the UN.[33] In the meantime, he instructed Lodge to move to adjourn the General Assembly for an indefinite period on the grounds that the Korean question was under active discussion at Panmunjom.[34] The Indian delegation, nonetheless, insisted that a date be set to reconvene the General Assembly to discuss the work of the NNRC before it disbanded on 22 February 1954.[35]

For that reason, Eden – who had recently returned to active duty and assumed responsibility for foreign affairs with Churchill, now 78, frail after his stroke – was placed in a difficult position. He agreed with the Americans that the UN debate should be postponed so as not to interfere with Dean's efforts, but he was also sympathetic to India's desire to report on its difficult task as chairman of the NNRC. To bridge these divergent views Eden sought to persuade Lodge to amend his draft resolution so that a special session of the General Assembly could be called if the Panmunjom talks broke down.[36] Yet Lodge refused to budge, suspecting that India wished to reopen the composition question.[37] Given the strength of Washington's convictions and since this was a point of procedure rather than substance, Eden instructed the British delegation to support the US proposal.[38] General Assembly Resolution 716 (VIII) was thus adopted on 8 December 1953 indefinitely recessing the UN debate. [39]

That same day Dean made a final effort to find a breakthrough on the composition question at Panmunjom. He conceded that some non-belligerent nations should be allowed to 'participate' at the conference but not be permitted to introduce items or vote. But Huang Hua dismissed this proposal as 'absurd, ridiculous and stale' and left the text received from Dean lying on the table at the end of the meeting.[40] Dean wished to break off the talks at this point but in light of the decision to recess the Korean debate at the General Assembly, Dulles instructed him to prolong the talks until 12 December 1953 to avoid controversy.[41] At a meeting that day, therefore, Dean unilaterally recessed the negotiations on the pretext that Huang Hua had charged the United States with perfidy.[42]

## Round three: The 1954 Berlin Conference and the membership question

With the prospect of finding a solution to the membership question at Panmunjom all but dead, the Eisenhower administration became convinced that the Korean political conference could only be established through bilateral negotiations with the Soviet Union. The president, in consequence, agreed with Churchill and French Premier Joseph Laniel, when they met at Bermuda in December 1953, to accept Moscow's suggestion that the foreign ministers of the Soviet Union, the United States, Britain and France meet in Berlin in January 1954.[43] This conference was called ostensibly to discuss the German and Austrian questions. But it was evident to all concerned that matters would quickly turn to more pressing Asian issues – namely the Korean political conference and the conflict in Indochina in which the Viet Minh, with increased Chinese support since the end of the Korean War, had gained the upper hand over the French colonial forces.

Nonetheless, before the Berlin Conference got underway Menon again called for the General Assembly to be reconvened. He argued that with the Korean political conference nowhere in sight the UN members had to discuss the fate of the remaining non-repatriate prisoners held by the NNRC before 23 January 1954 when the custody period specified in the Korean Armistice Agreement expired. The British delegation at the UN believed that this demand was reasonable given the collapse of the negotiations at Panmunjom.[44] Yet Dulles opposed the Indian proposal, fearing that renewed debate on the composition question would interfere with the upcoming talks at Berlin.[45] He thus sought to stymie Menon's campaign by instructing Kenneth Young, Dean's deputy at Panmunjom, to attempt to resume talks on the condition that the Communists retracted their charge of perfidy.[46]

However, the NNRC's decision to simply return the remaining non-repatriate prisoners of war to their former captors at the end of the custody period ended any possibility that the General Assembly would be reconvened at this time. Dulles now argued that since the NNRC had failed to complete its task, the UN was under no obligation to meet to hear its report.[47] Crucially, this argument resonated with Eden and the vast majority of other UN member states who opposed India's calls to reconvene the General Assembly. At the same time, after a number of weeks of trying, Young concluded that the Chinese delegation at Panmunjom had no interest in negotiating on the composition question.[48]

The Berlin Conference became, consequently, the only remaining venue in which to discuss the Korean political conference. Talks commenced on 25 January 1954 between Dulles, Eden, Soviet Foreign Minister Vyacheslav Molotov and French Foreign Minister Georges Bidault and, as predicted, immediately shifted away from the German and Austrian questions. The first item on the agenda tabled by Molotov was a proposal for a five-power conference consisting of the four countries present plus the PRC to tackle all outstanding Asian issues.[49] Dulles refused to accept this proposal on the grounds that the US government did not recognize the PRC. He also opposed discussing any other Asian issues until the Korean question had been resolved.[50] Eden and Bidault were more sympathetic to the Soviet proposal. The French Foreign Minister was unwilling to rule out a five-power conference since his government was desperate to start talks over Indochina given its desperate military situation there. Eden, moreover, felt that it would be difficult to publicly defend refusing a five-power conference now that talks were being held neither at the UN nor Panmunjom.[51] In addition, Churchill believed that it would be 'wise' to accept the Soviet proposal if this presented an opening for wider talks to lessen Cold War tensions.[52]

While the Western foreign ministers presented a united front in the meetings with Molotov, behind-the-scenes bickering between Dulles, Eden and Bidault intensified. Importantly, though, Dulles was determined to get the Korean political conference underway with domestic and international pressure building. He proposed a conference on Korea, therefore, which would be sponsored by the Big Four who would then invite the ROK, the other contributing UN member states, the PRC and the DPRK. If before the adjournment of this conference developments indicated positive results, the four inviting powers would consult on steps to establish a conference to restore peace in Indochina. The US proposal also included clauses stating that the conference was in line with General Assembly Resolution 711 (VII) and that the holding of the conference did not imply diplomatic recognition of the Beijing and Pyongyang regimes.[53]

Bidault was generally in favour of this proposal, although he also wanted a clear indication that a conference on Indochina would definitely take place. Eden also saw the benefits of the proposal since it would get the United States, the Soviet Union and the PRC sitting at the same table. But the British Foreign Secretary was convinced that Molotov would reject the proposal given the references to recognition of the PRC and the General Assembly resolution.[54] He thus took the lead in redrafting the proposal, effectively removing the comments Molotov found objectionable. Luckily, while Dulles was uncomfortable with some of these concessions, he accepted them since the key principles remained.[55] As a result, after lengthy and often rancorous debate, the four foreign ministers agreed that a meeting of their nations would take place at Geneva on 26 April 1954 to resolve the Korean question. The United States would invite the ROK and the other UN contributing states while the Soviet Union would invite the PRC and the DPRK. If the discussions on Korea made satisfactory progress then a separate but contemporaneous conference on Indochina could be established, with its composition to be decided at the time.[56]

Anglo–American relations had been tested at the Berlin Conference. At the heart of the problems experienced was Britain's desire to engage with the Communist powers and settle the Korean question to kick-start the process towards *détente*. If this involved Western recognition of the PRC then this was a concession London was willing to make since it had already done this in

144  *Robert Barnes*

early 1950. The Eisenhower administration, conversely, remained wary of engaging with the Soviet bloc and was under no circumstances going to recognize the government of a country it had recently been fighting against. Friction at Berlin was also partly a response to the poor relations that existed between Eden and Dulles. The two men had quarrelled over a number of issues in the past and Eden had even advised Eisenhower not to appoint Dulles as his Secretary of State in November 1952. Additionally, the Englishman's extroverted aristocratic personality distinctly clashed with that of the dour Presbyterian American.

## The Korean phase of the 1954 Geneva Conference

Despite the agreements reached at Berlin, the two-and-a-half month period before the opening of the 1954 Geneva Conference was full of controversy. The Eisenhower administration's priority was convincing the reluctant ROK government to participate. On his part, Rhee demanded vast amounts of military assistance from Washington before finally agreeing to attend just eight days before the conference was due to begin. The Western sponsors also ran into many difficulties with Moscow in regard to the technical arrangements for the conference. The three Western governments argued that the conference should take place in the UN's Palais des Nations and be serviced by UN Secretariat personnel, since this was the only practical solution and would maintain the world organization's link with the Korean question. The Soviet leadership, however, opposed any UN role until only a few weeks before the conference was due to start when they accepted there was no real alternative. In addition, Anglo–American friction flared up over the seating arrangements at the conference. The Eisenhower administration remained adamant that it would only accept a two-sided conference. But the British government argued that a round-table conference would be more conducive to compromise. Yet with the conference about to start Eden conceded to prevent a major crisis occurring. A horse-shoe seating arrangement, with the delegations seated in alphabetical order, was thus finally agreed with the Soviet Union.[57]

More significantly, planning for the Geneva Conference was greatly complicated by events in Indochina. On 12 March 1954 the Viet Minh launched a final assault on the French military's stronghold at Dien Bien Phu sparking a major crisis within the Western alliance. The US government, now funding 80 per cent of France's military effort, seriously contemplated direct intervention in the conflict and even the use of atomic weapons. But in the end Washington decided to supply the French only with additional aircraft and pilots. Central to this decision was the British reaction. The Eisenhower administration was only willing to deploy US troops to Indochina as part of a coalition with the British. The Churchill government, however, was convinced that the French would be defeated and that the best course was to find an acceptable political solution at the negotiating table.

*Korea and the 1954 Geneva Conference* 145

Ominously, the Korean phase of the Geneva Conference got underway at the height of this crisis. Hence from the outset it was clear that all the non-Korean participants shared the view that Indochina was now the much more important international crisis and should be dealt with straightaway. In addition, the majority of the delegations present agreed that a balance of power now existed in Korea, the resumption of hostilities was unlikely, and the peninsula could be allowed to remain divided since a solution acceptable to all would be impossible to attain. As a result, neither side was willing to make any significant concessions which risked its position on the peninsula. Nevertheless, in accordance with the Berlin agreements, the Korean phase of the conference had to be dealt with before Indochina could be discussed. The question that plagued the US and British delegations in Geneva, therefore, was how to terminate the talks on Korea as expeditiously as possible.

The first act of the conference was to appoint Eden, Molotov and Prince Wan Waithayakon, the foreign minister of Thailand, as its joint chairmen.[58] While the chairmanship was a strictly administrative position, Eden believed that his appointment placed him in a position of responsibility for the fate of the conference. For that reason he felt that the conference had to be treated as a genuine attempt to find a solution to the Korean question even if he had little faith that the unification of the peninsula could be achieved. Eden also desired real dialogue with the Communist side, especially with the Chinese whom he hoped to entice back into international society and away from the USSR. To achieve these ends Eden proposed that the UN side put forward a moderate proposal from the start in order to win over international opinion. If, as expected, the Communists rejected this position the Korean talks could be terminated without any harm being done to the Western alliance. Attention could then shift to the Indochina question. Importantly, this strategy garnered widespread support, particularly from Britain's Commonwealth partners.

Dulles agreed with Eden that the likelihood of finding a breakthrough on Korea was minimal and made this clear by declaring he would only attend the first week of the conference, during which he controversially refused to shake hands with Zhou Enlai.[59] But, despite these views, Dulles wanted to drag out the conference for two reasons. First, he believed that the longer the Communists were exposed to international scrutiny the more they would demonstrate their intransigence. This would allow the UN side to break off the negotiations while winning a propaganda victory. Furthermore, Washington needed time to coordinate its policy with the ROK government. This process had begun long before the conference opened since the US government appreciated that South Korea had the most at stake. Yet the Eisenhower administration feared that if Seoul adopted an aggressive independent policy at the conference this would highlight the divisions within the Western alliance and permit the Communists to end the talks in an advantageous position.[60] Accordingly, the US ambassador to the ROK, Ellis Briggs, and Dulles' special envoy Arthur Dean, pressed Rhee to temper his views. At the

146　*Robert Barnes*

same time, the US delegation worked more closely with its South Korean counterpart, led by Foreign Minister Pyun Yung-tai, than with any other delegation at the conference.

Still, when the plenary sessions on Korea commenced Pyun called for the Chinese 'aggressors' to withdraw from Korea and for UN-observed elections to take place solely in North Korea to fill the 100 seats left open in the ROK National Assembly. In retaliation, the North Korean representative, Nam Il, demanded that all foreign forces be withdrawn within six months and that all-Korea elections be arranged by an equal North-South committee in order to establish a new fully representative government.[61] In the debates that followed, the Soviet and Chinese delegations backed Nam Il's proposal while the Americans supported Pyun's suggestion. Significantly though, very few of the other UN contributing states, including Britain, became involved in the debate at this stage. This silence infuriated Dulles who, shortly before leaving Geneva, strongly complained to Eden that the British delegation had not spoken to defend the US position despite the attacks being made by the Communist representatives. He claimed this presented 'a pathetic spectacle of drifting without any agreed policy or purpose'. In response, Eden explained that Britain and the other Commonwealth delegations had not spoken in the debate since they did not want to get tied to the ROK formula which they opposed.[62]

And so by the end of the first week of the conference the UN side was thoroughly divided. The new head of the US delegation, Under-Secretary of State Walter Bedell Smith, nonetheless, was determined to find a means to bring the Korean phase of the conference to a close in a way acceptable to both Britain and the ROK. The impetus for this drive was the news on 8 May 1954 that Dien Bien Phu had fallen to the Viet Minh. As a result, the Indochina phase of the conference commenced and Washington now wished to focus its attention on this matter. The Eisenhower administration was also concerned that the united Communist side was so far winning the psychological battle. Smith thus called for the UN side to formulate a set of general unification 'principles' that would uphold the UN's authority to answer the Korean question. He thought this could best be achieved by calling for the world organization to supervise all-Korea elections. Smith had no apprehensions that the Communists would accept this proposal since they had consistently refuted the UN's right to interfere in Korea's future. But he hoped both the British and South Koreans might accept this proposal as a means to terminate the talks.[63]

Significantly, the US government discussed this proposal with the ROK in Seoul and Geneva before it approached the British. Rhee and Pyun, however, continued to argue against all-Korean elections and to demand China's immediate withdrawal. After almost a fortnight of fruitless discussions, Smith then sought to coordinate policy with the United States' other allies, starting with the British. Eden welcomed the idea of all-Korea elections but was less certain over the principle of UN supervision. He argued that if the

Communist side was willing to accept some form of international supervision then the British government would find it difficult to justify terminating the talks on the UN principle. Furthermore, Eden argued that the talks should not be terminated without any prospect of resurrecting them in the future. Working closely with Menon, who was present in Geneva even though India was not a participant, Eden therefore suggested that a statement be issued highlighting the 'points of agreement' with the Communists. However, the US delegation dismissed this proposal out of hand since it did not want to commit to another round of negotiations given the lack of progress at Geneva.[64]

Meanwhile, at a meeting of the sixteen allied delegations Pyun had unexpectedly presented a fourteen-point unification plan that essentially embodied Smith's principles.[65] The reasons behind the ROK's *volte face* are unclear, although it is probable that Rhee finally accepted the US argument that the Communists would reject these principles, thus allowing the Korean discussions to be terminated. Evidently, the South Korean president preferred no unification plan over one that might jeopardize the ROK's and his own future. In addition, Rhee knew that he could only push Washington so far since his country relied on American support and goodwill.

In this climate, Eden also now accepted the US proposal in the interest of Anglo–American relations, stating that the principle of UN supervision was defensible, and because he agreed that the Indochina phase was now the priority.[66] Consequently, all of the sixteen Allied delegations, including the British and South Koreans, worked in harmony to draft a declaration terminating the conference if the Communists rejected the principle of UN supervision.[67] This plan was put into action on 15 June 1954 when the Communist side refused to accept the UN's authority in this matter, claiming that the world organization was a belligerent in the conflict and had no right to interfere in the domestic affairs of a sovereign state. The Korean phase of the conference thus ended without any decisions being taken on the fate of the peninsula.[68]

The US delegation had achieved its difficult task of holding together its disparate allies in Geneva. The divisions within the UN side, however, had not been kept private. Smith's claims on his return to Washington that allied unity had been maintained throughout the conference thus sounded false.[69] The US Under-Secretary of State was far more truthful in his telegram to the Department of State a week earlier when he wrote of relations with the other members of the UN side, 'it was like herding a flock of rabbits through a hole in a fence, and there was cause for extreme exasperation'.[70] Clearly, Washington's and London's differing loyalties and conceptions of the Cold War had come to the fore at Geneva creating friction between the two Western allies. But in the end the US delegation, due in large part to Smith's patience and skill, was able to force Britain and the ROK to toe the line. Even so, the US delegation did make a number of concessions to appease Eden and his Commonwealth partners allowing attention to shift to the more pressing Indochina crisis.

## Conclusion

The eleven months following the signing of the Korean Armistice Agreement represented a dangerous period in the Cold War. The prospect of fighting in Korea resuming loomed large while the situation in Indochina threatened to create another 'hot' conflict on the Asian mainland. Additionally, with Stalin's death and recent Eisenhower's election much uncertainty existed. Some, such as Churchill, hoped that tensions between the two blocs could be lifted but others, most notably Dulles, were seeking ways to put pressure on Moscow. For these reasons it is understandable why the crisis in Anglo–American relations regarding the post-war political conference on Korea has been largely ignored by historians. Yet the level of tension created between the United States and Britain surrounding this issue was palpable.

On the membership question, Washington and London came extremely close to splitting at the UN over India's right to participate, demonstrating that the two capitals had differing alliance loyalties. But Britain did eventually concede, prioritizing Anglo–American relations over Commonwealth allegiances. Then again at the Berlin Conference Dulles and Eden clashed repeatedly over the Soviet proposal for a five-power conference, including the PRC, to resolve all outstanding Asian issues. Here the United States' and Britain's opposing conceptions on establishing dialogue with the Communist states proved troublesome. Still, Dulles and Eden were willing to compromise paving the way for the agreement to hold the Geneva Conference. Rifts between the US and British delegations during the Korean phase of this conference, however, were quick to reappear. The Eisenhower administration, eager to work closely with the ROK government and with no interest in appeasing the Communists, wished to take a hard line. In stark contrast, the Churchill government, with the support of its Commonwealth partners, wished to put forward a proposal that at least appeared to be a genuine attempt to bring about Korean unification. Nonetheless, events in Indochina made terminating the Korean negotiations everyone's priority. Eden thus accepted Smith's principle of UN supervision of all-Korea elections before any lasting harm was done to the special relationship.

The Korean phase of the 1954 Geneva Conference marked the final time the international community seriously attempted to find a solution to the Korean unification question. Nevertheless, for two decades after Geneva the Korean item continued to be debated at the UN. But discussions invariably descended into a propaganda contest over whether the DPRK should be invited to participate. Evidently, the two Koreas and their superpower patrons were satisfied with the status quo for the time being. Importantly for Anglo–American relations Britain happily followed America's lead at the UN. After the problems encountered between the two states over the making and breaking of the Korean phase of the Geneva Conference, neither Washington nor London wished to revisit this issue. For the British government Korea was no longer a problem over which it was worth risking the special relationship. For the US administration Korea had become its responsibility and it would not accept any more allied interference on this matter.

## Notes

1 Peter Lowe, *The Origins of the Korean War*, London: Longman, 1986.
2 Peter Lowe, *Containing the Cold War in East Asia: British Policies towards Japan, China and Korea, 1948–1953*, Manchester: Manchester University Press, 1997; *The Korean War*, Basingstoke: Macmillan, 2000; 'Great Britain, Japan, and the Korean War, 1950–1951', *Proceedings of the British Association for Japanese Studies* 9 (1984), pp. 98–111; 'An Ally and a Recalcitrant General: Great Britain, Douglas MacArthur and the Korean War, 1950–1', *English Historical Review*, 115:416 (1990), pp. 624–53; 'Hopes Frustrated: The Impact of the Korean War upon Britain's Relations with Communist China, 1950–1953', in T.G. Fraser and Keith Jeffery (eds), *Men, Women and War*, Dublin: Liliput Press, 1993; 'The Frustrations of Alliance: Britain, the United States, and the Korean War, 1950–1951', in J. Cotton and I. Neary (eds), *The Korean War in History*, Manchester: Manchester University Press, 1989; and 'The Settlement of the Korean War', in J. Young (ed.), *The Foreign Policy of Churchill's Peacetime Administration, 1951–1955*, Leicester: Leicester University Press, 1988.
3 For the best accounts of the implementation of the Korean Armistice Agreement see, for example, Sydney Bailey, *The Korean Armistice*, Basingstoke: Macmillan, 1992, pp. 141–9, 171–7; Shiv Dayal, *India's Role in the Korean Question: A Study in the Settlement of International Disputes under the United Nations*, New Delhi: Chand, 1959, pp. 192–259; and Rosemary Foot, *A Substitute for Victory: The Politics of Peacemaking at the Korean Armistice Talks*, Ithaca, NY: Cornell University Press, 1990, pp. 190–205.
4 For the most detailed accounts of the Korean phase of the 1954 Geneva Conference see, for example, Bailey, *Korean Armistice*, pp. 150–70; Henry Brands, 'The Dwight D. Eisenhower Administration, Syngman Rhee and the "Other" Geneva Conference of 1954', *Pacific Historical Review*, 56:1 (1987), pp. 59–85; Matsuda Haruka, 'A Clash of Empires in East Asia: The Geneva Conference on Korea, 1954', *Seoul Journal of Korean Studies*, 20:2 (2007), pp. 193–211; and Ra Jong-Yil, 'The Politics of Conference: The Political Conference on Korea in Geneva, 16 April–25 June 1954', *Journal of Contemporary History*, 34:3 (1999), pp. 399–416.
5 For more on Churchill's attempts to lessen tensions with the Soviet Union see, for example, Steven Lambakis, *Winston Churchill, Architect of Peace: A Study of Statesmanship and the Cold War*, Westport, CT: Greenwood, 1993, pp. 137–61; Klaus Larres, *Churchill's Cold War: The Politics of Personal Diplomacy*, New Haven, CT: Yale University Press, 2002, pp. 189–240; Daniel Williamson, *Separate Agendas: Churchill, Eisenhower, and Anglo–American Relations, 1953–1955*, Lanham, MD: Lexington, 2006, pp. 13–29; and John Young, *Winston Churchill's Last Campaign: Britain and the Cold War*, Oxford: Oxford University Press, 1995, pp. 131–82.
6 For more on the Eisenhower administration's views on the post-Stalin Soviet leadership see Robert Bowie and Richard Immerman, *Waging Peace: How Eisenhower Shaped an Enduring Cold War Strategy*, New York: Oxford University Press, 1998, pp. 109–22, 149–57, 224–7; Dwight Eisenhower, *The White House Years: Mandate for Change, 1953–1956*, New York: Doubleday, 1963, pp. 143–9; Townsend Hoopes, *The Devil and John Foster Dulles*, Boston, MA: Little Brown, 1973, pp. 170–5; and Richard Immerman, *John Foster Dulles: Piety, Pragmatism and Power in US Foreign Policy*, Wilmington, DE: Scholarly Resources, 1999, pp. 52–5, 59–61, 70.

150  *Robert Barnes*

7  The National Archives, Kew (TNA) FO371/105524 Lloyd (UN NYC) to Salisbury 13 Aug. 1953.
8  Dwight David Eisenhower Library, Abilene, Kansas, (DDEL), Papers of JFD – Telephone Calls series, box 1, file: telephone memos (except to and from White House) July–Oct. 31, 1953 (3), telephone conversation (Lodge) 12 Aug. 1953.
9  DDEL Papers of JFD – Telephone Calls series, box 1, file: telephone memos (Except to and from White House) July–Oct. 31, 1953 (3), telephone conversation (Lodge) 14 Aug. 1953.
10  TNA FO371/105525 Salisbury to Lloyd 14 Aug. 1953.
11  DDEL Papers of JFD – Telephone Calls series, box 1, file: telephone memos (Except to and from White House) July–Oct. 31, 1953 (3), telephone conversation (Lodge) 14 Aug. 1953.
12  TNA FO371/105525 Salisbury to Lloyd 15 Aug. 1953.
13  TNA FO371/105525 Lloyd to Salisbury 15 Aug. 1953.
14  TNA FO371/105524 Salisbury to Lloyd 13 Aug. 1953.
15  TNA FO371/105525 Lloyd to Salisbury 15 Aug. 1953.
16  *Foreign Relations of the United States (FRUS) 1952–54* vol. XV memorandum of conversation Lodge (UN NYC) 14 Aug. 1953, pp. 1494–5.
17  TNA FO371/105526 Lloyd to Salisbury 18 Aug. 1953.
18  United Nations General Assembly (UNGA), Official Records, 7th Session 1st Committee 613–618th meetings 18–21 Aug. 1953, pp. 699–730.
19  National Archives and Records Administration (NARA), Archives II, College Park, Maryland, RG59/250/49/26/07 entry 1380, box 2, file: 7th General Assembly, Assistant Secretary of State for UN Affairs (Robert Murphy) to Dulles 19 Aug. 1953.
20  DDEL Papers of JFD – Telephone Calls Series, box 1, file: Telephone Memos (Except to and from White House) July–Oct. 31, 1953 (3), telephone conversation (Lodge) 24 Aug. 1953.
21  TNA FO371/105526 Salisbury to Lloyd 24 Aug. 1953.
22  TNA FO371/105526 Lloyd to Salisbury 23 Aug. 1953.
23  UNGA 7th Session 1st Committee 623rd meeting 25 Aug. 1953, pp. 749–55.
24  TNA FO371/105527 Salisbury to Lloyd 27 Aug. 1953.
25  UNGA 7th Session 1st Committee 625th meeting 27 Aug. 1953, pp. 765–70.
26  TNA FO371/105527 Lloyd to Salisbury 27 Aug. 1953.
27  UNGA 7th Session Plenary 430th meeting 28 Aug. 1953, pp. 724–34.
28  NARA RG84/350/63/05/04 entry 2846, box 2, file: 310 – Political Conferences Jan.–Oct. 1953 vol. I, Dulles to Dept. of State 17 Sept. 1953.
29  NARA RG59/250/49/06/03 entry 1198, box 2, file: Korean Political Conference Oct. 1953 (1), Zhou Enlai to Hammarskjold 19 Oct. 1953.
30  For a detailed analysis of Dean's mission to Panmunjom, see Princeton University Library (PUL), John Foster Dulles Oral History Project, Arthur Dean interview 21 May and 13 July 1964, pp. 77–88.
31  *FRUS 1952–54* vol. XV Dean (Munsan-Ni) to Dulles 1 Nov. 1953, pp. 1578–9.
32  *FRUS 1952–54* vol. XV Dulles to Dean 4 Nov. 1953, pp. 1587–8.
33  NARA RG84/350/63/05/04 entry 2846, box 2, file: 310 – Political Conference November 1953 vol. II, Dulles to Dean 18 Nov. 1953.
34  NARA RG84/350/63/05/04 entry 2846, box 4, file: 312 – United Nations (UN) 1953–1954–1955, Dulles to Lodge 20 Nov. 1953.
35  TNA FO371/105596 Lloyd minute 25 Nov. 1953.
36  TNA FO371/105596 Eden to Jebb (UN NYC) 1 Dec. 1953.
37  TNA FO371/105596 Jebb to Eden 2 Dec. 1953.
38  TNA FO371/105596 Eden to Jebb 3 Dec. 1953.
39  UNGA 8th Session Plenary 470th meeting 8 Dec. 1953, p. 446.
40  *FRUS 1952–54* vol. XV Dean to Dulles 8 Dec. 1953, pp. 1651–2.

# Korea and the 1954 Geneva Conference 151

41 NARA RG84/350/63/05/04 entry 2846, box 4, file: 312 – United Nations (UN) 1953–1954–1955, Dulles to Dean 9 Dec. 1953.
42 *FRUS 1952–54* vol. XV Dean to Dulles 12 Dec. 1953, pp. 1655–7.
43 *FRUS 1952–54* vol. V Communiqué of the Bermuda Conference of the Heads of Government of the United States, United Kingdom, and France, Bermuda 7 Dec. 1953, pp. 1838–9.
44 TNA FO371/105597 Jebb to Lloyd 14 Dec. 1953.
45 NARA RG84/350/63/05/04 entry 2846, box 4, file: 312 – United Nations (UN) 1953–1954–1955, Dulles to Allen (New Delhi) 17 Dec. 1953.
46 *FRUS 1952–54* vol. XV Dulles to Young (Munsan-Ni) 29 Dec. 1953, pp. 1675–7.
47 NARA RG84/350/63/05/04 entry 2846, box 4, file: 312 – United Nations (UN) 1953–1954–1955, Dulles to Lodge 20 Jan. 1954.
48 *FRUS 1952–54* vol. V Young to Dulles 26 Jan. 1954.
49 *FRUS 1952–54* vol. VII Dulles (Berlin) to Dept. of State 25 Jan. 1954, pp. 814–17.
50 *FRUS 1952–1954* vol. VII Dulles to Dept. of State 24 Jan. 1954, pp. 790–3.
51 TNA FO371/110574 Eden (Berlin) to FO 25 Jan. 1954.
52 TNA CAB128/27 CC(54) 5th Cabinet meeting 26 Jan. 1954.
53 *FRUS 1952–1954* vol. VII Dulles to Dept. of State 4 Feb. 1954, pp. 953–4.
54 *FRUS 1952–1954* vol. VII Dulles to Eisenhower 6 Feb. 1954, pp. 982–3.
55 *FRUS 1952–1954* vol. VII Dulles to Dept. of State 15 Feb. 1954, pp. 1106–7.
56 *FRUS 1952–54* vol. VII Final Communiqué of the Berlin Conference 18 Feb. 1954, pp. 1205–6.
57 For detailed documentary evidence on the pre-Geneva Conference planning, see *FRUS 1952–54* vol. *XVI*, pp. 14–142.
58 *FRUS 1952–54* vol. XVI Dulles (Geneva) to Dept. of State 26 Apr. 1954, pp. 144–5.
59 This incident is graphically recounted in PUL John Foster Dulles Oral History Project, U. Alexis Johnson interview, 28 May 1966, pp. 20–1.
60 *FRUS 1952–54* vol. XVI, Second Meeting of the Heads of the 16 Allied Delegations, US Delegation (Geneva) to Dept. of State 28 Apr. 1954, pp. 156–8.
61 *FRUS 1952–54* vol. XVI Dulles to Dept. of State 27 Apr. 1953, pp. 148–51.
62 *FRUS 1952–54* vol. XVI Dulles to Dept. of State 30 Apr. 1954, pp. 165–8.
63 *FRUS 1952–54* vol. XVI Smith (Geneva) to Embassy in Korea 4 May 1954, pp. 201–2.
64 *FRUS 1952–54* vol. XVI Smith to Dept. of State 1 June 1954, pp. 333–4.
65 *FRUS 1952–54* vol. XVI Smith to Dept. of State 21 May 1954, pp. 304–6.
66 *FRUS 1952–54* vol. XVI Smith to Dept. of State 11 June 1954, pp. 361–5.
67 *FRUS 1952–54* vol. XVI Smith to Dept. of State 14 June 1954, pp. 371–2; Smith to Dept. of State 15 June 1954, pp. 374–6.
68 *FRUS 1952–54* vol. XVI Declaration by the Sixteen, 15 June 1954, pp. 385–6.
69 DDEL, Papers of Dwight D. Eisenhower, Legislative Meetings Series, box 1, legislative meetings 1954 (3) [May-June], Memo for the record 23 June 1954.
70 *FRUS 1952–54* vol. XVI Smith to Dept. of State 16 June 1954, pp. 389–90.

# 10 A withdrawal from Empire

## Hong Kong–UK relations during the European Economic Community enlargement negotiations, 1960–3[1]

*David Clayton*

During the height of the Cold War, 1949–85, Hong Kong, a developing country, was dependent economically on relations with the West, that is, on exchanges of capital, men and goods with high-income markets. Hong Kong's economic relations with Britain were particularly important. In an age of strict controls, private money still flowed relatively unhindered between London and Hong Kong, and the colonial state held its monetary reserves in the City of London, providing support for sterling and generating revenue for British banks.[2] During a golden period of growth, 1950–73, trade between Britain and Hong Kong, the focus of this chapter, grew quickly; this industrializing colony sold low-cost cotton textiles, garments, footwear and electronic goods to Britain, and bought capital and high-quality consumer goods in return.

During the Cold War, an era when Britain's policy of retaining Hong Kong was constantly under review, imperial economic relations were subject to two shocks: the 1967 devaluation of sterling, which affected capital flows, and EEC enlargement, c. 1960–73, which affected trade. As documented by Schenk, the 1967 devaluation of sterling was a major shock for Hong Kong.[3] The British government devalued Hong Kong's sovereign wealth fund but did not notify the colonial state in advance, and post-devaluation monetary policy generated tensions because Hong Kong was not allowed to diversify its currency reserves. During this crisis, the Hong Kong government managed to secure a small concession, a guarantee for its official sterling reserves because the British government predicated that private banks in the colony would have diversified out of sterling without an insurance scheme.

EEC enlargement was a different type of colonial crisis. British government attempts to enter into a customs union with the existing members of the EEC – Belgium, the Netherlands, Luxemburg, France, Germany and Italy (the Six) – lasted from the early 1960s until 1973. During the first round of negotiations, 1961–3, entered into by Harold Macmillan's Conservative government, one of the issues preventing a settlement was uncertainty regarding how the common external tariff (CET) would be applied to duty-free imports into the UK from Hong Kong.

As shall be documented, Macmillan's government, which had been under intense pressure from protectionist business interests since the late 1950s to curb imports from the Asian Commonwealth, perceived EEC enlargement as an opportunity to manage the decline of low-cost industries in Britain. But, by 1963, the government had not constructed a settlement that balanced British and Hong Kong interests. This strained political relations between Hong Kong and Britain.

To support British diplomacy the colonial administration and the organized business community in Hong Kong fed the British government commercial intelligence, conducted shadow diplomacy and lobbied a constituency of British politicians opposing Britain's integration into Europe. As historians have clearly documented, Hong Kong gained considerable political autonomy from London in the 1950s and 1960s.[4] But with respect to important issues such as devaluation and EEC enlargement, the British government retained considerable power.

This chapter adds to the literatures on decolonization and EEC enlargement. The first section uses this scholarship to show how EEC enlargement complicated Britain's withdrawal from its Empire; the second explains why at a time of rapid decolonization the British government wanted to retain Hong Kong; the third sketches Hong Kong's dependence on the UK market; the fourth presents EEC enlargement as a hypothetical shock to Hong Kong; the fifth and sixth explore how the British government devised mitigation strategies for Hong Kong; the seventh argues that British diplomacy undermined the credibility of the colonial state; the penultimate section details the activities of Hong Kong business groups based in the colony and London. The final section sums up.

## EEC enlargement as history

The value to the British economy of trade with the Empire/Commonwealth declined in the post-war period, while trade with Western Europe grew in significance. As such, Britain's failure until 1973 to join the European Economic Community (EEC), a treaty that committed the Six to common commercial policies, was a missed opportunity: British businesses could have gained improved access to expanding markets and British governments could have turned European integration into a vehicle for the liberalization of global trade/the stringent regulation of capitalism.

A new literature has refuted the standard thesis that Britain failed to secure entry in 1963 because of strategic differences between Britain and France. It argues that the decision taken in January 1963 by Charles de Gaulle, the French President, to veto British membership is explained by practical difficulties afflicting negotiations, most importantly over how Britain's tariff policy towards the Empire/Commonwealth would be modified.[5] Britain's convergence with Europe was, from this perspective, a diplomatic problem that took ten years of discontinuous negotiations to solve. This literature poses a question: why was it so difficult in the early 1960s for Britain to disentangle itself from imperial economic ties?

There is a simple answer: trade with Western Europe did not become more important to Britain than trade with the Empire/Commonwealth until the

154 *David Clayton*

mid-1960s,[6] and so it was not in the country's immediate economic interest to reform its tariff policy. There is an alternative one, that, in 1962, Britain had failed to solve a fundamental problem: how to ensure that an economic withdrawal from the Empire did not damage colonial and Commonwealth economies. In the early 1930s Britain had entered into multilateral obligations that allowed goods from colonial dependencies and the Commonwealth entry into Britain at low or zero tariff rates. By the late 1950s this policy had outlived its economic usefulness to Britain.[7] Conservative governments were committed to the liberalization of world trade. However, the British market was of considerable economic value to certain parts of the Commonwealth (notably New Zealand) and to some colonial dependencies.

Imperial preference also had symbolic value within Britain. It epitomized imperial commitments to aid economic development; to embed representative government; to nurture, via migration and nation-building policies, Britannic identities; and to sustain a strategic alliance that had contributed to Britain's victory in two global conflicts. Imperial preference could not however survive British membership of the EEC, a treaty that committed members to converge on the CET. Therefore during its negotiations with the Six, the British government had to secure transitional trading regimes to mitigate for colonial dependencies and Commonwealth nations the loss of price competitiveness in the British market. During 1962 Britain failed to solve this problem for all parts of the Empire/Commonwealth. Consequently de Gaulle vetoed British entry.[8]

Imperial preference mainly facilitated the exchange of manufactured goods from Britain for primary products from the Empire/Commonwealth. Hong Kong's status was exceptional. As a major exporter of manufactured products, it presented one of the thorniest problems at the EEC enlargement talks. This colonial dependency could have been granted associate membership, duty-free access to European markets, but this would have given the colony's industries a competitive advantage. This concession had been extended to French colonies but was not offered to Hong Kong. This outcome is well known.[9] What remains unclear is how the British government sought – but did not get – a trade regime with the EEC based on written rules that would mitigate the effects of the CET on Hong Kong.

Before turning to tell this technical tale, the next section explains why during an epoch of rapid decolonization the British government was determined to hold on to Hong Kong. Mark's landmark account has detailed the politics of decolonization for Hong Kong carefully, but he has underplayed how UK-Hong Kong economic relations affected the calculations made by bureaucrats in London.[10] The next section uses new material to refine the literature on Hong Kong's decolonization.

## British rule of Hong Kong: a cost-benefit analysis

Hong Kong posed an unusual problem for British governments seeking to withdraw from imperial commitments. Another great power, the People's

Republic of China (PRC), claimed sovereignty, so there was no realistic possibility of independence, and by the early 1960s China had committed itself in private to maintaining the *status quo ante*. Hong Kong, which ran a trading deficit with China, was a useful source of foreign exchange for the PRC. For the British government, Chinese instrumentalism was fortuitous: its possession of Hong Kong benefited the British economy. By the early 1960s symbiotic Anglo–Chinese commercial interests had created a state of equilibrium. Consequently British policy was to 'stay there and to show that we intend to do so'.[11]

The British Empire was a drain on public capital, and had an adverse effect on Britain's balance of payments, a constraint on growth. Hong Kong was however an exceptional colony because the costs of retaining this possession were low and Britain benefited economically from holding on. In 1961 the net cost of maintaining a British garrison in Hong Kong was £2.5 million per annum, and the colony, which ran persistent budget surpluses, had not drawn extensively on metropolitan aid finance. Britain's trading account with Hong Kong was in surplus due to the size of monetary flows. Remitted profits, pensions and earnings from investment, insurance and shipping services were high. Furthermore, Hong Kong banked its private and public reserves of sterling in the City of London, and, if Hong Kong returned to China, these liabilities would have to be met, a 'balance of payments cost' estimated at £100 million.[12] In 1962 one quarter of sterling holdings by British colonial dependencies originated from Hong Kong.[13]

From the mid-1950s the Colonial Office recognized that the 'real cost' of holding on to Hong Kong was being met by a particular British constituency, domestic producers of low-cost manufactures, being out-competed by Hong Kong imports in the UK market.[14] By the early 1960s some of these effects were being mitigated. In 1959 cotton textile producers based in Lancashire had, thanks to interventions by the British government, secured a three-year multilateral set of quotas controlling the growth of exports of yarn and cloth from India, Hong Kong and Pakistan.[15] EEC enlargement was an opportunity to create a permanent, comprehensive trade regime that would manage the growth of exports from the Asian Commonwealth to high-income markets in Europe.[16] Prime Minister Harold Macmillan acknowledged as much in the House of Commons in February 1963:

> In the case of those manufactured goods, which are of special importance to India, Pakistan and Hong Kong, we had hoped, by the negotiation of comprehensive trade agreements, to inaugurate in Europe as a whole a move towards those advantages which we in Britain have given to these Commonwealth countries, often at very great sacrifice to ourselves.[17]

This settlement needed to shore up confidence in British rule in Hong Kong. Since the late 1950s British government actions – imposing 'voluntary' export restraints and retrenching Britain's military expenditure – had 'shaken

156    *David Clayton*

confidence' in the colony. The danger, from the perspective of bureaucrats in the Colonial Office, was that these cumulative processes would cause a tipping point after which local people, in expectation of a transfer of power, would make 'terms with the other side', China.[18] As the next section outlines, Hong Kong's exposure to the UK market for manufactures made EEC enlargement an acute problem for British diplomats.

## The UK market for Hong Kong manufacturers

During the 1950s, a period of extremely rapid industrialization in Hong Kong, trade between Britain and Hong Kong, grew quickly.[19] This reorientation was timely because Hong Kong's entrepôt functions, the mainstay of the pre-war economy, had declined due to China's turn to autarky and because of Western embargoes. In the 1950s, as Table 10.1 shows, the expansion of external demand first in the UK and then in the US compensated for a sharp decline in Hong Kong's export trade with China. By 1960 Hong Kong's trade with Britain was two and a half times larger than Hong Kong's trade with the whole of Western Europe, and, as shown in Table 10.2, for the most voluminous and valuable manufactures, textiles and clothing, the UK market was eight times more important than the West German market, another large and rich economy, which, compared to those in France and Italy, was relatively open to competition from Hong Kong.

By the early 1960s British merchants were sourcing a considerable proportion of imported cloth and clothing from Hong Kong.[20] In 1962 Hong Kong was the UK's largest supplier of foreign clothing, footwear and handbags, providing a third of the total; Italy was the next largest, supplying a quarter. For certain types of clothing UK importers relied almost exclusively on Hong Kong: three-quarters of men's and boy's shirts, and infant gloves came from Hong Kong; over four-fifths of imported canvas 'gym' shoes, fabric gloves and wellington boots were made in the colony. In 1962 Hong Kong replaced India as Britain's largest supplier of imported cotton yarn and cloth, and Italy as the largest source of foreign-made girl's and women's jumpers, cardigans and pullovers.

*Table 10.1* Destination of exports from Hong Kong, 1936–8 to 1960 (%)

|        | UK | USA | Western Europe | China |
|--------|----|-----|----------------|-------|
| 1936–8 | 4  | 11  | 5              | 42    |
| 1949   | 6  | 11  | 3              | 15    |
| 1956   | 9  | 6   | 3              | 4     |
| 1960   | 15 | 20  | 6              | 3     |

Source: Colonial Office, *Quarterly Digest of Statistics*, no. 52, Jan. 1962, Table 7.

Notes: HK$ data was converted by the Colonial Office into standard sterling measures.

*Hong Kong/UK & EECE negotiations, 1960–3* 157

*Table 10.2* Hong Kong's exports and re-exports as a relative share of UK and German import classes, 1965–7

| Product class | UK | Germany |
| --- | --- | --- |
| Clothing | 3 | 1 |
| Cotton fabrics, woven (textiles) | 13 | 1 |
| Footwear | 10 | 1 |
| Made-ups (textiles) | 8 | 1 |
| Manufactured articles | 3 | 1 |
| Telecommunication apparatus (electronics) | 7 | 1 |

Source: *Hong Kong Statistics* (1967), p. 108.


British merchants were buying Hong Kong products because they were cheap. By the early 1960s trade data reveals that Hong Kong industries were out-competing other low-cost producers in the developing world and European producers on price. In 1962 Italian women's jumpers (at £13 per dozen) were a third more expensive than those from Hong Kong (at £10 per dozen). In 1962 in a new international market for transistor radios, German imports (£7) were a fifth more expensive than sets from Hong Kong (£5.6). These price advantages dated back to the early- to mid-1950s, when British manufacturers first began to complain about import penetration by Hong Kong products. In the 1950s UK producers were reporting that their wellington boots were 25 per cent more expensive than boots imported from Hong Kong; that UK-made fabric gloves were 50 per cent more expensive than imported Hong Kong equivalents; and that Hong Kong cloth (drill 3110) was 20 per cent cheaper.[21]

But Hong Kong's ability to penetrate the UK market was not based on price competitiveness alone. This can be demonstrated using a sample of product ranges for which Hong Kong had a large share of the UK market for foreign-made produce but high prices relative to their competitors. With respect to the category of cloth, 'drills, jeans and gaberdines', Hong Kong products were, as Table 10.3 shows, marginally more expensive than other low-cost producers but had secured a much larger market share. Likewise, although Hong Kong held the vast majority of the market for foreign-made cotton underwear (80 per cent), its products were, as revealed in Table 10.4, a third more expensive than those from Japan, the next largest low-cost supplier. The main reason why certain Hong Kong products enjoyed a non-price advantage in the UK market was because the British government was using import quotas to manage the growth of exports from some of Hong Kong's main low-cost Asian competitors, China and Japan.[22] (It is unlikely that Japanese goods were cheaper because they were inferior; and strong network ties between Hong Kong-based export merchants and British retailers and import merchants would only have made a marginal difference, compensating

158   *David Clayton*

*Table 10.3* Average per unit import price of 'drills, jeans and gaberdines' into the UK, and market share of imports by country of origin, 1959–62.

|  | Hong Kong | India | China | Japan |
|---|---|---|---|---|
| Per unit price | 0.09 | 0.09 | 0.08 | 0.07 |
| Market share | 61 | 2 | 10 | 1 |

Source: *Annual Statement of the Trade of the United Kingdom with Commonwealth Countries and Foreign Countries*, 1962, Volume II (HMSO, 1964).

Note: measured by weight, drills were heavy, twilled-cotton cloth; Gaberdines, closely woven twill fabric; and jeans another twilled-cotton cloth.

*Table 10.4* Average per unit import price and import market share in the UK of Hong Kong and Japanese underwear, 1959–62

|  | Unit price (Hong Kong) | Market share (Hong Kong) | Unit price (Japan) | Market share (Japan) |
|---|---|---|---|---|
| 1959–62 | 0.9 | 80 | 0.6 | 2 |

Source: *Annual Statement of the Trade of the United Kingdom with Commonwealth Countries and Foreign Countries*, 1962, Volume II (HMSO, 1964).

Note: class: underwear, measured in dozens, containing more than 50 per cent by weight of cotton.

for higher Hong Kong prices by ensuring that the colony's products were delivered in the requisite quantities and on time.)

As the next section outlines, the primary concern of Hong Kong business interests was that the CET would erode Hong Kong's price competitiveness, but there was also underlying anxiety within the colony that the non-price competitiveness of its exports would be undermined by nascent multilateral efforts to codify the use of import quotas.[23] There had been a sea change in 1961 when the US administration, working through the GATT, had codified the use of quotas against low-cost exporters of cotton textiles and clothing; this allowed GATT members to use quotas as emergency measures, a protectionist regime balanced by a collective undertaking to allow imports to grow, typically at a rate of 5 per cent year. As shall be demonstrated in subsequent sections, this shift created uncertainty, making the implications of EEC enlargement much more unpredictable.

## EEC enlargement as a hypothetical economic shock

Why was enlargement described as the 'biggest question' facing the colony?[24] And why did Governor Robert Black writing in *The Daily Express* argue that Hong Kong's exports would be priced 'off the market'?[25] Essentially because assessments made by business and bureaucratic elites in Hong Kong indicated that, on the application of the CET, Hong Kong would lose half of its share (by volume) in the British market, and that the margins on the surviving trade would be significantly eroded.[26] It was estimated that Hong Kong products paying the CET would become on average 20 per cent more expensive; and British imports from the Six would be on average 20 per cent cheaper.[27] It should be noted (before considering the social costs of this in Hong Kong) that these effects varied across industry. It was estimated that one-third of Hong Kong's grey cloth production was exported to Britain. Faced by combined tariff increases of 36 per cent, a large section of the textile industry would, it was predicated, be 'wiped out'.[28] One-third of Hong Kong's production of certain lines of clothing, such as gloves and brassieres, were also exported to Britain. Faced by tariff rises of between 23–40 per cent, these industries would struggle to compete.[29] Furthermore, new industries, such as transistor radios, dependent on 'home' demand in the UK, might be killed off; as would older industries, such as umbrellas and artificial flowers.[30]

The colonial administration predicted that firms would respond to heightened competition in the UK market by cutting costs. This was a risky strategy because by concentrating production on certain lines it might strengthen demands for stronger quota protection.[31] But it was rational for individual enterprises to cut costs, to maintain their market share. Each sector would have cut costs differently. Garment businesses would have slashed wages; in this industry wages were high relative to production costs. Weaving concerns would have laid off workers; in this industry, capital-labour ratios were high. Merchants may also have cut margins.[32] However they were arrived at, these measures would, according to W. C. G. Knowles, the chairman of the Hong Kong General Chamber of Commerce (HKGCC), cause 'social and political unrest'.[33]

As Hong Kong was a colonial dependency, Britain had a moral obligation to alleviate such distress. In a letter to *The Economist*, Knowles reminded Britain of this relationship. He believed that the suffering caused by EEC enlargement should be 'relieved by subsidy', a fiscal transfer from Britain. This was a powerful message. Thirty-five per cent of the four million residents of Hong Kong depended directly on manufacturing for their livelihoods; and 45 per cent of net domestic consumption derived from the export of manufactures.[34] John Cowperthwaite, Hong Kong's Financial Secretary, also demanded a fiscal transfer from Britain. He proposed that British tariff revenues reaped from Hong Kong imports should be sent to the colonial administration.[35] British bureaucrats viewed imperial patronage as the last resort. The Colonial Office believed that the colonial administration would, given its track record for low rates of investment in the social infrastructure, use any fiscal transfer to augment Hong Kong's overseas holdings of sterling.[36] The colonial state had moreover no mechanisms to target relief to those distressed by the fall in UK demand for their products; the government did not provide unemployment benefits or industrial subsidies. The British government wanted a strategy based on 'trade not aid'.[37] These ritualistic exchanges, a reminder of what was at stake, confirmed the consensual view that the British government had to secure a comprehensive trade deal that would create rules to compensate Hong Kong for any contraction in demand in the UK.

160 *David Clayton*

The next section considers how British bureaucrats using intelligence sent by the colonial administration in Hong Kong sought to create these new rules.

## Framing British strategies

The British government devised two sets of rules to prevent EEC enlargement from becoming an economic shock for Hong Kong: the first sought to maintain Hong Kong's share of the UK market; the second sought to compensate the colony for a contraction in its share of the British market by improving access to consumers in continental Europe. Hong Kong was overcommitted in the UK market, and the scope for expansion of garment exports to the US had been capped as part of the recent GATT settlement. Hong Kong needed therefore to increase its market share in the Six, thus expanding high-income markets. EEC markets bought only 5 per cent of Hong Kong's exports and were protected by high tariffs on textiles and clothing (20 per cent in France, Italy, and the Benelux countries; 12 per cent in Germany); by French import quotas on Hong Kong textiles; and by an Italian informal agreement between importers and domestic manufacturers to restrict access.[38] EEC enlargement presented therefore an opportunity to open up European markets. Could Britain forge a liberal settlement, facilitating market integration between the Six and Hong Kong?

In February 1962 Sir Pierson Dixon, the head of the UK Delegation to the Brussels Conference, stressing the fragility and importance of Hong Kong, a capitalist enclave next to a Communist China, requested that the Six grant associate status to Hong Kong. British bureaucrats did not believe that the Six would accede but they hoped that they would grant Hong Kong modified associate status, that is, some permanent special trading rights.[39] British policy makers drafted rules based on two premises: that Hong Kong should be compensated for losses in the British market by new trading opportunities in the EEC; and that its access to EEC markets should be similar to those of other Commonwealth and British colonial territories. Conscious that this would cause a protectionist backlash, the Board of Trade proposed that exports of textiles from the Asian Commonwealth (which comprised nearly three-quarters of Hong Kong's exports to Europe) should be treated as a separate category. The CET would be applied immediately to all Commonwealth imports of textiles but all existing quota restrictions on textiles would be scrapped. This innovative solution would have provided Hong Kong with an opportunity to expand its market share against India and Pakistan, where productivity levels were lower. As a *quid pro quo* for a protectionist regime all other Hong Kong exports would be allowed into EEC markets duty-free, which would provide Hong Kong with non-price competitive advantages vis-à-vis Japan, and with an opportunity to diversify its export product mix via the growth of its nascent electronics sector.

Doubtful whether the Six would accept this scheme, the government formed alternative strategies. Its second-best option replicated existing schemes to deal with the French trade with North Africa: Hong Kong would gain permanent duty-free entry into Britain but re-exports to the Six would be controlled to safeguard the interests of European producers. Its third-best option entailed the application of the CET by Britain on imports from Hong Kong but at a slower rate than proposed by the Treaty of Rome, a transitional regime governed by periodic reviews and subject to policy interventions to arrest distress. It quickly became clear to British diplomats that there was no chance that the Six would grant to Hong Kong permanent preferences, modified associate member status.[40] This left the government to try and implement its third-best strategy.

During these early diplomatic exchanges both sides waged a propaganda war. The rhetorical position of the Six was protectionist. There were differences between the existing members (from the uber-protectionist French to the more liberal Germans) but the common view was that Hong Kong's exceptionally cheap exports had the potential to ruin European textile and clothing industries. This was nonsense; even if every person in the colony spun, wove, knitted or sowed, and all production was diverted to Europe, Hong Kong industry would never have been able to satisfy all of European demand. This irrational fear was founded on a persistent belief that Hong Kong was re-exporting goods made in China and Japan, large economies that did have the capacity to meet all of European demand for cheap manufactured goods.[41] The British government countered this claim using its own propaganda. British delegates argued that the colonial state was effectively regulating the local economy, clamping down on the falsification of export documents, which had been rife in the early 1950s but which had 'virtually disappeared' by 1962.[42] They also highlighted that the Six ran a trading surplus with Hong Kong, and presented an idealized view of colonialism: that Hong Kong was the Berlin of the East, emblematic of a capitalist route out of poverty. These reasoned and rhetorical positions fell on deaf ears.

This failure to convince the Six that Hong Kong was a developing country worthy of support during the Cold War created a problem: might the Hong Kong issue cause EEC enlargement talks to collapse? The next sections examine how the government handled this diplomatic crisis.

## Implementing British strategies, June 1962 to January 1963

After these propagandist exchanges between Britain and the Six on Hong Kong during the early months of 1962, the British government judged the prospect of an agreement involving Hong Kong so poor that it considered excluding the colony from the negotiations. At this stage, the Six were insisting that, as a condition of entry, Britain must apply in full and with immediate effect the CET on the Hong Kong imports. Under this scenario, discussed with Hong Kong officials, Britain would, once it was a member, have had to provide relief for the colony, and work towards a more liberal EEC commercial policy towards Hong Kong. There was a minor legal problem with this

162   *David Clayton*

solution: the British government would have had to negotiate on behalf of a colonial dependency against itself, the seventh member of the EEC.[43] There was a major political problem: how would Britain manage the fall out in Hong Kong? Colonial officials were extremely concerned by Hong Kong's potential exclusion from a trade deal between Britain and the EEC.[44] If Hong Kong was not included in a final settlement, Britain would have to provide a considerable amount of imperial patronage. And these compensations might be long lived. Hong Kong officials believed that the prospects for liberalization of the EEC trade regime were poor, contingent on a strong alliance between Germany and Britain to oppose the French and Italians. Liberalization might also adversely affect Hong Kong's trading prospects in Europe. A common commercial policy might treat imports from Japan and Hong Kong equitably, destroying Hong Kong's non-price competitive advantages in the UK market.

British bureaucrats were relieved that, after a summer recess, UK-EEC talks resumed and positions had shifted somewhat. By the autumn, the end game was to craft a transitional regime that would provide Hong Kong with time to adjust before its exports to the UK incurred the full CET.[45] By this point, British delegates had a precedent to work with. In the early summer, Britain and the Six had agreed to a transitional regime for India, Pakistan and Sri Lanka. This involved the incremental application of the CET to British imports of cotton textiles, combined with safeguards to prevent market disruption in the Six caused by British merchants diverting cheaper Indian and Pakistan cloth into European markets. But although British diplomats sought to rework this scheme for Hong Kong, this proved far from straightforward. Three problems arose.

The fundamental difficulty was Hong Kong's price-competitiveness. Hong Kong merchants had to be given the same entitlement to trade as those in India and Pakistan. But this meant Hong Kong's market share would expand.[46] This outcome would have destroyed the principle behind the 'voluntary' multilateral agreement capping the rate of growth of Hong Kong, Indian and Pakistan imports into Britain.

The secondary problem related to the compensation mechanisms built into the UK-India scheme. The plan for India was to offset a protectionist regime for manufacturers by a liberal regime for tea. There was no equivalent way to sweeten the deal for Hong Kong. Cowperthwaite suggested one: to allow Hong Kong's cotton textile import quotas to be switched to clothing. But this was not feasible: Lancashire textile interests would have opposed it, arguing reasonably enough that they deserved the same level of protection enjoyed by US garment industries which had already secured quota protection against Hong Kong. [47]

The tertiary problem related to the capacity of the British state to prevent British merchants from re-exporting Hong Kong-made goods into European markets. This was of particular concern to French delegates. The French state had direct experience of operating a control regime for French re-exports of colonial produce from North Africa, and French bureaucrats were still convinced (despite British diplomatic efforts) that a large proportion of Hong Kong goods were made in China. The underlying fear was that British merchants based in Hong Kong, Manchester and London would dump communist goods on the Six. They were therefore not satisfied with a solution that required the model agreed for India applied to Hong Kong.[48] After months of talks they still refused to back a settlement based on a transitional period during which Hong Kong products entered the British markets at rates below the CET.[49] The notion that Hong Kong would dump China-made goods on French markets was outlandish, but French concerns about Britain's capacity to prevent UK merchants re-exporting Hong Kong-made goods was legitimate; the British Board of Trade admitted that UK rules of origin would have to be revised to determine precisely how much re-processing would change the status of a re-export from Hong Kong into a 'British' export.[50]

In sum, by late in 1962 the British government had been backed into its third-best strategy for mitigating the effects of EEC enlargement on Hong Kong. Even so, there were practical difficulties in the way of an agreement. French delegates were distrustful of Hong Kong's mode of capitalism, and were unconvinced that the British government and colonial administration could regulate mercantile behaviour effectively. This strengthened the French case for the use of the veto. The British government had not solved a fundamental problem: how to withdraw from imperial commitments to Hong Kong without damaging the colonial economy or British prospects for entering the EEC.

From the perspective of UK-Hong Kong relations, the decision of the French to end negotiations in January 1963 was fortuitous. For, as the next section outlines, the colonial administration was already struggling to manage an ill-informed public in Hong Kong.

## Managing expectations in Hong Kong

During 1962 anxiety in Hong Kong regarding UK-EEC talks heightened. Early optimism that there might be a liberal settlement faded during the spring, to be replaced by a fear that Britain might converge on EEC levels of protection (rather than the other way around). This shift presented the colonial state with a problem: how to manage local public opinion. As this section describes, the British government denied the colonial state autonomy on this matter.

During the spring of 1962 Britain and the Six had, as previously noted, prioritized reaching an agreement on India, Pakistan and Ceylon. The thorny issue of how to handle Hong Kong was put off. By June, Britain and the Six had agreed to a provisional deal for these Commonwealth countries, and so talks on Hong Kong were finally scheduled for July. With time running out before a summer recess, and with negotiators conscious of how 'very difficult' these discussions were likely to be, these talks were delayed.[51] A joint UK-EEC statement, which merely mentioned that 'appropriate measures'

## 164   David Clayton

would be taken before Britain's entry, heightened concerns in Hong Kong. It was obvious that this vague declaration hid considerable disagreement between Britain and the Six. It provoked a strong reaction in the colony. The Press demanded Hong Kong's representation at the talks.[52] Business interests in Hong Kong labelled the statement as 'totally unsatisfactory'.[53]

The major problem from Hong Kong's perspective was that, despite months of talks, Britain had failed to secure recognition that an enlarged EEC would have a developmental obligation to Hong Kong.[54] Business and professional elites in Hong Kong sensed that the British government would trade-off Hong Kong interests to secure entry into the EEC.[55] Given the local crisis situation, Governor Black and Cowperthwaite requested the right to disclose intelligence on Britain's negotiating positions to local elites and thus begin the process of managing public opinion. Members of the organized business groups had had meetings with UK officials.[56] But UK officials had not discussed detailed policy proposals with them, fearing that they would be leaked and that Hong Kong businessmen would lobby aggressively for a better deal. Colonial officials had long been aware of this information gap. Before the issue of the EEC statement, this was recognized as a problem.[57] After its release, Black felt he must be allowed to prepare his public for bad news, and to begin the process of restoring 'confidence' in colonialism.[58] The Colonial Office refused. It felt that a public relations campaign by the colonial state would at this stage 'grievously weaken' Britain's negotiating position.[59] This decision was only overturned late in 1962 but by then Black did not want to add fuel to the fire.

In October 1962 the Six finally agreed that Britain (but not the EEC) had a right to take into account its 'responsibility' (a developmental obligation) to Hong Kong. This gave Britain the opportunity to devise a transitional regime for Hong Kong, along the lines created for India.[60] This was progress of a sort. The Six also established a working party to formulate a response to British proposals on Hong Kong. Talks had entered the end game. At this point the lack of participation by Hong Kong business elites in decision-making became a major point of controversy between Hong Kong and London. In October a delegation of local 'unofficials' attended meetings in London with Edward Heath, the Lord Privy Seal with responsibility at the Cabinet level for the EEC negotiations, and Duncan Sandys, the Secretary of State for the Colonies. These delegates questioned Britain's ability to prevent a 'loss' of 'confidence' in Hong Kong.[61] They predicted that, if Britain failed to secure preferential terms for Hong Kong, capital would drain from the colony, leading to social and political unrest. The British government's position changed soon thereafter. The colonial administration was instructed to prepare the public for bad news: that the 'solution we shall eventually obtain for Hong Kong is not likely to be welcomed in the territory'.[62] Black refused. It was, he felt, too late. He believed that if the colonial state had leaked information about the provisional deal there would have been 'a substantial loss of confidence'.[63]

The penultimate section explains his reasoning. It shows how, in response to the slow and uneven pace of UK-EEC talks during 1962, Hong Kong business interests engaged in a propaganda war (repeating ineffective British rhetoric deployed early in 1962), practised shadow diplomacy (forwarding negotiating positions already rejected by the Six) and launched a lobbying campaign in the UK that built up parliamentary and press opposition to Britain's entry into the EEC.

## Rent-seeking behaviour by Hong Kong business groups

The EEC enlargement talks strengthened a shift from entrepreneurship – that is, making new products for new markets – to rent-seeking behaviour, monopolistic organizations seeking to control market shares. From August 1962 business groups in Hong Kong lost faith in Britain's ability to influence EEC commercial policy, and so, in an effort to tip some 'finely balanced decision', they invested heavily in commercial public relations.[64]

In response to the impasse in talks, the Hong Kong General Chamber of Commerce, which was dominated by British merchants with strong network ties in London, designated an extra-ordinary budget for public relations, and set up a joint Common Market Committee with the Federation of Hong Kong Industries (FED), a new state-sponsored umbrella organization representing industrial trade associations. This business nexus initially used subscription fee income to pay for lobbying. But, at the end of 1962, the colonial administration agreed to double the stamp duty on exports and imports (from 1 to 2 per cent) and allocate these funds, matched dollar for dollar with revenue from general taxation, for commercial public relations overseas.[65] The administration had used a hypothecated tax to turn private lobbying into a public good. This was a curious decision. Powerful figures in the administration, such as Cowperthwaite, perceived commercial public relations as 'largely a waste of money'.[66] That a parsimonious colonial state granted this concession confirms that it was truly fearful that its relationship with powerful business elites was being seriously damaged by EEC enlargement. It was a decision to shore up its rule. Cowperthwaite was correct. Most of this expenditure was wasteful.

Business rhetoric was ill timed. The leaders of the Hong Kong lobby in Europe, Sir Sik-nin Chau, the chairman of the FED and 'the most influential Chinese in Hong Kong',[67] and businessmen such as P. Y. Tang, one of Hong Kong's most successful textile manufacturers,[68] embodied the territories' status as a developing country with a large émigré population who had escaped communist persecution and avoided penury by embracing the 'free' market. These carefully chosen figureheads stressed the 'political importance of [the] colony to Europe', and the importance of trade to 'absorb and maintain [the] present population including refugee element[s]'.[69] This propaganda message merely repeated official British rhetoric that had already failed to change prevailing views in the Six.

166   *David Clayton*

Shadow diplomacy conducted by white expatriate business elites was also ill timed, and failed to enhance the prospect of a settlement. As late as October, business leaders were demanding that the EEC should recognize Hong Kong's right to 'exceptional treatment', to 'maintain unimpaired' its status as a colonial dependency.[70] British diplomats had already tried out this reasoning. It had cut no ice with the Six. By late in October there was only one end game: getting the French to trust Britain's transitional scheme for managing Hong Kong re-exports to Britain, and on to Europe. At this stage the interventions of Hong Kong business elites must have sowed distrust. The underlying problem was that the Colonial Office had refused to allow the colonial state to keep Hong Kong business elites in the loop at the start of the talks.[71] By their end, they were on the warpath, mobilizing opposition within London.

By the end of 1962 Hong Kong business interests were cultivating pro-Empire members of the Conservative Party, and MPs within the Labour Party that were anti-EEC and pro-Commonwealth. This was astute. During the talks the British public assumed that the Macmillan government would put the interests of the Commonwealth before those of the Six.[72] Expatriate business interests were strengthening the conditions for a press and parliamentary backlash against a trade settlement that failed to honour Britain's developmental obligations to Hong Kong. During a December House of Commons debate on the EEC, Anthony Royle (Conservative: Richmond), a leading figure in the parliamentary Hong Kong lobby who throughout 1962 had requested improved access overseas for Hong Kong goods and improved publicity for the colony's 'magnificent efforts' in housing and education, asked the government how long would elapse before 'arrangement could be completed' for Hong Kong.[73] EEC enlargement talks had entrenched a particularistic imperial network, connecting business elites in Hong Kong with journalists and politicians in London.

## Conclusion

British diplomacy to mitigate the effects of the CET on the Hong Kong economy damaged Hong Kong-UK political relations. By late in 1962 there was a pervasive fear that Britain might enter into the EEC without creating a workable set of rules governing UK-Hong Kong trade. At a time of rising protectionism in the West, this bred uncertainty about the economic future of Hong Kong.

Throughout the early post-war decades confidence in the colonial project rested on the ability of Hong Kong's industries to enter on preferential terms high-income markets in the West. Hong Kong's broker was the British government. But, due to the rise of protectionism at home and overseas, the capacity of the British state to secure good terms for Hong Kong was in decline. Hong Kong's bureaucratic and business elites responded by engaging in their own diplomacy overseas, building up their capacities to influence the formation of bilateral and multilateral rules governing Hong Kong export trade. This had some curious side effects. As documented here, it entrenched a

## Hong Kong/UK & EECE negotiations, 1960–3   167

particularistic imperial network linking together Hong Kong business elites and British politicians and journalists.

Shadow diplomacy gave Hong Kong a voice overseas; delegates from the colony, who took up seats at trade talks in Geneva and Brussels, helped to shape discussions about how the world would manage the integration of developed and developing economies. But during this particular episode, the EEC enlargement talks of 1961–3, the ability of Hong Kong actors to influence outcomes was extremely limited. Using economic intelligence from Hong Kong, the British government devised a range of innovative strategies to mitigate the effects of the CET on Hong Kong exports. But, facing opposition from the Six, it was quickly backed into its third-best option. Attitudes in the Six towards Hong Kong were intransigent, distrustful of Hong Kong business ethics and fearful of Hong Kong's price-competitiveness. Despite this the British government prevented the colonial state from managing public expectations in Hong Kong. At the beginning of the talks there were hopes that EEC enlargement would open up protectionist markets to Hong Kong products, vitalizing the colonial project. This quickly turned into a realization that Britain would have to converge with European levels of protection against Hong Kong. This was a withdrawal from Empire, an acceptance that Britain could not meet its existing developmental obligation to Hong Kong *and* secure entry into the EEC. These talks had deleterious effects on Hong Kong-UK relations, heightening anxieties in the colony, sapping confidence in the colonial project and encouraging the colonial state to turn private rent seeking into a public good, a transfer of money from Hong Kong to journalists and politicians overseas.

## Notes

1 Thanks to audiences at the Department of History, University of Hong Kong, September 2015, and at the British Association for Chinese Studies Conference, Leeds, September 2015; to Mark Hampton; Tak-Wing Ngo; Leo Goodstadt; and especially to Peter Lowe, a sensational supervisor and a wonderful person who first raised questions in my mind about the impact of the Empire/Commonwealth on Britain's tortured history of a member of the EEC.
2 Catherine R. Schenk, *Hong Kong as an International Financial Centre: Emergence and Development 1945–65*, London: Routledge, 2001.
3 C. R. Schenk, 'The Empire Strikes Back: Hong Kong and the Decline of Sterling in the 1960s', *Economic History Review*, 57/3. 2004, pp. 551–80.
4 Ray Yep (ed), *Negotiating Autonomy in Greater China: Hong Kong and its Sovereign Before and After 1997*, Copenhagen: NIAS Press, 2013.
5 N. Piers Ludlow, *Dealing with Britain: the Six and the First UK Application to the EEC*, Cambridge: Cambridge University Press, 1997, and Alan S. Milward, *The Rise and Fall of the National Strategy, 1945–1963*, London: Routledge, 2012.
6 Charles Feinstein, 'The End of Empire and the Golden Age', in Peter Clarke and Clive Treblicock (eds), *Understanding Decline*, Cambridge: Cambridge University Press, 1997, p. 229.
7 Jim Tomlinson, 'The Empire/Commonwealth in British Economic Thinking and Policy', in Andrew Thompson (ed.), *Britain's Experience of Empire in the Twentieth Century*, Oxford: Oxford University Press, 2012.

168   *David Clayton*

8 Stuart Ward, 'Anglo–Commonwealth Relations and EEC Membership: the Problem of the Old Dominions', in Georges Wilkes (ed.), *Britain's Failure to Enter the European Community, 1961–63: the Enlargement Negotiations and Crises in European, Atlantic and Commonwealth Relations*, London: Frank Cass, 1997, p. 105.
9 Ludlow, *Dealing*, p. 85, and Milward, *Rise and Fall*, p. 411.
10 Chi-Kwan Mark, 'Lack of Means or Loss of Will? The United Kingdom and the Decolonisation of Hong Kong, 1957–1967', *The International History Review*, 31, 2009, pp. 1–36.
11 The National Archives, Kew (TNA), CO1030/1298 Cabinet GATT Policy Committee, 'Market Disruption, The Problem of Hong Kong' CO memorandum, 27 July 1960.
12 TNA CO1030/1300, Selwyn minute 6 July 1961.
13 Colonial Office, *Quarterly Digest of Statistics*, no. 52, Jan. 1962, Table 47.
14 TNA CO1030/59 'Hong Kong: Its Value to the United Kingdom, and its Cost', 1957.
15 David Clayton, 'Inter-Asian Competition for the British Market in Cotton Textiles: the Political Economy of Anglo–Asian cartels, c. 1932–60', in A.J.H. Latham and H. Kawakatsu (eds), *Intra-Asian Trade and the World Market*, London: Routledge, 2006, pp. 186–209.
16 This 'cost' was a benefit for British consumers.
17 Hansard Online (http://hansard.millbanksystems.com/), House of Commons Debates, HC Deb., 11 Feb. 1963, vol. 671 cc.943–1072 [accessed 19 Mar. 2014].
18 TNA CO1030/1298 Background notes on Hong Kong for Visit of Secretary of State, June 1960.
19 TNA CO852/2071 'Hong Kong and the Common Market', Hong Kong General Chamber of Commerce (HKGCC) and FED memo, Nov. 1961.
20 For the raw data, *Annual Statement of the Trade of the United Kingdom with Commonwealth Countries and Foreign Countries, 1962*, volume II, London: HMSO, 1964, various pages.
21 TNA BT64/4562 British Rubber Footwear Manufacturers Association to the President of the Board of Trade, 1953; T236/5580 Treasury notes for a Meeting with Lancashire, 20 Jan. 1955; CO129/623/11 Labour Conditions in the Rubber Industry in Hong Kong, [1951].
22 Yokoi Noriko, *Japan's Postwar Economic Recovery and Anglo–American Relations, 1948–62*, London: Routledge, 2003; and David Clayton, 'British Foreign Economic Policy towards China, 1949–60', *electronic Journal of International History*, 2000.
23 Vinod K. Aggarwal, *Liberal Protectionism: the International Politics of Organized Textile Trade*, Berkeley, CA: California University Press, 1985, pp. 63–73, 77–94.
24 TNA CO852/2071 HKGCC General Committee minutes 5 Oct. 1961.
25 TNA CO852/2071 Wooller, (British Trade Commissioner HK), to Sharp (BOT) 16 June 1961; and *The Daily Express*, 26 Sept. 1961.
26 TNA CO852/2074 Clark minute 30 July 1962.
27 TNA CO852/2071 'British membership of the European Common market and its effects on Hong Kong's trade', Economist Intelligence Unit (EIU) report, Oct. 1961, and Sir William Gorell Booth report 15–21 Dec. 1961.
28 TNA CO852/2074 'Effects on Hong Kong exports of withdraw of Commonwealth Preference and Imposition of the CET of the EEC' [summary of Hong Kong memo] 31 July 1962.
29 TNA CO852/2073 Cabinet Common Market Negotiations (Official Committee) Additional Brief on Hong Kong [draft], Note by Colonial Office, March 1962, Appendix B, 'Effects on Hong Kong's Tariff Position of Application by Britain of Common External Tariff '.
30 TNA CO852/2074 Clark minute 30 July 1962.

Hong Kong/UK & EECE negotiations, 1960–3   169

31 Archives and Special Collections, SOAS Library, China Association papers, (CHAS)/C/11–13 'Britain and the EEC with reference to HK', Commerce and Industry Department (HK) 2 Aug. 1966, and Collar (HKA) to Knowles (HKGCC) 14 June 1962.
32 TNA CO852/2074 'Effects on Hong Kong exports', HK memo 31 July 1962.
33 TNA CO852/2071 letter to *The Economist* 27 Oct. 1961.
34 TNA CO852/2072 'The Value of Industry to the Economy of Hong Kong', Colonial Secretariat Jan. 1962.
35 TNA CO852/2073 Cowperthwaite (Fin Sec HK) to Vernon 15 Mar. 1963.
36 TNA CO852/2071 Gorell Booth minute 29 Dec. 1961.
37 TNA CO852/2071 Gorell Booth minute 29 Dec. 1961, and CO852/2072 Morris minute 13 Feb. 1962.
38 TNA CO852/2071 EIU, 'British membership', pp. 4 and 29.
39 TNA CO852/2072 'Supplementary Brief on Hong Kong' CO memo, and 'Common Market Negotiations, Manufactured Goods from the Asian Commonwealth: Cotton Textiles' BOT memo [c. Feb. 1961].
40 TNA CO852/2072 CO to HK, tel. 72 22 Jan. 1962, and Brussels to FO tel. 22 1 Feb. 1962.
41 TNA CO852/2073 Black (Gov HK) to Gorrell Barnes, 16 Mar. 1962.
42 Lawrence Mills, *Protecting Free Trade: the Hong Kong Paradox 1947–97. A Personal Reminiscence*, Hong Kong: Hong Kong University Press, 2012, p. 40.
43 TNA CO852/2074 Brussels to FO tel. 291 18 July 1962.
44 TNA CO852/2074 Cowperthwaite to Trafford Smith, 25 Aug. 1962.
45 TNA CO852/2074 'Common Market Negotiations: Draft Revised Negotiating Brief on Hong Kong', 4 Sept. 1962.
46 TNA CO852/2072 Vernon minute 12 Feb. 1962.
47 TNA CO852/2074 Fisher (BOT) to Morris 11 Sept. 1962.
48 TNA CO852/2075 CO to HK, tel. 1917 19 Oct. 1962.
49 TNA CO852/2076 Robinson (Brussels) to Vernon 20 Dec. 1962.
50 TNA CO852/2075 CO to HK, tel. 1994 30 Oct. 1962.
51 TNA CO852/2074 Brussels to FO tel. 171 6 July 1962.
52 TNA CO852/2074 Woller to Trenaman (BOT) 22 Aug. 1962.
53 CHAS/C/11–13 HKA meeting memo 27 Aug. 1962.
54 CHAS/C/11–13 HKA memo, 27 Aug. 1962.
55 CHAS/C/11–13 Keswick (JM) to Collar (HKA), 11 Aug. 1962, and HKA agenda, 28 Nov. 1962.
56 TNA CO852/2071 Collar to Gorrell Booth 5 Feb. 1962, and CO852/2072 Gorrell Booth report, 15–21 Dec. 1961.
57 CHAS/C/11–13 HKA committee minutes 31 Jan. 1962.
58 TNA CO852/2074 HK to CO tel. 708 18 Aug. 1962.
59 TNA CO852/2074 CO to HK tel. 901 22 Aug. 1962.
60 TNA CO852/2075 Gorrell Barnes minute 23 Oct. 1962.
61 TNA CO852/2075 'Note of meeting with delegation', Trafford Smith 4 Oct. 1962.
62 TNA CO852/2075 Trafford Smith to Cowperthwaite 8 Nov. 1962.
63 TNA CO852/2075 HK to CO tel. 907 30 Oct. 1962.
64 CHAS/C/11–13 Keswick to Collar 24 Aug. 1962; and meeting memo 27 Aug. 1962.
65 This created a considerable war chest, $HK38 million from trade receipts, plus $38 from general taxation in 1962, equivalent to 6 per cent of government expenditure (this calculation is based on the assumption that the tax covered all exports). For the data, *Hong Kong Statistics*, pp. 88, 158, on the policy shift, Public Record Office, Hong Kong, Hong Kong Record Series (HKRS) 270/5/46 Holmes (Director Commerce and Industry) to Cowperthwaite 27 Nov. 1964.
66 PRO HKRS63/1/2701 Cowperthwaite minute 29 Jan. 1962, and Murray to Morris 31 Aug. 1961.

170  *David Clayton*

67  TNA CO1030/1302 Brief for Secretary of State 18 July 1962; and PRO HKRS270/5/45 'Trade Promotion and Public Relations', HKGCC memo 15 Aug. 1962.
68  CHAS/C/11–13 Keswick to Collar 7 Sept. 1962.
69  CHAS/C/11–13 Kite to Keswick 14 June 1962.
70  CHAS/C/11–13 Collar note to the Unofficial members of Council and Common Market Committee 11 Oct. 1962 (appended to minutes 24 Oct.); and Collar to B-C 19 Nov. 1962; and Paris meeting minutes 1–2 Oct. 1963.
71  TNA CO852/2076 Cowperthwaite to Trafford Smith 17 Dec. 1962.
72  Neil Rolling, *British Business in the Formative Years of European Integration, 1945–1973*, Cambridge: Cambridge University Press, 2007, p. 9.
73  Hansard Online (http://hansard.millbanksystems.com/) HC Deb 17 July 1962, vol. 663, cc.220–1; and HC Deb., 11 Dec. 1962, vol. 669, cc.190–1; and HC Deb., 19 Dec.1962, vol. 669 cc.1255–63 [accessed 19 Mar. 2014].

# 11 From Vietnam to Hong Kong
## Britain, China and the everyday Cold War, 1965–7

*Chi-kwan Mark*

On 6 January 1950 the British Labour government accorded diplomatic recognition to the newly-founded People's Republic of China (PRC). Mao Zedong, however, agreed only to the opening of negotiations over the establishment of diplomatic relations. The negotiations started in March but were brought to a fruitless end by the outbreak of the Korean War in late June. Under the spirit of cooperation during the Geneva Conference in 1954, the British and the Chinese agreed to establish diplomatic relations by exchanging chargé d'affaires. Since 1961 Britain voted for China's admission to the United Nations (UN), but also supported the US insistence that this was an 'important question' that required a two-thirds majority for adoption. Nevertheless, the escalation of the Vietnam War and the outbreak of the Chinese Cultural Revolution in the mid-1960s brought Anglo–Chinese relations to their nadir, culminating in the sacking of the British Chargé d'Affaires office in Beijing in August 1967. Not until March 1972 did the PRC finally agree to establish full diplomatic relations with Britain, twenty-two years after the first round of negotiations.

This chapter focuses on British policy and relations with China between 1965 and 1967, a period when the Vietnam War escalated and the radical phase of the Chinese Cultural Revolution was underway. These were critical years when the Labour government, under economic and political pressures, decided to withdraw all British forces from East of Suez by the mid-1970s. According to his detractors, Harold Wilson had once been blinded by delusions of Britain's greatness, but the East-of-Suez decision, together with the (unsuccessful) application for membership in the European Community, epitomized his final recognition that Britain could no longer play a world role in view of its post-war economic decline.[1] This 'declinist' interpretation also explains the 'failure' of British policy towards Communist China until 1972. It has become almost a cliché that, after 1949, declining Britain had no choice but to 'appease' the rising China and to 'kowtow' to Chairman Mao. Nevertheless, one should note that the notion of 'appeasement' associated with Neville Chamberlain's foreign policy in the 1930s has been subject to revisionism in recent years. Rather than being dictated by 'economic decline' and condemned as the 'guilty man', Chamberlain is portrayed by some

## 172   Chi-kwan Mark

revisionist historians as a realistic leader who opted for appeasement after exploring and then rejecting alternative policies as impractical and too risky (albeit with the caveat that Chamberlain was 'right to be wrong').[2]

In his wide-ranging publications on British interactions with East and South-East Asia during the Cold War period, the late Peter Lowe depicted British ministers and officials as pragmatic and flexible, working to achieve accommodation with nationalist movements while containing communist challenges. Although committing policy mistakes and adopting an arrogant attitude towards Asians at times, overall Britain, through flexible diplomacy, 'appeared centre stage' in South-East Asia during the period between 1945 and 1965 (with the 1954 Geneva Conference as a watershed), and 'did exert moderating influence on the United States on significant occasions' (notably during the Korean War).[3] Building on Lowe's analysis of British policy in pre-1965 Asia, this chapter takes a critical look at the Labour government's policy towards China at the height of the Vietnam War and the Cultural Revolution. It argues that Anglo–Chinese interactions in the mid-1960s can best be understood through the theme of the 'everyday Cold War'.[4]

What was the Anglo–Chinese Cold War of the everyday? A highly contested concept, 'the everyday' generally possesses such features as 'ordinary', 'routine' and 'business-as-usual'. The 'everyday life' refers to the mundane, repetitive and taken-for-granted experiences, practices and relations of ordinary people. What facilitates everyday interactions are 'rituals' or 'symbolic actions' that convey deep meaning, foster identity and construct power relations.[5] The Cold War encounter between Britain and China appeared insignificant and uneventful: the relationship was not vital to their national interests, and was not characterized by high drama as compared with the Sino–American confrontation. Besides, the post-1949 power relationship between Britain and China was asymmetrical: preoccupied with Europe and constrained by the domestic economy, Britain was clearly the weaker of the two in Asia. Nevertheless, Britain and China could not but interact with each other in the mid-1960s, thanks to the imperative of the Cold War and the legacy of British imperialism. From Vietnam to the mainland to Hong Kong, the British were confronted with the 'everyday Cold War' waged by the Chinese Communists.

China's 'everyday Cold War' was marked by diplomatic ritual, routine propaganda, and symbolic retaliation. Premier Zhou Enlai attached great importance to the 'form' of diplomacy: the protocol of treating foreign countries and foreign guests in China was closely linked with politics.[6] Ritual carried symbolic meaning and served useful purposes.[7] Symbolically China performed rituals to assert its new identity and status vis-à-vis Britain after the 'century of humiliation' and to signal its displeasure at London's policy. By refusing to recognize the British diplomats as a formal mission but merely 'negotiating agents' until 1954, Mao and Zhou asserted the principles of 'making a fresh start' and 'cleaning the house before inviting the guests' in China's foreign relations.[8] And by refusing to exchange ambassadors until

*The everyday Cold War, 1965–7*  173

1972, the Chinese signalled that Britain, in supporting Taiwan in one way or another, fell short of endorsing their policy of 'one China'.[9] From an instrumental point of view, Beijing's 'everyday Cold War' was intended to split the Anglo–American alliance in accordance with the united front doctrine. Seeing Britain as a declining imperialist power within the 'second intermediate zone', Mao sought to win this 'middle roader' over in order to isolate and eventually defeat the principal enemy, the United States.[10] Yet China also needed to 'struggle' against Britain, through diplomatic protests and hostile propaganda, from time to time due to its vacillating position on Taiwan.[11] Such was the 'everyday Cold War' between China and Britain that encompassed both cooperation and struggle.

\*\*\*

Following the Gulf of Tonkin Incident in August 1964, the Lyndon Johnson administration gradually escalated the war in Vietnam by committing American air and ground forces to South Vietnam. Mao responded by increasing China's military and economic assistance to North Vietnam. To him, the escalation of the Vietnam War was part of Washington's intensified efforts to encircle China.[12] Ideologically, Mao identified the North Vietnamese struggle with the global wars of national liberation, and used it to mobilize the Chinese people for the struggle against the 'revisionists' at home (such as Liu Shaoqi).[13] Caught between Washington and Beijing, Britain needed to walk a tightrope between maintaining the Anglo–American 'special relationship' and averting a direct Sino–American confrontation. At the same time as the situation in Vietnam deteriorated, Britain was committing over 50,000 troops to Malaysia in the 'confrontation' with Indonesia. To prevent a third world war, to keep the Commonwealth united, and to pacify the Labour left wing, Wilson could not afford to associate Britain too closely with American policy. On the other hand, Britain, facing serious balance of payments deficits, desperately needed American dollars to defend sterling against devaluation. Wilson realized that only by demonstrating solidarity with the United States in public would London be in a position to influence Washington in private.[14]

On 9 March 1965 Wilson got the chance to demonstrate loyalty to America. In a parliamentary debate on Vietnam, he indirectly defended the American bombing of North Vietnam:

> A year ago, the general supposition was that the fighting in South Vietnam was a spontaneous, so-called nationalist rising on the part of the Viet Cong people. But now there is no attempt at all to deny the responsibility of North Vietnam who have said that they are fighting a war in South Vietnam. That makes a very big difference, I think, in terms of our analysis of the problem.[15]

174   *Chi-kwan Mark*

Another chance to show public unity with the Americans came on 1 April when Michael Stewart made his maiden speech as Foreign Secretary. In his speech he made some detailed remarks on China:

> We wish to have good relations with China [and] support her claim to her rightful seat at the United Nations... [But] as long as China's attitude to world affairs is dominated by hatred of the United States China will not be able to take the place in the world to which its size, industry, the ingenuity of its people and great cultural heritage entitles that country.[16]

China felt incensed about the British leaders' public display of Anglo–American solidarity. During early 1965 the Chinese propaganda machine intensified its attacks on British policy in Vietnam and elsewhere.[17] On 21 March the *People's Daily* criticized Wilson for 'repeatedly explaining away American aggression in Vietnam on their behalf'. Four days later the paper accused the Prime Minister of defending the American use of gas in Vietnam, which he said was 'not poisonous' and 'no contravention of the Geneva Protocol of 1925 and other treaties'. On 5 April a *People's Daily* commentator article condemned the Labour Government for supporting 'American aggressive actions and war blackmail all along the line' in return for 'United States Imperialism's support for the tottering colonial rule of Britain in the "Malaysian" region'.[18]

The Chinese government, moreover, linked the Vietnam War with the progress of Anglo–Chinese relations. On 31 May the Chinese Foreign Minister, Chen Yi, met the British chargé d'affaires in Beijing, Donald Hopson, for over an hour, covering a range of topics. Chen claimed that the '[b]iggest obstacle to improvement of relations' was the question of Chinese representation in the UN, where Britain had voted in favour of Washington's proposals to 'deny China's rightful place'. But he added that there was now a 'new obstacle' to improvement of Sino–British relations in that the Labour Government was 'supporting United States policy in Viet Nam even more strongly than [the] former Conservative Government'.[19]

Eager to resume Britain's traditional role as peace mediator in Indochina, to pacify the anti-war Labour backbenchers, and to bolster his personal prestige, Wilson made a number of peace initiatives on Vietnam.[20] Nevertheless, China snubbed all the British peace efforts. Until 1969 Mao opposed peace talks as a solution to the Vietnam conflict, for he was confident about the ultimate success of the people's war strategy and needed an external crisis for domestic mobilization.[21] In late March Wilson decided to send Patrick Gordon Walker, a former foreign secretary, as his personal emissary to South-East Asia on a three-week fact-finding tour between mid-April and early May. However, the Chinese government stated that it would not welcome Walker's proposed visit to Beijing.[22] It also showed no enthusiasm for the Commonwealth peace mission proposed by Wilson in June. The timing of this mission coincided with the convening of the week-long Commonwealth Prime

Ministers' Conference in London (beginning on 17 June), and was not far ahead of the Second Afro-Asian Conference at Algiers (scheduled for 29 June–3 July). At the Commonwealth Prime Ministers' Conference it was decided that the Commonwealth peace mission would consist of the leaders of Britain, Ghana, Nigeria and Trinidad. Beijing's propaganda machine fiercely attacked Wilson for manipulating the Commonwealth Prime Ministers' Conference into promoting his peace initiative and, worse still, sabotaging the upcoming Second Afro-Asian Conference. Indeed, at London the thirteen Commonwealth countries invited to attend the Algiers Conference decided to demand its postponement in light of the Algerian coup on 19 June, which overthrew Ben Bella.[23] An article of the *People's Daily* on 22 June lambasted Wilson's scheme 'to organize a so-called "Peace-bid Mission" in Vietnam in the name of the Commonwealth', which 'was entirely inspired by the United States'.[24]

With the escalation of the Vietnam War, then, the Labour government and particularly Wilson himself became a target of Beijing's everyday propaganda. Although Wilson had refused to commit even token British troops to the conflict, his public display of support for Johnson obviously was not lost on the Chinese leaders.[25] More importantly, Mao needed to mobilize the Chinese people for the Vietnamese struggle of national liberation and for the prevention of a 'capitalist restoration' at home. The tone of China's propaganda became more militant, and the themes of 'supporting national independence movement' and 'propagating China's socialist construction' were emphasized.[26] As an old colonial power which was still playing a world role, Britain inevitably caught the eye of the Chinese propaganda machine. British officials were not unaware of the gulf between China's policy and rhetoric, between its power and limits. 'Is China after all only a paper dragon?', asked Hopson when assessing Beijing's diplomatic setbacks on the Afro-Asian front during 1965 – the indefinite postponement of the Second Bandung Conference, the conclusion of a ceasefire in the Indo-Pakistani War, and the sidelining of General Sukarno and the subsequent purge of the Indonesian Communist Party.[27] The Foreign Secretary drew a distinction between propaganda and policy. 'If we were to take [China's] words at their face value', Stewart replied to calls for 'containment of China' in Parliament, 'it would be very alarming indeed.... If we look at China's actions they are, fortunately for mankind, much less bellicose than her words.'[28] After all, unlike America, China had only dispatched non-combat troops to Vietnam. For all the militant tone of Beijing's policy statements and propaganda, the British 'managed to maintain a fairly constant level of mediocrity' with the Chinese during 1965.[29]

On 28 July Johnson announced the dispatch of an additional 100,000 troops to Vietnam. China issued a statement condemning America's 'expansion of its war of aggression against Viet Nam', but without mentioning Britain.[30] However, on 1 September the *People's Daily* seized on the publication of the British White Paper on Vietnam (which featured 63 statements

176  *Chi-kwan Mark*

and articles issued by the interested governments concerned) by criticizing Britain for 'closely following the United States' in Vietnam.[31] The same day, Beijing's propaganda machine found a seemingly mundane issue to make a fuss about – US naval visits to Hong Kong.

\*\*\*

As a British Crown Colony with a deep-water harbour, Hong Kong had been used as a liberty port by the US Seventh Fleet since the Korean War. With the gradual escalation of the Vietnam War, Hong Kong's role as a 'rest and recreation' (R&R) centre for the United States became more important than ever. In 1964, the year when the Gulf of Tonkin Incident occurred, 315 US naval vessels visited Hong Kong. In 1965 the number increased to 330; and during the first six months of that year, approximately 80,000 US armed forces personnel spent R&R vacations in Hong Kong.[32]

Between 1965 and 1967 China lodged three diplomatic protests with the British government about the visits of US warships, planes and military personnel to Hong Kong. The first diplomatic note of 1 September 1965 warned against the use of Hong Kong 'as a base of operations for the United States war of aggression against Viet Nam', which not only 'endangered the peaceful life of the inhabitants of Hong Kong', but also 'posed an increasingly grave threat to the security of China and of Southeast Asia'. At the end of the note, China firmly demanded that Britain should immediately take 'effective measures' to stop all of the US aggressor's activities, otherwise it 'must bear full responsibility for all the consequences arising therefrom'.[33] The second protest note was delivered on 1 February 1966, asserting that the United States was 'attempting further to use Hong Kong as a springboard for its future attack on China's mainland'.[34] On 20 March of the following year, the British chargé in Beijing was summoned to the Chinese Foreign Ministry to receive what was then the third protest about the visits of US ships to Hong Kong in recent months.[35]

In assessing the three separate Chinese protests, the Foreign Office and the Colonial/Commonwealth Office generally concluded that they were routine propaganda. First of all, there was absolutely no truth in the Chinese allegations: Hong Kong had been used by the Americans primarily as an R&R centre, not as a base for military operations. Besides, the British noticed that the timing of the Chinese protests was such that they were all preceded by incidents and announcements that stole the media headlines: in 1965 the crash of a US Marine Corps transport plane into the bay off Hong Kong and the American bombing of the dam and hydroelectric plant southwest of Hanoi; in 1966 the visit to Hong Kong of the nuclear-powered carrier USS *Enterprise* (the first US nuclear warship in action) and Johnson's announcement on the resumption of bombing of North Vietnam after a forty-day pause; and in 1967 the return of the iconic *Enterprise*, among other ships. For the sake of 'face', Beijing simply could not turn a blind eye to these high-profile

# The everyday Cold War, 1965–7  177

events. Nevertheless, despite the 'violent wording' of the first two protest notes, as the Hong Kong Governor observed, there was 'no sustained effort [by China] to bring about a change in the Hong Kong Government's policy': the Chinese protests 'were becoming a matter of routine'.[36] After all, China benefited indirectly from American military tourism in Hong Kong, which was the main source of its foreign currency earnings. Besides, through signalling to London via third parties at the onset of Johnson's escalation of war, by late 1965 the Chinese leaders had become more assured that Britain would not involve Hong Kong in the Vietnam conflict, lest its colonial status be jeopardized.[37] (Likewise, Chen Yi had signalled to the Americans via Hopson about the limits of China's intervention in Vietnam, thereby helping to avert a Korean-type confrontation.)[38]

After 1949 the British were acutely aware that Hong Kong existed in the shadow of its giant communist neighbour. Over time they got accustomed to China's routine protests and propaganda about the everyday issues it exploited, most of which were related to Taiwan or the so-called 'two Chinas' conspiracy – the size of the US consulate-general in Hong Kong, the colonial authorities' toleration of Nationalist activities, publicity about the Chinese refugee problem and so forth.[39] To the British, the three Chinese protest notes were symbolic in that they were primarily designed to communicate more significant messages than the alleged American military use of Hong Kong. In addition to demonstrating its commitment to Hanoi, China also had an eye on Moscow in light of the Sino–Soviet dispute. Back in December 1962 Nikita Khrushchev had criticized China's toleration of British colonial rule in Hong Kong in response to Mao's accusation of his diplomatic climb-down during the Cuban Missile Crisis.[40] In the subsequent years the Soviets continued to meddle in Hong Kong affairs, accusing China of using Hong Kong as 'a kind of loophole into the capitalist world' where it earned foreign currency as well as allowing it to become a 'major foreign centre of slanderous propaganda and subversive activity' against Moscow.[41] The Vietnam War intensified the Sino–Soviet split. As the Foreign Office noted of the second protest:

> China's main purpose ... seems to be to demonstrate publicly their support for Hanoi against the Americans at a time when the latter have resumed full-scale operations in Viet-Nam. This is particularly important for the Chinese when they are under pressure from the North Viet-Namese to increase their support and when they are accusing the Soviet Union of failing in its duty to give all-out support to North Viet-Nam.[42]

Based on these assessments, the Foreign Office sent a non-polemical reply to each of the three Chinese protest notes, stressing the fact that Hong Kong was used primarily for rest and recreation by the United States. To relax tension, some visits by the Seventh Fleet, particularly those close to Chinese national days, were rescheduled. Moreover, the British and American governments formalized some ground rules for the use of the Hong Kong facilities, for example, avoiding undue concentration of US ships at any one time and establishing a Hong Kong-US Consultative Group to oversee the implementation of the new guidelines.[43] All this, the British believed, was the most sensible response to China's everyday propaganda at the height of the Vietnam War.

\*\*\*

Beijing's 'everyday Cold War' against the British was played out most vigorously and, in August 1967, most violently, on the mainland. Since the exchange of chargés d'affaires in 1954, China and Britain maintained merely 'semi-diplomatic relations', thanks to the latter's Taiwan policy.[44] The Chinese Communists placed the British Mission below most of the foreign diplomatic corps in the pecking order, subjecting the British diplomats to rituals that reflected the hierarchical relationship after the 'century of humiliation' (emphasizing that the Chinese people had 'stood up' and that Britons no longer enjoyed extra-territoriality and other privileges in the 'new China'). Not infrequently, the British diplomats were summoned to the Chinese foreign ministry at most inconvenient times and with the greatest urgency to receive routine protest and communication. The tone of Chinese officials was 'abusive, dogmatic and rigid'. On the other hand, the British diplomats were not always accorded access to the Chinese Foreign Ministry.[45] The Chinese authorities placed severe limits on the movement of foreigners within and without China. The British diplomats in Beijing normally enjoyed freedom of movement within a twelve-mile limit from the city centre (plus two nearby beauty spots), but needed permission to travel further. Entry and exit permits were required of them, but applications for exit visas often met with long delays.[46] All this was not in accord with the 1961 Vienna Convention on Diplomatic Relations, signed by Britain but not China, which stipulated the functions of a diplomatic mission and the privileges of diplomatic agents.[47]

The British diplomatic outpost in Shanghai was particularly vulnerable to Chinese pressure. According to an oral agreement in 1954, the British Mission in Beijing was allowed to send one officer to Shanghai to take care of the ever-shrinking British community there, which by mid-1965 numbered less than forty people, many of whom were aging wives or widows of Chinese nationals. However, the Chinese Foreign Ministry insisted that the British representative in Shanghai should 'function only as an individual and not as a mission', and should not carry out so-called 'illegal activities' like issuing passports to 'Chinese nationals' and acting on behalf of third parties such as the United States. Even symbolism mattered: the British officer was told that he had no right to use the Royal Arms on his paper or to fly the Union flag on his car.[48]

During the radical phase of the Cultural Revolution in 1967, the British diplomats on the mainland suffered intense harassment at the hands of the

The everyday Cold War, 1965–7    179

Red Guards and the rebels in the Chinese Foreign Ministry (the liaison station). In May the radicalism of the Cultural Revolution spilled over into Hong Kong, where left-wing elements exploited an industrial dispute to launch large-scale anti-colonial riots. Zhou Enlai was confronted with a dilemma between supporting the leftist struggle and maintaining the colonial status quo, the result of which were contradictory policies designed both to exert pressure on the British and restrain the local Maoists.[49] On 22 May, the day when the Hong Kong police violently suppressed the leftists outside the Governor House, the Chinese Foreign Ministry unilaterally announced the closure of the British office in Shanghai and ordered Peter Hewitt and his family there to leave China within forty-eight hours.[50] From London, Foreign Secretary George Brown sent an urgent message to Chen Yi to the effect that 'an agreement mutually reached between two parties cannot be unilaterally annulled', but, in view of the worsening situation, Hewitt was ordered to withdraw from Shanghai at the earliest opportunity.[51] It was the British diplomats in Beijing who bore the brunt of China's radicalization. Day after day the Red Guards demonstrated outside or passed along the road of the chancery compound and residence, broadcasting anti-British slogans. In their everyday work the British diplomats faced various sorts of Chinese 'pin pricks' or minor harassments, such as refusals to grant exit visas and to handle luggage matters by the Foreign Ministry and strikes by the Chinese staff of their office.[52]

The situation took a sharp turn for the worse during August. In Hong Kong the colonial authorities arrested and imprisoned the journalists of the New China News Agency (NCNA) and other leftist media outlets and suspended the publication of three 'fringe' communist newspapers pending legal proceedings. In response, Beijing put Anthony Grey, the British correspondent of Reuters in China, under house arrest. On the mainland the Foreign Ministry appeared to be in a state of paralysis. On 19 August, emboldened by Wang Li, the rebels of the Liaison Station in cooperation with the Red Guards of Beijing Foreign Languages Institute seized power in the Department of Political Affairs of the ministry.[53] Chen Yi and his vice ministers were forced to make self-criticism; Yao Dengshan (the 'red diplomatic soldier' expelled from Indonesia) was proclaimed the new foreign minister in some big character posters; and the ministry, as Zhou later claimed, was out of control for four days.[54] In this chaotic situation, Zhou approved the suggestion by the Hong Kong and Macao Office in the West European Department that an 'ultimatum' should be issued to the British government, demanding the release of all Hong Kong 'patriotic journalists' and suspension of all the 'illegal lawsuits' against them within forty-eight hours, otherwise Britain would 'be held responsible for all the consequences arising therefrom'. At 10:30 pm on 20 August Hopson was summoned to the foreign ministry to receive the note, which he rejected.[55]

On the night of 22 August (the 'ultimatum' was due to expire at 10:30 pm) the radical Red Guards – mainly from Beijing Foreign Languages Institute,

180 *Chi-kwan Mark*

Qinghua University and other universities in the capital – rallied outside the British Office, where twenty-three British diplomats and wives were effectively besieged. Worrying about an explosive situation, Zhou had instructed the demonstrators not to break into the British Office and had ordered the Beijing Garrison Command to dispatch troops and plain-clothes police to keep order.[56] However, shortly after the expiry of the 'ultimatum', the mob 'pour[ed] through and over the gates like monkeys, breaking windows, smashing furniture, and burning cars'. The British retreated from one room to another, but eventually surrendered themselves to the mob. They were then 'paraded up and down, forced to their knees and photographed in humiliating postures'. Hopson was 'hauled by [his] hair, half-strangled with [his] ties, kicked and beaten on the head with bamboo poles'. Performing a Cultural-Revolution ritual, the Red Guards forced Percy Cradock, the Political Counsellor, to say 'Long Live Chairman Mao', but fortunately they did not press their demand after the British Sinologist had lied that he 'did not understand and remained silent'. After suffering a lot of beating and kicking, the British diplomats were all rescued by the army and plain-clothes police officers. As a result of the four-hour Red Guard rampage, the British Office compound was completely burnt down, and the chargé's house ransacked; but miraculously, none of the Britons was seriously injured.[57]

Ministers in London responded quickly to the sacking of the British Office. Since May they had been contemplating various retaliatory measures against China, such as expulsion of Chinese diplomats from Britain and closure of the NCNA in London. However, ministers regarded placing restrictions on the movement of the Chinese diplomats and NCNA staff in London as the least risky (for Anglo–Chinese relations) and objectionable (to both the Foreign and Home Offices) of all options.[58] On 23 August Wilson flew back from his holiday in the Isles of Scilly to London to discuss the situation with Brown, who himself had returned from his Norwegian vacation.[59] On the same day the Chinese diplomats in London were informed that they would be restricted to an area within a radius of five miles from Marble Arch (unless permitted to travel further), and would require exit permits before departing from Britain. To enforce these measures, the London police and the Special Branch placed the Chinese Legation at 49 Portland Place under close surveillance.[60]

The Chinese response was the so-called 'Battle of the Portland Place'. The Chinese diplomats posted to Western European countries had always felt that they were 'sitting on a cold bench' in a hostile Cold War environment. With the return of all but one of the Chinese ambassadors to the mainland to participate in the Cultural Revolution, the zealous low-ranking staff who stayed behind turned their embassies into 'outposts' for disseminating Maoism in the host countries.[61] Even before the new restrictions on their movement, the Chinese diplomats in London had already felt provoked by a handful of British demonstrators outside their office (for example, members of the Campaign for Nuclear Disarmament protesting against China's hydrogen

The everyday Cold War, 1965–7    181

bomb explosion).[62] The growing presence of British policemen in Portland Place after 23 August only intensified their 'siege mentality'. On 29 August after an earlier incident involving British policemen arresting a pro-China British demonstrator, more than two dozen zealous Chinese diplomats came out to demand the removal of a Special Branch car in the mews behind the mission office. Wielding baseball bats, large axes and iron bars, the Chinese clashed with the British police officers, pushing and pulling each other. The 'battle' did not last long, but in the end eight Chinese required minor hospital treatment and three British policemen were slightly injured.[63] At 5 am on 30 August Hopson was duly summoned to the Chinese Foreign Ministry and was told that with immediate effect, no personnel of the British Office might leave China without permission; exit visas already issued were all cancelled; and all British personnel should confine themselves to their office and residences and to movement between them.[64] The British diplomats in Beijing became de facto hostages of their host government.

\*\*\*

How did the Wilson government react to the events in Beijing and London within the wider context of China policy? After the dust had settled, the Foreign Office received detailed reports from the British diplomats about their personal ordeal on the night of 22 August. A fuller picture of the Red Guard assault emerged. As Hopson observed, 'the whole operation was carefully planned by someone, though by whom and at what level we may never discover'. The assault teams were 'well-organised,' 'knew exactly where to go', and some of them even brought their own petrol. While the whole operation had been carefully planned, it appeared that not all of the Red Guards had followed the script. Hopson estimated that 'the attack was planned by members of the cultural revolution group with the connivance of the security authorities', but it was 'possible that in setting fire to the Office the mob exceeded its instructions'. Related to this, the British diplomats were of no doubt that the 'P.L.A. clearly had orders to ensure [their] eventual safety after a good deal of roughing-up and humiliation'. Besides, the Red Guard posters found by them suggested that Zhou had deplored the burning of the British Office, and had 'taken over direct responsibility for the running of foreign affairs from 23 August'. In retrospect, the sacking of the British Office appeared to be a performance staged by the Red Guards, whose intended audience was the Chairman. As Cradock wrote of his harassment at the hands of the Red Guards, 'Cameras were in readiness to record the fun.'[65] In forcing the British diplomats to bow their heads and photographing this, the Red Guards performed a ritual for the benefit of the camera.[66] No incident was more theatrical than the 'Battle of Portland Place'. 'This curious piece of theatre', as Cradock recollected, 'was undoubtedly engineered by the Chinese so that they could claim to match us in terms of outrage and work themselves into the position of moral superiority from which they loved to operate.'[67]

182 *Chi-kwan Mark*

It is true that Cultural-Revolution China was a political theatre, where Mao communicated his revolutionary messages and his 'audiences', the Red Guards, performed the ritual of Maoism. But instead of 'mere manipulation' by the Chairman, 'many of the most engrossing episodes of the Cultural Revolution spectacle were performed with little or no direction, often contrary to the preferences of Maoist stage managers'.[68] During 1967 the Red Guards' assaults on foreign missions assumed ritualistic and performative qualities. Not just the British, but the Soviets, the French, the Indians, the Indonesians, the Burmese and many other foreigners were all subject to the Red Guard rituals of demonstration, condemnation and violence.[69] Deeply divided into different factions, the Red Guard youth all wanted to prove their revolutionary credentials and thereby win the support of the central leaders in political infighting.[70] The British Office was burnt down by a moderate group at Qinghua University called the April Fourteenth (together with the Red Guards of Beijing Foreign Languages Institute), which wanted to prove that it was more 'Maoist' than its rival, the Jinggangshan Corps.[71] Zhou was shocked by their 'spontaneous action'. While sanctioning the 'ultimatum' about Hong Kong on the night of 19 August (due to tiredness, as he claimed),[72] Zhou had consistently opposed the storming of foreign embassies by the revolutionary masses.[73] Upon receiving the news of the burning on the early morning of 23 August, Zhou held an emergency meeting with some of the Red Guards involved, asserting that the 'seizure of power' within the foreign ministry in the past four days was 'illegal' and that diplomacy was the prerogative of the central leaders.[74] Thereafter, Mao and Zhou purged the 'ultra-leftists' within the ministry (such as Wang and Yao) and reined in the Cultural-Revolution diplomacy of the Red Guards.

The Labour government was able to discern the difference between the everyday violence of the Red Guards and the largely cautious foreign policy championed by the (moderate) Chinese leaders. Throughout 1967 the Foreign Office and British overseas posts carefully assessed whether the anti-foreign incidents on the mainland represented a fundamental break in China's foreign policy. In early August Hopson reported that there was 'no evidence that incidents have been planned ahead and deliberately provoked in order to justify a prepared change of policy': China had shown no desire 'to intervene directly with ground forces either in Viet-Nam or Hong Kong'.[75] By early November James Murray, the head of the Far Eastern Department, took notice of '[t]he trend towards a greater degree of control and discipline' on the mainland after the August chaos. Encouragingly, Zhou's influence and that of other 'administrators' was 'on the increase', while 'the influence of the notorious "Embassy burner", Yao Teng-shan (Yao Dengshan), [was] clearly on the wane' – and this 'may well have a salutary effect on the conduct of the Chinese Foreign Ministry'.[76]

Even the temperamental George Brown 'acted with admirable restraint' in response to the sacking of the British mission, 'sensibly realizing that this episode of madness would blow itself out in due course'.[77] While he had

*The everyday Cold War, 1965–7* 183

decided to impose restrictions on the movement of Chinese diplomats in London in retaliation, on 2 September Brown sent a personal message to Chen Yi, stating that '[t]he present state of Anglo–Chinese relations' required both governments to 'discuss these relations frankly and dispassionately' and suggesting that both sides withdrew their mission and personnel from each other's capital for the time being so as to 'ensure that no further incidents develop to make a breach inevitable'.[78]

Two days later Brown submitted a memorandum on relations with China to the Cabinet Defence and Overseas Policy Committee. Approved by the Committee on 5 September, the memorandum recommended that Britain should 'not take the initiative to break diplomatic relations with China'. Brown made a strong case against a diplomatic rupture because he believed that positive engagement best served the interests of Britain and of the Labour Party.[79] First of all, there was the consideration of trade. The chaos of the Cultural Revolution did not seem to have a devastating impact on Anglo–Chinese economic relations: during the first seven months of 1967 British exports to China had increased from £16.5 million in the same period of the previous year to £27.3 million, although British imports dropped somewhat from £21 to £18.3 million.[80] To Brown, the volume of trade would 'depend not so much on anti-British feeling in China, which seems hardly to have affected trade at all, but rather on the internal political state of China'. And 'the trend over the last year has been for it to increase and for the balance to increase to our advantage'.[81] Both the Board of Trade and the Sino–British Trade Council were cautiously optimistic that China wanted to keep foreign trade going.[82] Second, Brown and his Cabinet colleagues were concerned about the small number of British residents in China, including Grey who had been under house arrest since July. Any decision to break diplomatic relations with China and to withdraw the British mission might arouse 'adverse criticism' within Britain that the government was leaving its subjects at the mercy of the Chinese Communists. Related to this was the importance Brown attached to the presence in Beijing of 'a fully operative diplomatic mission' that could observe and 'exploit without delay' the latest developments in China. By early September the Cultural Revolution was far from over and the political future of China remained uncertain. This was also true of Hong Kong, which, in view of the leftist riots, Whitehall pessimistically assumed that Britain could not expect to hold on its present terms until 1997 and were therefore prepared to negotiate its future with a new Chinese leadership that might arise. Thus, the maintenance of a diplomatic mission in China, Brown argued, was highly desirable 'both to warn us of opportunities as they may arise and to advise us of the Chinese personalities with whom we might be able to do business'.[83]

Approaching Anglo–Chinese relations from a longer-term perspective, Cabinet ministers decided that Britain should continue to vote for China's admission into the UN in the coming session of the General Assembly (while also continuing to support the 'important question' resolution). This decision

184   *Chi-kwan Mark*

was based 'not on the approval of the actions of the Chinese Government but on the existence of China and the need for universal representation in the United Nations'.[84] It was consistent with the Labour Party's foreign policy principle of 'socialist internationalism', characterized by cooperation, interdependence and disarmament.[85] In this vein, Brown aimed to 'build the United Nations as a world authority and invest it with real authority'.[86] With the escalation of the Vietnam War and China's explosion of a hydrogen bomb, it became all the more important than ever that the PRC should be removed from its largely self-imposed isolation. China's continued exclusion from the UN would only make a diplomatic solution to the Vietnam conflict more difficult. Nor would it help the international negotiations over arms control and disarmament, particularly the question of nuclear proliferation in which Wilson took a deep personal interest.[87] Nevertheless, in light of the Red Guard outrages, ministers agreed that, during the General Assembly debate on Chinese representation, the British delegation to the United Nations 'should take no other action (e.g. lobbying) to promote Chinese admission', while his speech 'should reflect the deterioration in Anglo–Chinese relations brought about by recent Chinese actions'.[88]

When the General Assembly voted on 28 November, the 'important question' resolution was adopted, and the Albanian resolution on seating Communist China failed.[89] Britain's voting behaviour remained a major stumbling block to Anglo–Chinese relations, which were now – and for the next two years – bedevilled by the 'hostage crisis' of British diplomats and nationals on the mainland.[90] Nonetheless, by the end of 1967 Mao and Zhou had restored a semblance of normality to China's foreign policy. Beijing's 'everyday Cold War' against Britain continued, but without the Red Guard outrages.

## Conclusion

In sum, Anglo–Chinese relations during 1965–7 appeared to be on a downward spiral, culminating in the burning of the British Embassy. China's 'everyday Cold War' was, though, largely symbolic and ritualistic. True, the Vietnam War made it even more difficult for Anglo–Chinese political relations to move forward, but the reality was that Britain had not become the real enemy of the PRC that the Chinese propaganda machine made it out to be: the US, the Soviet Union and perhaps India were. At a time when Mao was mobilizing the Chinese people for the global wars of national liberation and Britain still possessed a residual empire, anti-British rhetoric inevitably became part of Beijing's international propaganda against imperialism, capitalism and revisionism. By making symbolic protests about the US naval visits to Hong Kong without following up their threat, British officials estimated, the Chinese probably had other more significant issues in mind, notably the Sino–Soviet split. In their routine attacks on foreign missions, not just the British, the warring Red Guards were performing a ritual of the Cultural Revolution to impress and win the support of the Chairman.

*The everyday Cold War, 1965–7* 185

Notwithstanding the horrendous events in August 1967, British ministers and diplomats calmly drew a subtle distinction between the Red Guards' everyday violence on the mainland and China's largely cautious foreign policy in Asia. They held firm to a policy of constructive engagement with China. This was not 'appeasement' determined by the post-war decline of Britain (although London had few illusions about its ability to influence Beijing). Nor had the British 'kowtowed' to the Chinese (even on that terrifying night, Cradock had refused to verbally kowtow to the Red Guards by chanting 'Long Live Chairman Mao'). Rather, the British had considered various policy options, such as the expulsion of Chinese diplomats in London and a rupture of diplomatic relations, and rejected those that were counterproductive to the long-term strategic objective of bringing China into the family of nations and to the immediate aim of safeguarding Hong Kong and Britons on the mainland. They had made a reasoned and realistic assessment of the August events in the wider context of China's fierce domestic power struggle and its largely non-interventionist diplomacy. To Wilson and Brown, who attached great importance to nuclear non-proliferation and the UN as an effective authority, engagement or negotiation was the best way of fighting the 'everyday Cold War'.

## Notes

1 See, among others, John W. Young, *The Labour Governments 1964–70*, vol. 2: *International Policy*, Manchester: Manchester University Press, 2003; Saki Dockrill, *Britain's Retreat from East of Suez: The Choice between Europe and the World?*, Basingstoke: Palgrave-Macmillan, 2002; and Glen O'Hara and Helen Parr (eds), *The Wilson Governments 1964–1970 Reconsidered*, London: Routledge, 2006.

2 For a good historiographical overview, see Sidney Aster, 'Appeasement: Before and After Revisionism', *Diplomacy & Statecraft*, 19/3, 2008, pp. 443–80.

3 Peter Lowe, *Contending with Nationalism and Communism: British Policy towards Southeast Asia, 1945–65*, Basingstoke: Palgrave-Macmillan, 2009, p. 252, and ibid., *Containing the Cold War: British Policies towards Japan, China and Korea, 1948–53*, Manchester: Manchester University Press, 1997, p. 265.

4 It must be noted that 'Everyday Cold War' was not a term contemporary British officials used. Nor is this chapter about the social history of Britons and their 'private life' in mainland China.

5 See Michel de Certeau, *The Practice of Everyday Life*, Berkeley, CA: University of California Press, 1984; Erving Goffman, *Interaction Ritual: Essays on Face-to-Face Behavior*, Garden City, NY: Doubleday, 1967; and Catherine Bell, *Ritual Theory, Ritual Practice*, New York: Oxford University Press, 1992.

6 Pei Monong, *Zhou Enlai waijiaoxue* [*School of Zhou Enlai's Diplomacy*], Beijing: Zhonggong zhongyang dangxiao chubanshe, 1997, pp. 222–40; Cong Wenzi, 'Zhou Enlai tichu xuanba, peiyang waishi ganbu di shiliu zi fangzhen' ['The Sixteen-Point Principles of Selecting [and] Training Foreign Affairs Cadres advocated by Zhou Enlai'], in Zheng Yan (ed.), *Waijiao jishi* [*Diplomatic Episodes*], vol. 1, Beijing: Shiji zhishi chubanshe, 2007, p. 222.

7 On the role of ritual in Anglo–Chinese relations before 1949, see James L Hevia, *Cherishing Men from Afar: Qing Guest Ritual and the Macartney Embassy of 1793*,

186 *Chi-kwan Mark*

Durham, NC: Duke University Press, 1995; and Robert A. Bickers (ed.), *Ritual and Diplomacy: The Macartney Mission to China 1792–1794*, London: Wellsweep Press, 1993.

8 Zhongyang wenxian yanjiushi (ed.), *Jianguo yilai Zhou Enlai wengao* [*Zhou Enlai's Manuscripts since the Founding of the PRC*], vol. 2: Jan.–June 1950, Beijing: Zhongyang wenxian chubanshe, 2008, p. 26; and Waijiaobu dang'anguan (ed.), *Jiemi waijiao wenxian: Zhonghua renmin gongheguo jianjiao dang'an, 1949–1955* [*Declassified Diplomatic Documents: Archives of the Establishment of China's Diplomatic Relations, 1949–1955*], Beijing: Zhongguo huabao chubanshe, 2006, pp. 475–6.

9 Zhongyang wenxian yanjiushi and Zhonghua renmin gingheguo waijiaobu (eds), *Zhou Enlai waijiao wenxuan* [*Selected Works of Zhou Enlai on Diplomacy*], Beijing: Zhongyang wenxian chubanshe, 1990, pp. 94–105; and Zhongyang wenxian yanjiushi and Zhongguo renmin jiefangjun junshi kexueyuan (eds), *Jianguo yilai Mao Zedong junshi wengao* [*Mao Zedong's Military Manuscripts since the Founding of the PRC*], vol. 2: Jan. 1952–Dec. 1958, Beijing: Junshi kexue chubanshe, 2009, pp. 259–62.

10 The PRC Foreign Ministry and the CCP Central Committee's Party Literature Research Centre (ed.), *Mao Zedong on Diplomacy*, Beijing: Foreign Language Press, 1998, pp. 387–8.

11 Gao Cunming, 'Xuexi Mao Zedong guanyu Xiou lianhe ziqiang di sixiang' ['Learning Mao Zedong's Thinking on West European Unity and Self-strengthening'], in Pei Jianzhang et al., *Mao Zedong waijiao sixiang yanjiu* [*Research on Mao Zedong's Diplomatic Thinking*], Beijing: Shijie zhishi chubanshe, 1994, pp. 233–5; and Su Yang, *Zhang Wentian yu Zhongguo waijiao* [*Zhang Wentian and Chinese Diplomacy*], Hong Kong: Hong Kong Open Page, 2012, pp. 194–5.

12 *Mao Zedong on Diplomacy*, pp. 429–30.

13 See Qiang Zhai, *China and the Vietnam Wars, 1950–1975*, Chapel Hill, NC: University of North Carolina Press, 2000, pp. 139–52; and Chen Jian, *Mao's China and the Cold War*, Chapel Hill, NC: University of North Carolina Press, 2001, pp. 209–12.

14 Dockrill, *Britain's Retreat from East of Suez*, pp. 105–21; John Dumbrell, 'The Johnson Administration and the British Labour Government: Vietnam, the Pound and East of Suez', *Journal of American Studies* 30/2, 1996, pp. 211–31; and Sylvia Ellis, *Britain, America, and the Vietnam War*, Westport, CT: Praeger, 2004, pp. 118–27.

15 *House of Commons Debates*, 5th series, vol. 708, col. 238, 9 Mar. 1965.

16 *House of Commons Debates*, 5th series, vol. 709, col. 1869, 1 Apr. 1965.

17 Examples include Malaysia and Indonesia. See *People's Daily*, 6 Jan. 1965, 13 Jan. 1965 and 20 Apr. 1965.

18 *People's Daily*, 21 Mar. 1965, 25 Mar. 1965 and 5 Apr. 1965.

19 The National Archives (TNA), Kew, FO 371/180990 Beijing to FO tel. 721 31 May 1965.

20 Young, *The Labour Governments*, pp. 70–1, and Geraint Hughes, *Harold Wilson's Cold War: The Labour Government and East-West Politics, 1964–1970*, Woodbridge: Boydell Press, 2009, pp. 60–2.

21 Zhai, *China and the Vietnam Wars*, pp. 157–75.

22 TNA PREM 13/694 Beijing to FO tel. 476 12 Apr. 1965.

23 *People's Daily*, 22 June 1965; Xiong Xianghui, 'Cong dierci Yafei huiyi geqian kan Zhou Enlai guangming leiluo de waijiao fengge' ['The Total Honesty of Zhou Enlai's Diplomatic Style Seen From the Abortion of the Second Asian-African Conference'], in Yu Wuzhen (et al.), *Xin Zhongguo waijiao fengyun* [*Winds and Clouds in New China's Diplomacy*], vol. 4, Beijing: Shijie zhishi chubanshe, 1996, pp. 168–84.

24 TNA PREM 13/690 Beijing to FO tel. 808 22 June 1965; and *People's Daily*, 22 June 1965.

The everyday Cold War, 1965–7   187

25  The left wing in the Labour Party saw Wilson as a subservient follower of Johnson. Rhiannon Vickers, 'Harold Wilson, the British Labour Party, and the War in Vietnam', *Journal of Cold War Studies* 10/2, 2008, pp. 41–70.
26  Gan Xianfeng, *Zhongguo duiwai xinwen chuanboshi* [*A History of China's International News Communication*] (Fuzhu: Fujian renmin chubanshe, 2004), p. 145.
27  TNA FO 371/180991 Beijing to FO tel. 31'S' 22 Nov. 1965.
28  *House of Commons Debates*, 5th series, vol. 727, col. 571 26 Apr. 1966.
29  TNA FO 371/186977 'China Annual Review for 1965' 24 Jan. 1966.
30  TNA FO 371/180528 Beijing to FO tel. 996 8 Aug. 1965.
31  *People's Daily*, 1 Sept. 1965.
32  For a detailed analysis, see Chi-kwan Mark, 'Vietnam War Tourists: US Naval Visits to Hong Kong and British-American-Chinese Relations, 1965–1968', *Cold War History*, 10/1, 2010, pp. 1–28.
33  TNA FCO 40/56 Beijing to FO tel. 1070 1 Sept. 1965.
34  TNA DEFE 11/537 Beijing to FO tels. 88 & 89 1 Feb. 1966.
35  TNA FCO 40/56 Beijing to FO tel. 311 21 Mar. 1967.
36  TNA DEFE 13/534 Hong Kong to CO tel. 2879 15 Dec. 1966, reprinted as FED 150/402/01 Feb. 1967.
37  TNA DEFE 11/537 Hong Kong to CO tel. 965 11 Aug. 1965.
38  See James G. Hershberg and Chen Jian, 'Reading and Warning the Likely Enemy: China's Signals to the United States about Vietnam', *International History Review*, 27/1, 2005, pp. 47–84.
39  See Chi-kwan Mark, *Hong Kong and the Cold War: Anglo–American Relations, 1949–1957*, Oxford: Oxford University Press, 2004, particularly Ch. 3 and 5.
40  Lorenz M. Lüthi, *The Sino–Soviet Split: Cold War in the Communist World*, Princeton, NJ: Princeton University Press, 2008, p. 232.
41  *Hong Kong Standard*, 30 Apr. 1964; *South China Morning Post*, 28 May 1964; United States National Archives, College Park, RG 59, Central Foreign Policy Files, 1964–1966, box 2269, Hong Kong to State Department no. A-610 9 Mar. 1966.
42  TNA FO 371/187005 FO note enclosed in Bolland memo 4 Feb. 1966.
43  See Mark, 'Vietnam War Tourists', pp. 10–11.
44  *Zhou Enlai waijiao wenxuan*, p. 155.
45  Humphrey Trevelyan, *Worlds Apart: China 1953–5, Soviet Union 1962–5*, London: Macmillan, 1971, pp. 108–9, and Percy Cradock, *Experiences of China*, London: John Murray, 1994, p. 75; and TNA FO 371/180994 Wilford to MacLehose 12 May 1965, and FO 371/181002 Hopson to Bolland 9 Dec. 1965.
46  TNA FO 371/115197 Beijing to FO 10 May 1955, FO 371/115197 Beijing to FO tel. 155 15 June 1955, FO 371/127403 Wilson to Dalton 12 Oct. 1957, and FCO 21/79 FO memo 22 July 1967.
47  See Eileen Denza, *Diplomatic Law: A Commentary on the Vienna Convention on Diplomatic Relations*, Oxford: Oxford University Press, 1998.
48  TNA FO 371/181037 FO minute 10 Sept. 1965, and Wilford to FO tels. 1103 and 1104 8 Sept. 1965.
49  Barbara Barnouin and Yu Changgen, *Zhou Enlai: A Political Life*, Hong Kong: Chinese University Press, 2006, p. 261.
50  *People's Daily*, 23 May 1967.
51  TNA FCO 21/63 FO to Beijing tel. 387 23 May 1967, and FCO 21/64 Beijing to FO tel. 11S 6 June 1967, enclosed in Hopson to Brown 12 June 1967.
52  *People's Daily*, 17 and 18 May 1967; and TNA FCO 21/33 Peters to Bolland 7 June 1967, enclosed in memo, Bolland to de la Mare 15 June 1967, and Peters to Bolland 21 June 1967.
53  Xiaohong Liu, *Chinese Ambassadors: The Rise of Diplomatic Professionalism since 1949*, Hong Kong: Hong Kong University Press, 2001, p. 114.

188   *Chi-kwan Mark*

54  Liu, *Chinese Ambassadors*, pp. 114–15, and Roderick MacFarquhar and Michael Schoenhals, *Mao's Last Revolution*, Cambridge, MA: Harvard University Press, 2006, pp. 227–8.
55  Ma Jisen, *Waijiaobu wenhua dageming jishi* [*The Cultural Revolution in the Foreign Ministry of China*], Hong Kong: The Chinese University Press, 2004, p. 161; and TNA PREM 13/1458 Beijing to FO tel. 1116 20 Aug. 1967 and Beijing to FO tel. 1124 21 Aug. 1967.
56  *People's Daily*, 23 August 1967; Bu Weihua, *Zhonghua renmin gongheguo shi*, vol. 6:'*Zalan jiushijie': Wenhua dageming de dongluan yu haojie (1966–1968)* [*The History of the People's Republic of China*, vol. 6: *'Smashing the Old World': Havoc of the Chinese Cultural Revolution (1966 1968)*], Hong Kong. The Chinese University of Hong Kong, 2008, pp. 567, 572–3.
57  TNA FCO 21/34 Hopson to Brown 31 Aug. 1967, and Hopson to Denson 14 Sept. 1967.
58  Chi-kwan Mark, 'Hostage Diplomacy: Britain, China, and the Politics of Negotiation, 1967–1969', *Diplomacy & Statecraft* 20/3, 2009, pp. 477–8.
59  Harold Wilson, *The Labour Government 1964–1970: A Personal Record*, London: Weidenfeld & Nicolson, 1971, p. 425; *The Times*, 24 Aug. 1967.
60  TNA FCO 21/80 de la Mare to Thomson 23 Aug. 1967, and FCO 21/64 Comm. Office to HK tel. 1782 25 Aug. 1967.
61  Liu, *Chinese Ambassadors*, pp. 99 and 117.
62  *Peking Review* 10:29 (14 July 1967): 40. On CND activities, see British Library of Political and Economic Science, LSE, Archives and Special Collections, CND papers, CND/1/4 CND memo 21 Apr. 1967, and CND/1/5 Minutes of meeting of National Council of CND 20–1 May 1967. The Chinese chargé d'affaires in London, Xiong Xianghui, had returned to the mainland to participate in the Cultural Revolution early in 1967.
63  TNA PREM 13/1458 Metropolitan Police Special Branch report 29 Aug. 1967, and FCO 21/86 FE Dept note 29 Aug. 1967.
64  TNA FCO 21/64 Beijing to FO tel. 26 30 Aug. 1967; and *People's Daily*, 30 Aug. 1967.
65  TNA FCO 21/34 Hopson to Brown 31 Aug. 1967, Cradock to Denson 29 Aug. 1967, and Bolland to de la Mare 11 Sept. 1967, FCO 21/65 Denson to Bolland 7 Sept. 1967, and FCO 21/12 Appleyard to Wilson 4 Sept. 1967.
66  The Chinese official media, however, published no photograph of the British diplomats being humiliated on 22 August, perhaps an indication that Zhou and Mao did not endorse the Red Guard's behaviour. The *People's Daily* gave a rather low-key coverage of the event, reporting that the Red Guards had taken 'strong actions' against the British mission but making no mention of the burning (*People's Daily*, 23 Aug. 1967). In contrast, pictures of the Chinese diplomats engaging in the 'Battle of Portland Place' featured in Chinese propaganda as well as in the British press.
67  Cradock, *Experiences of China*, p. 68.
68  Richard Curt Kraus, *The Cultural Revolution: A Very Short Introduction*, Oxford: Oxford University Press, 2012, p. 28. On the ritual and rhetoric of the Cultural Revolution, see Daniel Leese, *Mao Cult: Rhetoric and Ritual in China's Cultural Revolution*, Cambridge: Cambridge University Press, 2011.
69  Barbara Barnouin and Yu Changgen, *Chinese Foreign Policy during the Cultural Revolution*, London: Kegan Paul, 1998, pp. 66–9, 72–5.
70  Jin Ge, 'Zai Waijiaobu "duoquan" qianhou' ['The Beginning and End of "Seizing Power" in the Foreign Ministry'], in An Jianshe (ed.), *Zhou Enlai de zuihou suiyue, 1966–1976* [*Zhou Enlai's Final Years, 1966–1976*], Beijing: Zhongyang wenxian chubanshe, 1995, p. 251.
71  Xiaowei Zheng, 'Passion, Reflection, and Survival: Political Choices of Red Guards at Qinghua University, July 1966-July 1968', in Joseph W. Esherick, Paul

The everyday Cold War, 1965–7  189

G. Pickowicz and Andrew G. Walder (eds), *The Chinese Cultural Revolution as History*, Stanford, CA: Stanford University Press, 2006, p. 57.

72 Barnouin and Yu, *Zhou Enlai*, p. 262.

73 'Zhou Enlai's Instruction about Demonstration against the Soviet Embassy in China', January 1967, in Song Yongyi (ed.), *Zhongguo wenhua dageming wenku* [*Database of the Chinese Cultural Revolution*] (electronic database), Xianggang: Xianggang Zhong wendaxue Zhongguo yanjiu fuwu zhongxin, 2006.

74 Ibid., 'Speeches by Zhou Enlai and Chen Boda to Representatives of the Mass Organizations of Foreign Affairs Circles about the Incident of the Burning of the Office of the British Chargé d'Affaires', 23 Aug. 1967.

75 TNA FCO 21/52 Hopson to Brown tel. 22S 1 Aug. 1967.

76 TNA FCO 21/12 Murray to de la Mare 3 Nov. 1967.

77 Peter Paterson, *Tired and Emotional: The Life of Lord George Brown*, London: Chatto & Windus, 1993, p. 217.

78 TNA FCO 21/64 Brown to Chen 2 Sept. 1967, and Beijing to FO tel. 32 2 Sept. 1967.

79 TNA CAB 148/33 OPD(67)67 Brown memo 4 Sept. 1967, and FCO 21/64, Bolland to Private Secretary 6 Sept. 1967.

80 TNA BT 241/1870 CRE21018/1G CRE.4 4 Sept. 1967.

81 TNA CAB 148/33, OPD(67)67 Brown memo 4 Sept. 1967.

82 TNA BT 241/1870 CRE 21018/1G Webb to MacMahon 12 Sept. 1967, and Rogora to Hunter 19 Sept. 1967; and Archives and Special Collections, SOAS Library, China Association papers, CHAS/C/7, Sino–British Trade Council Correspondence Jan. 1967–July 1968 Webb to Collar 22 Aug. 1967 and 12 Sept. 1967.

83 TNA CAB 148/33 OPD(67)67 Brown memo 4 Sept. 1967.

84 TNA CAB 148/33, OPD(67)67 Annex to Brown memo 4 Sept. 1967.

85 See Rhiannon Vickers, *The Labour Party and the World*, Part 2: *Labour's Foreign Policy since 1951*, Manchester: Manchester University Press, 2011.

86 Bodleian Library, University of Oxford, Lord George-Brown papers, Ms.Eng. c.5025, Brown speech and news release by The Labour Party Press and Publicity Department, 8 July 1967, fols 74–115.

87 *House of Commons Debates*, 5th series, vol. 750, col. 415, 11 July 1967, and col. 2502, 20 July 1967.

88 TNA CAB 148/33 OPD(67)67 annex to Brown memo 4 Sept. 1967.

89 TNA FCO 21/48 UN NYC to FO tel. 3473 28 Nov. 1967.

90 See Mark, 'Hostage Diplomacy'.

# 12 Towards 'a new Okinawa' in the Indian Ocean

## Diego Garcia and Anglo–American relations in the 1960s

*Yoichi Kibata*

### Diego Garcia as 'a new Okinawa'

At the apogee of the period of decolonization in the mid-1960s a new British colony was created in the Indian Ocean. The Chagos Archipelago, which was until then a part of Mauritius, was separated from the latter and turned into the British Indian Ocean Territories (BIOT) in 1965. This measure, which completely ran counter to the spirit of the age, was undertaken jointly by the British and American governments as a result of their negotiation for securing a site for American military facilities in the Indian Ocean. And in the 1970s a military base began to be constructed on one of the islands, Diego Garcia.

Prior to the start of the construction of the base, which was a small-scale communication facility at the initial stage and then expanded considerably, the entire inhabitants of the Chagos Archipelago, some 1,500 people, were ousted from their islands. In September 1975 *The Sunday Times* carried a large article titled 'The Islanders That Britain Sold' and reported in detail the story of the expulsion of the islanders. According to that article, 'US Navy officials have worked assiduously, secretly and ultimately successfully to turn a British colony into what is now on the road to becoming a new Okinawa.'[1] In fact, the base on Diego Garcia continued to grow thereafter and played a significant part in American military activities in the Gulf War, the Afghanistan War and the Iraq War, just as the American bases in Okinawa had occupied a crucial position in the execution of the war in Vietnam.

During all those years the Chagossians were condemned to live in harsh and miserable conditions in Mauritius and the Seychelles, to which they were sent, or in Britain, into which they were admitted after they became eligible for British passports in 2002.[2] The fate of these people had begun to attract public attention in 2000 when the High Court ruled that the Immigration Ordinance of 1971 which had legitimatized the exile of the Chagossians had been unlawful. But this High Court judgment was later overturned by the British government, and the Chagossians' desire to go back to their home islands is yet to be fulfilled.[3]

The tragic history of the Chagossians has been dealt with by investigative and critical writers like Mark Curtis and John Pilger.[4] In addition, David

## 'A new Okinawa': Diego Garcia in the 1960s 191

Vine, an American cultural anthropologist, has written a good book about American policy concerning the military base in the Indian Ocean and the process of the expulsion of the people from the BIOT.[5] The Anglo–American negotiations that led to the construction of the base are discussed by Vine, and he puts emphasis on 'the strategic island concept' held by the American side. This is an important point, but Vine's book stops short of analyzing the Anglo–American negotiations in the context of decolonization and especially of the British move to withdraw from 'East of Suez', which was occurring around the same time in the 1960s.

The aim of this article is to fill this gap in the literature. Due to limited space, the problem of the displacement of the Chagossians is treated only tangentially, but let me stress here that my interest in Diego Garcia stems from my sympathy towards them. I came to know about their case at the time of the Falklands War, when the British government's harsh treatment of them about a decade before was starkly compared with its warm support for the Falklanders, whose number was approximately the same as that of the Chagossians.[6]

## The Indian Ocean in the limelight

The Chagos Archipelago, whose main islands consist of Diego Garcia, the Salomons and Peros Banhos, were spotted by the Portuguese in the early sixteenth century, but the Portuguese did not try to exercise sovereignty over this uninhabited territory.[7] It was, instead, the French that began to rule these islands as dependencies of Mauritius (the Isles de France) in the eighteenth century, but as a result of its defeat in the Napoleonic War France ceded Mauritius to Britain together with those islands.

Though situated in a strategically important position in the middle of the Indian Ocean, these islands were not used for military purposes. Plantations of copra (dried coconut) were developed, and labourers imported from Africa (Mozambique, Senegal, etc.) and south India were employed there. They lived on fishing and growing vegetables and poultry, and their life was peaceful, though not idyllic.[8] Even during the Second World War, when German and Japanese submarines became very active in the Indian Ocean, these islands were not much affected, though a small contingent of the Indian Army was stationed in Diego Garcia in 1942 only to be withdrawn at the end of that year.[9]

Until the Second World War the Indian Ocean, which was ringed by British possessions, was militarily dominated by Britain, and the American interest and presence in this area were not so marked. But in the 1950s, especially after the Suez Crisis, the United States began to pay strong attention to the Indian Ocean in the context of the Cold War. According to Monoranjan Bezboruah, the Suez Crisis:

... cast grave doubts on the future effectiveness of any British-led peace-keeping role in the region. The growing evidence of the diminishing

192    *Yoichi Kibata*

British potency, as well as the near-total end of the French hold over the region with the end of its formal colonial rule over Madagascar in 1958, prompted some US defense planners to foresee a possible power vacuum in the region.[10]

And the idea of using islands in the Indian Ocean for military purposes began to take concrete shape.

In the spring of 1959 the Americans began their first investigation into this idea, and the British government became aware that the US Navy was examining the possibility of building military facilities in the Indian Ocean.[11] Though W.F. Dickson, the Chief of Defence Staff, welcomed this offer, the British side as a whole was still non-committal at this stage.[12]

The issue then lay dormant until May 1961 when the British side observed that interest had revived in the United States.[13] In the autumn of that year an informal approach was made by Admiral Arleigh Burke, the American Chief of Naval Operations, to his British counterpart about the idea developed by Stuart Barber in the US Navy's long-range planning office. According to this 'strategic island concept', bases should be constructed in small, lightly populated islands in order to avoid hindrances, and Barber regarded Diego Garcia as an ideal location, for its population was 'measured only in the hundreds'.[14] However, at this stage the attention of the American military was not necessarily focused on Diego Garcia, for in 1962 the island of Gan, the southernmost island of the Maldives, most attracted the attention of the American side.[15] When Paul Nitze, the Assistant Secretary of Defense, visited Britain at the beginning of 1963, it was Gan that he mentioned as the island that the Americans liked best.[16] Therefore, when a formal approach from the American government about the initiation of discussions 'looking toward the possible strategic use of certain small islands in the Indian Ocean area' was made in April 1963, Diego Garcia was not yet singled out.[17] But in the summer of that year the American side began to focus on Diego Garcia and sought British permission to send a survey team to look into the possibilities of setting up military communication facilities on the island.[18]

## The creation of the BIOT

The British government responded positively to the American request to have discussions about the islands in the Indian Ocean, and the Anglo–American talks eventually took place between 25 and 27 February 1964. As the result of this meeting the British delegation agreed to recommend to the British governmental authorities that they should '(a) consider favourably the possibility of the development by the U.S. of such facilities on U.K. island possessions as they may require ... (b) pursue as rapidly as possible the feasibility of transfer of the administration of Diego Garcia (and other islands in the Chagos Archipelago) and the Agalega Islands from Mauritius', and '(c) as soon as politically practicable, facilitate a joint survey of Diego Garcia and other islands

## 'A new Okinawa': Diego Garcia in the 1960s 193

under British sovereignty in the Indian Ocean area that the U.S. may require'.[19]
This joint survey was undertaken between mid-July and mid-August 1964.

There are several points that should be emphasized about the outcome of these talks. First, Diego Garcia occupied the top position in the list of the islands on which American military bases would be constructed, but other islands, such as Aldabra, which was part of the Seychelles, and the Cocos and Keeling Islands, which were under Australian administration, were also regarded as candidate areas. Second, the British government was to be responsible for acquiring land and resettling the population. In this way the resettlement of the people came into the picture from the outset of the Anglo–American negotiations. Third, it was deemed necessary to detach Diego Garcia and the other islands in the Chagos Archipelago from Mauritius. This last point requires detailed examination.

Around the time of this meeting the world was witnessing the process of decolonization. Beginning in the year 1960, 'the year of Africa', many European dependencies in Africa headed towards independence one after another, and Mauritius was not an exception. In 1961 a constitutional conference about Mauritius was held in London, and it was decided that it should duly proceed to independence. If Mauritius was to become independent with the Chagos Archipelago within its national territory, Britain would be deprived of its power to dictate the future of these islands and thus make Diego Garcia available for American military use. Therefore the American and British governments thought it imperative to detach the Chagos Archipelago from Mauritius before the latter became independent. Though the prospect of the independence of the Seychelles was more distant than that of Mauritius, the same measure was also deemed necessary for the Seychelles, too.

The policymakers of both Britain and the United States were well aware that the act of transferring territory from countries that were to gain independence did not conform to the trend of the age, and that, if this operation were highlighted internationally, Britain would meet strong criticism from various quarters, especially from the Third World and the United Nations, where newly independent countries were vociferous in demanding the acceleration of decolonization. Therefore they thought about ways in which to evade that outcome. In a telegram to the London embassy in May 1964, George Ball, the American under-secretary of state, suggested:

> In order [to] undercut Afro-Asian, USSR and [East European] Bloc attacks anticipated on supposed 'Neo-Colonial' efforts, we wonder whether HMG could conceive of placing administration of these islands (i.e., Chagos, Agalega, and Aldabra) directly under London administration, using some other Ministry than Colonial Office (perhaps Admiralty or Foreign Office), on [the] basis [that] problems [of] these islands were now wholly foreign policy or military in nature and did not involve same range of issues which correctly occupy Colonial Office.[20]

194    *Yoichi Kibata*

In the same vein, the chairman of the British Cabinet's Defence and Overseas Policy (Official) Committee of Britain pondered around the same time:

> We have the constitutional authority to take this step without the consent of the local Governments [in Mauritius and the Seychelles]. But arbitrary action of this kind would be impolitic, since it would tend to jeopardise future relations with those Governments. Moreover, we may in any event encounter criticism in the UN if we exclude the islands in question from the prospect of eventual independence and can be represented as relegating them indefinitely to the status of colonial dependencies; and we may take some of the edge off this criticism if we proceed throughout on the basis of consultation with the Governments concerned.[21]

Accordingly, British policymakers thought it necessary to inform Seewoosagur Ramgoolam, the chief minister of Mauritius, of the Anglo–American plan before the joint survey of the islands was undertaken, especially because the *Washington Post* had got wind of the content of the negotiations, which had been kept secret until this point. When the British government approached Ramgoolam with the plan at the beginning of July 1964, he reacted favourably towards the proposal for military facilities, but showed reservations about the idea of changing the constitutional status of the islands.[22]

Legally the detachment of the islands could be undertaken without the assent of Mauritius and the Seychelles, and, given Ramgoolam's reservations, the Foreign Office and the Ministry of Defence were inclined to think that the agreement of political leaders of these countries was not necessary, but the Colonial Office, which was more sensitive to the international repercussions of this problem, considered that their agreement was necessary.[23] Out of this there emerged the idea of paying a certain amount of money to Mauritius and the Seychelles as compensation for the detachment of the islands. The total amount was to be £10 million. This included the money for purchasing land and other expenses, in addition to the direct compensation to be paid to Mauritius (£3 million) and the Seychelles (£3 million for the construction of an airfield on the main island). Upon a British request that it take an equal share of this financial burden, the American government agreed to pay half the amount (£5 million).[24]

While the British officials expected little difficulty in the case of the Seychelles, they foresaw that it might not be easy to persuade the leaders of Mauritius. But they were determined to make Mauritius swallow the planned amount of money. On 23 September 1965 when the second constitutional conference for the independence of Mauritius was taking place in London, an offer of compensation of £3 million was made to Ramgoolam. He regarded this sum as too small, and at first refused the offer outright, but eventually in February 1966 he decided to settle for that amount.[25]

In the meantime, on 8 November 1965 an Order in Council was issued establishing the BIOT, which was composed of the Chagos Archipelago, detached from Mauritius, and the islands of Aldabra, Farquhar and Desroches, detached from the Seychelles. Thus a new colony was created in the Indian Ocean just at the time when colonies all over the world were following the path towards independence.

Arthur Greenwood, who as the Colonial Secretary was directly responsible for this problem, was very candid in admitting the anachronistic nature of the creation of the BIOT for constructing military bases, and wrote immediately before the Order in Council was issued, 'We shall be accused of creating a new colony in a period of decolonization and of establishing new military bases when we should be getting out of the old ones.'[26] Significantly the timing of the announcement of the Order in Council was calculated so that the establishment of a new colony could be presented to the world as a fait-accompli and the United Nations, especially in the Fourth Committee (the Committee of Twenty-Four), which looked after the progress of decolonization, would not interfere with the Anglo–American project.[27] This tactic seems to have worked. Though the United Nations did react adversely against the decision of the British government, with the General Assembly in the following month passing a resolution calling on the British government 'to take no action which would dismember the territory of Mauritius and violate its territorial integrity', it was too late.[28] The resolution did not have any coercive force, and the British government just ignored it.

## Anglo–American negotiations and the 'East of Suez' factor

In considering the background of Anglo–American negotiations that led to the creation of the BIOT, one factor, which has been rather neglected in existing works on this topic, should be taken into account. That is the problem of the British military commitment 'East of Suez'.

The phrase 'East of Suez' denoted the British military presence east of the Suez Canal, with the core position being the bases in Aden and Singapore. The maintenance of this military presence was regarded as crucial for the continuance of Britain's world status even after the process of decolonization gained momentum. According to Karl Hack, a new 'East of Suez' concept developed after the Suez War in 1956, envisaging a central, Singapore-based Carrier Task Force operating in a triangular zone stretching from Aden and Mombasa to Hong Kong.[29] However, keeping this military presence was costly and voices were being raised demanding that the forces 'East of Suez' should be curtailed or even withdrawn. In the discussions of the governmental working group for the 'Study of Future Policy' that was set up in 1959, opinions were split into two factions. One faction supported the maintenance of an active world-wide role; the other argued that Britain's overseas military positions had become superfluous in the postwar era and Britain should withdraw into a regional role within Europe.[30] In this working group the representatives from the Foreign Office and the Treasury were the ones who argued for disengagement from the 'East of Suez' role, but their arguments

196 *Yoichi Kibata*

were not powerful enough to change the existing course, and the final report endorsed Britain's overseas role.

This situation continued in the early 1960s. However, as Saki Dockrill points out, during the Macmillan Government's last months in office, which came to an end in October 1963, Britain's 'East of Suez' role began to be discussed more frequently than the other two roles (nuclear deterrence and the defence in Western Europe) as a possible area for defence savings.[31] This means that, when the Anglo–American negotiations concerning military facilities in the Indian Ocean took off in 1964, the possibility of British withdrawal from 'East of Suez' had become less remote than previously.

This trend was observed by the American Government with worried eyes. Up until the Suez War, American policymakers had not been keen on supporting Britain's world role, in part because of its anti-imperialist ideals, but after 1956 they came to value the British role in the global Cold War struggle. In particular, the British military presence 'East of Suez' began to be interpreted as vital for the executing of American Cold War strategy.[32] Therefore in pursuing its aim of establishing military facilities in the Indian Ocean, the US government envisaged that American military involvement in the area would not replace the British presence, but would rather buttress the continuation of the latter's commitment. This way of thinking was clearly expressed in a memorandum that Secretary of State Dean Rusk wrote to President Lyndon Johnson in July 1964 about Anglo–American discussions on military facilities in the Indian Ocean:

> We initiated the discussions. We thought that, by drawing the British into forward thinking about possible future requirements for military resources in the area from the Gulf of Oman eastward, the UK would be encouraged to remain East of Suez in strength.[33]

It should be noted that the British side was also taking the 'East of Suez' factor into consideration in its dealing with the United States about the islands in the Indian Ocean. At the time of the meeting in February 1964, the Directors of Defence Plans wrote in a brief:

> If we lose our main bases in Aden or Singapore it would be necessary to re-establish the facilities elsewhere if we wished to continue our military presence in the Indian Ocean. The opportunity of sharing the facilities on Diego Garcia and Aldabra or another island in the Western Indian Ocean at a fraction of the cost which we would incur in developing alternative bases ourselves represents an extremely valuable insurance policy against an uncertain future.[34]

When the Labour government led by Wilson came into power in October 1964, it was still trying to preserve Britain's world role, and the 'East of Suez' question was far from being settled, and that situation lingered for some time.

_'A new Okinawa': Diego Garcia in the 1960s_  197

In the background of the creation of the BIOT lay this continuing uncertainty about the future of the British military role in the Indian Ocean. Thus in April 1965 Edward Peck, an assistant under-secretary of state at the Foreign Office, wrote as follows:

> If we wish to maintain our presence east of Suez without over-straining our resources, we shall need American help, particularly if we lose our footing in Aden and Singapore. But the Americans will not be able to help us in the Indian Ocean unless they acquire facilities there. The present proposals, in addition to their intrinsic strategic value, are admirably fitted both to give them the power, and to put them in the mood, to help us. We may not get another chance.[35]

A memorandum written jointly by the Foreign Secretary and the Minister of Defence for the Defence and Oversea Policy Committee around the same period also expressed a similar hope and argued that, if Britain lost one or both bases 'East of Suez' (i.e. Aden and Singapore) and still wished to operate in the area, the system of American facilities would help Britain to do so.[36]

The British policymakers who were engaged in the Anglo–American negotiations over the Indian Ocean islands were therefore thinking that the establishment of American military facilities would guarantee the maintenance of British influence in one way or another even if a decision was made to withdraw from 'East of Suez'. But the American side was not satisfied with such a halfway measure and continued to demand the maintenance of the full British military presence in the region.

## The BIOT Agreement and the problem of the islanders

Once the Chagos Archipelago and other islands were separated from Mauritius and the Seychelles, the British and American governments proceeded to conclude an agreement about their future use. On 30 December 1966 an agreement on the 'Availability for Defence Purposes of the British Ocean Territory' (hereafter referred to as the BIOT agreement) was signed.[37] By this agreement, the BIOT, which was now under British sovereignty, was to be made available to meet the needs of both governments for defence. It was, of course, assumed that the main user of the military facilities on the BIOT would be the Americans, and that they would select contractors and the sources of equipment, materials, supplies and personnel. As for the time-span of the agreement, after an initial period of fifty years, it was to continue in force for a further period of twenty years unless, not more than two years before the end of the initial period, either government gave notice of termination to the other government.

However, it took some time before the actual construction of military facilities on the BIOT started, for two plans that were under way at the time of the signing of the BIOT agreement faced obstacles and one of them had to be abandoned: one was for the building of an airfield on Aldabra and the other for constructing military facilities in Diego Garcia. Since the treatment of these two plans was closely connected to the problem of 'East of Suez', it is in order here to mention briefly the process leading to the announcement by Wilson in January 1968 about the decision to withdraw British forces from 'East of Asia' by the end of 1971.

As was mentioned before, when the BIOT was created at the end of 1965, the issue of the future of British military presence 'East of Suez' was still largely undecided. Shortly after that, in February 1966, the nationalist movement in Aden, one of the pivotal bases, compelled the British government to announce the decision to withdraw its forces from there.[38] The Defence White Paper published in the same month, which referred to this policy towards Aden, showed that the British government continued to believe that Britain should continue to maintain a military presence 'East of Suez', but at the same time it also suggested that it should reduce its forces in this area as soon as conditions permitted.[39] Though the period after that saw the strengthening of voices for military withdrawal, at the time of the conclusion of the BIOT agreement in December 1966 the Wilson government was still debating Britain's future role 'East of Suez'.

The opinions in the Wilson government were divided, but in the spring of 1967 a plan for a staged withdrawal from 'East of Suez' was put forward by Denis Healey, the Minister of Defence. With the support of Wilson and George Brown, the Foreign Secretary, Healey gained the upper hand, and in consequence the decision to halve the forces stationed in Malaysia and Singapore by 1970–1 and to withdraw them altogether in the mid-1970s was announced in parliament in the form of a supplementary statement on defence policy on 18 July 1967.[40]

The American government was disappointed with this British decision, but the process did not stop there. In November 1967 Britain was shaken by the sterling crisis and the Wilson government was forced to announce the devaluation of the pound. This situation led to further discussions about the speeding up of the retreat from 'East of Suez', and finally on 16 January 1968 Wilson made a statement in the House of Commons about the government's decision to accelerate the pace and to withdraw all of its forces by the end of 1971.

To return to the problem of military facilities in the BIOT, the idea of building an airfield on Aldabra was originally nurtured by the British government in mid-1966, i.e. after its decision to withdraw from Aden. In May 1966 Healey proposed the establishment of this new airbase to the Cabinet Defence and Overseas Policy Committee, arguing that in order to continue to play a peace-keeping role after the retreat from Aden, Britain needed to have some facilities for staging and deploying forces in the Indian ocean in association with the American government.[41] This plan, which envisaged equal cost-sharing between Britain and the United States, was conveyed to President Johnson at the time of Prime Minister Wilson's visit to Washington in July 1966, and was approved by Secretary of Defence Robert McNamara on 4 August.[42]

'A new Okinawa': Diego Garcia in the 1960s 199

In July 1967 the Aldabra airfield scheme was again discussed in the Defence and Oversea Policy Committee; this took place ten days after the publication of the above-mentioned Supplementary Statement on Defence Policy. The memorandum prepared by Healey justified the plan by pointing out that it would give (a) flexibility during the period of disengagement from the commitments in the Indo-Pacific area and (b) flexibility in carrying out the withdrawal from the Persian Gulf as well as (c) flexibility of action in relation to Africa and (d) flexibility in access routes to the Far East.[43] It is clear that this plan was considered in the context of the recent further disengagement from the military commitment 'East of Suez'.

However, this plan had to be abandoned in November 1967 at the time of the sterling crisis. According to Paul Gore-Booth, the Permanent Under-Secretary of the Foreign Office, the reasons for this decision were the American reluctance to pay their share, the strong opposition from scientists in both countries who were concerned about the destruction of the unique ecological features of Aldabra,[44] and opposition from the Indian Government.[45]

As for the construction of a military facility on Diego Garcia, which was under consideration right from the beginning of Anglo–American negotiations, a concrete proposal was made by the American Joint Chiefs of Staff in July 1967. This proposal for establishing a small-scale, austere facility costing about $26 million was promoted by the navy but met with vigorous opposition from the Office of Systems Analysis (OSA) at the Pentagon. The OSA, which had been created in 1961 when Robert McNamara took up the position of Secretary of Defense and was staffed with specialists devoted to the cost-benefit calculation of weapons purchase, troop deployment and base decisions,[46] severely criticized this proposal. McNamara, who of course trusted the judgement of the OSA, registered his disapproval of the plan in October.[47]

The main point in the OSA's criticism was that neither the navy nor the JCS had established a definite requirement for a base for conducting stabilizing operations in the area, but the former also pointed out that the establishment of an American military facility in Diego Garcia would not necessarily maintain the British presence 'East of Suez'. Accordingly, John Reilly of the State Department speculated that McNamara's position could probably only be altered by a firm indication that a base on Diego Garcia would indeed keep Britain 'East of Suez'. According to Reilly, that was by far McNamara's primary concern throughout the whole BIOT affair.[48]

This American desire to keep Britain 'East of Suez' was harboured in vain. Wilson's announcement about the acceleration of the withdrawal from 'East of Suez' dashed the remaining hope on the American side. However, faced with increasing Soviet naval activity in the Indian Ocean, the United States continued to proceed with the plan to build military facilities on Diego Garcia.[49] With McNamara having left the scene (he resigned from his post at the end of February 1968), on 15 June 1968 Paul Nitze, the Deputy Secretary of Defense, approved the construction of a 'modest' military facility on Diego Garcia, which followed the plan of the previous year and included ship-to-shore

## 200   *Yoichi Kibata*

communications, telemetry and intelligence monitoring capabilities, at a cost of $26 million, while discarding a new and bigger ($44 million) plan proposed by the Joint Chiefs of Staff.[50] This decision was communicated to Britain in July, and the British side approved it in principle.[51] After that the American plan did not make progress for some time because of opposition within Congress, but at the end of 1970 Congressional approval was finally received. On 15 December 1970 both governments made public announcements about the building of a naval communication centre on Diego Garcia.[52]

This announcement said nothing about the inhabitants of Diego Garcia and the other islands in the Chagos Archipelago, but behind the scenes preparations were made for their expulsion. BIOT administrator John Todd told the islanders of Diego Garcia on 24 January 1971 that they should leave the island because it was going to be closed to civilian habitation. As stated at the beginning of this paper, this problem has been dealt with by David Vine and others, and this paper does not discuss it in much detail. But at least the following should be mentioned.

It was immediately after the concrete plan for the building of a military facility on Diego Garcia was approved in the summer of 1968 that the American government officially told the British side that it preferred, 'the total removal of all the inhabitants on the island'.[53] After this the problem of 'resettling' the inhabitants began to be discussed more intensely by policymakers, but it should be emphasized that this issue was always present in the Anglo–American deal from the very beginning. As has been mentioned before, the Anglo–American talks in February 1964, which were the starting point of the whole process, touched upon this problem. Also immediately after the creation of the BIOT an official at the Colonial Office had written: 'It would be helpful if we were soon in a position to say that the existing inhabitants of Diego Garcia were being moved (? resettled) as soon as possible.'[54] Actually, as early as 1967 those Chagossians who visited Mauritius for regular vacations or medical treatment began to be prevented from returning to the islands.[55]

What is important is that, just as with the original creation of the BIOT, both governments were aware that the ousting of the inhabitants from their islands was tantamount to those colonial practices which were no longer tolerated in the age of decolonization, and would invite international criticism, especially from the Committee of Twenty-Four at the United Nations. In order to avoid or weaken such criticism, policymakers on both sides attempted to portray those people as only temporary residents. For that purpose Frederick Lee, the British Secretary of State for the Colonies, proposed to 'avoid any reference to "permanent inhabitants", instead, to refer to the people in the islands as Mauritians and Seychellois'.[56] In the same vein, Dean Rusk, the American Secretary of State, wrote to the American embassy in London: 'We suggest that the term "migrant laborers" be used in any conversations with HMG as withdrawal of "inhabitants" obviously would be more difficult to justify to littoral countries and Committee of Twenty-four.'[57]

'A new Okinawa': Diego Garcia in the 1960s 201

It should be added that there were those who were clearly aware that such an argument was nothing but a deception. J.W.D. Gray of the Defence Department of the Foreign Office told David Bruce, the American ambassador, that the expression 'migrant laborers' was a 'good term for cosmetic purposes although it might be difficult to make completely credible as some of the "migrants" are second generation Diego residents'.[58] In fact, many of the inhabitants of Diego Garcia and the other two islands in the Chagos Archipelago, who were all to be deported to Mauritius and the Seychelles,[59] were not migrant labourers and were entitled to continue to live on their home islands. However, their expulsion from the islands was forcefully conducted by both governments in complete disregard of their rights.

## The expansion of the American base

The history of Diego Garcia after this is one of the continuing expansion of the American military base. In October 1972 a further agreement to establish a 'limited U.S. naval communication facility' on Diego Garcia was concluded between Britain and the United States and in March 1973 the communication station was opened.[60] But the American military facility on Diego Garcia did not stop at this 'limited' scale. As a result of the Fourth Arab-Israeli War (the Yom Kippur War) in the autumn of that year, the military significance of Diego Garcia came to be increasingly stressed by the American military, and the government in Washington therefore began to plan the building of a much bigger naval support base. At first, the British government was a little perplexed about this American plan which exceeded the level envisaged in the preceding agreements, but it eventually approved the plan. At the beginning of February 1974 an announcement was made in the House of Commons that Britain had agreed to the new American proposal and that the facilities on Diego Garcia would be expanded. 'A new Okinawa' was now well on the way to being created.

This was the starting point in the growth of Diego Garcia as a pivotal location in American world strategy, but the years dealt with in this paper can be regarded as the vital preparatory period. This period is important in reflecting the changing nature of international power relations in the Indian Ocean and revealing the imperialistic collusion between Britain and the United States. And in concluding this article, it should again be stressed that the result of this collusion is still before us in the form of the suffering of the former inhabitants of the Chagos Archipelago.

## Notes

1 *The Sunday Times*, 21 Sept. 1975.
2 See Laura Jeffrey, *Chagos Islanders in Mauritius and the UK: Forced Displacement and Onward Migration*, Manchester: Manchester University Press, 2011.
3 For the judicial aspects concerning Diego Garcia and the Chagossians, see Peter H. Sand, *United States and Britain in Diego Garcia: The Future of a Controversial Base*, Basingstoke: Palgrave Macmillan, 2009.

202 *Yoichi Kibata*

4 Mark Curtis, *Web of Deceit: Britain's Real Role in the World*, London: Vintage, 2003, Ch. 22, and John Pilger, *Freedom Next Time*, London: Bantam Press, 2006, Ch. 1.
5 David Vine, *Island of Shame: The Secret History of the U.S. Military Base on Diego Garcia*, Princeton, NJ: Princeton University Press, 2011.
6 John Madley, *Diego Garcia: A Contrast to the Falklands*, Minority Rights Group, report No.54, 1982.
7 For the early history of the Chagos Archipelago, see Garth Abraham, 'Paradise Claimed: Disputed Sovereignty over the Chagos Archipelago', *The South African Law Journal*, 128/1, 2011.
8 Sandra J.T.M. Evers and Marry Kooy (eds), *Eviction from the Chagos Islands: Displacement and Struggle for Identity*, Leiden: Brill, 2011.
9 Ashley Jackson, *War and Empire in Mauritius and the Indian Ocean*, Basingstoke: Palgrave, 2001, pp. 44–7, and K.S. Jawatkar, *Diego Garcia in International Diplomacy*, Bombay: Popular Prakashan, 1983, pp. 5–6.
10 Monoranjan Bezboruah, *US Strategy in the Indian Ocean: The International Response*, New York: Praeger, 1977, p. 35.
11 The National Archives, Kew (TNA), DEFE7/1652 Watson to Gough 1 Apr. 1959.
12 TNA DEFE7/1652 Dickson to Sandys 27 May 1959, and DEFE7/1652 'U.S. Navy Interest in the Indian Ocean' Admiralty brief Aug. 1959.
13 TNA DEFE7/1652 Hall to Deverell 25 May 1961.
14 Vine, *Island of Shame*, pp. 4–5, 68–9, and Vytautas B. Bandjunis, *Diego Garcia: Creation of the Indian Ocean Base*, San Jose, CA: Writer's Showcase, 2001, pp. 2–3.
15 TNA FO371/166308 Ledward to Warner 9 Feb. 1962, and FO371/166309 Benwell to Waterfield 11 Apr. 1962.
16 TNA FO371/173504 'Anglo–U.S. Defence Interests outside Europe: Views of Mr. Paul Nitze' 18 Jan. 1963.
17 *Foreign Relations of the United States (FRUS), 1961–1963*, Vol.XIX, *South Asia*, doc.284, Note from the Department of State to the British Embassy 25 Apr. 1963.
18 *FRUS, 1961–1963*, Vol.XIX, *South Asia*, Doc.324 Department of State to the Embassy in the UK, 23 Aug. 1963; and TNA CAB21/5418 Rose to Cumming-Bruce 29 Aug. 1963.
19 TNA CO968/879 'U.S. Defence Interests in the Indian Ocean' memo Feb. 1964.
20 National Archives and Records Administration (NARA), RG59, DEF15 IND-US, box 1638, Department of State to Embassy in London 13 May 1964.
21 TNA CAB148/2 'United States Defence Interests in the Indian Ocean' Chairman of the Defence and Overseas Policy (Official) Committee memo 4 May 1964.
22 TNA FO371/179122 Foreign Office [FO] to Washington 6 July 1964.
23 TNA CO968/841 Fairclough to Greenwood 22 Jan. 1965.
24 TNA FO371/184523 FO to Washington 30 April 1965, FO371/184525 US embassy London memo 24 June 1965, and PREM13/1387 Healey to Brown 12 May 1967.
25 TNA FO371/184528 Mauritius Defence Matters meeting 23 Sept. 1965, and CO1036/1650 Greig to Smith 14 Feb. 1966.
26 TNA FO371/184529 'Defence Facilities in the Indian Ocean', Greenwood memo 5 Nov. 1965.
27 TNA FO371/184529 'Defence Facilities in the Indian Ocean', Greenwood memo 5 Nov. 1965, and PREM13/1387 Stewart to Wilson 6 Nov. 1965. For the Committee of Twenty-Four and the British attitude towards it, see Wm. Roger Louis, 'Public Enemy Number One: The British Empire in the Dock at the United Nations, 1957–71', in Martin Lynn (ed.), *The British Empire in the 1950s: Retreat or Revival?*, Basingstoke: Palgrave Macmillan, 2006.
28 Sand, *United States and Britain*, p. 4.
29 Karl Hack, *Defence and Decolonisation in Southeast Asia: Britain, Malaya and Singapore 1941–68*, Richmond: Curzon, 2001, p. 262.

## 'A new Okinawa': Diego Garcia in the 1960s   203

30 Jeffrey Pickering, *Britain's Withdrawal from East of Suez: The Politics of Retrenchment*, Basingstoke: Macmillan, 1998, p. 113.

31 Saki Dockrill, *Britain's Retreat from East of Suez: The Choice between Europe and the World?*, Basingstoke: Palgrave-Macmillan, 2002, p. 41.

32 Pickering, *Britain's Withdrawal*, p. 147.

33 *FRUS, 1964–1968*, Vol.XXI, *Near East Region; Arabian Peninsula*, doc.37, memo, 'Indian Ocean Facilities' enclosed in memo, from Rusk to Johnson 15 July 1964.

34 TNA CAB21/5418 'Brief on UK/US London Discussions on United States Defence Interests in the Indian Ocean', Directors of Defence Plans note 6 Mar. 1964.

35 TNA FO371/184523 'Defence Facilities in the Indian Ocean', Peck memo 9 Apr. 1965.

36 TNA CAB148/20 OPD(65)68 'Defence Facilities in the Indian Ocean', Stewart and Healey memo 7 Apr. 1965.

37 Sand, *United States and Britain*, appendix 1.

38 Spencer Mawby, *British Policy in Aden and the Protectorates 1955–67: Last Outpost of a Middle East Empire*, London: Routledge, 2005, Ch. 6.

39 *Statement on the Defence Estimates 1966*, Part I, *The Defence Review* (Cmnd.2901), London: HMSO, 1966, p. 8

40 *Supplementary Statement on Defence Policy 1967* (Cmnd.3357), London: HMSO, 1967, p. 5, and P.L. Pham, *Ending of 'East of Suez': The British Decision to Withdraw from Malaysia and Singapore, 1964–1968*, Oxford: Oxford University Press, 2010, Chs. 4–6

41 TNA CAB148/28 OPD(66)65 'Defence Facilities in the Western Indian Ocean' Healey memo 31 May 1966.

42 Vine, *Island of Shame*, pp. 85–6, and Bandjunis, *Diego Garcia*, pp. 20–1.

43 TNA CAB148/33 OPD(67)57 'Aldabra: Plan to Develop Airfield Facilities', Healey memo 26 July 1967.

44 For example, "Scientists fight defence plans for Island of Aldabra", *The Times*, 16 Aug. 1967, and Julian Huxley to the editor, *The Times*, 22 Aug. 1967.

45 TNA FCO46/10 Gore-Booth to Brown 17 Nov. 1967.

46 Vine, *Island of Shame*, 96–7.

47 NARA RG59 DEF15 UK-US box 1644 Reilly to Farley 22 Nov. 1967.

48 NARA RG59 DEF15 UK-US box 1644 Reilly to Farley 22 Nov. 1967.

49 For example, in March 1968 four Soviet warships from Vladivostok entered the Indian Ocean from the west and called at ports on the Indian Ocean subcontinent, the Persian Gulf and the coast of East Africa. Bandjunis, *Diego Garcia*, p. 31.

50 NARA RG59 DEF15 UK-US box 1644 Earle to Farley 2 July 1968.

51 TNA PREM13/2565 Brown to Wilson, 25 July 1968.

52 *The Times*, 16 Dec. 1970.

53 TNA FCO46/16 Grey to Sykes 20 Aug. 1968.

54 TNA CO1036/1344 Jerrome to Hall 18 Nov. 1965. The parenthesis is in the original.

55 Vine, *Island of Shame*, p. 92.

56 TNA CO1036/1643 Lee to the Commissioner, BIOT 25 Feb. 1966.

57 NARA RG59 DEF15 IND-US box 1452 Rusk to American Embassy in London 7 Aug. 1968.

58 NARA RG59 DEF15 IND-US box 1452 Bruce to Department of State 9 Aug. 1968.

59 Some of the inhabitants of Diego Garcia went to Mauritius via the Seychelles. The others moved to the Salomons and Peros Banhos, but eventually together with all the inhabitants of these two islands they had to move either to Mauritius or to the Seychelles.

60 Sand, *United States and Britain*, Appendix 3.

# Index

Allied occupation of Japan 5, 18; aims 100; an American affair 107, 108, 112; American public opinion on 104–105; Japanese textile industry 110–11; new Constitution of Japan 107, 109; *see also* Allied press and the post-war occupation of Japan

Allied press and the post-war occupation of Japan 5, 100–16; Britain's retreat 108; censorship 100; importance of the press 5, 104–105, 113; MacArthur's publicity machine 103–104; SCAP 103, 106, 107, 111, 115 (criticism 104, 113); SCAP GHQ 100, 103, 104, 105, 106, 110, 114; US/Japan partnership 113; vast volume of material 101, 103; war correspondent 100, 114; *see also* Allied occupation of Japan; *Manchester Guardian* and the Allied occupation of Japan; *New York Times* and the Allied occupation of Japan

Alston, Sir Beilby 40, 66

AMSH (Association for Moral and Social Hygiene) 73, 80

Anglo-American relations 96, 173, 174, 177–8; Britain/US imperialistic collusion 201; China as source of disunity in 173, 174; East of Suez 196–7, 198, 199; Lowe, Peter: Anglo-American relations in East Asia 3, 7, 135; rivalry 18; *see also* Anglo-American relations in the Korean War; BIOT

Anglo-American relations in the Korean War: British/American disagreement 6, 136, 137–40, 142–4, 145–7, 148–9; British concessions 136, 139–40, 143–4, 148; Cold War 136–7, 143, 147, 148; different international loyalties 136, 138, 147, 148; 'special

relationship' 6, 135, 136; Washington/ London tensions 6, 135, 139, 143–4, 148; *see also* Anglo-American relations; Geneva Conference, Korean phase; Geneva Conference, planning for

Anglo-Japanese Alliance 8–19, 57, 64, 87; 1905 revised treaty 3–4, 12, 18; 1911 revised treaty 4, 9, 10, 12, 17, 18; Britain/Japan trade 9–10, 13–14, 18; British 'retirement' 3–4, 18, 19; China 12–14, 15–16, 17, 18; end of 17, 53; Four-Power Pact 17; Germany, war against 35, 36; Japanese expansionism 13–14, 15; Korea 12, 18; League of Nations 64; Lowe, Peter 2–3, 87; post-war period 8, 15–18; pre-1914 period 8–12; Royal Navy 10–12, 15; Russo-Japanese War 9, 10–11; tensions 2–3, 8–9, 18; Twenty-One Demands 40, 43, 48, 50, 52, 53; US 8, 15–17, 64; World War I 8, 14–15; *see also* Japan; Paris Peace Conference; Twenty-One Demands; Washington Naval Conference

Anglo-Japanese relations: British policy of accommodation and friendship with Japan 89, 90, 95, 96; British suspicion of Japan 57, 89; changing nature of 57; China as major source of disunity 57; impact of Twenty-One Demands on 52, 53; rapprochement 96; trade 9–10, 13, 18, 90; World War I 57; *see also* Twenty-One Demands; Siberian intervention

Attlee, Clement Richard 108, 110, 111, 113, 120, 121

Australia 11; building up its army and air force 88; Singapore strategy 5, 87, 89,

*Index* 205

90, 93–5, 97, 98; vulnerability to attack 5, 97
Avenol, Joseph 76, 77–8, 79

Baldwin, Stanley 92, 120
Balfour, Arthur 15, 16–17, 59
Ball, George 193
BCOF (British Commonwealth Occupation Force) 107, 115
Bell, Major Mackintosh 60, 61
Bennett, John Sterndale 132
Bennett, R. B. 96
Bernstorff, Johann Graf 22, 26
Bethmann Hollweg, Theobald von 24, 31
Bevin, Ernest 120, 121, 122, 123, 128, 129
Bezboruah, Monoranjan 191–2
Bhattacharya, Narendra Nath 23, 29
Bidault, Georges 142, 143
BIOT (British Indian Ocean Territories) 7, 190–203; Aldabra 193, 195, 196, 198, 199; BIOT Agreement 197–201; British/American negotiations 7, 190, 191, 192–5, 196–7, 199–200, 201; Chagos archipelago 7, 190, 191, 192; Chagossians 190 (forced exile 7, 190, 200–201, 203; 'temporary residents'/ 'migrant laborers' 200–201); creation of 192–5; decolonization 7, 190, 191, 193–5, 200; detachment from Mauritius and the Seychelles 193–5; Diego Garcia 191, 192 (American military base 7, 190, 192, 199–200; expansion of the American base 201); East of Suez 196–7, 198–9; Mauritius 7, 190, 191; 'a new Okinawa' 190, 201; OSA 199; Peros Banhos 191, 203; Salomon Islands 191, 203; Soviet Union 199; UN 193, 195, 200; *see also* Indian Ocean
Black, Robert 158, 164
Bopp, Franz 22
Bose, Rash Behari 23, 27
Brenan, Sir John F., 77, 78
Britain's retreat 1, 6, 7, 8, 11, 57; Allied press and the post-war occupation of Japan 108; Anglo-Japanese Alliance and British 'retirement' 3–4, 18, 19; British decline from a position of strength in East Asia 14, 68, 87; planned retreat 8, 18, 19
Brown, George 179, 180, 182–3, 184, 185, 198
Bruce, David 201
Bryan, William J.: 'Bryan Statement' 36, 44

Burma 1, 3, 4, 18, 21, 30–1
Butler, Josephine 73
Butler, Sir Paul 109

Canada: Indian migration 23–4, 26–7; Singapore strategy 5, 89, 95–6, 97; US 96
Casey, R. G. 88
Cecil, Lord Robert 59, 62
CER (Chinese Eastern Railway) 57, 63, 74–5; NMR 81; Russian women refugees in China 73, 75, 80–2; sale to Manchukuo 80–2; *see also* railway
Chamberlain, Neville 89–90, 91–2, 120, 121, 171–2
Chandra, Ram 27, 28, 31
Chattopadhyaya, Virendra Nath 25
Chen Yi 174, 177, 179, 183
China 2, 6, 137, 155, 171–89; Anglo-Japanese Alliance 12–14, 15–16, 17, 18, 57; China as source of disunity in Anglo-American alliance 173, 174; Cultural Revolution 6, 171, 172, 178–9, 181, 182, 183, 184; Foreign Ministry 176, 178–9, 181; Geneva Conference 141, 142–3, 148; Germany 4, 22; Hong Kong 172, 176–8, 179, 182, 183, 184, 185; hydrogen bomb 180–1, 184; nationalism 1, 3, 8, 15, 17, 52, 38, 52, 79, 87; New China News Agency 179, 180; Nine-Power Pact 17; *People's Daily* 174, 175, 188; Red Guards 179–80, 181, 182, 184–5, 188; Shanghai 178, 179; Sino–Japanese Treaty (1915) 15, 16; Sino–Japanese Treaty (1918) 15, 16; Sino–Soviet dispute 177, 184; storming of foreign embassies 182, 184; Twenty-One Demands 38, 48, 50, 52, 53 (Chinese press 38, 39; territorial integrity 35, 39, 40, 43); US 171, 173, 174, 175–7, 184; Washington Naval Conference 17; Xinhai Revolution (1911–12) 13, 38; *see also* China/Britain relationship; Manchuria; Qingdao; Shandong; Shanghai; Vietnam War
China/Britain relationship 171; admission of China into the UN 171, 174, 183–4; appeasement of China 6, 171, 185; Battle of the Portland Place 180–1, 188; British diplomats, treatment of 171, 172, 178–80, 181, 184, 188; burning of the British Office 180, 181–2, 184; diplomatic relations 6,

206 *Index*

171, 172–3, 178, 180, 182–5; everyday
Cold War 6, 172–3, 178, 184, 185;
trade 1, 183; *see also* China; Vietnam
War
Churchill, Winston: Geneva Conference
136–44 *passim*, 148; South-East
Asia regional authority 117, 118, 121,
122
CID (Committee of Imperial Defence) 5,
12, 88, 95
Clyde, William 123, 132
Cold War 148, 152; Anglo-American
relations 136–7, 143, 147, 148; *détente*
136, 143; East of Suez 196; Hong
Kong 152, 161; *see also* Geneva
Conference, planning for
Commonwealth 18, 173; British trade
with 153–4; Commonwealth
Secretariat 133; Geneva Conference
136–40 *passim*, 145–7, 148; *see also*
Hong Kong/UK relations
during EEC enlargement
negotiations
Cooke, Alistair 112
Cowperthwaite, John 159, 162, 164, 165
Cradock, Percy 180, 181, 185
Crane, Burton 103, 106
Crowdy, Dame Rachel 73, 79–80, 84
Cumming, Admiral Mansfield 60
Curtis, Mark 190
Curzon, Lord 16, 23, 64

*Daily Express* 93, 158
*Daily Herald* 93
*Daily Telegraph* 40
*Daily Worker* 93
Dayal, Har 24, 25–6
De Gaulle, Charles 153, 154
Dean, Arthur 141, 142, 145
decolonization: BIOT 7, 190, 191, 193–5,
200; Hong Kong 153, 154
Dening, Esler 119, 120, 121, 124, 128
devaluation of sterling (1967) 152, 198,
199
disarmament 16, 90, 180, 184
Disraeli, Benjamin 21
Dixon, Sir Pierson 160
Donald, William 36, 38, 39, 40, 54
DPRK (Democratic People's Republic of
Korea) 138, 143, 146, 148
Duff Cooper, Alfred 117–18, 119, 128,
131
Dulles, John Foster 112, 113; Geneva
Conference 137–46 *passim*, 148

East Asia 1; British decline from a posi-
tion of strength in 14, 68, 87; East
Asia/South-East Asia comparison 2;
Lowe, Peter: Anglo-American relations in East Asia 3, 7, 135; US,
involvement in East Asian affairs 15
East of Suez 195–6; BIOT 196–7, 198–9;
British withdrawal from 7, 171, 191,
196, 197, 198–9; Cold War 196;
Wilson, Harold 196, 198, 199
*The Economist* 159
Eden, Anthony 121; Geneva Conference
3, 6, 136, 137, 141–8 *passim*
EEC (European Economic Community) 71
EEC enlargement 153–4; British trade
with the Empire/Commonwealth
153–4; complicating Britain's with-
drawal from its Empire 153–4, 163,
167; *see also* Hong Kong/UK
relations during EEC enlargement
negotiations
Eisenhower, Dwight 136–9, 142, 144,
145, 146, 148
Eliot, Sir Charles 66
Empson, William 123, 128
*Evening Standard* 93

Falk, Ray 103
Falklands 21, 191
*Far Eastern Survey* (1945) 104
Fisher, Admiral Sir John 11
Fisher, Sir Warren 92, 98
Four-Power Pact 17
France 17; Anglo-French entente (1904)
10; Indochina 142, 144; Russo-
Japanese War 10–11; Siberian
intervention 61, 64
Fraser, David 36, 38, 41, 44, 45, 51, 52, 54

Gandhi, Mahatma 25
Garstin, Charles F. 75, 76
GATT (General Agreement on Trade
and Tariffs) 158, 160
Gayn, Mark 103, 114
GCCS (Government Code and Cypher
School) 58, 61, 65, 66
Geneva Conference (1954) 3, 171, 172;
*see also the entries below for* Geneva
Conference
Geneva Conference, Indochina 3, 6, 136,
142, 143, 144–5, 146, 147, 148; Dien
Bien Phu crisis 6, 144, 146; Viet Minh
142, 144, 146; *see also* Geneva
Conference, planning for

*Index* 207

Geneva Conference, Korean phase 6, 143, 144–7, 148–9; all-Korea elections 146–7, 148; British/American disagreement 144, 145–7, 148–9; British concessions 147; chairmanship 145; collapse of 6, 147; Commonwealth 145–7, 148; DPRK 146; Indochina crisis 144–5, 146, 147; Korean unification 135, 136, 145, 147; ROK 145–6, 147, 148; US 145–7, 148; *see also* Geneva Conference, planning for

Geneva Conference, planning for 6, 135–42, 148; 1954 Berlin Conference 135, 142–4, 148; British/American disagreement 6, 136, 137–40, 142–4, 148; British concessions 136, 139–40, 143–4, 148; China 137, 141, 142–3, 148; Commonwealth 136–40 *passim*, 148; composition question 135, 136, 137–44, 148; DPRK 138, 143, 148; India 135, 136, 137–40, 141, 148; Panmunjom 135, 138, 140–1, 142; political conference on Korea 135, 137, 142–3; ROK 137, 138, 143, 144; Soviet Union 137–8, 139–40, 142–4, 148; UN and the membership question 137–40, 148; UN General Assembly 137, 139 (Resolution 711 (VII) 140, 141, 143; Resolution 716 (VIII) 141); US 137, 138, 140–1, 143–4; *see also* Geneva Conference, Indochina; Geneva Conference, Korean phase

Gent, Sir Edward 124, 127, 133

German campaign against British India 4, 21–34; Andaman Islands, attack on 4, 29–30; Bangkok, German consuls in 4, 30, 31; British resistance to German sabotage 4, 29, 30, 31; Burma 21, 30 (entering Burma from Thailand 4, 21, 30–1); China 4, 22; East Asiatic Squadron of cruisers 21; India, fomenting unrest in 21, 24–5, 31 (assistance with arms 4, 26–9, 30, 31; supporting Indian revolutionaries 4, 22, 24–6, 31); Netherlands East Indies, German community in 4, 21–2, 28, 29–30; Philippines 4, 22, 30; Qingdao 4, 21, 22, 37; Shandong 15, 16; Shanghai, German consuls in 4, 22, 30, 31; US 4, 22, 24, 26–7, 30, 31; *see also* India/British India

Germany 72, 82, 89, 90; *see also* German campaign against British India

Gleboff, General Th. L. 78–9

Gore-Booth, Paul 199

Gray J.W.D. 201

Greene, Sir William Conyngham 14, 60; Twenty-One Demands 38, 40, 41, 43–4, 46

Greenwood, Arthur 195

Grey, Anthony 179, 183

Grey, Sir Edward 9–10, 12, 13, 14, 15, 18; Twenty-One Demands 14, 39, 40, 43–4, 48, 50

Guillain, Robert 112

Gull, E.M. 17

Hankey, Sir Maurice 5, 88–98; Australia 5, 89, 93–5, 97, 98; Canada 5, 89, 95–6, 97; Dominions tour 5, 88–9, 91–2, 93–6, 97, 98; imperial defence policy 5, 90–4, 97–8 ('Empire, big navy' school 89); New Zealand 5, 89, 95, 98; Royal Navy 90, 91; South Africa 5, 89, 93, 95, 97; *see also* Singapore strategy

Harding, Warren 16–17

Hardinge, Lord 23, 61

Healey, Denis 198, 199

Heath, Edward 164

*Herald-Tribune* 101, 114

Hewitt, Peter 179

Hioki, Eki 39, 41, 45, 48, 50, 51

Hitler, Adolf 89

Hodgson, Robert 59, 65

Honda Kumatar⊠, 43, 44

Hong Kong 1; 1967 devaluation of sterling 152; China 172, 176–8, 182, 183, 185; Cold War 152, 161; Cultural Revolution 179; R&R 176, 177, 184; US 176–7, 184; *see also* China; Hong Kong/UK relations during EEC enlargement negotiations

Hong Kong/UK relations during EEC enlargement negotiations, 6, 152–70; Britain, conduit for low-cost Asian manufactures 6, 157; British determination to retain Hong Kong 154–6; British mitigation strategies for Hong Kong 160–3, 167; CET 152, 154, 158–62 *passim*, 166, 167; China 155, 156; damaged Hong Kong/UK relations 166, 167; decolonization 153, 154; EEC enlargement as a hypothetical shock to Hong Kong 158–60; FED 165; GATT 158, 160; HKGCC 159; Hong Kong business groups,

208  *Index*

rent-seeking behaviour 6, 165–6, 167;
Hong Kong dependence on UK
market 154, 156–8, 166; Hong Kong
public opinion 163–5; imperial
network: Hong Kong business elites/
British politicians/journalists 166–7;
parliamentary and press opposition to
British EEC membership 165; protectionism 152, 160, 161, 162, 163,
166, 167; shadow diplomacy 153,
165–6, 167; veto against British EEC
membership 153, 154, 163; *see also*
EEC enlargement
Hopson, Donald 174, 175, 177, 179, 180,
181, 182
human trafficking: AMSH 73, 80; efforts
to stop trafficking in women and children 73–4; League of Nations 73–4,
84; Russian women refugees in China
71, 75, 76, 83; US 74; *see also* Russian
women refugees in China

IJA (Imperial Japanese Army) 37;
Siberian intervention 58–9, 61, 62, 63
(withdrawal from Siberia 65, 66, 67)
imperialism 118, 184; British imperialism
93, 95, 122, 126, 129, 172; Japanese
imperialism 106; shift away from
imperialism as a frame of mind 5; US
174
India/British India: Bengal 23; the
'brightest jewel' in Britain's imperial
crown 21; Canada, Indian migration
to 23–4, 26–7; exports of cotton 9,
156; Geneva Conference 135, 136,
137–40, 141, 148; Ghadr party 24,
26–7, 28, 30–1 (Ghadr Trial 31);
importance for Britain 22; independence 3, 31; Indian Army 22, 23;
Indian Independence Committee 25,
26, 30, 31; Indian National Congress
23, 25, 26; Indian nationalist movement 57; Indian revolutionaries 4,
22–7, 29–30; Japan 57; *Komagata
Maru* 26–7; Korean War 138, 139;
NNRC 138, 141, 142; Punjab 23, 24,
26–7; World War I, manpower contribution in 22, 23; *see also* German
campaign against British India
Indian Ocean: Britain 191–2; Suez Crisis
191–2; US 191–2; World War II 191;
*see also* BIOT
Indochina *see* Geneva Conference,
Indochina

Indonesia 173, 175, 179
Inoue Kaoru 46, 47, 49
Inoue Katsunosuke 39–40, 43–5, 48
International Settlement 22, 77
internationalism 5
*Izvestiya* 93

Jamieson, E. G., 81
Japan 1; Germany, war against 35, 36,
37; Japan-British exhibition, London
(1910) 13; Japanese expansionism 1,
15, 68, 87 (Manchuria 13–14, 64, 87;
Twenty-One Demands 35, 36, 37, 38,
43, 52); Japanese imperialism 106;
occupation of Korea 12; occupation of
Singapore 18, 118, 127; shipbuilding
11–12; surrender of Imperial Japan
100; USS *Missouri* 100, 120; *see also
the entries below for* Japan; Allied
occupation of Japan; Anglo-Japanese
Alliance; Anglo-Japanese relations;
Emperor of Japan; IJA; Russo-
Japanese War; Twenty-One Demands
Japan and the Twenty-One Demands:
criticism towards Japan 38–40, 43, 45,
46, 52; expansionism in China 35, 36,
37, 38, 43, 52; foreign mistrust
towards Japan 4, 40, 42, 44, 48, 51, 53;
Japanese military intimidation 42;
Japanese newspapers 39, 41, 46; senior
statesmen 46–50, 52–3; *see also*
Anglo-Japanese Alliance; Japan;
Twenty-One Demands
Japan, Emperor Hirohito, 103, 104,
105–106, 107, 111; renunciation of his
divinity 105, 109
Japanese Foreign Office (Gaimushō) 37,
38, 66
Jebsen, Frederick 27–8
Jellicoe, Lord 87
Jerram, Admiral Thomas 21
Johnson, Lyndon 173, 175, 176, 177, 198
Jordan, Sir John 38, 39, 40, 42, 50

Katō Takaaki 9, 13; Twenty-One
Demands 14, 37, 39–49 *passim*, 51, 52,
53
Khrushchev, Nikita 177
Killearn, Lord (Sir Miles Lampson)
121–3, 128–30, 133; criticism 127, 129;
food crisis 123–4, 126, 127, 129;
foreign service in Egypt 122, 123, 125;
Indonesian dispute 126; Killearn/
MacDonald comparison 125–6;

Killearn/MacDonald successful partnership 5–6, 117, 126–7; Special Commissioner 5, 117, 122–3, 128–30; *see also* South-East Asia regional authority
Knipping, Hubert 22, 30–1
Knowles, W. C. G. 159
Kolchak, Admiral 61, 62, 63, 64, 67
Korea 1; Anglo-Japanese Alliance 12, 18; Japanese occupation of Korea 12; *see also the entries below for* Korea
Korean Armistice Agreement (1953) 137, 148; Britain/US disagreements 135, 136; military ceasefire at the thirty-eighth parallel 135; NNRC 138, 141, 142; *see also* Korean War
Korean War 6, 135–51, 171, 172, 176; Allied casualties 111; India 138, 139; Lowe, Peter 2, 3, 6; US 3; *see also* Geneva Conference, Korean phase; Geneva Conference, planning for; Korean Armistice Agreement
Kraft, Vincent 30

Labour Party (Britain) 120, 121, 125, 166, 196; British policy and relations with China 171, 172, 173, 174, 182, 183, 184
Langley, Walter 45, 48
Latham, Sir John 94, 96–7
Laurence, William 102, 114
League of Nations 83; Anglo-Japanese Alliance 64; Britain as chief support for 71, 83; budget 72, 74, 82, 83; Commission of Enquiry into Traffic in Women and Children in the East 72, 73–4, 76, 83; Convention for the Suppression of the Traffic in Women and Children 73; human trafficking 73–4, 84; refugee 72, 83; Russian women refugees in China 71, 73–9 *passim*, 82, 83–4; TWC 73, 75, 79; *see also* Nansen International Office for Refugees; Russian women refugees in China
Lee, Frederick 200
Liu Shaoqi 173
Lloyd, Selwyn 137–8, 139, 140
Lodge, Henry Cabot 137–9, 141
Lowe, Peter 2, 5, 7, 8, 172; Anglo-American relations in East Asia 3, 7, 135; Anglo-Japanese Alliance 2–3, 87; Britain's retreat 18; *Contending with Nationalism and Communism* 2, 117;

contributions 2–3, 7; expansion of American power into the region 7; *Great Britain and Japan* 2, 36, 57, 87; Korean War 2, 3, 6; *The Origins of the Korean War* 135; Pacific War 18; Twenty-One Demands 36; Vietnam War 2
Lu Zhengxiang 48, 50
Lyttelton, Oliver 117, 122

MacArthur, General Douglas 101, 103–13 *passim*; International Military Tribunal for the Far East 107
MacDonald, Malcolm 120–1, 130, 133, 134; campaign against Sarawak's cession to the Crown 126; Governor-General of Malaya 5, 117, 120, 125; head of the Commission-General 128–9, 130; Killearn/MacDonald comparison 125–6; Killearn/MacDonald successful partnership 5–6, 117, 126–7; Malayan Union crisis 126; *see also* South-East Asia regional authority
MacDonald, Ramsay 90, 91, 92
Macmillan, Harold 152–3, 155, 166, 196
Malay States 1
Malaya 5, 118, 119, 121, 124, 133
Malayan Union 124, 126
Malaysia 173, 174, 198
*Manchester Guardian* and the Twenty-One Demands 36, 39, 40, 45–6, 50–1; critical of Japan's demands 36, 45, 52
*Manchester Guardian* and the Allied occupation of Japan 5, 101, 102, 113; atomic bomb, Hiroshima 109; English regional/small paper 101, 109–10; Japanese textile industry 108, 109, 110, 111, 112–13; poor/shallow coverage of the occupation 108–109, 110; pro-SCAP perspective 111; San Francisco Peace Conference 112–13; trade policies 101, 110–11, 115; *see also* Allied press and the post-war occupation of Japan
Manchuria/Manchukuo 1; Japanese expansionism 13–14, 64, 87; Russian women refugees in China 73, 77, 79, 80–2; Twenty-One Demands 13–14, 35, 37, 42, 43, 49
Mao Zedong 171, 172–3, 174, 175, 177, 180, 182, 184, 185
Matsukata Masayoshi 46–7, 48, 49, 50
McNamara, Robert 198, 199

210    *Index*

Menon, V. K. Krishna 138–40, 142, 147
Metzler, C. E. 77, 78
Milner, Lord 59
Molotov, Vyacheslav 142–3, 145
Mongolia 4, 35, 47, 61, 63
Morris, John 113
Morrison, George 36–7, 38, 39, 45, 54
Mountbatten, Lord Louis 119–20, 121, 123, 124–5, 128
Mukherji, Jatin 23, 29
Murray, Ralph 123, 128, 132

Nansen, Fridtjof 72
Nansen International Office for Refugees 71, 72, 75
Nehru, Jawaharlal 136, 138
Netherlands East Indies 121; German community in 4, 21–2, 28, 29–30
*New York Times* and the Allied occupation of Japan 5, 100, 101–108, 113; advantages enjoyed by the paper 101–102; atomic bomb, Hiroshima/Nagasaki 102, 114; conservatism 105, 107; division of labour at 103; extensive coverage 102, 111; favourable to US 103; MacArthur, Douglas, General 101, 103, 106, 111; a national/international paper 101, 109; positive characteristics of coverage 105; pro-SCAP perspective 103–104, 106–107, 111; purge programme 106, 107; San Francisco Peace Conference 111–12, 116; surrender of Japan 102; *see also* Allied press and the post-war occupation of Japan; Emperor of Japan
New Zealand 11; building up its army and air force 88; Singapore strategy 5, 87, 89, 90, 95, 97, 98; vulnerability to attack 5, 88
Nine-Power Pact 17
Nitze, Paul 192, 199
North Borneo 1, 119, 125

Ōkuma Shigenobu 35, 41, 46, 47, 49
Oppenheim, Baron Max von, 24–5, 26
Othmer, Hermann 27–8, 29
Ottoman Empire 22, 24, 58
Ōura Kanetake 47, 50
Ōyama Iwao 46, 49, 50

Pacific War 2, 3, 18, 103, 109, 117; end of 100
Papen, Franz von 22, 26, 27, 28, 29, 31

Paris Peace Conference (1919) 15–16, 18, 62, 64, 77
Parrott, Lindesay 103, 106, 107–108
Pearce, Sir George 88, 91, 93–5
Peck, Edward 197
Peterson, Maurice 16, 19
Philippines 4, 22, 30
PID (Political Intelligence Department) 62
Pilger, John 190
Pillai, Chempakaraman 25
Pindor, Karol 74, 76
POW (prisoner of war) 60, 108, 120; NNRC 138, 141, 142
Pratt, Sir John 76
PRC (People's Republic of China) *see* China
Pyun Yung-tai 146, 147

Qingdao 4, 21, 22, 37, 49, 77

Rai, Lajpat 26, 28, 29
railway 13, 62; TSR 61, 62; Twenty-One Demands 35, 37, 41, 43–4, 45, 48; *see also* CER
Ramgoolam, Seewoosagur 194
refugee 71–2; increase of numbers in the 1930s 72, 82; League of Nations 72, 83; Russian refugee 71–2, 83; *see also* Russian women refugees in China
Reilly, John 199
Reinsch, Paul 37, 38
Reston, James 111, 116
Rhee, Syngman 136, 137, 138, 144, 145, 146, 147
Robinson, Kenneth 121
ROK (Republic of Korea) 136, 137, 138, 143, 144, 145–6, 147, 148
Royal Navy: Anglo-Japanese relations 10–12; Britain's appeal to Japanese naval assistance 15; Britain's security in East Asia 10; end of British naval ascendancy in eastern waters 11, 87; withdrawal of battleships of the China squadron from Hong Kong 11; World War I 87; *see also* Singapore strategy
Rusk, Dean 196, 200
Russia 1; Bolshevik revolution (1917) 59, 64, 71, 72; Russian Civil War 4, 61, 64; Russian refugee 71–2; Russian women refugees 71; White Russian resistance to the Bolsheviks 57, 61, 67, 71; *see also* Russian women refugees in China; Soviet Union

*Index* 211

Russian women refugees in China 5, 71, 72–3, 74–86; Britain 78; British Consulates, information collected by 76–8; CER 73, 75, 80–2; Commission of Enquiry into Traffic in Women and Children in the East 72, 73–4, 76, 83; condition of 74–6; Harbin 75–7, 80–2; human trafficking 71, 75, 76, 83; League of Nations 71, 73–6, 77, 78–9, 82, 83–4 (budget 74, 82, 83; travelling commission 73, 74); Manchuria 73, 77, 79, 80–2; prostitution 74, 75, 76, 78, 80, 83; racial group-making 72, 77, 78–9, 82; Shanghai 75–6, 78–9, 80, 82; 'The "Shocking" Report on Russian Women in Shanghai', 77; SORO's report 78–9; Tianjin 76–7, 78; TWC 73, 75, 76, 79; voluntary organizations 73, 74, 83–4 (British voluntary organizations 71, 79–80); *see also* human trafficking; League of Nations
Russo-Japanese War 9, 10–11, 37, 52, 74

Salisbury, Lord 138, 139
San Francisco Peace Conference/Treaty 18, 111; *Manchester Guardian* 112–13; *New York Times* 111–12, 116
Sandys, Duncan 164
Sansom, Sir George 60, 109
Sarawak 1, 125, 126
Sargent, Sir Orme 123, 127, 129
*Saturday Evening Post* 104
Schenk, Catherine R. 152
Scott, Robert 123, 128, 131, 132
Scott, Walter 44
Semenov, Grigory 61–2, 63, 65, 66, 78
Shandong: German lease in 15, 16; Japan 15, 16, 17, 64; Twenty-One Demands 35, 37; Washington Naval Conference 17
Shanghai 1, 178, 179; German consuls in 4, 22, 30, 31; Japanese attack on 87; Russian women refugees in China 75–6, 78–9, 80, 82
Shidehara Kijūrō 105, 106–107
Siberian intervention (1918–20), 4, 57–70; Allies' involvement in 58, 61–2, 64, 67; armed POWs 60; Bolshevik revolution (1917) 59, 64; British intelligence 58, 60–1, 63, 62–5, 66, 68; coup against government in Vladivostok 66–7; Dairen talks 67; FER 65–7; France 61, 64; GCCS 58, 61, 65, 66;

IJA 58–9, 61, 62, 63 (withdrawal from Siberia 65, 66, 67); Japan, new sphere of influence of 4, 57, 61, 64–5, 68; loss of confidence in Japan as an ally 4, 57, 58, 62–3, 64, 67–8; MI1c 60, 62; MI2: 59; 'mission creep' 61; need for 59–50; Nikolaevsk incident 65, 67; pan-Asianism 4, 62; PID 62; Russian Civil War 4, 61, 64; SIS 58, 60, 63, 65, 66; strategic implications 58–61; US 61, 64; White Russian resistance to the Bolsheviks 57, 61, 67; *see also* Anglo-Japanese relations
Simpson, Sir John Hope 81–2
Singapore 2; British reoccupation 118; British withdrawal from 198; Japanese occupation of 18, 118, 127; *see also* South-East Asia regional authority
Singapore strategy 5, 87–99; 1932 Shanghai crisis 88; Australia 5, 87, 89, 90, 93–5, 97, 98; British imperial defence policy 5, 88–94, 96–8 (the Dominions 90–1, 97–8; 'Empire, big navy' school 89; 'European menace' school 89); British weakness 87–8; Canada 5, 89, 95–6, 97; DRC 88, 89–92, 93; New Zealand 5, 87, 89, 90, 95, 97, 98; Royal Navy 90, 91–2 ('main fleet to Singapore' strategy 5, 87, 92–3, 94, 95, 97; weakness 89, 97); South Africa 5, 89, 93, 95, 97; unreality of 5, 87, 97; *see also* Hankey, Maurice, Sir; Royal Navy
Singh, Jawala 27
Singh, Sohan 24, 27
SIS (Secret Intelligence Service) 58, 60, 63, 65, 66
Sly, Henry 63, 65
Smith, Walter Bedell 146, 147, 148
Smuts, General Jan 90, 93, 96–7
South-East Asia 1–2; British retreat from 3, 5–6; East Asia/South-East Asia comparison 2
South-East Asia regional authority 5–6, 117–34; British retreat from 5–6; diplomacy 119; food crisis 121, 123–4, 128, 132; SACSEA 119; SEAC 119, 124, 126; Singapore 127; Special Commission 127, 128 (Commission-General 130; merger with the office of Governor-General 128–9, 130, 132; responsibilities 123–4); US 120; *see also* Killearn, Lord; MacDonald, Malcolm; Malaya

## 212  *Index*

Soviet Union 67, 108, 199; Geneva Conference 137–8, 139–40, 142–4, 148; sale of the CER to Manchukuo 80–1; Sino-Soviet dispute 177, 184; *see also* Russia; Siberian intervention

Steed, Henry Wickham 36, 39, 40, 44–5, 52

Stewart, Michael 174, 175

Stockwell, A.J. 5–6, 117–34

Straits Settlements 1, 79

*The Sunday Times* 190

Taiwan 173, 177, 178

Thailand (Siam) 1–2, 10, 119, 124, 145; Germany, entering Burma from Thailand 4, 21, 30–1

Thomas, Sir Shenton 118

*Times*: Twenty-One Demands 36, 39–40, 44–5, 54 (favouring Japan 36, 44, 51, 52; friendly with the Foreign Office 36, 39)

Todd, John 200

trade, 1, 9; Britain/China trade 1, 183; Britain/Japan trade 9–10, 13, 18, 90; competition for Chinese markets 13–14, 17, 35; decline of Britain's exports 10, 17; Japanese textile industry 108, 109, 110, 111, 112–13; *Manchester Guardian* and trade policies 101, 110–11, 115; *see also* Hong Kong/UK relations during EEC enlargement negotiations

Tsushima, battle of 11, 21

Twenty-One Demands 3, 4, 14, 35–57; American newspapers 38–9; Anglo-Japanese Alliance 40, 43, 48, 50, 52, 53; Anglo-Japanese relations, impact of Twenty-One Demands on 52, 53; British government 4, 35, 39, 42–6, 50, 53; British newspapers 36, 43, 44; China 38, 48, 50, 52, 53 (Chinese press 38, 39; territorial integrity 35, 39, 40, 43); deadlock 42, 48, 52; evaluation of 50–1; final notification and settlement of 48–50; Group I–IV 35, 37, 53; Group V 35, 37–45 *passim*, 47–53 *passim*; leak of Group V 4, 38–9, 52; Lowe, Peter 36; *Manchester Guardian* 36, 39, 40, 45–6, 50–1 (critical of Japan's demands 36, 45, 52); Manchuria 13–14, 35, 37, 42, 43, 49; railways 35, 37, 41, 43–4, 45, 48; scholarship on 36; Shandong 35, 37; submission of 37–8; *Times* 36, 39–40,

44–5, 54 (favouring Japan 36, 44, 51, 52; friendly with the Foreign Office 36, 39); US 35, 36; *see also* Anglo-Japanese Alliance; Japan and the Twenty-One Demands

UN (United Nations) 84; admission of China into 171, 174, 183–4; BIOT 193, 195, 200; Geneva Conference 137–40, 148

UN General Assembly 137, 139; Resolution 711 (VII) 140, 141, 143; Resolution 716 (VIII) 141

US (United States) 2, 7; Anglo-Japanese Alliance 8, 15–17, 64; Britain/US rivalry 18; Canada 96; China 171, 173, 174, 175–7, 184; Four-Power Pact 17; Geneva Conference 137, 138, 140–1, 143–4, 145–7, 148 (ROK 136, 137, 138, 143, 145–6, 148); German campaign against British India 4, 22, 24, 26–7, 30, 31; Hong Kong 176–7, 184; human trafficking 74; involvement in East Asian affairs 15; Paris Peace Conference 15; Siberian intervention 61, 64; South-East Asia regional authority 120; Twenty-One Demands 35, 36; Vietnam War 173, 175–6; Washington Naval Conference 17–18; *see also* Allied occupation of Japan; Anglo-American relations; Anglo-American relations in the Korean War

USSR *see* Soviet Union

Vansittart, Sir Robert 96, 98

Versailles Treaty 16

Vietnam War 6, 171, 172, 173–8, 182, 184; Britain 173–5 (British White Paper on Vietnam 175–6); Commonwealth Prime Ministers' Conference 174–5; Gulf of Tonkin Incident 173; Lowe, Peter 2; outbreak of 136; Sino–Soviet dispute 177; US 173, 175–6

Vine, David 190–1, 200

Von Spee, Admiral Maximilian Graf 21

Walker, Patrick Gordon 174

Wang Li 179, 182

Wangenheim, Hans Freiherr von 25

Washington Naval Conference (1921) 4, 15, 16, 17, 18, 67; China 17; Japanese abrogation of naval treaties 96; US 17–18

*Washington Post* 194

Weihaiwei 1, 4, 17
Wesendonck, Otto Guenther 24–5, 26, 30
Wilson, Harold: British withdrawal from East of Suez 196, 198, 199; China 171, 173, 174, 175, 180, 181, 184, 185
Wilson, Henry, General 62
Wilson, Thomas Woodrow 16, 36, 61
World War I: Anglo-Japanese Alliance 8, 14–15; Indian Army 22, 23; Royal Navy 87; *see also* Siberian intervention
World War II 72, 98, 191
Wright, Michael 123, 128, 132

Yamagata Aritomo 42, 46–50 *passim*, 52–3
Yangtse valley 13–14
Yao Dengshan 179, 182
Yoshida Shigeru 106, 108
Young, Kenneth 142
Yuan Shikai 13; Twenty-One Demands 14, 35, 37–8, 39, 42, 52, 53

Zhang Zuolin 75
Zhou Enlai 172, 179–80, 181, 182, 184; Geneva Conference, Korean phase 140, 141, 145
Zhou Ziqi 38

# eBooks
## from Taylor & Francis
Helping you to choose the right eBooks for your Library

Add to your library's digital collection today with Taylor & Francis eBooks. We have over 50,000 eBooks in the Humanities, Social Sciences, Behavioural Sciences, Built Environment and Law, from leading imprints, including Routledge, Focal Press and Psychology Press.

**Choose from a range of subject packages or create your own!**

Benefits for you
- Free MARC records
- COUNTER-compliant usage statistics
- Flexible purchase and pricing options
- 70% approx of our eBooks are now DRM-free.

Benefits for your user
- Off-site, anytime access via Athens or referring URL
- Print or copy pages or chapters
- Full content search
- Bookmark, highlight and annotate text
- Access to thousands of pages of quality research at the click of a button.

**Free Trials Available**

We offer free trials to qualifying academic, corporate and government customers.

## eCollections
Choose from 20 different subject eCollections, including:

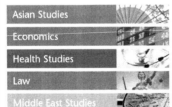

- Asian Studies
- Economics
- Health Studies
- Law
- Middle East Studies

## eFocus
We have 16 cutting-edge interdisciplinary collections, including:

- Development Studies
- The Environment
- Islam
- Korea
- Urban Studies

For more information, pricing enquiries or to order a free trial, please contact your local sales team:

UK/Rest of World: **online.sales@tandf.co.uk**
USA/Canada/Latin America: **e-reference@taylorandfrancis.com**
East/Southeast Asia: **martin.jack@tandf.com.sg**
India: **journalsales@tandfindia.com**

**www.tandfebooks.com**